Vj

C000215838

"and The Geordie Mafia"

Stephen Richards

Mirage Publishing

A *Mirage Publishing Book*
Publishers of Investigative authors

New authors welcome to submit manuscripts

First edition

Published in Great Britain
By Mirage Publishing 1998

A CIP catalogue record for this book
is available from the British Library.

ISBN 1 902578 01 5

Mirage Publishing
PO Box 161
Gateshead
NE8 4WW
Great Britain

Printed and bound in Great Britain by

C P Print Ltd, Swalwell, Newcastle upon Tyne, NE16 3DJ

Cover designed by Printex, Gateshead, NE8 4HX

Contents

IV

FOREWORD

I had just got married and had bought an MFI unit and had nothing to put on it. I said boxing was a mugs game when I was asked to go to the gym and box. I was classed as a natural. I started out in boxing as an amateur at the age of 25, considered late by most. I was not working and thought I would box and get a couple of trophies to put on the MFI unit.

I turned from amateur to the professional circuit and I was looking for a sponsor. Someone mentioned Viv's name, I asked Viv if he knew anyone who would sponsor me he said, "I'll sponsor you" and he was the first man to sponsor me with £1,000. I managed to buy all my equipment with the money, my gown, boots, a proper gum shield, my head guard, gloves and all the rest. My sparring friendship with Viv grew from that. Personally speaking I thought he was a gentleman, I did not know anything about his lifestyle. Viv always had a smile for everyone, when he was an amateur Viv thought about turning professional and I believed he would have beat many of those around because of his punching power.

John Davison

Boxing booth and amateur champion. Captained English boxing team 17 times and selected for the Olympics. Winner of two professional World International titles. (World International Featherweight title and World International Super Bantamweight title.) The first man from Newcastle to win a British title in 60 years.

Introduction

For those readers who have just picked this book up off the shop shelf it may be dismaying to find 'Chapter One' starts in the middle of an interview with the late Viv Graham's potential sister-in-law, Sharon Tate. No apologies are given for this since it has taken two books to cover the detail with regard to the late Viv's life. I do, however, apologise for the wait that the loyal following have had to put up with in order to finalise the chapter that was cut short at the end of the previous book, *Viv (Graham) – 'Simply the Best'*.

Since then a number of things have happened, most of which benefit the content of this book therefore adding to the truth that I always intend to give you, just about, no matter what.

Paddy Conroy, double category 'A' prisoner serving 11 ½ years for alleged kidnap and torture is featured herein in spite of the authorities interfering with mail addressed to him. Mail that was directly concerning his attempts for a renewed appeal against conviction was withheld, returned unopened due to his refusal to sign for Recorded Delivery letters when prison authorities wanted him to sign for mail prior to them censoring it so they could assess if it was fit enough to be passed on to him. This would have given the impression that he had in fact received mail, when in actual fact he would not have.

What is the connection between Conroy and Viv? The answer is; a man called David Glover, one of Conroy's co-accused. Glover had that many deals going for him he might as well have been a Texas oil tycoon. One of those deals was allegedly a deal he had made with police officers from Northumbria Police Force. Glover was alleged to have been willing to be a prosecution witness in the Viv murder trial!

A number of other people were interviewed in this matter and the conclusion is given over to you to decide on, as to whether there was some jury rigging by means of incentives by way of a party being offered to jurors serving in the Conroy torture trial.

The descriptive term 'Geordie Mafia' may well be a name that becomes synonymous with Geordie criminals, but that would be an un-earned accolade to give to just any old lag. To become a member of the Geordie Mafia you must have first earned your colours. An original Geordie Mafia member is a man called Kenneth 'Panda' Anderson (Goosey, goosey Gander), 60, he is featured within these pages and he is not to be mixed up with any ordinary criminal, he is and was a criminal that aptly defines what separates the men from the boys.

Panda's connection with Viv is revealed as well as his connection with London hard man, Lenny McLean. Lenny is now, sadly, deceased. He died, late July 1998 at home from lung cancer at the age of forty-nine. Freddie Foreman the co-writer of *Respect* is also a friend of Panda's. Did Reggie Kray really get kicked out of Newcastle way back in the 60s?

What started out as an investigation into who killed Viv has ended up as a sort of who's who amongst Geordie criminals? Nothing of this sort has been attempted ever before and there are bound to be some omissions in terms of people who would have wished to be included. That may well be able to be rectified if a further book that is anticipated to be written with the help of Panda in the near future, but first we must get this book into your hands.

Much has been written of London gangsters, rightly so, they are the envy of the rest of the world and an export that helped colonise Australia, as we know it today. They did not turn out too badly so it goes to show good old Britannia can export some things that turn out good. Some things have been written of Scotland's gangsters from Glasgow. Manchester has had their Quality Street Gang put into ink. Now it is the turn of the Geordie Mafia. Little has been written about them and it is rather like Richard Attenborough in his early days when he filmed apes in the wild. People were enthralled by it all because it was something new. So be it then! Let this be the forerunner of many books that are waiting to be written.

Gone are many of the pages of statistics and that will no doubt please a lot of you out there. This is not meant to be a socio-documentary book or a novel as was suggested of the last book. All what is written within is taken from those in the know. Many with personal connections to Viv have for the first time come forward and given their all to make this as true a picture as possible.

The interview with Viv's parents is particularly enlightening and reveals what Viv was really like. Considering that Jacky, Viv's father, had not given anyone an interview at all so it was deemed something of an honour that he allowed me the privilege of interviewing him under such circumstances to speak of his late son. The press had tried all ways to speak with Jacky and Viv's mother Hazel. They even followed Hazel to her son's graveside making it all but impossible for Hazel to be allowed time to grieve in her own way.

The church comes into this matter in the form of an interview granted by Father Conaty. This interview is important in terms of how the church look at revenge and interpretations from the old beliefs of the *Old Testament.*

Wallsend is an industrial area that has suffered knocks for many years in terms of job losses. The Catholic Church has intervened on many occasions giving solace and spiritual strength to those in need and often to those in need that did not know they were in need. Viv was an atheist, or so he professed, but his actions in helping those in need and being respectful to believers shows his acceptance and tolerance of others and what they believed in.

Anna Connelly, Viv's fiancée, called on the help of spiritualists to reach the spirit of Viv. In the end she returned to the Catholic faith after seeing a lot of different so-called spiritualists.

During the investigation into the murder of Viv our team called upon the services of a spiritualist. We asked a number of local spiritualists for their help, we offered fees and free publicity to many across the North East, all refused to take part in our request for help in visiting the murder site and other areas around Tyneside.

However, we were put in contact with someone via a North East based professional medium service. She asked for no fee and did not want free publicity; all that she requested was that she remains anonymous. This was a big sacrifice for someone of her status to make under the circumstances and it restored some faith into a charlatan-brandished profession. The revelations are startling especially since the lady did not know Viv from Adam.

There is no index at the end of this book as there is no need to impress academics as none have been pursued in the matters detailed within. So should you be searching for yourself apologies are given, look hard.

Viv's insurers have been contacted and the question over the insurance claim being frozen has been raised with them. An interview with Sinton & Co Solicitors has resulted in some details being available for all to see what insurance companies are really like. They, insurance companies, take your premiums and when it comes to paying out they come up with all sorts of different reasons as to why they do not want to pay up. Another firm of solicitors sought the opinion of the author of this book as to Viv's connection with drugs and club doormen racketeering.

The press is exposed for what they really are although that will be of little surprise to most people. Privacy laws are meant to address this problem of over exertion by over zealous journalists! Really? This book might be a pre-cursor in moving a sluggish government to react to what is required in cases such as the death of Viv and how people were hounded by the press.

This book, contrary to opinion, is not meant as a biography of Viv's life or as a dedication to what he did or became, but is meant to act as a warning to those who might try to emulate him or his actions. A warning sign is usual when danger lurks nearby. Let this book be a warning to those who would take up the mantel that Viv left, as if for someone to come along and pull it from the rock it is embedded in. Rather like King Arthur pulling the sword from the stone, thus proving his worth. Let that not be the case here. He who lives by the sword shall die by the sword! No one is special enough to have the charm and charisma to pull themselves through what Viv could not get through. A legend may have been made when Viv passed away, time will tell if that is the case. If that is so then let it remain a legend and many people have commented on Viv being a Robin Hood character. Did he really exist? Some say he did, if so then the truth is stranger than fiction and has been romanticised so that nostalgia can become acceptable if it portrays someone as a larger than life character, surely Viv was that and for that reason alone warrants the attentions of you, the readers, to help escape your own lives for a short while. Do not let that detract from your own lives and the importance your life has to others around you. You would only realise how loved you are if you were to pass away. Do not be hard faced to others who might want to love you although it may be love you seek from those around you be happy to have their respect.

The police featured heavily in the previous book, they too feature within this book. The author has raised a number of issues for you to reach a conclusion over. I do not wish to look at things from a biased view regardless of how the police acted towards me and the holding up of the previous book from being released to the public because of their lack of consideration for deadlines. Maybe that will reflect on how they do not consider the feelings of people. We have all become statistics to them, just a record on a computer disk, broken down into little bits of information for them to ogle over from their detached position of self-ingratiated power. Where rules are rules with no grey areas of doubt.

Jealousy and professional pride are two different things. Those with professionalism act with good conduct towards most, but those who are jealous are the most dangerous of all. Avoid these people at all costs if you can for they will surely cause your downfall by hook or crook. Some police officers became jealous over how we had unearthed a number of things they could not. For that reason their pride was hurt some officers could accept this with grace and dignity others could not and became jealous. Our insurance policy against these officers is to record the goings on with a dedication second to none. For those police officers that are with professional pride I thank you for the help given although it is accepted that their names cannot be revealed for fear of themselves becoming victimised. But they know who they are. I once witnessed a sight as a young boy. That sight was of a Negro being dragged along a main road by the gloved hand of a policeman.

The policeman held the man's ear, pulling his head slightly down to the side as he led him away. Whatever the reason was I do not know as I was sitting on a bus looking through the steamed up window. The picture it gave me was a one of fear. Fear of the police and how they could do that. I knew no such thing as colour prejudice at such a young age in such a naïve time.

All what I knew was that this was a man having his dignity taken away from him in public. Dignity was a big thing way back then, pride was often a thing that had to be broken and it was, at times, the only thing a person possessed. I saw a man having his pride drained from him. Should such an event have taken place at present time of writing it would cause a riot beyond comprehension? Since things were dealt with differently way back then it may well not be relevant to today's policing methods therefore I do not venture further into a fool's territory.

Kray, Foreman, Sibbet, Landa, Richardson and Anderson are names synonymous with big time crime. Kenneth 'Panda' Anderson has given an interview and he reveals many things not even touched on by the press. The press could not get near to the truth nor would they cover it so as to give you the readers the truth. You would be left with a convoluted view if you followed what the press write about such names. It can be revealed that Lenny McLean who co wrote *The Guv'nor* with Peter Gerrard boasted of winning all of his fights some 3,000+ of them. I can tell you that was not the case and can reveal who beat Lenny McLean, that man is now sixty two years old! The memory of Lenny McLean is not wished to be hurt or to convey he was not all he was cracked out to be. He was every bit that was written about him and more, but for the sake of romance he did not count any of his losses in battle. Lenny is not here to defend what is said. I can reveal that it was planned to interview Lenny, but he was too ill and for that reason his privacy was respected. Viv was invited to fight against Lenny. Find out what happened later on.

The original Geordie Mafia has their day. Read about how Viv ran from a pub where allegedly a man had his finger cut off by a member of the original Geordie Mafia. Viv was not a weapons man and only used his fists as weapons so when he saw what had happened to the man he was asked to hold it turned his stomach. This blows the lid off what people believed Viv to stand for.

Many thanks to those of you who gave assistance in the matter of seeking out information, your help has been invaluable. Where our promises have been given we stick to them as always about anonymity. Should I write about everything that was told to me off the record it would result in a lot of people being charged with various offences that have not been cleared up by the police. I have acted as a priest and my word is my bond in all matters that have been related to me with a promise of none revelation.

My intention is not to act as a source of information for the authorities in any matters that have been discovered that do not directly involve this book and any findings on the way are therefore discounted even were people have bragged of murders and where bodies are buried. The police are employed to secure this information and act on it best they can. 'Kicker' was the nickname of a man that went missing and he was allegedly buried in Kielder

Forrest. In the course of investigating the murder of Viv it came out that a Manchester firm murdered this man called Kicker. Maybe that gives you some idea of the extent and strength of information we discovered and the trust placed in our word. How many people could be given such trust and respect? That is the reason that people will not impart information to the authorities, because trust is lost due to their poor track record of keeping confidences.

I was informed on Friday 6th November 1998 that charges were not being brought against me relating to my arrest some months previously in June. This was of no surprise to me and it was Monday 9th November 1998 that the remainder of the property and computer discs were returned! The difficulty has been that this book should have been published by November 5th 1998. The police are not directly blamed for the delay it is now the turn of the Northumbria Police Authority, Gillian Lowes' solicitor and the insurance company who have delayed payment on Viv's life insurance policies. Read more of that in the relevant chapters.

Charges against two of my researchers were also dropped, not surprisingly. Many thanks go to those who have given their help, particularly the legal team of Gary Ward. Gary is serving life imprisonment for a Blackpool Beach Murder he says he did not commit. Dezmond Lartey for the loan of archive papers relating to his uncle, Aryee Jackson. Jim Richardson for showing that fortitude is something that still exists. The close family of Viv for showing everyone that life is precious. Paddy Conroy who gave up and then renewed his fight. Gary Ward who gave up and then renewed his fight.

Many people commented on the last book *Viv (Graham) – 'Simply the Best'*, Glen Miller one of my researchers said, "The words 'Fish & Chip wrapper papers' mentioned far too often." Dez Lartey, "I felt disappointed and let down because I thought the killers would have been named." Blame the police for that one, Dez. 'Read on and enjoy! An ex-special constable who sued Northumbria Police Force for racial discrimination said, "Steve, I have had police officers come up to me and say the book is brilliant." A female researcher, "Not enough violence!" Chas, "It was really good and I'm not just saying that." Joan, "Get the next one proof read." Other quotes have been, 'Good luck with the book' from John Stevenson, Deputy Commissioner Met Police. 'Mish-Mash, Re-hash', Newcastle *Evening Chronicle*. 'An interesting book', Keith Bell. 'What a load of crap", someone close to me, were they serious?

I have refused to be hurried by those of you who have kept telephoning the publisher and asking when the book is due out. There have been things of importance to wait for in this matter so as to give you a better read. I hope this is something you consider to be worth waiting for, read on and enjoy.

You read the last book as it was written and that could be looked upon as a new concept in writing, let me call it 'Live Writing'.

For Aryee Jackson

(Ghana) Featherweight Boxing Champ who came to
England and showed them all a lesson in class. Now
Living in a nursing home in England needs your kind
Letters of support via Publisher.

1

Sharon Tate

Continued from *Viv (Graham)* – *'Simply the Best'* "... out and they had a plastic tunnel to walk through right from where your car would pull up. This tunnel went for ages and every time we turned around he was still there, waving. I would say 'Look at him what's he doing.' We were laughing and I was saying, 'Go on then get in the car.' He said, 'Nah, nah I am standing here!' We were carrying on walking it felt like for miles and I kept turning back and he was there, there until I turned a corner and then I went to turn the corner and I looked back he was still there and I waved. We kind of went down the rest of the way by this time we were nearly to the area where you check in. There was nowhere to sit beforehand because it was all pulled to pieces. That was it, off I went. It was a queer feeling because it was New Year's Eve and I was there (Tenerife) for New Year. For some reason I didn't want to go."

Paddy Leonard was an ex-patriot Geordie living in Tenerife and it was suggested that he was in the North East of England about the time of Viv's murder. This allegation is thwarted by the fact that he was actually in Tenerife as Sharon goes on to explain. "We got there it was New Year's Eve so everybody just left their cases and got straight to the bar. We got to the bar and David went, 'What do you want?' I said, 'I don't fancy a drink', I didn't. I felt funny the next morning because on the Christmas Eve he (Viv) had been with me all night and wouldn't go home. He gave me the presents to wrap up for Anna and he had a daft Christmas hat on, a Santa Claus hat.

The taxi called to pick him up and every time it called he kept saying, 'Tell

1

him to come back.' I had to keep going to the door so in the end I rang Anna up and said, 'I'm sick of him now I want rid of him.' Anna spoke to him on the phone and he said, 'Anna, I'm getting your presents.'

"I had a tape for Christmas and I was singing it to him. I took the tape away on holiday and the next morning I put the tape on and was sitting listening to it. We had no milk for a cup of tea with just getting straight in the previous night I was wide-awake. As David was going out the door for the milk Paddy (Leonard) was on his way up to us so when David came back in the door I knew by there faces something really bad had happened.

"It's more or less a blur from there. I left straight away to return to home via Gatwick. My sister-in-law and brother-in-law were with us and they didn't have any kids so they moved into my apartment to look after the kids. How we got home I just don't know. There was snow all over the road that thick", Sharon demonstrates the depth with her hands. "There were cars conked all over the motorway and we had this stupid little car something like a little Fiat. We got home and all the way along the motor way there were BMWs and everything broken down. The snow turned deep and was getting into the engines but we done it. I just can't remember how it was like a bad dream.

"I was keep wondering what's happened and I kept looking at David and I was saying, 'What's happened David, why are we here?' Like when you're away from home and somebody tells you something..." At this point Sharon is re-entering her world of grief and is actually as if in some hypnotic trance becoming one with her inner feelings and this is the part of the interview that my lack of eloquence is more than made up for in Sharon's ability to put her loss into words. Had I the abilities of a great writer then I would not have been at odds in expressing things with the magical use of words Sharon more than made up for the frustrations of a mediocre writer.

"It couldn't be real, it couldn't be real. To know what it actually does to people around because they might have probably wanted rid of him but, did they realise, like, how many people had been... We just absolutely, our whole family meaning brothers and sisters because we had loads of cousins around, but brothers and sisters we went to pieces and just couldn't take it in."

They must have all loved the man, they were a big family and were fun to be with by the sounds of it and they all had a good time. He was not a brother-in-law by marriage but he was nearly by virtue of having Anna as his fiancée. This man was loved and it effected those members of the family beyond normal reasoning. That extended family was effected including children. Sharon says she does not want to try making him out as being any different to any other brother-in-law, he was not; he was the same as.

They were all close and Sharon says in her own words. "We are all that "close, we all drink together, we all do everything we do together like if one needed something then the other ones are there because that's just the way we were brought up. And I think Viv liked that feeling as well because we were close." Viv was from an average sized family and he did not lack any love and attention as a child maybe he needed this continuation of having a feeling of warmth and acceptance.

"He liked what he got from us, he liked the vibes that we were all giving each other around." It was put to Sharon that Viv wanted to get away from everything that he was involved with up to a certain point. It was spoken of between him and Anna to maybe get a nice place in the countryside a smallholding or something with chickens running around. To delegate and have someone else doing something and do everything through the books. Sharon interjects with, "That was all happening."

That may have been only a stone's throw away from where he was in life. Then the legend would have been intact. It could have been for him to destroy and say, 'Well... look, this man, you made him up I've shifted out of the area I've got my head clear now that wasn't me I've had a chat with my dad and you know... get lost the lot of you.' That could have happened.

It was put to Sharon that Anna must have changed in many ways since Viv died. How had she seen Anna Change? "For her to pull through after the way she was is unbelievable. She's always been a caring type of lass because before she even met Viv she was working in a old people's home and she cared for people and always put herself out for old people, things I could never have done. I used to watch her and think how could she do that. She had a little sports car and used to take the little old people with her and this was before she met Viv she used to take them everywhere with her. She was still working in the homes when he met her and then she let off it for a few years and now she's back there so she's kind of back to the lass she was really in that kind of a way."

It proved how little attention the press paid to Anna because they reported that Anna was working for a contract cleaning company.

"We've all learned a lot from what's happened everything for all of us in this sense. My outlook is a completely different outlook to what I had. Now I'll live for the day and I'd do everything that I wanted to do." It was pointed out that this was exactly how Viv had lived his life. Sharon continued, "Because he was doing it and we were saying, 'That's not the way, you're not making a little nest for later on in your life.' He said, 'There might not be any more life later on.' So we live for the day now and don't make a nest for years to come there might not be anymore years to come.

We went through a big thing, you know when you're looking anywhere for help like, 'Please, who can help me?' You know like spooky meetings we were running for fortune tellers like when you're searching. Searching, 'Can anybody help the way I feel?' Because I went to shopping places like the Metro Centre and I was, like, watching the people pass and I was thinking how can you get on with your lives and I can't get on with mine? I would be thinking these people don't even know what this feels like. Horrible, it was horrible everything I went through, but now when I look back on it I know now that I could help somebody in that situation now because now I know what it feels like to be kind of lost in the wilderness. Thinking is this real is it really happening. What happens, it's the inside, people can look at you and think she looks good and ask, 'Are you alright?' You automatically go, 'Oh! Aye, great, great', but in there", Sharon puts her hand on her heart, "it's a different kettle of fish isn't it, torn apart. I was thinking if I feel like this then what can my sister feel like if this is the way I feel what way does she feel? How is she coping with this at times, she was strength for me and probably at times I was strength for her. In my own mind I was thinking, 'God I've got no strength at all I don't think I'm going to get through this.'

"It really had done something my whole insides were like an empty ripped apart feeling that you just didn't think other people had had. Obviously though they had these feelings, people that's lost people, things have happened tragedy in people's lives, but I'd never felt this before so I didn't know the feeling. I mean I would read a paper and go, 'Eh! Please God give me grace', but I didn't know that ripped apart gutted feeling. I would read it and feel sorry but, now I know that when people have got tragedy I say, 'Please God help them through this.' That feeling is just an absolute killer. I would imagine Viv's dad I think slowly, but surely it's eating that man away. I'm nearly four years later and I've learned a lot and I sometimes wonder was all this meant to happen was this for us to be there for other people to understand other people and now I'm never away from the church. I love the church I'm back to my own Catholic faith I went away from that for a while"

It was mentioned that a conflict between her Catholic faith and attending medium spiritualist churches might exist, Sharon says, "At the time I was more thinking of myself and what was best for me. As it happened I went around in a full circle looking and looking and I ended up back at my own church and found it there." Sharon was asked if she came back to her church with a stronger faith or was it the same or had it opened up. "I was open because I wanted help and I went back saying, 'Right I'm back I need something.' When I went back I was weak and open and just wanting help and I got it." Sharon was asked then if the other sources she had went to such as mediums and spiritualist had failed her? "I know there was life after death and I know there is something but I was getting the feeling that these people had read that many papers and knew our faces and knew who we were."

Were there any feelings of paranoia such as feeling that people were putting your every movement under a microscope? "We would just make it seem "like we were coping like we were alright it's took some time even like today.

We're different people to what we were four years ago." At this point David comes into the room and joins us and he looks unsure of what to make of it all it seems as if he is stepping in for a curious look at something. To make him feel welcome a question is put to him. "What about you David are you religious in any way?" His reply is a curt and quiet, "No."

To help him relax I throw a long-winded question at David to get his mind thinking and take the edge off the newly strained atmosphere. "So! David, perhaps, where Sharon turned to the Catholic Church how did your strength come about to support yourself through the upset and turmoil that had obviously took place and not just with the passing away of Viv. A number of other family members who passed away one through tragedy and one who died of cancer must have added to your burden. To get through all of that how much can you carry and where do you offload it? Between Sharon and Anna they may well have said 'Right we'll get together and try a medium and try a spiritualist but no! Now we've ended up back at church.' Where does David start to unload all of this pressure?" His eventual delayed reply of, "I don't know", ends with a nervous laugh from him, which of course is understandable.

We are on the road to opening up some of his feelings but he seems to carry much more of his wounds within himself and being a man it is not easy to talk about sensitive emotional issues. Especially in this part of the world where a bit of stigma still attaches itself to those men who are emotional. It is explained to David that we are not looking for answers to questions that dig into the depths of Viv's torment about how he died. "The wish is to show people how it has affected you." David said the loss of Viv was a "devastating experience" and the family had to stick together and help each other through it. "We were with each other all the time", David looks to Sharon to offer support as he finishes the sentence, "weren't we?"

David succinctly answers a few more questions and when it was put to him that people who were aware of him being close to Viv might not have known what to say about the death of Viv he says. "No because I think everybody over this part of the town had loads of respect for him and they never made you feel uncomfortable." Sharon helps David out by saying, "Not really because most people who knew Viv knew us they were quite close so they would come in and just put their arms around you. They were feeling just as bad as you and they really meant what they were saying so you were kind of all right about it. This was set up in one house we were all there in that house for weeks." David interjects, "A couple of months or something it just went on and on everybody just helped each other through." Sharon continues, "Because it wasn't like a normal thing you see because he didn't get buried "immediately. So normally you would last in a house until somebody gets buried and then you say, 'Well this person's got to get on with their life and they've got to start getting back to work and getting back to seeing to the kids and get their life back running.' This didn't happen with us because we didn't get that done. We just lived in one house and we all had to feed. My mother and my aunts would come with big pans of soup and make sure that everybody had something to eat and that kind of thing. Then he (David) would come and bring a big takeaway meal when returning from work and say, 'Get this down you.' We lived like that it must have been for about three or four months." David said that they all moved into one house together and the company was better than looking at the walls.

When the family was together and showing Geordie solidarity in such a depressing time was it a case that they avoided talking about what had happened? David and Sharon are now both fully relaxed and it is a case of cherry picking an answer from either one of them. David starts to answer, "No, no that was the centre of..." Sharon comes in, "We just sat and kept going over and over it and why did everything go to perfection? Why did they do what they done? Then they got in the car and nobody seen the car the car got set alight and nobody seen that and we just sat and we kept thinking how did nobody see anything? Plus we had the videos of him and talked about all the things that we did and we just constantly talked about him which I think is the best way to do things."

The family counselled each other and did not avoid the subject of Viv it was not a taboo subject. The family and even those on the borders of the family all helped out. The house was full all the time and maybe that was for the best so that the subject of Viv could be talked about openly and allowing people to have their say about how they felt.

York University discovered that counselling might be a waste of time. That finding was the prompting I needed to give up professional counselling. I now realise that counselling actually existed in every street of the UK many years before modern housing estates were designed to alienate people from each other. The ethos of neighbours helping each other in hard times has faded over the years along with the disappearance of the typical street design. There would always be an 'auntie so and so' to go and speak with over a problem or a worldly-wise mother figure in just about every street that could be used as a sheet anchor in times of need. Those street counsellors have long gone and a more official set up makes people's problems seem more exaggerated than what they really are. Gone is the shoulder to cry on, no physical contact is recommended when counselling anyone? Least it should give rise to a suggestion of sexual innuendo.

The next question was a one that was about a female member of the press masquerading as a mourner. An allegation had been brought to our attention about how a journalist had supposedly pretended to be a mourner. Sharon and David were asked if it was correct that a woman reporter had been sitting in the kitchen of Anna's house and how no one was aware who she was and how she was eventually exposed as a reporter? Sharon says, "Because there was that many people in the house every room was full and the kitchen was full and the little dinning area where you come into the side door. There were loads of my aunts and uncles you just thought maybe that someone had come with them. One man hitched from hundreds of miles away and he turned up at the door with a little bag. He had hitched it just to say 'sorry' out of respect."

David reiterates it, "I can't remember where he was from but he came just to show respect. He said he had met Viv in jail and he left his address somewhere so that if something like this come up he wanted to give his opinion on Viv."

We broached the subject of the reporter again and it was asked where they were from. Sharon says with some venom in her words, "There's two of them just tell me there names." A few names are thrown at Sharon but a name that has not been thrown at her is 'Hickman', Brenda Hickman. Sharon says without any prompting about this name, "Hickman! One's Hickman. Funnily enough when I read the paper now and there's something tragic that happened I look at the name that's done it and it's always them stinking two."

It is mentioned that certain newspaper articles had suggested that Viv Graham was part of a drug ring or a crime ring and some had just come straight out with it. "But they've blatantly been able to do that and just come straight out with it. They've been allowed to do that and I can't see how." David says, "It's like anything else, no one would have said anything about him if he was still here it's just that because he's gone it's like a can of worms opening up isn't it? They just want to say what they want. Everybody knew he was the hardest in the North East and he ran the doors so when he was gone the door was open for them to say what they wanted. It confused everything and then they started to say it was all drug related. You've got to remember that a member of the police force got up in an interview on TV and said how well respected Viv was in the police force for the trouble, which they knew he stopped in the drugs and all that so what are you supposed to do? That's why I don't really like to say all what I know about anybody because everybody has their own views and I know what I know. You've got the media saying he's a drug baron, he's this and that. You've got an old woman in the Co-op saying, 'He's a gentleman'. Did she (Sharon) tell you that one when it come to Christmas she was in the queue and she had her turkey she couldn't get through and there was just a little old woman, maybe 75 years old? He (Viv) says, 'Come here pet', he paid for "the turkey and said, 'Merry Christmas'. Then you've got a police officer standing up and saying what he thought Viv had done for society, which was good. So then you've got the media saying, 'he's this, he's bad', so that's why I just like to say nothing."

From David being withdrawn and introvert some while ago he has opened up. That is because he can see we are not there to do them any harm or secure them to say things about Viv they do not want to say or to put words into their mouths. It is explained that newspapers like to write this sort of thing so as to sell newspapers and amplify what has been said.

How do you weigh a man up? Is it by the allegations against him or is he weighed up by what he is truly worth? Depending on those allegations that could be good or bad then we could say we would use those allegations that this man was wonderful and worked hard or was a bad person.

"Even the fellow who had a papershop next door everybody was devastated because everybody was used to him, everybody knew him, people weren't scared of him, nobody was scared of him they were only scared of him if he had to go and see you to sort something out. If you'd done something wrong but he wasn't going to come along to shoot you. He would speak he'd say, 'You've done something wrong don't do it again', so he had a lot of respect and a lot of people admired him. He used to nip next door for the paper he used to talk to people. People just wanted to talk to him because he was such a nice person he come across as a nice person he was a proper gentleman. You would never think he could knock ten men out. You wouldn't even see that side of him. I've never seen him fight not that I wanted to", said David.

We talk a while of the media and how the press and particularly the local press portrayed Viv and this has made my job somewhat more difficult. That was the case with just about everybody who was interviewed they all had reservations about the press. It was explained that this interview was taking place so that the whole story could be put together and it would not be fair on the people involved not to give them a chance to have their say.

David starts talking without any prompting, "If you just even take for instance what he done for the whole City of Newcastle the only people who didn't like him were BAD PEOPLE." David put the emphasis on the last two words and it was said that it was understood what he was saying. He goes on, "If you look at Wallsend now it's a bit of a ghost town the bars are all dead quiet you can drive down anytime they're quiet and this is four years after, but before that Wallsend was like Whitley Bay or the Bigg Market. Every bar was jumping. There was a lovely feeling in the air people enjoyed going out in company. There were no bullies nobody was going to pull knives out on you and guns and all that because all over there was awareness of Viv Graham. People who had pubs, clubs and shops respected him so he wasn't looking after everywhere and getting paid off everybody. As long as

8

"he was in the manor, as long as he drove along that road everywhere seemed to be happy. Nobody was going to run along and start smashing windows and pinching cars and pulling knives and guns out because everybody knew, you know, what he could do!"

Comment on the changes in the area of Wallsend over the last four years was sought from David. "The area has died a death people just weren't coming out. People were coming out happy and safe. Everybody felt happy every time you seen him he always had a smiling face he wasn't a person if looks could kill he was killing everybody, everybody was happy it doesn't matter where you were."

David was asked if Viv looked at people with the normal club doorman stare. "No! You'd see him having a drink and a laugh talking to somebody he wouldn't even stand on the door. Just his presence even being in one pub amongst a hundred pubs it seemed the hundred pubs were covered because the villains wouldn't even come in from one of them up to a hundred. He was asked what Viv's feelings were towards nuisance criminals like burglars? "He gave anybody a warning, 'Whatever you do, you know, don't do it anywhere where I am', type of thing. And then if they ever pursued it again then he would probably give them a clip and they wouldn't do it again."

The increase in drug usage had spiralled and would Viv have been able to put a stop to this happening in the Daisy Hill area in the East End of Newcastle like it was apparent now? "I don't think it would be as bad as what it is if he was here put it that way but, I wouldn't say that it would not be there. I'm 99% sure it would be a nicer place to be." David is asked have there ever witnessed occasions when Viv used kindness and good words? "He was like that all the time. He just naturally came out nice. He'd say, 'Nowts a bother'. He would see somebody carrying bags, he'd be there or he'd buy something for an old woman he always seemed to be there and you always seen a nice part of him and I think that's how a lot of people liked him."

We talk about a video that had been viewed some weeks earlier of Viv at a school sports day where parents have to get involved. Viv was portrayed as a man at ease with himself and happy go lucky how true was that? David says, "We had great company everyday we used to laugh. I used to come in from Scotland at three o'clock in the morning then I'd wake up like that.

"Everybody was here Sharon, Viv, Anna and me. Then that was it I'd go across the butcher's for the sausage the bacon the leek the mushroom and the egg. He used to have a breakfast like that with about eight sausages, four bits of bacon, three eggs, loads of leek and mushrooms loads of beans and tomatoes that was it that was the routine everyday. We used to just laugh and he was taking the Mickey out of me because that was me, 'See you later'. I "was away back to Scotland or something away back to work. We just used to generally have a laugh and a carry on."

Viv did not seem the type of man who had his head in a dark cloud of depression nor was he a bit of a psychopath who could just flip. We are not looking for it but by the same token cannot seem to find anything there. During this question Sharon fills the background up with her gentle Geordie tones with a "Nah" every so often so off we go with our duet again. Sharon has her reply ready, "He didn't used to flip and be like a rotten person you didn't see a nice man and then an animal of a man, that's why you loved him as much." David gets his chance by saying, "You know like in a situation in a pub where if you get somebody in a right temper who pushes everybody away, 'I'M GOING TO KILL YOU…', he wouldn't do that. I've never ever seen him fight you'd see him stand talking one minute and he'd go, 'Whoa', and say to somebody, 'You can't do that type of thing', and that's all he had to do. He didn't get in a bad temper and pick chairs and tables up and want to kill everybody. They would never think he was as hard as what he was. I never seen him hit anybody."

It did not look like David and Sharon were knocking on poverty's door but it was asked if they had ever needed some type of help from Viv other than financial? "The only help I've needed from him", says Sharon, "was when I was putting a big girder across the top of the scullery and a lot of builders were here and they couldn't lift the girder up. I phoned Viv up and said, 'Viv I need you, like', he said, 'What's the matter?' I said, 'These weaklings here…', and there was all the builders standing, '…they can't even pick this girder up!' He said, 'I'll be there in a shot.' He came with his slippers on and he just lifted the whole thing up and shoved it because it had to go into the wall there. He needed David though and would say, 'You couldn't lend us a few quid?' We never, em…" I interject because it knocks spots off the arguments that Viv had a £2 million drug empire as reported without foundation in the Newcastle *Sunday Sun*. Viv having to ask David for a loan of money is contrary to what was suggested in an article by John Merry.

Sharon backs this up further by saying, "He could have paid him back probably the next day because he used to get good money from the job he done, running the doormen. He used to get good money but he squandered it and he loved a bet."

We talk of insurance policies now and about the dispute over monies yet to be paid out from them this leads on to more money talk and David says, "Viv rang me up and said, 'Have you a £1,000?', 'Aye', I replied, 'Lend me it will you?', he said. I stopped for a moment and then said, 'What do you want it for?' 'Just somebody's asked for a lend of it', he said. The money was for a taxi driver and Viv never seen it again. I went, 'You must be daft you, like', "I said, 'I'd only lend it to you because I know I'd get it back.' If any Tom,

"Dick or Harry comes up and says, 'Lend us some money', you go you know... They were desperate they would come, 'Please, please they've cut the gas off' or 'They've cut the electric off', You know."

Viv was a softy for a sob story and it usually always ended up with the people getting what they asked for and maybe a bit more besides. £20s, £50s and sometimes £100s would be loaned out with no request for it to be returned. Was it that Viv was trying to balance things up if you have done something wrong the scale goes down and you have to do something good to bring it back up. Everybody has this thing in him or her no matter how bad anyone is. It does not seem that Viv was trying to balance the scales up because he was not that type of person. What was it? David says, "You know when this did happen a few weeks and months later **everybody**", David puts a heavy emphasis on the word 'everybody', "said if they ever made a film about Viv it would be a total sell out. You know if you could make a proper real good film. He was such a character, **everybody, everybody** thought a lot of him you know, those who we knew this side of the town whether you dealt with him or not, you knew, because there was just a nice feeling there." Sharon interjects, "Just everywhere he went he went with a smile on his face." David says, "You were driving along the road and people were going, 'Yeah!'"

David is now well into his stride with this interview and has the confidence and enthusiasm enough to take the lead where needed. This is no doubt explained by our lack of aggression in terms of the line we take with regard to the questions asked. Do not let that make you think that the questions are easy, they are not. David says without prompting, "Listen, it was even great just say a wrong one, a burglar or villain or whatever done something wrong and he (Viv) said, 'Tell him I want to see him', the kid would probably shake in his boots. They knew what kind of person he was they could take a gamble and knock on his door and say 'I'm sorry', type of thing and he wouldn't hit them. He wasn't the type of person who would fly off the handle hit you and put you in the corner and strangle you. So they would go, 'look I'm sorry'; he would more or less shake their hand type of thing. They would go, 'Right!' and never do anything of that sort again it was a lesson for them. He wouldn't have to hit them."

Did Viv always see the good in someone? "Viv wasn't just nice to one or two he was nice to everybody. Even the bairns have pictures up of Viv he didn't just have one best friend or two or three it was just everywhere you went", David said. I brought up the subject of the so-called close friends who deserted Viv. Recently it was passed on that one of Viv's past associates and really close friend Robin Armstrong did not wish to make comment in light of his impending court appearance on serious drug charges. Originally Rob's point of view was sought, but for some reason he did not come forward or call me. Then it was decided that Rob's opinion would not be sought as it was believed that information may have been passed onto him via some private detectives that did the dirty on us by dropping our case and running to Newcastle United Footballl Club for big money.

My publisher's asked that his opinion be sought some weeks ago and it was a case of asking Gillian Lowes if she would mind passing the message on to Rob asking for his help. The news came back that Rob was too concerned about his own problem and therefore would not be commenting. This is well understood but in light of the fact that Rob gave interviews left right and centre to all and sundry after Viv's death it seemed a bit unjust for him to turn his back on a publication that was digging up the good as well as the bad. TV documentaries had taken extracts from Robin's interview and twisted them to how they wanted. Newspapers had twisted his words and yet the only publication to print the truth is ignored! May Viv rest in peace with regard to how he is remembered by those who were once close to him. It seems that most people close to Viv had disbanded and went their own way although later on it is suggested that some went to the 'other side' and did not pursue Viv's murderers for fear of themselves becoming victim to attack.

We talk a while of how David and his potential brother-in-law got on and the answer was that they got on very well. David goes on to say, "We never had a fall out, we carried on at times. I remember I jumped on Viv just carrying on he just squashed me and threw me about. My friend did the same who was a good friend of Viv and he tried the same just to have a go and he just got him a squashed him. I think he did his ribs in but just in carry on you know and he was a big lad. Just to see how far he would go, but never in temper or nothing like that. It was just the way Viv was he was never showing off."

Leading up to the end of the interview David was asked if he knew of any weakness Viv may have had? "He was soft at heart. It was nice to see a man of that size being nice to somebody but he certainly wasn't too soft. He would stand and talk with you about football and anything. "What sort of pressure was Viv under? David wants to know what sort of pressure I am on about. The question is lengthened to support what I have asked. David went on to say that if Viv had been under any sort of pressures he only had to lift up the telephone and talk with his family.

The question of threats is raised and it is asked if David knew of any threat that Viv had received to his life, David knew of no sort of threat that Viv may have had. At this stage there is a cooling down of David's replies, perhaps this could be put down to the line of question I make, which under the circumstances of him losing someone so close to him is understandable. The short replies that are made to my questions could also reflect the length of time I have been interviewing. What do you think was the cause of the shooting of Viv? "Power! He was probably stopping somebody getting something or he was an obstacle in somebody's way. They couldn't confront him in a manly way. There's got to be a lot of reasons for somebody who is shot and murdered. If anything I think he didn't involve himself into the drug scene. If he were in a pub he would tell people to stop smoking dope. He was more of a deterrent than anything was. Wherever we went where he was there was none of that there (drugs). I didn't like it I had nothing to do with it. I wouldn't go to a local if people were smoking dope. Whether it was the *Anchor* up on Shields Road there was none of that there. People didn't do that in front of him. I think that if people go for a drink they don't want people smoking dope. I don't think drugs and drink mix, that's my own view."

David was asked if he was happy about the way that the police had carried out their investigation? "Not really, no, not really." Do you think they have not acted wholeheartedly? "I s u p p o s e so", David says in a long drawn out way, "I mean we wanted to put rewards up and everything but there was no help." It was pointed out to David that there was a reward posted for up to £100,000 and that the police approved of that. "There was nothing on TV about that nothing in the news and nothing good to say. They weren't going to say there was a £20,000 or £40,000 reward leading to information or the arrest of the person who done this. There was nothing like that. The money was sitting in the bank and that was it. We never got no publicity or nothing."

I can counter what David says by disclosing that there was a small article that appeared in the press saying a local bank operated the reward fund and that traders had contributed to it. But that is as far as it went. I contacted the bank myself and found that they knew nothing of the existence of the fund but obviously this was some years after it was started. The reason for this as I found out from Peter Connelly was that the fund was terminated when there was no response. Had the press given support it would have been different.

A place like Newcastle would have had every known junkie limbo dancing from underneath toilet doors if they knew of such a fund in an effort to collect on it. David was right, there was no real interest in the money. The simple reason for that though is that the fund received very little publicity. Had it been operated correctly by, say, a solicitor with a cast iron guarantee of it being paid out then it would 100% have led to killers being convicted. The person collecting it could have done so anonymously without anyone ever knowing who informed with the vital information, the missing piece of the jigsaw that would put the last nail into the coffin of the killers.

David has a rasp of weariness in his voice although it is not aimed at me but at the way the situation went without any help from the press. "A lot of people would have come out for £20,000 or £50,000 or £100,000 if it was put "up sort of like, 'You tell me and if you can stand up in court and say obviously you know it was this man.' I think it would work." David goes on to say that he would put his house up for a reward again. Company that Sharon leads into the room distracts us at this point. Time has flown by so fast and just about most points have been covered.

The lady and gentleman are asked if they would wish to contribute anything that they knew of about Viv. Carole and Alan Morpeth mentioned how they met Viv a number of years ago. Alan goes on to say he met Viv when Viv was working at *Baxters*. Carole was worried about meeting Viv as she was a friend of Sharon's and it was put to Viv that Carole was wary of meeting such a man who's reputation went before him. Her fears were unfounded and she says, "When I first met Sharon and got to know that Sharon knew Viv and I heard about his reputation I had seen Viv once or twice when he was younger. The first time I met him Sharon said to him, 'Now don't be intimidating with her try and be sort of…', it lasted all night it didn't change he was the perfect gentleman everybody got drunk and merry, but he made sure he kept coming saying, 'Are you alright, you alright'. Then the next time I met him it was in this very room with Anna, he was just wonderful when Anna was just chatting and laughing."

Sharon has returned to the room and her renewed spirit is showing in terms of the rest she has from my continuous line of questioning that would wear down a rock of granite, not that I came in wanting to wear anyone down. We talk a while of the funeral and Sharon goes on to say how some people from the West End of Newcastle would have been pleased to see Viv gone. A few more questions later and I take the cue to leave while I am still reasonably bright eyed myself as there is much more work to do in this matter.

Should you have gone through bereavement yourself you are sure to be able to have an affinity with what Sharon said in the earlier part of the interview. A loss is not easy to handle no matter how clever you are at controlling your emotions, grief just happens it is an uncontrollable emotion. You know someone has made an impact on your life after they are gone.

The family counselled themselves by staying close. Not that close so as to live out of each others pockets and become jealous of every little thing the other one had, that is a different and dangerous kind of closeness that can destroy a family I have seen that happen.

The closeness that helped Sharon and her family through it was a form of self-help where they talked openly and listened to each other. They searched for answers via mediums with no solace for their pain. In the end they turned to each other. What better form of counselling is there? None! Such extravagance is not needed on the costly fees of therapists or jumped up clinical nurses looking for an easy ride to retirement by making the right sounds during listening to your problems.

Super Gran was usually the answer to a family problem, her wry smile would give her that look of a seasoned professional who had heard it all before. Clever men wearing Dickie bow ties and white coats have drawn out the traits of most Northerners. Gone is the sure and confident, 'I'll put the kettle on while you tell me all about it.'

'They're coming to take you away, ha, ha.' The happy house was a place literally where people were kept happy on large doses of drugs prescribed by national health doctors. Try telling a little old lady who has been on valium for twenty five years that she has to stop taking the drug right now, this minute. When it is looked at who is really responsible for the drug problem it is modern medicine, lazy doctors whose right hand does more work than anything else knocking out prescriptions twenty to the dozen. If you are really sick they kick you off their surgery list, 'Excuse me, wasn't that what doctors were really there for?'

The grieving family is something that has not been really looked at but some bright spark is sure to come along now and do some research and submit the paper for a degree award.

2

Peter Connelly

Peter is a busy man and he was very withdrawn about granting me an interview due to how the press had acted towards his potential brother-in-law. That is something I cannot blame him for and as usual I was humbled to be allowed this opportunity to have an interview. It would have been easy to think I was the one doing the favour but that has not left me for one moment. Anyone who has contributed is the one doing the favour and for that I thank those who co-operated regardless of what their initial fears were.

Peter has certain business interests that keep him within Newcastle's social circle. To add to this he has maintained working for a multi-national company so I had to catch him in between these two commitments. As I wait for Peter in a pub I look around the area it is situated in. Looks can be misleading and for that reason I attach no importance to how good or how bad a place looks. The pub featured in an interview that Peter gave to a TV documentary team. I must admit I did not pay a lot of attention to that or just about any other documentary done on Viv because I know how they get cut to pieces in the editing studio. Therefore I came with a reasonably clean mind with my own set of questions rather than ponder on what was said by Peter to another interviewer.

My luck was in because it had been some few years earlier that Peter had given any sort of interview although the distrust that the press had instilled into him was still present. As usual before any interview we have some small talk but I sense that Peter wants more than that. Something always gives with people in these circumstances and that seemed to be the case here. Peter was ready to give his all, time had not healed his wounds but time had cleared his head allowing him to grasp what I wanted.

We talk about some photos that Viv's family and friends have contributed and how they portray Viv through the different stages of his life, out of the blue Peter says, "And you never ever got a chance to talk to his Headmaster I suppose, did you?" That certainly caught my breath. As I said looks are not important but here Peter looked sharp and he was sharp. That question put me on my toes, "Sid Henderson", I replied. That let Peter know I was aware of who Viv's former Headmaster was in his early years. I stumbled through Peter's retort as my mind worked fast to get a grip back on the situation. I guess it was Peter's way of finding me out if I was for real. I felt I got the question right and from then on we got on well. I could understand the need for Peter to find out if I was sincere in what I wished to find out. I spoke of how Viv's former school was vandalised by being set on fire and that I would be contacting Sid Henderson who was now a councillor on Gateshead Metropolitan Borough Council.

Peter asked if I had interviewed 'Hussain' and Andy Webb. "They were really close to him", Peter told me. I explained that Andy was not sought for an interview due to it being believed that Viv thought he may have had a soft spot for a woman called Julie Rutherford. (One of Viv's former lovers, mentioned in later chapter.) Viv always blamed Andy for being the father of a child that Julie had conceived whilst Viv was in prison and Andy had been driving Julie to visit Viv. Viv put one and one together and came up with two. Peter says, "He (Andy Webb) came here and he was crying and he asked if I would take him across to Viv's graveside and he knelt there and sat there for an hour crying showing his feelings." It has to be said that if this was the case then Andy Webb is a man to be admired since a man who can show his feelings in public is the greatest man on earth. For someone of Andy's stature to cry would help him considerably in terms of releasing any pent up emotions. Andy a former Mr Great Britain body sculpture winner in the heavyweight division a number of years ago with interests in leisure facilities around Newcastle was no whimp and for Peter to have witnessed such a huge man giving his emotions an airing would have been witnessing a true friend indeed.

Peter was closer than any friend of Viv's he was nearly a relation and obviously that put Peter in a status that automatically raised him above that of a friend in terms that he was nearly a relation. You cannot get rid of relations easily because they are still related they are still there, and there is still a connection there no matter what. If Peter had ever fell out with Viv then Anna could say, 'Come on, Viv, Peter was only kidding', so with a friend he could fall out and that could be the friendship finished. Viv had friends in the Sayers' and Rob Armstrong, but Viv fell out with them whilst in prison.

17

Once a chain of friendship is broken it is only as strong as its weakest link. With Peter it was suggested that could not happen so it was put to him that if Andy Webb wished to speak from his own free will without feelings of being pursued then by all means I would certainly be willing to accept comments he would wish to be known. I had not approached certain people because they may well be in a detached position and have lost some of that feeling that I needed to translate into words. Up to date Andy Webb has not made it known that he wished to pass comment to me via Peter and for that reason he is not within this book.

When Viv was murdered on New Year's Eve it was mentioned that Peter had closed his pub? Peter says, "I was standing making a pan of soup and a pan of curry waiting to put on the bar that night New Year's Eve and we got the phone call it was my brother and I went straight down to the hospital with my brother. We seen Paul Lister standing outside the hospital and we saw Terry Scott inside the hospital running about punching walls and things. The doctor came up to me and the police had almost surrounded the place expecting there to be some sort of backlash to the hospital staff and different things. A young Canadian doctor, I got him to one side and I said, Can you tell me what's happening?' He said, 'I'll tell you the truth he died twice on the way to the hospital and we have him now in the recovery room.' Which of course he wasn't he was already dead. He was never ever in the recovery room, which we thought he was. It eased the anger and everything then. Which I thought great, 'I can get back to the pub.' The police were getting worried because by this time there were more and more people there my mam was there my sisters were there the whole family was there. The police thought there would have been ructions if they said Viv was dead there and then. So I decided to give them a bit of breathing space and come back to the pub. "About an hour and a half later I got a phone call saying Viv was dead. I said, 'The doctor told me he was in the recovery room?' So I went back down and everybody was screaming and crying."

It was thought that the hospital Viv had been taken to was an inferior one where if you cut your finger they had to put the lights on and get the place opened up before treating you. Dispelling that rumour Peter said that the place was better equipped and more advanced than the Newcastle's RVI (Royal Victoria Infirmary) at that time.

"After I had heard about it I just wanted to walk, I was crying, I just wanted to walk and keep walking. Suppose I walked to London and I walked back and someone would tell me that he was all right. That's what I felt like doing. We didn't really think about who did it at the time it was more or less the next day we said that somebody knew there had to be a 'Judas' amongst them. They were on about the little fellow that ran away and I knew who that was, it was Eddie Wilson ('Little Legs'). Terry Scott was the gentleman

18

"with the white shirt leaning over him."

What seemed rather strange was that, and maybe it was the same to Viv, it did not matter who did it. It was perhaps only a case if I can just only get to where ever I will be all right and he did not think to say, 'I didn't see who did it', 'I did see who did it', 'Did you see who did it?' or 'Have you got them?' None of that was said. A policeman went in the ambulance with him to the hospital.

A short while after this Peter had the window of his premises shot out with a firearm, Peter says, "I got them shot out from this corner across here", Peter points out to me the corner where the shot came from. He says, "It was a few nights later it happened about one o'clock in the morning. It was a warning shot from a shotgun. Maybe because I was so close to him I was with him quite a bit. People would get in contact with me to ask Viv if he would come and look after their pubs. The breweries would say, 'Get in touch with Peter Connelly he'll see his brother-in-law, maybe he can sort something out for you?'

It was suggested to Peter that it was common knowledge that even the police passed on Viv's name to those in need of his assistance and advice about security. Peter says, "We did it in a fair way we didn't do it, 'Either you give us this or!' or 'Pay us X amount of pounds and I'll look after your pub.' All the publicans drank with me in this pub and if they had a problem they would come to me. If you had five or six characters in your bar and they want to make it into a loud bar, noisy bar start effing and blinding and swearing other people aren't going to use your bar so the trade was dropping off in some of the pubs."

Peter was asked what would make these people come into a bar behaving in such a manner? "It would probably be there local bar it would be close to where they lived. Lots of the pubs in Walker and Wallsend (areas in the East End of Newcastle) where all getting lots of trouble. A particular publican asked if I could bring Viv down. They were pissing in glasses, urinating at the counter. They weren't great big hard people."

Were these people high on drugs and just decided to act like animals? "When Viv first came on the scene they didn't realise his capabilities they didn't realise how big and powerful he was until he got up to them. I seen it on one occasion where a guy said, 'Peter I've had enough of this.' There was a particular family in Walker who weren't hard but they were a bit crackers. They are a known family, I know them and get on with them but Viv was working then for the publican. I couldn't say, 'Viv don't give them warnings because I know them.' The warning that he gave them was always three warnings. You got a first warning a second warning and then after the third warning you had to be clipped. This particular guy used to cause trouble in quite a nice pub in Walker called *The Stack* and he went in and got a hold of "this man and within seconds, and this man was a big lad as well, the pee was running down his legs. Running down his legs! So! Even though the manager was a little bit frightened to say anything at the time the next time the lad came in the manager threw the lad a packet of pampers, everybody started laughing at this man who was supposed to be a tough guy, that was one.

"Then we would go onto another bar called *The County*. Viv would say, 'What can you afford?' He didn't say, 'I want £100!', he would say, 'What can you afford?', and the reply was, '£50 a week, Viv, I wont miss £50 a week if I get rid of these two particular people this bar will pick up again.' So Viv went behind the bar and started pulling pints in the bar and started serving people as if it was a family pub, his pub. It was, 'A pint of Guinness, Viv'. Viv was laughing away and carrying on, 'A pint of lager, Viv' and these people stopped literally point blank and never went back in the bar again the pub was great." From this point of view we can see that Viv made the place safe to go in and the people were happy. Peter interjects, "The atmosphere was different in the pubs, the nightclubs, the social clubs. He didn't drink you know?" Peter says this with some admiration on behalf of Viv. "He only drank orange juice and occasionally a Guinness if you ever brought him a Guinness he would really get happy and enjoy himself you know and you could have a good laugh with him it was great everybody was happy.

"I got a phone call from a Bass publican it was a pub off Norham Road up in North Shields. This landlady had been petrol bombed she had a child on the premises she couldn't take much more, but the breweries said they would pay to foot the bill. So obviously then we said, 'Well it's £500 it's a one off thing we aren't coming up every week.' We got the address of these people who done this and knocked on their door and they were warned there and then. There was nobody got hit or anything like that and that was the end of the trouble for that publican up until Viv was shot and then all hell broke loose. Obviously everybody that ever got barred from pubs turned up. There was big parties everybody would go on a rampage all those pubs got it that night."

Here we have a total antithesis of what the newspapers wrote of Viv and are still writing to this very day of Viv about him being a gangster and a hoodlum. The romantic air of such a man is not good for selling newspapers yet the British are steeped in a history of romantic attachments with so called 'likeable rogues'. 'Fagin' the character from *David Copperfield* is cast as a down to earth character giving shelter to homeless waifs in return for them doing a bit of dipping. (Pick pocketing. The perpetrators were better known as cut purses due to them cutting the strings on purses way back in those days.) 'Robin Hood' takes from the rich and gives to the poor he is steeped in myth yet his spirit is heralded as something to behold.

Ronnie Biggs the Great Train robber was hunted down and at one point saved by the skin of his teeth. Did the British public really want to see such a romantic figure looked up and the key thrown away?

Peter sets the record straight as to how he was granted a publicans license even though he admits he has a past criminal record of violence for two assaults and GBH and he says it seemed highly unlikely that he would ever get a license under such circumstances. There has been a lot of conjecture as to how it came about that the police granted this application without objection. This innuendo of him being a police informer only added to his grief and here he sets the record straight. "I was doing quite well and at that time I didn't hold a publican's license or anything like that. The police asked to see me and I came down they said, 'Peter it's come to our attention that you are trying to run a pub and we are thinking about letting you have your own license to run a pub.' Which I thought was great because of my criminal record it was unlikely I would be allowed ever to get a license. It was ten or fifteen years since I was last convicted. I took the wrong route and mixed with drug dealers that's the people I knocked about with but at the time they were petty. They went in heavy handed that lot did they burst into bars and smashed the place up and even took coffins to bars and did horrible and nasty things. I was with that clique for a short time because at that time I didn't have any money."

Peter was asked if the use of coffins left at pubs was a way of gaining territory for their drug pushers to sell from? "It was mostly money them days it was just before the drugs came in heavy and just before Viv came across here." Was it the days just before the end of the Harry Perry era? "Harry was there it was one of Harry's operations in his time. He was the boss way back then; Harry and me had quite a close relationship then. We were sent in to do the business and obviously they got the message one way or another."

Harry Perry was considered a forerunner to the pre-Viv days. Although Harry could use his fists he was said by some people to have a short fuse and could blow for the slightest of reasons. That was way back in the 60s and 70s. The main nightclub where most underworld figures met used to be in a place called *Billy Bottos*. That is a place where all the gangsters headed for in those days, the Kray's where in there and Joe Louis was in there. Times have somewhat changed, but the nostalgia that exists within the North East about such places and names lives on. Peter knew some of the patrons of *Billy Bottos* and he remembers one in particular. "One of the greatest men that I admired", Peter says, "more than anything was a man called Jimmy Walker. I was at his funeral just a fortnight ago. His father had him fighting three fights a day for a half a crown (12 ½ pence) a time, his knuckles were out here." Peter signifies with the use of his cupped hand over the top of the

21

other how his knuckles had swelled. "This was a great man a great fighter in "lots of respects." Where did these fights take place? "These were the bare knuckle days under Pottery Bank under the bridge in different places and the Quayside. He met Viv lots of times and Viv loved him. Viv would sit and listen to some of his stories. And he had the greatest stories in the world to tell. I've always wished that before he died that someone wrote a book about Jimmy Walker because his stories were far greater than you could ever say about Viv there were some belters. I would sit for hours and listen to them. They cut his legs off three times you know", Peter indicates the places by pointing to his own leg and saying, "there, there and there he had fluid in his leg until eventually his legs were off and it was just a body that they were carrying about. He lived through all of that but died from pneumonia a year later."

Could it be assumed then that Viv looked up to this man, was he one of Viv's hero's? "He fought a Dutch man and at the bottom of the plate (winners trophy) it had on, *'The man who invented bottle'*, which was great, because he was until Viv and Viv obviously to me was the man who had all the right bottle in the world and I've seen some awesome things when Viv was fighting. We once got called to a pub in North Shields in which we got paid £200. The man used to have a pub across here called the *Queens*. When he very first came to Newcastle that was the first pub Viv started to run in the East End of the city and the odd few. Denny Haig was working with Viv at that time." (Denny Haig is from Highfield near Rowlands Gill where Viv originated from.)

It is pointed out here that Denny Haig was featured in the *Cook Report* an exposé TV Documentary (featured in the chapter on media betrayal), Peter goes on to say. "I didn't hold any grievance against Denny until what he did to Jack and I was really annoyed. I know he's quiet old, Denny, about forty odd or fifty but Jack, to hit Jack and Jack's never ever harmed anybody. They all seemed to jump on the bandwagon after Viv was gone they all seemed to jump on his back everybody was in his pockets they'd only ever got money off Viv he supplied their wages."

Viv, as his father, Jacky, pointed out was a moneybox for others. It may well have been that Denny Haig was misquoted in the TV documentary about protection rackets. This led to a confrontation between him and Viv's father and all sorts of trouble ending in violence that would have seen Viv turning in his grave. The televised interview that Denny gave to Roger Cook was cut to shreds and portrayed what Denny had said very differently to what he actually said in one go. (More on that in a later chapter.)

It was put to Peter that he was typically anti-police, but after the killing of Viv he had turned the other cheek. "I always felt the police were right but I just don't think they put enough into it, they put plenty of man hours into it."

22

I asked then if Peter was happy at what the police had done because he said he was happy with them. "Not as happy as I would have like to have been. To me it's like an apple. They seem to have wanted to start at the centre of it I wanted them to start at the outside and come in slowly. I don't know where I've got it now, but I wrote down everything that I was ever told and I swore on TV and I swore on Viv's life that I would if I could I would tell and I would literally tell and I would stand in court and tell what I had been told whoever killed Viv because it was like killing my brother in a sense and everybody knows that so people speak less about Viv to me than anybody else." Peter speaks with a sense of justice and meaning here that pulls no punches. Any true friend of Viv's would have taken a leaf out of Peter's book and pursued answers to questions. Listening to what he says is very convincing and full of loyalty. The sorrow that Peter shows is a proud sorrow one that will not be washed away by the tides of time. There will be no wearing down of his endeavour and something springs to mind that I once said to someone. 'Fortitude', which according to my faithful Collins English dictionary is defined as: 'Courage in adversity or pain.' That person I passed that word on to took great solace in what I said but sadly did not turn out to be a person who could make it through such pain. Peter, I know will make it.

Perhaps those that are intent in causing further turmoil to Peter's life by whispering that he is an informer perceive this quest of Peter's the wrong way. Peter by virtue of his ongoing loyalty to Viv wants the killers brought to justice so that the family can get on with their lives. After all if someone goes missing and years have went by the family then wants to know one way or the other if they are dead or well. This uncertainty adds to the anguish of those left waiting for news. Then, say, the person's body is found and it turns out they have been murdered! The anguish is still there because the family and friends wait for justice to be done.

Viv's family is left in an agonising situation. They witnessed there son die with his body riddled full of holes. They have no reason for this to help them understand what it was all about or what it was over. Rumours are rife, overly rife. Drugs. Protection Rackets. Territorial Rights. They are only a few of the explanations offered. In fact it was none of those reasons as you will find out in this book a little later. Then, when it is found out why Viv was amateurishly murdered the anguish is still not then over as the killers are still on the loose and have yet to be brought to justice. That could have happened, but for mistakes made by the police.

Peter is on the look out for anything that could help catch the killers. What though of Viv's other friends? "We should have made a pact we should have done things ourselves. I would have at that time got revenge if I knew exactly at the time who did it. There were about nine people mentioned that could have done it."

In a story revealed to me from an underworld source of the highest order I can relate the following story. One of those arrested on suspicion of the murder of Viv was a man called Brian William Tait. It has been alleged to me that a few days after Viv was murdered that this man went into a pub called *Jacksons*. It had been under Viv's care in which some £200 a week was the fee for security. Brian Tait walked in and took money out of the till. Robin, 60, the under manager took a beating from Tait. Tait was shouting his mouth off about what he was going to do and so on. The bar had previously been under the management of Peter Connelly and Robin was Peter's second in command who stayed on after Peter left. It has been further alleged that Tait went in and out of pubs up and down Shields Road and in Wallsend demanding money saying he was now in charge.

Peter was in a pub he owned some days after that in the early hours of the morning was having a private party. In that company with a few other cronies was a man whose nickname crops up again, 'Little legs'. (More of him later) A knock came to the pub window just after midnight and it was this man Brian Tait. Peter went outside and they both had a fight, which it was obvious what Tait had come for. Peter was not in a situation to back off as in this area once that happens it means you are giving up your rights not to have any old Tom, Dick or Harry walk all over you.

The story told to me about the ensuing fight was alleged by someone who was present that night but wishes to remain anonymous. They say that Tait was a taller man than Peter but Peter was standing his ground. Tait was alleged to have said, 'I'm going to shoot you as well.' Peter replied, 'Oh! You're going to shoot me are you?' Peter allegedly went and got a gun, which according to my source he says that Peter was not a weapons man. Peter went to shoot Tait who by this time was 'squealing like a pig'. Tait ended up grabbing the gun off Peter and pointing it at him and the gun was going back and forward. What seemed to be the difficulty was that the safety catch was on which was the only thing that prevented the gun from being fired. The gun was like a rifle that held three cartridges a one went in underneath.

There was a fine layer of snow and a blue light was seen coming down the street and Tait decides to leg it. My source tells me "Peter knew that he and Tait were not shot neither of them was dead. As soon as Peter came in the pub carrying the gun and it went off, B O O M! A woman who was standing nearby in the pub pittled herself with shock. Peter got a shock and he ended up pressing the trigger again, BOOM! BOOM! It went off twice more one shot just missing the electric box. Peter got the shock of his life and seemed to be shaking. The police car still hadn't arrived a white Merc came flying around the corner it looked like a taxi and the driver said, 'Get in Peter, get in Peter.' The police helicopter was over head by this time. I saw a man take the gun from Peter stick it down his trousers, link the arm of a woman and he "calmly walked off with it."

Peter takes up the story from where my source has told me up to where the police pursue Peter to his home. "The house was surrounded by the police and the helicopter was above with the light on us and they've got us and they were saying, 'Where is the gun? Where is the gun?' I said I haven't got a gun I've never had a gun, 'It was a plank of wood' I told them. Someone telephoned the police from the garage forecourt. The police decided to follow the footprints in the snow and found Brian Tait in a house with a man called Billy Tait who isn't a relation." (Not the Billy Tait who owns a car dismantlers business in the Gateshead area.)

It has to be mentioned here that there is a large amount of people with the surname 'Tait' and most of them end up with the nickname 'Spud' after the potato which is commonly called a 'tatty' a word more commonly used in Scotland and the North East of England.

The story continues; Peter says, "Tait decided to stay at Billy's house as he knows he'll be put up for the night he doesn't want to go to his own house. The police surrounded the house, Walkie-talkies the business. They got Billy out, he came out with his hands up and eventually Brian Tait came out with his hands up. He told police straight away that I was the one with the gun he made a statement that I had the gun. Yet he was the one who came down and shot the windows out everybody seen him he didn't do it discreetly or nothing he walked down the road pulled the gun out, a sawn off shotgun and blew the windows out. This was a few nights after the scuffle."

My source who alleged the Tait/Peter Connelly fight was asked why Tait had called at the bar the night he and Peter had the fight? "Davy Lawson and Bill McFarlane were associates of Tait and it may well have been that he wanted to join them for a drink. Peter knew of Tait slapping Robin about and taking money so Peter obviously thought that he was involved. Tait was alleged to have went into just about all the bars on that road demanding money. He is due out of prison soon and I think it will start all over again. Peter may well be at the top of his list. A co-accused of Tait's got out of prison recently and he was jointly done with him when he held a gun to a student's face in *Circus Circus* (pub in Newcastle's Bigg Market area). These students didn't know who the guy was from Adam and he couldn't find out where they lived and they went witness against him saying he definitely had a gun on him. The police loved it because they wanted to see this man locked up."

This connection shows how violence is interweaved within people's lives. Darren Arnold an associate of Brian William Tait was sentenced to seven years for an offence of violence. Tait and Arnold were close associates and lived in a world of violence. Peter says, "I went to pick up David Roche (Ex

Newcastle United Midfield Footballer) who got four years imprisonment he looked in great shape. David got himself into bad company and he now realises that to be the case. David told Peter that he got the four years imprisonment because of being guilty by association when a club doorman was attacked in a crowded street of shoppers during the daytime.

The story goes like this. Darren Arnold had been involved in some trouble and a doorman refused him entry into a Newcastle club. For this the doorman was attacked with a machete and received horrific injuries. Arnold received seven years imprisonment and Roche got four years. An insider tells me. "Roche was easily led and couldn't handle drink. He wasn't very aware of things around him he got himself a bit more anxious to fight and he wanted to have a go at different people, he didn't want people to pick on him and he changed a little bit. Only because he was getting mixed up with these he was drinking with them and he was associating with them. They were hangers on because David always had money to buy the drinks and whatever they wanted. That day David and young John Wheatly tried twice to get rid of Tait they didn't want to be seen with him or anywhere near him and for some reason he still stuck with them and it was through him that David ended up getting jail."

Roche, 24, was to become the victim of a kneecapping in June 1995 whilst attending a wake for a family member at *Jackson's* bar in the East End of Newcastle. Roche had been invited outside to have a fight with Roger Vinton, 28. Vinton had goaded Roche and Roche had taken the bait and went to go outside and have a one-to-one fair fight with Vinton. Although it is not what it seems and having a fair fight with some people is like fighting the very Devil himself. Once he was lured away from the other mourners Roche was squirted in the eyes with ammonia by Vinton. On the scene was Vinton's henchman, Lawrence Donnelly, 23, who had on him the usual tool of a city hardman? A shotgun! Roche was shot in the right knee as usual in the typical heroic fashion, from behind. If you play with fire you must expect some dire consequences. The big league in David's case was playing over thirty games for Newcastle United (The Magpies) before being transferred.

Big league crime is far beyond the capabilities of most criminals. Delving into the occasional hardman act to collect a few quid here and there is playing small time yet the consequences are often far more than what the crime is really worth. Real gangsters are not a myth but at times people like to play-act and take off those up the ladder as a role model.

Three operations later Roche is not the same person. He has learned some valuable lessons. There is no such thing as a code of conduct amongst the lower echelons of the crime world. Vinton and Donnelly were charged with Grevous Bodily Harm with Intent and Attempted Murder. Both denied the charges and entered pleas of not guilty. Donnelly told police when he was arrested that 'Roche won't be taking anymore penalties.' Other mourners who had come out to see what the commotion was held Vinton outside the pub while Donnelly was arrested the following day.

The end result was a prison sentence for both Vinton and Donnelly, ten and twelve years respectively. On the charge of attempted murder against Roche both were cleared. Mr Justice Ian Kennedy said that there was no excuse for the crime that threatened Roche's career. He said that this was a deliberate offence and there was no mitigation! If that is the case then how can any judge justify the jailing of someone who defended their family grave from a vandal by giving them a good hiding? Remember this when you read a later chapter about Patrick Conroy.

Wallsend High Street in the East End of Newcastle came under threat from those who closed in after the kill (after Viv's death) for the spoils. Viv was no more and advantage could be taken by those who dared. As has been alleged that after Viv's death Brian William Tait pursued the action of going into pubs and using force to obtain money from the managers as they no longer had the use of Viv to deter such things happening. Shields Road leads into the East End it was an area that Viv took under his wing. The lion was no longer there to defend his territorial rights and those seeking to take advantage by foul means failed. In 1997 four hopeful racketeers tried to take over a piece of the East End and failed when three of them were charged with affray.

The *Grace Inn* came under attack when the men demanded free drinks in return for keeping trouble out of the bar. This kind offer was declined and the consequences of refusing such a kind offer of help from these four gentlemen resulted in the bar being wrecked. Windows were put out, furniture smashed and violence dished out to those standing about in dismay at what was happening. The elderly manager, 67, pulled a barmaid to safety from under a counter. The four had been previously told to leave the premises when one from the group had broken into the one-armed bandit. The woman barmaid ordered the four men to leave. Faced with a female telling them what to do with an elderly manager in attendance it gave them no impetus to leave in peace. As a consequence of this Paul Roche, 25, David Kerr, 26 and William Tait, 30 all received prison sentences for affray to which they all pleaded guilty in March 1998. What is the importance of this matter? William Tait is allegedly the brother of Brian William Tait who had paraded up and down the very same road and allegedly demanded money from the licensees immediately after Viv's death! The barmaid was willing to give evidence against the three that were caught regardless of the consequences. A fourth man made good his getaway and was not apprehended for the part he played in the affray. Although I have been told from underworld sources who that fourth man was it serves no purpose to expose him, that is for the police to pursue.

The prison sentences dished out were two years to each with Roche receiving a three-and-a-half-year custodial sentence, which included an extra offence of attempting to pervert the course of justice. Was this the power vacuum referred to after Viv's death? If so it was a futile attempt at capturing power. Looking at how Viv worked compared to these will give you some idea of why he was in so much demand. Viv was given an invitation to help publicans out compared to how these villains tried to take what was not theirs to take. Viv empowered people while others tried to overpower people. That best sums up the difference between Viv and those who tried to fill his boots.

Assuming that this fight did take place as mentioned earlier between Peter and Brian Tait it is lucky that either one did not end up dead, but for the good fortune of the safety catch not coming off the gun that both tussled over. Tait was told to keep out of Wallsend by Viv, as people felt uncomfortable with him around. A tie in with this is a connection between Tait and a woman called Karen Young from Wallsend. An insider alleges that a gun was supplied to Peter Connelly from someone close to Karen. Bearing in mind that this is all what it can be an allegation since Peter denies ever having a gun in his possession. Young and Tait were amongst those arrested but not charged over Viv's murder. What reason does Tait have for allegedly shooting windows out of a pub that Peter was in only a matter of days after Viv was murdered? Where did he get that gun? Where did Peter Connelly get his alleged weapon? Why did Peter's association with Karen Young end immediately after Viv's death when they had previously associated with each other?

David Lancaster was Peter's brother-in-law. He was involved in the assault on Stuart Watson inside of *Hobbo's* nightclub. (*Viv (Graham) – 'Simply the Best.'*) The whole thing is intertwined and Peter says, "Viv got into the wrong clique and once you got into the wrong clique it was hard for him to get out. They used Viv to get them into *Hobbo's* because they were barred and Viv took them in." It was put to Peter that a story was made up to Viv so as to arouse his anger along the lines that Stuart Watson was alleged to have broken the jaws of two young men and had got away with it. Whether or not Viv was told this is conjecture. Peter says, "You could see by his face (Watson's) he knew what was going to kick off." Peter briefly describes the ensuing three-minute attack on Watson. "Viv slung him about a bit but Watson never went down he blocked well he covered well. You didn't see any photographs of Stuart Watson after it. You didn't see how bad he was?" Watson is alleged to have said that he was used as a pawn in the game to get Viv.

Peter continues describing the fight, "They went on about how heavy he "was (Viv) and how he flung him (Watson) about like a rag-doll, this, that and the other. I think it was just his jacket (Watson) was too big for him it looked worse than what it was, it was never as awesome as that. There were four tapes, four cameras actually on this fight. You were getting the back before the front you were getting the wrong sequence. It came out the wrong sequence, not the way the event actually happened. It was nothing I seen a lot worse than that." Peter repeats this as if replaying the picture through his mind. Re-running the sequences in the right order.

Ray Hewitson ('Dodgy Ray') is brought into the conversation. Ray a former lieutenant of the Harry Perry camp had served time in the early 1980s and it was suggested that his connection with Viv had given rise to the drug stories about Viv. When Peter had first met Viv 'Dodgy Ray' was one of Viv's closest pals. They, Viv and Ray, had eventually fallen out. Ray was of a big build but as far as being anywhere near Viv's status in power and commanding respect from others he fell short, but wherever I went to interview people about Viv it was said in the majority of cases, "Have you spoken with Dodgy Ray?" Ray straddled the past and the future but with regard to pursuing him about Viv it was accepted that he would have to join the queue of people wishing to be interviewed about Viv.

Any person in this country is entitled to go anywhere in this country, travel with free passage, free from hindrance, free from being intimidated, free from anything. Viv obviously served in some of that sense to allow that free passage from intimidation yet the press were quite willing to accept from any Tom, Dick or Harry who said that they were Viv's friend anything and put it into print. Peter confirms this, "Any night club people went to, they said, 'I'm Viv's pal', just so they would get in. They never ever knew him from Adam they had never ever met the man. I even here it today. You hear some stupid things from people what they say. 'I did know him then.' I was his brother-in-law and I had never ever seen them with him."

Peter had said to the press that he felt the people who had killed Viv (January 1995) were going to be caught very shortly. Peter said, 'I can feel it in my blood'. What made you feel that way? "It was the people the way they were talking. The people who were around me and the way they were talking. I thought, 'They are talking about it now and talking about it freely surely somebody is going to slip up here?' The fact that there was too many involved in it you see. I thought well, 'To do a murder you think it's got to be a one-to-one you wouldn't tell your brother, you wouldn't tell your sister, you wouldn't tell your wife.' These they sat around a table it was sort of quickly planned and they didn't get a lot of money for it. They didn't get fortunes for it we don't know if they even got the full payment and sometimes when you don't get the full payment (you cannot really complain can you?) something else could come up. There's that many deals being made with the police you've seen what happened to the last guy to go Queen's evidence he gets eight years less than anybody else does. You can make deals. That's what the judges want and so do the police want it to make deals with these so called criminals something they expect fifteen for and they get eight.

"I thought that was going to happen. I thought somebody was going to do something quite serious and go queen's evidence. I don't know if you saw the Photostat copies of Davie Glover's deps? They were too real some of the things that you had read. Including about a house where they hit the wall with the car. The police couldn't really take anything he said because in the end he was going to plead insane." What Peter is referring to here is the David Glover, Jnr kidnap and torture trial when he and his co-accused received lengthy prison sentences. Glover had allegedly made a deal whereby he would go witness against the killers if the police could get them to trial. Glover then at the last minute withdrew his offer of help and left everyone in the lurch. This is covered more in depth in a later chapter within this book.

Peter had gone on to say to the press in 1995, 'If the killers aren't caught it would give a free hand to anybody who wants to kill.' Now he says, "If they can take somebody off the street like that, and I mean he wasn't killed he was assassinated. If they can do that they can do it to anybody. They wouldn't have used that calibre of a gun and they wouldn't have fired as many shots."

Do you think they knew what the gun was and what it was capable of doing? "When I went to the inquest and what they had said about the gun and all that I didn't know the gun's capabilities. What it done was to take every vital organ out of Viv and he couldn't survive it, they couldn't have saved him. They could have given him blood and blood and blood and he wouldn't have survived. They said how they shot him and where they shot him and the burn marks went out the back and another bullet put a skid burn up the centre of his back. As the bullet went through him he put his hand there and it came through his hand. They didn't know if that was the same shot or another one." This emotional subject is left alone and we move on.

Viv was well known in Teeside and he would travel down there once a week to nearby Spennymoor where a once a week rave was held in the *Venue* and Viv had to show his face. I spoke with the club's DJ who told me that Steve Forrest had took over the Venue but its days were numbered as a rave scene. Peter confirmed that Viv made this once a week trip as his face there alone would prevent any trouble. "He had to show his face to let them know he was in charge of it." It was put to Peter that Viv might have had contacts in Glasgow but Peter could not confirm or deny this.

Pip Wright was a friend of Viv's and Viv gave him £500 on the Christmas day a week before he was gunned down. Wright was hard up for cash and Viv was generous that way. Peter says, "Some people say Viv bought his own murder weapon." (By this act of generosity.) Wright is brought into the scenario on the allegation that he was close to Micky Lang ('little legs'). Peter takes the story up from here, "Viv had showed Mickey Lang up a day or two before this (when Wright was given £500 from Viv). In the afternoon Viv grabbed Mickey and threw him on the pool table, but they were drinking later on. Lang was close to this Pip Wright. I never met Pip Wright to this day. I took over a pub a few months ago just before Christmas. There was great big brick through the window and it had a note saying, 'Put through the window the next time it will be off your head', it was signed on the brick, 'Pippy Wright'. I had never ever met him but I knew he had got £500 but I don't know what for or anything like that it was just a favour from Viv." This story about Viv just about buying himself the weapon that was responsible for his murder must be viewed as an allegation only and there is no inference that Pip Wright had any connection with the murder of Viv. Public opinion at times can be based on strange facts and it is not intended to sway public opinion in any direction.

With regard to Terry Scott (Viv's associate that held his head as Viv lay dying on the ground.) Peter says, "I've only seen Terry Scott once since he phoned me from the hospital and said that Viv was dead. I seen him once when I went into a nightclub in the town. It was a nice summer's night and he just sat outside the door with his arms folded and he just looked at me and I walked in. It was just that we didn't have anything to talk about."

What about Rob Armstrong! (One of Viv's closest friends up to a few years before his death.) What I am getting at here is that if Viv had a brother that was just like him in the same way and they worked hand in hand like the Kray's used to or like the Richardson's then they would defend each other if something happened to one of them. Because Viv did not have this support system there was no continuity to his defence. Therefore although, yes, the Connelly's were as close as he was going to get to a family it was not as though they were like a brother.

What about all of those people and his friends? "They were just like rats leaving a sinking ship. They were super hard when he was there but soon as he was gone they became nothing they were just weaklings. He was their strength. What was going to happen to them as long as he was there? It was him that was always going to be in the front line it was always going to be him that was going to be...", Peter talks fast at this point half finishing a sentence before moving on to the next, "...they knew his capabilities and knew nothing was going to happen to them and it was just a free ride for them and there was as many as there could that got onto the band wagon."

Peter is saying that there is no loyalty there and there in terms of Viv's mother and father that are not financially sound compared to some of Viv's so called friends who have got money. "Ask Brenda Hickman then where's all of these millions then, £2m and there's them (Viv's parents) can't even get the phone on." (Brenda Hickman is a crime reporter that has worked for the *Evening Chronicle* for some years. She covered the Viv murder.) "Viv's car was on the chuckie (HP). They've got a house that any average person's got they don't own it or nothing."

The Alan Rooney case is talked about. Rooney, 34, (1994) received eight years imprisonment for blackmail. In June of 1993, six months before Viv was murdered, Rooney had heard of a Sunderland publican putting Viv down with insults. For these insults Rooney was prepared to collect in the name of Viv. The sum of £5,000 was demanded and if it was not forthcoming then Rooney told the man that he would be tortured and have his home burned down as well as being murdered. The victim was told that he was acting on behalf of Viv and said, 'He's the man.'

Rooney allegedly told Viv that some insults had been forthcoming from a publican's husband and Rooney asked Viv if he could pursue the matter. Viv had allegedly told him, 'Do what you want'. (More on this in the Anna Connelly interview.) The victim was pursued via telephone for a payment but the police had now been called in and were recording the threats given over the telephone. An arrangement was made for a down payment off the demanded £5,000 to be ferried via taxi cab and a middle man was hired to collect the money but the police arrested him and soon afterwards Rooney was locked up.

The victim was scared shitless to say the least especially when confronted with the name of Viv. No doubt there was some truth in the slanderous remarks made by the victim but many a person has said things that they often regret. Rooney took it upon himself to pursue this bit of private enterprise although he had explained the situation to Viv. Viv had taken little interest in the matter and for that reason Rooney decided to have a 'little earner' on the side. By time Rooney was tried for this crime he was already part way through an eighteen-month prison sentence for a wounding offence. Viv would have been called as a witness in this matter but for the fact that he was dead. Eight years seems excessive for this, but when you consider that the name of Viv was sufficient to make most people shake at the knees it was worse than saying your home would be burned down just using Viv's name alone could get results, it did; eight years worth.

The victim in all of this was a father of three and for the sake of the children his name is withheld. Had Viv been a real up and get 'em gangster he would have went along to the man's gaff himself and done the business for the dis (disrespect) he was shown. Viv just laughed it off like the affable man he was. Those that said Viv took liberties with people were proved wrong.

When Viv received a driving ban Rooney started driving him around and their association became a friendship.

Peter comments on this. "That was on the other side of the water, Sunderland. I used to like Alan Rooney he was quite a funny lad and he came out with some funny things. When Viv was murdered though Alan Rooney then tried to twirl it to say he was working for Viv when that happened." Viv was not into blackmail and obviously had said whatever you are doing has nothing to do with me but if you make anything from my name do it but I am not into that.

The Independent newspaper was mentioned and given a good report from Peter but as for the other newspapers he gives a brusque criticism of them. Should there be a law to prevent the invasion of the press at such times? "Definitely. As far as the *Independent* were concerned that was not the case but the rest of the press I had nothing to say to them. I was a pallbearer at the funeral and my stepbrother Michael was comforting my sister. The press said that this was 'Peter Connelly comforting his sister', it wasn't even me it was my brother Michael they didn't even know me or nothing. Then I was angry and I did want to say something. I was at the inquest and I said a lot there. Tony Cartlidge who interviewed me in the *Close Up North* TV documentary did a fair representation and I told him all that I knew."

Peter is asked how Viv found the time to relax? "Taking the phone off for one, he used to love just getting out the road going somewhere different from people and just maybe just him and Anna. I knew that he loved his kids and would go across as often as he could to see them he just absolutely idolised them. There was nothing greater, I was there the day he went to the hospital when Gillian Lowes gave birth to the bairn it was a lovely day he was happy.

He was a great provider for her he never ever left her short. She always thought there was something there and that he would come back. He was a great man."

What of the stress that Viv must have been under having to do so much? "I think Viv took too much on he was doing far too much. Later on drugs became a big thing and they started coming in they weren't there at first they started moving very fast there was quite a few drug dealers. A lot of drugs I didn't realise their was so much drugs about and they were all wanting to be in on the nightclub scene. That's where they were sold. The 'E's became popular and different types of ecstasy tablets. Viv was never involved in any type of drug dealing."

Viv had been accused (After he died.) of being a big drug baron, people say there is no smoke without fire. Suggestions of a £2M turnover and racketeering were plastered in enough newspapers to cover the side of any barn door. Our investigations showed no such activities but we did unearth associations with people of a dubious character. But saying that just about everyone in this country is standing or sitting within about twenty feet of a drug user. That drug user might be an alcoholic or a smoker at the very least.

Most people will know of someone who is a drug user or know of someone who knows someone who is a user of drugs. Why should Viv be any different in this context. We live in a decadent society. Even President Clinton of USA drawed but, '...did not inhale.' Viv was a naïve person when it came to that side of things but he certainly did not approve of drugs that were used to get a high. Unwittingly he may have become involved in some activities that could have been misconstrued.

A story was related on hearsay to Peter about Viv being asked by Geoffrey Tote in Newcastle's *Madison's* nightclub to sort some trouble out with the doormen who had allegedly took his 'E's off him and his money whilst he was in the toilets. He went crying to Viv saying that his drugs and money were taken from him. Viv went and knocked the two doormen out and gave Tote his things back. Peter says, "I don't know why he did that but I heard about it. It was a stupid thing to do but Viv was like that and he thought he was helping out. They weren't Viv's drugs. There was another girl in who was a big drug dealer who had plenty of money. The Sayer's got involved and beat her and her man up there and then in *Madison's*. Viv didn't intervene he just kept out of it. He stood back and didn't get involved in it. Then I realised that there was that many people wanting to sell drugs. A drug dealer asked Viv for a loan of £500. The man offered to pay Viv £600 back I don't know if he loaned him the money but that's the way people went on. Viv had no idea of other people's motives for wanting to borrow money."

Peter must have seen a number of changes in Viv since he first met him up until the time of his death. This man who was a bit green who was from outside of the city and then over the years he develops his persona and charisma. "He used to love going to the gym for half an hour or an hour he would use Andy Webb's gym and they would end up having such a laugh. The laughs that went on in the gym you haven't heard the likes of it. I never ever touched weights but I was watching him as they put some weights on the bar. It was awesome the weights they were putting on for him. Off he goes he was bench pressing it and it was great to see him doing this and everybody would clap and cheer. Then they would put a bit more weight on and he would just press the weight that nobody could bench press and he used to love it if he could exceed it and get a better weight he thought it was great. Each time he was getting bigger you could see him getting bigger, but then he was getting little side effects he was complaining about certain things he was aching, he didn't feel well at some stage. He had an abscess on his leg." Viv at this time was taking steroids and they did not agree with him as they do not (in the end) agree with anyone. Viv gave them up because he did not have time to train as often as he wished due to pressure of work. Bad temperedness started creeping into it."

Viv didn't train as hard then and then he didn't have time to train because he was running all over the place. His mobile phone number changed that many times because there were that many people who had his number. You would say, 'Have you got Viv's number?' Then you would pass that number on to others. On my book I've got about five or six numbers for him."

He had received a lot of death threats over the phone but did he take them seriously? "He didn't ever take any notice of them did he? He never took them to heart or anything. Viv did talk and I said to him, 'Who do you think is the one most likely to shoot you?' the most likely one to shoot you? He said, 'If anyone is going to shoot me I think it would be the Sayer's'. I said, 'If I get shot will you sort it for me and if you get shot I'll sort it for you', which I've never ever done. I only ever had one piece of good advice off anybody since it happened."

A third party told me that Peter had carried a gun that was an eleven shooter with half-inch bullets. Peter had allegedly practised using it in readiness for threats he heard against him. Apparently he was walking around wearing a Barber jacket with a big bulge that was obvious. Peter then allegedly had a phone call from a policeman who asked him to bring the gun and all the ammunition and meet him straight away. Someone had informed the police that he was carrying a gun. Peter was told he would get two to three years with his record. The police put it to Peter that he had to leave it to the judicial system to find out who actually did it. The only thing Peter would say to this was, "You can get a gun anywhere." This of course is too true and Ireland has different gun laws to England. You just had to burgle a gun club but since the change in laws on that behalf Ireland has become the place to pick up anything from a handgun to a grenade.

Could Peter explain what he believed to be the direct cause of Viv being murdered? Viv obviously had much more on his plate. "I seen it getting out of hand the way they were going on. It is definitely down to drugs and drugs related why he was shot. They didn't get what they wanted they didn't get free access to all the nightclubs and they knew the amount of money that was to be made and they knew they had to have him out of the road. That was the only reason why they shot him because he was stopping him making a lot of money."

Peter mentions a woman's name which is withheld for legal reasons, he goes on, "I honestly think whatever happened to XXXXXXXXX and with her having a meeting with these and she said she could get it done and then there was somebody else there who said they could get it done and they went and said, 'Get it done!' It was a case of face. If they didn't do it they fell out with these people see! She and XXXXXXX have said we'll do it and the XXXXXXX have kept them to it." If what you say is true then how come no charges have been brought? "They had XXXXXX in twice and they've had XXXXXX in but they couldn't prove it." Who was the boxer from Cheshire who was also arrested with those you have just mentioned? "Who they brought up? He was the cousin of XXXXX, but I only heard that. Then somebody else said it was the guy who was extradited from abroad and they said he was the actual shooter. So then we're back to square one so who was the shooter at the end of the day? Who put the money up? I've got my own theories and mine still lead to it's got to be with XXXXXX, XXXXXX, XXXXXXX and the XXXXXXXX's."

Going off at a tangent. What about the Higgin's Security Company. They were employed; apparently, to get Viv out of a pub he was running is this true? "They phoned Viv up and asked to meet him and he met them and took them for dinner. They actually wanted Viv to work for them. The Higgin's Security Company." They were called in though a North East pub, to a Newcastle pub? "To stop Viv from entry? They couldn't stop Viv from entry!" Not to stop Viv from entry but to secure the pub because a publican called them in. "I knew that he had a meeting and had to go to Birmingham but he didn't go." I recall a story I was told which was that Viv had slapped one of the Higgin's crew around and they all left after giving Viv some money. The other story was that a publican called in Higgin's Security because Viv was causing some trouble they went to see Viv and told him not to go into the pub and Viv complied. "Viv wouldn't go down (to Birmingham) they offered to take him for a meal and meet him and obviously give him a bite of the cherry they knew he was the only one up here who could control the doors."

Peter relates how Higgin's Security men were controlling the doors of certain places in Newcastle. The men working for such a lucrative company had to abide by the companies wishes but they were frightened whilst in the Tyneside area. Peter says, "The guys were frightened on those doors even though Higgin's was the company. They were frightened they had to do it everybody was going to stick by them if there was a fight but they didn't whoever got hit got hit and the rest would run if it was in Viv's case. They tried to befriend Viv because they didn't want to get on Viv's bad side."

Higgin's Security is not a fly by night company they are a very respected security firm and at times do work hand in hand with the authorities. "It was costing them a lot of money to bring these people up from Birmingham and keeping them in hotels. It was costing them a lot more money than what Viv was getting." What were they brought in for? "I think it was the fact that there was that many getting in for nothing as well in some of the clubs. They started off in some of the clubs as well some of the nightclubs they seemed to get bigger and bigger."

Here we have a reputable company supplying their staff to work the club doors. What was the difference between this company and Viv? Just because one company is registered does not mean it is any better or more above board than an individual employed privately for the same service. Viv was consequently asked to help Higgin's out. "You could see that they wanted nothing to do with Viv when he went to the places. You could see that the fear of the thought of him coming to the places put the fear of God into them. There was never any trouble. Viv didn't cause trouble for the sake causing trouble sake."

Peter is asked if he has anything, which he would like to say to the killers of Viv. "I hope it never happens to one of their family. It cuts you right up it's the most horriblest thing to stand over a grave and see your mate getting lowered into it you see all them tears around. For such a young age his life was just going to start and begin. I always said that the game Viv was in was the most dangerous game that anybody could be in so the law averages weren't on Viv's side."

What about those people who started Viv off in the game, Paddy Leonard and Billy Robinson, what about these people who all came in they all wanted to do something, 'Lets get this guy on his feet.'? "They all get old they've lived there lives they just want an easy life they just want to retire you see. That's it basically and live their lives in Tenerife."

Viv did some good in his life and supported many sports he sponsored football teams and had a heating system installed into Wallsend boxing club.

"It was for a lad called Alan Mularkey who run the club they were a good club who were tremendous in the way of amateurs. Viv used to like to go training with the young'uns. Give them a little bit more support and when they seen him it used to really cheer them up they thought it was great. Another thing that was said about what Manny Burgo was supposed to do to Viv in the ring. (Many Burgo was a professional heavyweight boxer. As mentioned in *Viv (Graham) – 'Simply the Best'* Manny was around in the amateur boxing scene the same time as Viv. When I seen Manny cower away from him he nearly died. When he was caught in *Macey's* in the town. When he caught him he couldn't get out he shouted, 'VIV! I've come to sort it out.' Manny was more or less in charge of the coast. He didn't ever venture onto Viv's territory but then obviously Viv got well known. It didn't stop here it was getting bigger and bigger so eventually these people were getting sick of the people they had paid for a long time and they wanted Viv. They wanted Viv it was as simple as that. Then he started going into Whitley Bay, Tynemouth and he started getting bigger, pubs and clubs and them felt he shouldn't be doing this because he was cutting them out of a job. Viv would say I'll keep two of your pubs and you can have the rest yourselves." Manny Burgo had come into Newcastle to see Viv to sort the situation out. Peter continues, "In *Maceys* there was him (Manny) and a few of his pals and he come to try and see Viv. There was something or another said. You've never seen anybody run. Viv was running this way and the other to try and catch him. He talked his way out of it and Viv gave him the benefit of the doubt and didn't hit him or anything and this man is huge. Manny actually got in the car to drop me off it was never mentioned again. When Manny ever sees me now he never speaks or anything he just walks straight past and mind I watched him box but I never rated him. He didn't ever fear me in any way I wasn't feared of him. I'm not feared of anyone that I've mentioned I don't fear for Adam. I don't value life anymore now. It just cut everybody up, he didn't deserve it." Peter's voice goes dry and gravely and just a hint of his inner strength fading shows through. His point of not valuing life anymore was amplified by a number of people connected to Viv. Viv seems to have been the beacon of light that led these people into another world. Could Viv be blamed for leading these friends somewhere that they would not wish to be left?

What about these people who made Viv Graham what he was. Built him up and put him onto a pedestal and went away and left him there. He had to be Viv Graham on his own he couldn't be Viv Graham with Billy Robinson or Paddy Leonard? "I think you start to meet new people and new friends. I don't think Viv ever thought to any extreme that things were going to come to this that he would be wanted as badly by different pubs and clubs and even shops. What about the coloured community he had to go and sort out trouble at the mosque. Viv was asked to help them resolve a situation which he did."

It could be argued that Viv had no colour bar when it came to money but the fact is Viv had no discrimination against any race or colour. What if Viv was a member of the National Front? Would that make the press happy enough? There were no reports of his do-good actions by the press because it just didn't sell newspapers."

The same applies to most people in the limelight. Maybe the exception to the rule was the late Princess of Wales (Diana) when she went anywhere her picture on the front of any newspaper guaranteed extra sales no matter what the issue she was addressing and of course Elizabeth Taylor (actress) when she appears anywhere.

Other than that who can you think of apart from those that are dead who were newsworthy for issues other than violence or trauma related subjects? Mother Theresa of Calcutta, Gandhi, Martin Luther King, the militant suffragettes (women who chained themselves to the railings of 10 Downing Street in Victorian day's to win the vote for women) and so on. Who is alive and commands the attention of the press because of the good deeds they do apart from the odd human-interest story to fill the empty spaces between violence related subjects and crime? Tough question!

3

Anna Connelly: My life and times with Viv

How do you seek an interview from the fiancée, Anna Connelly, of the late Viv Graham? The press had hounded Anna and any refusal to grant an interview would be accepted as the end of the story and no further approach could be made. Camping out on Anna's doorstep might get her to change her mind if she refused. Chase her around until she became worn down with it all and eventually she might relent just to get it over and done with? That sort of interview might be acceptable to the press but not for you the readers of this book. You are given more credit than newspaper reporters would give you.

The interview would have to be given willingly without Anna being coerced or with an incentive of cash. That would have made what is written here just another tale. Anna was approached in the matter of an interview and without hesitation she graciously allowed me, accompanied by a female chaperon, nearly a full day of interviewing at her home. Had I been the press then I have a feeling the answer would have been an emphatic, 'No!' There were no promises made of keeping Viv's name clean or pursuing any issues outstanding. This interview is as it comes. It is at times emotional and anyone who can get through it without some feelings of sympathy towards Anna must have no heart at all. That is not the way the interview is intended nor is it the intention of capturing your softer side towards the memory of Viv. What follows is something that no one could put into words by themselves looking in from the outside. Here you have Anna's side of things from her angle things do look different.

Anna met Viv in 1986 and at that time he did not have a reputation and he was not known on Tyneside. Anna tells it like it was.

"When I met him in 1986 he didn't have a name and at that time I was still married but, separated. I was out on the town in Newcastle with my sisters and I noticed his lovely teeth. I knew he was a nice person but I didn't know who he was. He came across and asked if he could buy me a drink the very first time we met he bought us vodkas and we were laughing together. We went back the next night and got more vodka. We kept going for a few weeks getting drinks off him and then Viv asked me out. My sister-in-law was in the town and one of Viv's friends said to her that I was seeing Viv Graham. I hadn't been seeing Viv at all up to this time because I was married, but, my relationship wasn't very good. She then went and told my husband that I was seeing Viv we had a fight and after about five weeks we split up and I went to stay at my mam's. Viv found out about three weeks after that and he came to see me and said, 'You're not seeing your husband now will you go out with me on your own without your family?'

Viv was a gentleman in every way. Pulling seats out for me to sit on and opening doors. He was like that with everyone. Someone who was being nice to me made the difference as I was used to that. I remember Viv walking towards me with a big smile on his face and he said, 'Do you Ladies want a drink?' There was about six of us sitting there. He kept looking over all the time so I knew he wasn't going to come over and just ask the time. I wasn't aware that Viv was having a relationship with anyone else at that time. Although he said he had a few ex-girlfriends with kids to him and that he would always see his kids but he was a single free man.

At that time he had a girl to Julie Rutherford and had one boy to Gillian Lowes. I had been in love before, but not in this way. I couldn't fall in love again now mind. I'll probably not meet anyone again. Viv was still close to his children Viv's parents love their grandchildren and were visited every day by them as well as Viv calling to see them everyday. Our relationship didn't interfere with this. It wasn't like a duty for him he loved his kids. He loved to see them happy. He travelled to see them every day no matter what all those miles. At one time Viv started work as a labourer for John Wilkinson and he started travelling up to see his children at night time so he could fit the job in. Viv was working on roofs from Wallsend and that helped supplement his income at that time.

In the beginning he wasn't really known the only thing he did was have a few fights. His name wasn't big then as time went on it became bigger. He wasn't a villain all what he used to do was have a fight. If you were in the pub and you were a big lad and were being cheeky and the manager said, 'This man is being cheeky here', then Viv would come across and say, 'Look will you please leave the bar and stop causing trouble', he didn't come across and cause you trouble or beat you up. He would ask you a few times and if you didn't leave he would then hit you and knock you out. He didn't like picking things up and hitting you with it. When he hit them he used to catch them before they fell and take them outside and wait with them until they came around and sent them on their way by saying, 'Son, don't come back I've asked you three times and then you wouldn't leave', and that was Viv he wasn't a rotter like the West End lot. Hitting you with anything, punching you all over and then kick you down the stairs Viv wouldn't dream of anything like that. People come for him to sort out the bother he never ever asked them. People came to the door to ask him to go and sort trouble out in the bars saying that the police had sent them.

I had a marvellous life style dresses and things from *Peaches & Cream* (shop in Newcastle City centre dealing in clothing for the elite) dresses valued at £600 and £700. He would spend £1,000 on a dress and shoes to match.

Whatever I liked he would buy it for me and that pleased him as long as it made me happy then he was happy. He liked to give things but he didn't like them if they were short dresses! He would buy you them and when he got home if he didn't like them he wouldn't speak to you because they would be too revealing and he would say 'Have you seen how short that dress is?' I would say, 'What did you buy it for then you made me try it on in the shop?' Then we would start arguing and then the dress would get ripped up and I never got it and that was the end of that. My mam would say, 'What have you paid all that money for?' Viv would reply, 'Well, Irene, it's bad enough being in the town watching your own back without lads looking at your lass with short frocks on it just makes matters worse!' I said to my mother, 'He just wants me to wear polo necks and long skirts.' I didn't want to wear them because I was only in my twenties myself then.

He underestimated himself all of the time and he was a bundle of nerves and his stomach used to turn over he really underestimated himself. He was never like 'I'm Viv Graham don't mess with me' he was never like that he didn't have loads of confidence. If he ever lost a bit of weight he would think he was too small. He was never six foot yet his father was he was only five foot eleven. He would be worried if he got involved in a fight with a gang he never had loads of confidence and he loved to be really big and if he looked in the mirror and he was really big he was happy then. He was big but, if lost any weight he didn't like that and felt uncomfortable with that. It was because of his name really but he never used to be that big when he boxed, as his weight was only thirteen stone. He could do the same when he was big as he could do at thirteen stones he was fitter. Then he got into the body building stuff and he went even bigger. He got involved because a lot of his friends were doing that and eating the tuna and chicken. When he was in the gym it was one against the other he didn't want to be fat though. He went to the gym two and three times a day and he did once try steroids by injection but, he took bad with them and he ended up with an abscess on his backside and he ended up needing an operation (this was declared on his insurance application when asked about his health) he was frightened of needles and that I said, 'I'm telling your dad on you.'

He used to get in bad tempers but he never touched the kids or me. He used to pull the doors off but, I wasn't bothered because he used to replace them the next day. The confidence he lacked the steroids gave him he couldn't ever get the confidence because he wasn't an aggressive man. He couldn't get into a bad temper easy. It used to take him a long time to get like that people used to worry thinking he was getting softer. When he was supposed to do things he couldn't get the aggression there. But with steroids the aggression come straight away, but, then that wasn't him.

He knew himself where the aggression was coming from (steroids) and he decided himself to come off them because his dad said, 'You don't need steroids son you're a big lad.' Viv was disciplined by the boxing he started when he was thirteen years old. Boxing training was really well disciplined and he did that right up until he was in his twenties. Most people that ever met him knew that he was a gentleman and very soft hearted. He could easily cry over his nanna's memories. He always had a wreath at Christmas to put on her grave.

Viv used to give me chocolates and flowers as a romantic gift he never wrote me any poetry, as he wasn't a good writer he could only write a bet. He used to nip into town and get me makeup and lipstick and go into *Secrets* and buy me nice underwear and that. He went into that shop regardless of his size and being well known. It never bothered him a little bit and if I ran out of a lipstick then I would say, 'Oh! My makeup!' he said, 'Where's it from?', '*Fenwicks*!', I replied straight away he would run there. If I wanted stockings, 'What colour do you want?' Straight to *Fenwicks* and picked them he got you ten pair not one pair. If you wanted lipsticks he got you ten lipsticks, him and his friend Alan Rooney who was with him every single day went for the makeup.

Alan was later charged with blackmail because of something he got involved with and it was traced back to Alan because the bairn had picked the telephone up and said 'Hello?' That is how he got caught in a blackmail plot when he had threatened a publican's husband with Viv because the man had used Viv's name. Alan wasn't using Viv's name it was this other man. Alan had got eight years for something stupid like that. Alan was just out of hospital after that having had some sort of virus he was really bad. It took over his whole body and you know when you see someone with multiple sclerosis he was just like that for months and months.

Alan was at our house everyday but Viv had been told when he was in the town that this man had been using Viv's name.(The man that Alan eventually blackmailed.) Alan had no money and said, 'Should I phone him up and say whatever?' Viv said, 'Do what you want.' I think he said, 'I'll burn your house down.' But, he had no intentions of doing it. That man was in the wrong he knew he had used Viv's name and was taking money off people and he really thought Viv was going to get him because he had done the wrong.

Before Alan had done all this Viv and I had went to that man once and he had given Viv money for something he had done. From then on he thought he was well in with Viv sort of thing, 'I've give Viv a bit job and paid him some money me and Viv are like that'.

That's when he started using Viv's name and getting a lot of money out of it for himself. Viv never knew nothing about it he never seen that man again he was from over the water, Sunderland. He had a pub, *Hylton* or something like that. Alan got eight years for that (imprisonment) when really that man was in the wrong. It never happened that way it just so happened Viv died and then the man wouldn't drop the charges but if Viv had still been alive he wouldn't have Alan charged because he knew he was in the wrong. Even if the man hadn't of paid Alan he wasn't really bothered he was just testing him. It was a stupid thing it ended up Viv died and obviously he couldn't go to court but, had he of been alive he would have went to court as a witness. By this time Alan knew who the man had been taking money off by using Viv's name.

When Viv lost his driving licence for twelve months (banned from driving) Alan was the one to drive him around. That was another story, Viv went to pick the kids up and this woman stepped straight off the curb and he bumped her she wasn't hurt. I went straight to the scene and found her with broken glasses. A couple living opposite had seen it happen and phoned me up and I went straight there. Viv was absolutely devastated the woman said, 'Son I'm alright! I'm alright!' She had a pound coin in her hand she was running for the bus.

Viv gave her £200 for the glasses we went to the flower shop and got a big bouquet of flowers for her, found out where she lived and went back to the house with the flowers and gave her another £100. Her husband was there when this took place she again said, 'Son I'm alright I've just got a little bit of a headache where the glasses have caught me'. Within six weeks she took a private summons and got him done. As it happened his car wasn't insured. She thought she would get a lot of money and then she claimed. She said she was getting severe headaches but when she made a private summons and they wanted Viv's documents he wasn't insured and he lost his license. She still carried on with the private summons someone must have told her who Viv was and that he had money. She couldn't do anything about it because Viv died before it came to court. Viv was genuinely sick with it he gave her that money and was worried about her regardless of the insurance as he did not know his insurance had expired. The old lady said she was over the moon with the money her glasses weren't even worth £200 but, she still done that and took him to court. That will show you what type of person he was.

When people asked Viv to do them a favour he always had respect for the elderly and many a time turned down a job if the person he had to go and see was old. Many a time though he didn't really have to do anything a lot of businessmen came to him say for instance you had fitted windows to a house and you knew you weren't going to get the money they would go to Viv for help to get it. Then the money would be there the next day when Viv called to collect it.

Some of the things said about Viv were all lies saying things like he was a big drugs baron he never ever dealt in drugs that was one thing he never ever touched. He never needed to deal in drugs he made a lot of money from other things. He had bars, nighclubs from Whitley Bay through to Wallsend and Shields Road into the town (Newcastle City centre). You are talking some weeks he picked up maybe £15,000 that was apart from businessmen and other people knocking at the door. I was there when Viv had to collect £60,000 and he got £30,000 in a carrier bag he never needed to touch drugs.

Viv never thought of what he could do with his money he did at the finish with this house but before that he wasn't interested he just liked to spend it he didn't drink and he didn't smoke he just had a bet. Viv could have bought the house outright he could have bought his car outright but, he got it all financed. His dad pays for his car still now every week. He liked it better that way getting the house on a mortgage he didn't save a penny as quick as it come the quicker it went. He could have had £30,000 in that hand and within an hour he wouldn't have £1 for the meter it never bothered him he knew if he spent it by the Monday he would have more by the weekend. Tomorrow didn't matter he lived for the day I was just the same. At times it was a competition to see who could win the most money. Every day we were in the bookies (turf accountants) he would say, 'There's your money', like I would put a bet on and say, 'Give me £100 so I can put this bet on'. I would maybe win because I was more lucky than he was, I still put the odd bet on now. I had done that prior to meeting Viv. We bought a greyhound and it cost us a fortune it didn't come anywhere in the races it ran but we could watch it in the races and have a night out. We thought of buying a racehorse but, that's as far as it went.

We had thirty-two rabbits, two geese, five dogs and thirty-six chickens and they took a lot of looking after. Viv loved the chickens and getting the eggs in the morning although he ate chicken for his meals when he trained he

44

wouldn't have been able to eat one of these chickens for Sunday dinner. He went shooting with his dad but he couldn't have shot anything we had just so we could eat it. He shot at pheasants in the wild on these shoots.

Viv and I didn't lead a boring life we went to the best of restaurants and everything. Viv didn't like paying his debts although he did pay up in the end. If we got anything on HP it would end up not getting paid so we used to buy things outright. A television man knocked on the door and Viv wouldn't pay him. When he seen it was Viv he didn't come back. The Poll tax man came and he saw Viv and asked who he was and I just said something like, 'He's my brother', we were all laughing. Viv said, 'You'll get no money from here', the man said, 'I'm away me', he didn't come back.

He loved life and he was up at six o'clock in the morning with the dogs. He was even happier when we got Buster (the dog). There was a big field at the back and he was looking forward to getting up and running because he loved training. He used to make me get up with him and want me to run around the field with him. I still had my pyjamas on and used to walk around the field with the dogs. The neighbours next door used to laugh when he seen me out with him. Viv didn't like me smoking because he didn't, so he limited me to ten cigarettes a day, but, I had my secret supply hidden. I used to keep the same packet and top it up he would say, 'You've only had two tabs today'. Although Viv went into an environment where there was cigarette smoke he didn't like me smoking because it was bad for my health. He couldn't stand the smell of the smoke and he used to get bathed and showered two and three times a day. Every time he came back from the gym or from somewhere smelly he would have a shower. We had some one come in and help out with the cleaning so we didn't have a big pile of ironing building up in the corner.

As for Viv's safety he confided in me about this and many a time raised his concerns about him or I going to be shot. He used to say all the time, 'I'll never reach forty because I'm telling you they'll shoot me.' I thought he was invincible and nothing could happen to him. I just thought that when he said it that they would be too frightened to come and they wouldn't try it.

I mean they came to my house in Daisy Hill and the windows come in there were two car loads of them and they had masks on and were carrying guns then. Viv didn't hide from anyone and his telephone number was available from the telephone directory.

I don't know how the person managed to shoot him he never missed a trick all the time his eyes were everywhere. He always thought they'd come on a motorbike on the side of the car and shoot him. All the time he watched he used to hate me going in the car because he used to say, 'It could be dark, Anna, it could be tonight'. This shooting lark was constant, ever week, 'You're getting shot, you're getting shot.' He was always on his guard. At one time we bought an answerphone and a threat was recorded on the tape. If

I had of known what was going to happen to Viv I would have kept the tape but it was thrown into a draw I never thought in a million years that would happen to Viv. Then when he died we still had stuff in the other house. I was on vallium my family went across and cleared everything out. There were other things that were sentimental but, they went as well.

He walked to his car the window was out and he was shot. I can't understand it? I think someone had drugged his drink. As soon as he walked to his car and seen the window was out he would have been away but he wasn't he just stood there and they shot him. He was told that if he ever came back to his car and the tyre was flat or a window was out to be careful. A week before that people had been putting drugs into his drink, which was seemingly just a carry on. Someone had tampered with his Guinness he usually drank Perrier water but, with this being a dark drink he could see the white stuff on the top. I didn't see it but someone else did. He was as fast as lightening and for that reason I feel he was spiked prior to being shot.

I've seen him jump ten tables and he could see a fight where you would never even have seen it in a nightclub that was packed full. I thought, 'What's he seen?' He didn't miss a trick. The night he died he was slow and I think there were drugs in his drink. Viv said that they did it all the time about the white powder in his drink. I think they were very lucky and Viv was unlucky. That time of night on New Year's Eve with a bingo hall right opposite and all of these people and then to get away with all these witnesses and all these people going to the bingo.

We used to go on holiday and our favourite place was Greece. I would see a different Viv we never ever went where it was lively sometimes we were the only people on the beach. We would come back get changed and go for a meal. We did not ever go to Tenerife though as it was reported that Viv had been there and had a fight with a man called Andy Winder. Winder did timeshare in Tenerife. (Author's note: Winder was originally from Darlington and it was alleged that he placed a £30,000 hit on Viv if anything ever happened to him. The reason for this allegation was that he had supposed to come off the worst from a fight the pair had. That fight did not take place though and this story is unfounded and will always remain exactly that; a story.) Paddy Leonard wanted Viv to come across and do the timeshare. Viv had discussed this with his dad as he always did and he said 'No way.' There are things coming out these last four years that even I didn't know about because I was so high on vallium in all of that time there are things I am just asking now. When we went on holiday we went there as a family and we didn't want to come back. We wanted it to last forever and wanted to move away but, we said we'd just stay here for a few years. He loved the country and he wanted to be away but his work was here and he was becoming more established. Half the time he didn't have to show his face he had people like Rob Armstrong and them in nightclubs. Viv was going to get contracts on the books and do it properly some jobs could pay £1,000 a week. That was just happening before he died. It was all coming together he was going to give the town up and leave it at that. He was sick of it having to put his face up against it all of the time. People wanted to use Viv above board. Higgins Security came from Birmingham and asked Viv to visit them there and meet their top bosses. Viv told his dad and he was told not to go there and to make them come here to meet him. They told Viv they didn't want to take over the town because they knew he was Viv Graham.

A lot of the doormen were complaining because they were coming here to Newcastle and taking there jobs kind of thing and they were saying to Viv, 'You'll have to stop them because they're taking our jobs you'll have to show them!' They knew all about Viv and he went to see them and they said they had no intentions of taking over the bars. Viv sorted that entire lot out for them.

Viv hated me wearing short skirts and sometimes he went overboard. I remember once when we were out, off he went to the toilet through a crowd of women he would keep his hands in the air. If he seen anyone touch a woman and they complained he didn't take kindly to that happening especially if it was to me. I remember once when someone was talking to me and Viv went across and said, 'That was my wife!' They didn't do it again. When I first met Viv he had Gillian and then Julie (previous girlfriends) he was with me constantly but, sometimes there would be one night when he wouldn't be there and the next day I would say, 'Where were you?' He would tell me a pack of lies and say, 'Oh, I was in the casino in the town until seven o'clock this morning I had my breakfast.' Which was a load of crap eventually I caught him out when he went to jail one of them, Gillian Lowes, was pregnant by this time we had just got engaged and just come back from our holiday. I had found out when she had come to jail to visit and someone I knew had seen her visit and told me she was pregnant.

I pulled Viv and said that Gillian was pregnant and Viv told me that she had got herself a man. He still wouldn't say it was him until I found out. I went to the jail and gave him the engagement ring back and I told him 'That was it', he said 'Please listen to me I'll tell you the story', I said 'No way.' He said, 'You walk out of this jail and I'll smash this jail up', I said, 'You best smash this jail up because I'm away', and I went. I got a letter sent from his mam to say that he had been full of drink that night (the cause of Gillian Lowes becoming pregnant).

I never went to the jail to visit him but Gillian Lowes and Julie Rutherford had been to visit him. Julie already had one child to Viv and she claims a second to be his which meant she had to have had sex with him on a visit for that to be his child. Viv loved his children and I think that if he thought that had been one of his children he would have accepted it as his but, for some reason he wouldn't have that. I said to him, 'But you did have sex with her and it could be'. It wasn't a thing that bothered me because I hadn't been visiting him and he said, 'Na!' For some reason he didn't think it was his. He knew Julie was seeing another lad. Viv used to say to her, 'You want to get your maintenance paid for that bairn.' Viv felt that the real father was a man he used to train with in a gym who gave Julie a lift to prison to see him. Viv fell out with that man and went to train in another gym but, not over this, but because the Sayers' were coming into the gym.

Viv's best quality was his kindness he was over generous. People would call crying to the door saying they had a gas bill. He would pull the money out and give it to them but, he never got it back from them. I don't think Viv was trying to overcompensate because he was a non-believer. I was a good Catholic. Viv's funeral was in a Protestant church although he wasn't a believer in God and had no intentions of accepting my faith so he had no reason to want to prove something. I believe he started to believe in God more although his father was a staunch non-believer. I think it was because Viv got on well with Father Conaty and the fact that missionaries from Bosnia started coming to our house when we put them up. It was through me that he started to change his views.

I remember it was one of my daughters' first Holy Communion and the table was full of religious gifts and he bought the full wack for all the kids there. Once you met him you never forgot him and I used to say to the Father that he was something special because he was somebody special to me I couldn't believe how very kind in his ways he was and still have this power inside of him. He was very strong he could lift a five hundred and eighty-pound bench-press not a problem to him. He gave a lot of help to the local boxing club and had the heating put in and did a lot more Viv paid for everything.

When Viv died they had a charity do and I said that Viv would be over the moon for them to keep the money, which was important to me because they used to collect money at times like that all of the bars had buckets for collecting money. Viv wouldn't have wanted that, people putting coppers into buckets. The football people had a do and come with the money, I gave them it back, Viv wouldn't have wanted that.

We had our arguments just like anybody else Viv would come back from the gym lie on the settee have loads of sweets and watch video tapes. That's what he liked the most he would lock the door and take the phone off the hook.

After he come out of the jail he came to me and said, 'Will you come back to me?' He had sent me letters and cards and that. I said to Viv that he was a single man and he could do whatever he wanted and to go with Gillian or to go with Julie and whoever he wanted, but he didn't want this he wanted me. We were going to get married and we got engaged on Mother's Day. I said if he came back that would have to be the finish with Julie and Gillian and he couldn't have the one night away here and there because that's not what I want neither, I wanted a proper relationship. He loved my children and they loved him.

Viv was an organised and neat person he would even get the Hoover out. He wasn't a very good cook though, but he could do egg and chips. If I wasn't very well and he made a meal it was egg & chips. If we went to his mam's she always had a dinner on the go one for each of us, she knew I wasn't a very good cook. Viv could be timed he would take my children to their school and then he would leave time so that his children would be in the playground for, say, eleven o'clock. He would leave at half in the playground for five minutes and then straight to his mam's. His mam past ten and be up there by eleven o'clock quickly to the school to see his children would have him something to eat a scone and a cup of tea he would be there about fifteen minutes and then he would be back I could time him. Because even after he had died it was suggested that he was seeing Gillian. I don't know where he got the time because he was never off the phone to me ringing me from his mobile telephone soon as he got to his mother's. If I needed cigarettes he would say I'll be there in ten minutes, 'I'll get you them.'

I couldn't go to the shops. I couldn't go and visit friends they had to come and visit me. That was the only bad thing about him the jealousy and that wouldn't have happened if we didn't go out and had stayed in. Sometimes I would think, 'Instead of going out just stay in.' I don't mean every time when we went out it just depended on what I wore. I dropped the short things and went into long dresses after that. I could never go out with the girls mind he couldn't go out with the boys either. If he said, 'Can I go out with the lads?' I would say, 'Alright, but can I go out with my sisters?', he would say, 'No!' I would say, 'Well you're not going then.' He was over the moon and would then say to them, 'She'll not let me go out.' He wouldn't let me go so I wouldn't let him go. His friends would twist their faces people used to say, 'Wherever you see Viv you see Anna he never leaves Anna the two of them are constantly together.' If I went to the toilet he would wait outside the toilet door everybody knew that. People used to say, 'He's outside the toilets? Oh, Anna must be at the toilet. If I was in any longer than five minutes he used to open the door and shout, 'Anna! What are you doing, who are you talking to?' He didn't like that he used to say, 'What were you talking about?' I would say, 'What do you think I'm going to do? You know how much I love you I'm never ever going to leave you we're so, so happy so why is it that you act like that?' I used to think that because maybe he had been sly with me by going with them (Gillian Lowes and Julie Rutherford) and telling me lies and then when he was sent to jail and came out he knew I had never ever been with anyone, I've never been with anyone since the day he died or ever lived with anybody, so he knew what type of person I was. So I thought, 'Maybe he thinks I'm going to do back to him what he did to me and this is his insecurity with me.' He said to me when I gave him the ring back on the prison visit, 'You'll love somebody else.' I said, 'That's one thing I'm not going to do go with somebody just to pay you back for what you've done to me. That's just not my style.' I wouldn't do that get a man and think, 'Well, he'll be sick for what he's done to me.' So he knew I wouldn't do that I think he had this insecurity where he thought I would like to do back to him what he did to me, that's what I thought anyway.

As for children I didn't think we needed a child to cement our relationship and Viv didn't because I had my children and he had his children but, then there came a point when he did. We did try but it just never happened. I went to the doctors and put a pregnancy test in and I was frightened to say the real results after the way he went on. We came out of the doctors and I told him I was pregnant and he jumped for joy and wanted to tell everyone. We rushed back home and he was starting to telephone his mother. I put the receiver down and said, 'I've got something to tell you.' I was frightened after the way he went on I thought, 'Eh! Why did I say that to him, for a joke.' I said, 'I was only pretending' and he went, 'You what!' I said, 'I just pretended to you just to see what you would think.' He was gutted, really gutted and then I realised he really did want a baby.

I was frightened in case I had a one, as he wouldn't love my kids in the same way. We did want a one then, this was about three months before he died so we did start and try. He loved them and they loved him and they even called him their dad. He spent more time with them than he did with his own kids. I was from a mixed family and I knew there might be problems as I had some problems in my family although they weren't problems of a bad nature. Because I had the experience from that I thought that Viv might encounter some problems with that scenario. Viv said, 'I would treat them exactly the same', I said, 'Other people's are never the same as your own. Your two come here and I love them but, I don't love them as I love my own.' So I knew if I had ever had a baby that love would have been a special love different to the love he would have for them. This would have caused arguments and I didn't want that because we had a happy relationship I didn't want that I didn't want to start fighting. I knew he really did want a baby and we did try, my children said, 'We can have a little baby sister or a baby brother.' They (Anna's two daughters: Dominique and Georgia) talk about him everyday they've got their pictures in their rooms and they talk about him all the time they absolutely love him. She's got her own little book that

50

she (Dominique) makes her own little poems in and that." Here Dominique offers her own thoughts towards the interview as she has joined us only a short while ago, "When I lost a tooth once I got £50, a doll and a pram. I got a bike once when I was bad (ill)". This shows Viv's generosity in accepting Anna's children as his own.

Dominique is asked if she has any memories of Viv and whilst we await an answer Anna asks Georgia if she has any. The answer that Georgia gives puts everything into freeze frame. I want to remember how everything is so I can describe the scene and the situation so as to be able to relay it to you the reader. My fumblings and stumblings are more than made up for on the reply that is worth ten of these books. Anna sits slightly forward in her chair lending support to her two daughters that have had their space invaded by a chaperon and me. What Georgia says is everything rolled into one word. "Millions." Millions of memories in that split second of freeze frame what could match that? Nothing!

Anna continues, "The monkey hanging on the rear view mirror that was in Viv's car was put their by the kids and he just left it there. Sometimes Viv's business and private life overlapped. He would call me and come and get something to eat then he would go straight back out to the gym and from there on to the bookies. He would come out go for something to eat and go and get them, then seven o'clock he would ask us if we wanted anything from the shop. He would go and get a video and watch it with his bag of sweets with the phone off the hook and the door locked. If something cropped up, which usually it did, he would take me with him and I would sit in the car. My sister, Mary, and him were very close she would stand up to anybody even a man.

Just after I had lost Viv there was further tragedy when my brother-in-law, Harry Thompson, was tragically lost to violence. Mary's husband had went to sort out someone who had burgled his home and he was stabbed. I couldn't believe it. He died about nine months after Viv. I was just starting to get back on my feet. I couldn't believe it; I just couldn't believe it.

Viv's teeth were his pride and joy Viv was going to have gold fillings in some of them, he liked to look after his teeth. A ship had pulled into the Tyne and the sailors were causing bother one of them was a championship boxer about six feet ten tall. He touched a woman's behind Viv said, 'Here you wouldn't do that where you come from so you won't do that here in Newcastle start touching lasses backsides!' So he takes his sunglasses off (sailor) and said, 'Who are you, man?', Viv said, 'Never mind who I am', he (the sailor) just went bop! Viv's tooth went through his lip anyway Viv banjo's him and the sailor went down. The police were sitting in the car watching it. They said they seen the big coloured man and stood up for Viv as a lot of the police liked Viv so Viv got away with that one. Where we used to live it's terrible there is smack and heroin you can go and knock on any door and get it. When the football club was there Viv would take about fifty kids on the field and he would say, 'Don't take drugs get training.' Kids loved him if they could get into the car with him it made their day. I knew all the hard men you could think of or name and Viv was nothing like that. If Viv hit you he wouldn't let you fall in case you hit your head on the ground. I always think that none of those hard men were ever murdered. Viv never took liberties with people yet they did and they are all still alive? Viv first started in *Wheelers* and he had trouble with a Gateshead man called Paul Ashton.

Viv wouldn't use his power against someone weighing only about eight or nine stones he would pull his punch back. Viv gave Stevie 'Hammer' (Eastman) a nasty bash, I was there when it happened. I didn't like fighting and it wasn't as if it was a fight that would last for ages. Viv was as fast as lightening if you were a big person he knew how to punch through the boxing if you were a big person he would give a harder punch. He wouldn't punch a man of eight stones the way he punched Stevie 'The Hammer' because it would have punched their face in. After all of that Stevie did not hold any grudge against Viv he thought the world of Viv and they still remained friends even though that happened and Viv thought a lot of Stevie.

The press told lies about Viv every New Year they try it on even ten o'clock at night. They phoned me up one day. I had been going to the spiritualist I didn't know where I was at that time I felt that I needed it. They tripped me up by pretending to be someone I knew. A woman rung me up and said, 'How are you? Have you had anymore messages from the spiritualist have you, were you there on Sunday?' There's me blabbing away because I didn't really know who it was. I said, 'Yes, I got a message.' I was telling her the full message and by the end of the conversation I still couldn't work out who it was and I said, 'Who is it anyway?' 'She said she was from the *Sunday Sun.* That weekend it was plastered all over the newspapers. I even got one ringing up the other day. They twist things all over.

The police called about this Blackpool thing where a lad was charged with murder of a man on Blackpool beach. Viv had never ever been to Blackpool, never ever. It just so happened that month being September my birthday is the 1st of September he definitely wasn't there if he was innocent then I wonder where Viv Graham come into it. I wish that woman had come to me (the man's mother) I would have said that no way was Viv there. The police said the man was eighteen years old and fighting Viv on the beach. He wouldn't have had a chance with Viv. He could still be innocent look at Stephen Craven of the *Studio* nightclub murder of Penny Laing. It was supposed to be another man and that man went to London. Viv phoned him up and told him to come back. He was in the marines or something and the doorman at the *Studio* nightclub was alleged to have let him out of the side door. Viv had a confrontation with the doorman who supposedly did that and eventually Viv ended up being good friends with Stephen Craven.

Every night I go to bed I can't sleep very well I might sleep maybe about two-and-a-half to three hours. I must be in a deep sleep because the next day I'm fit enough and not worn out I'm always on the go so that must be all I need. Before Viv died you couldn't get me out of the bed, I could sleep and sleep and sleep. If I could say something to those people who killed Viv it would be this why did you want to kill him? Why didn't you shoot him in the legs and make him a cripple? Why use a gun so powerful as that? They tell me just the force of that bullet is enough to kill you. A .357 Magnum didn't need three bullets. Why didn't you just get out and just break his legs because what did he ever do to deserve this? There are millions of guns a .22, but why did they pick that size gun. I knew that if they shot and they missed Viv would have been in jail today for murder because he would have killed them.

They hit that main artery down there they couldn't have saved him because he had a hole in his back as big as a melon. He was still alive when he got to the hospital I was at the hospital before he got there and he was still alive and within seconds his heart stopped they got his heart going. The doctor said to me, 'I think he's fighting for his life.' So I knew then that Viv wasn't going to make it and his dad said to me, 'He'll survive that.' His dad used guns for shooting pheasants and rabbits on their uncle's farm all the time. I think if they don't get caught and never answer for it in this life then they will in the next. There's something there you can't have nice people and bad people and all go to the same place.

Viv's views on someone who committed crimes against old people were what you would expect from someone like him. Viv had no proper friends except for those in my family who were really close to him. Since he died I can say he has no friends. No one has given me any support that could be looked at as anything real. Robbie Warton, he was a good true friend to the children Rob Bell has helped, they were very good to Viv's family the rest of them just used him. Rob Bell nearly died when he was attacked in Newcastle on a night out in the Bigg Market it was because of an argument and words were said, but, I couldn't swear on this I wouldn't dare, but Rob might have hit one of them. They went to *Santino's* it was a night out on the spur of the moment. Some men walked in with the gun towards where Viv and Rob was sitting Viv said, 'Put that gun away before I shove it up your arse.' Viv grabbed the gun and then they went outside. After a fight it ended up allegedly that Viv broke the jaw of one of Rob's attackers, as Rob lay there nearly bleeding to death after being stabbed in the heart by one of the men.

I feel let down by some of Viv's friends it was only natural for me not to like the way they deserted him.   Some of his friends went over to the other side and joined Viv's enemies. Everybody ran scared and thought that if they can kill Viv Graham they can kill anybody. If they come for him what chance would they have? My brothers and sisters had all the fights over here with people and not one of them come and helped not Rob Armstrong not any of the big body builders it was all my family who got the backwash. People were saying we were grasses and all sorts of things. When Viv died I was assigned a woman police officer every single day for a few years her name was Denise Hall. As it happened she turned out to be my very best friend. So when she was seen coming here people would say, 'They're grasses.' I had no connections with so called gangsters or drug people or robbers so what could I tell her? She was just my friend I stick with my own family all my family are workers.   Now we are supposed to be grasses saying my brother's a grass they put him into hospital four weeks ago and tried to gouge his eyes out. Where's all Viv's best friends now then, eh? Only we have had the backwash of it, no one tried to find out who murdered Viv but, my brother did and none of them come across trying!

A lot of people used to ask Peter to get Viv to sort trouble out and he acted as a go-between. Peter has had no connections with drugs or grassing. The police never harmed me in anyway one of the police officers on the case used to go to school with my late brother-in-law, Harry. John Ramshaw hadn't seen my family for fifteen years so when he seen them they were the best of friends. If it weren't for my two kids I would have taken an overdose. I've been in the town and had words with one of the women who I thought to be one of those arrested for alleged involvement in Viv's murder." Anna was the only one out of all of Viv's acquaintances and associates who actually did something about it. How come it took a woman to stand up for the loss of Viv? This surely is an indictment on the friends and associates of Viv.

"I left the church and everything, then I went back about nine years ago. Hatred in my heart and vengeance was eating me away I've never harmed anybody in my life. My brother set up a fund for a reward to catch the killers but it was cancelled. If they thought that would help catch them the money could be put back again. If they were caught I would jump for joy I mean I can't keep this rotting feeling inside me constantly I've got to get on with my life. I just couldn't get it off my mind I went to pieces with it. I have only spoken in depth about this with a few people but I do talk about it all the time. Viv's dad has to put the paper down because it upsets him. I've still got his clothes in the wardrobe nothing's been changed all his clothes and all his shoes, his slippers and coat are hanging there. I feel as if he's still here and if I did take his clothes and everything away I'd feel he had gone, there wouldn't be anything here for me.

I consulted a medium out of comfort wanting to know how he was. Mind, the priest wasn't very happy. I got them from Scotland, London and all over wherever there was one, as anything at that time would have helped. I wonder at times, like three o'clock in the morning, if I were to walk somewhere would I hear his voice would he come something like that. Loads of things have happened in the house. Lights would come on the house was all wired up direct to the police station when he died so even the police wondered. Cameras were on the house all the time vans and cars would pull up and shout abuse, they all got recorded. The police said if they hadn't of got Viv that night then they were coming into the house. Viv wouldn't have gone into anybody's house but when they are on drugs they don't care all the honour has gone from these people.

I was sick of all the newspaper reports linking Viv to drugs. A reporter called John Merry wrote an article for the *Sunday Sun*, he was a right rotter the best article was in *The Independent*. Articles said he was put into prison for a savage attack on Stuart Watson. Why didn't the newspapers say that the man Viv attacked was eighteen-and-a-half-stones? Eventually Viv and Stuart became friends because after Viv got out of prison things were said and the air needed clearing so Viv went to see Stuart and the matter was settled without the use of violence. Viv was invited to parties that Stuart held so that proves Viv wasn't a thug as the newspapers portrayed him. Look at that with Gazza? That was a load of crap. Viv never even seen Gazza the night he was attacked. Viv had a football signed from the Newcastle United team. David Roche an ex-Newcastle player got it for Viv. The newspapers were saying that Viv threatened publicans and threatened people in the bars and ran a protection racket. Plenty of people said it after he died but, if that was the case how could he do it if he was well watched. CCTV used to follow him if he was in the town, people would hear police radios saying were he was. So at the end of the day when Viv died I had to say everything I knew. I couldn't hold anything back as it meant catching his killers and there was nothing there about drug dealing. I would have had to say if there was any involvement with drugs so I had to tell everything I knew about him.

If I could have changed some things I would have stopped all the pressure he had that gave him splitting headaches. He was sick of it and if I could say something to people thinking about doing what Viv did I would tell them to move away. I've got some friends who are looking for a place I wished we had never got this house. Our plan was to get a little place with chickens running around which reminds me of a story. We got a cockerel it was the first one we got. Viv said, 'It's a chicken it will be laying eggs shortly.' He thought he was a country bumpkin every morning he was running for eggs. Dominique took two out from the fridge and put them under it and he went and got them he said, 'I told you it's laid them it's laid these two eggs!' so she said, 'I put them under', Viv replied 'What did you do that for?', she said 'Because I thought it had to sit on them to hatch them.' So Viv is watching this chicken and he said, 'See that red thing on it's face? When it gets redder and redder and deep red it's ready to lay an egg', so we had this chicken for weeks and he's keep on looking for eggs. Then one Sunday morning we heard, cock-a-doodle-do! I looked at Viv and said, 'What's that?' Half past five on a Sunday morning we run out and what he said was a chicken turned out to be a cockerel and it was sitting on top of the hut going, cock-a-doodle-do! I said, 'And you're from the country? And you said that was a chicken and it was going to lay an egg', it was a cockerel! We eventually got rid of them all to different people.

Viv's boxing career led to an involvement with a fellow heavyweight amateur boxer, Manny Burgo, from South Shields. The boxing selectors choose Manny over and above Viv to go and box for the championships. Viv wasn't very happy at this and Manny said, 'Viv it wasn't my fault.' This is what made Viv throw the towel in as he knew he was a better boxer than Manny, but Manny was chosen because he looked a better boxer. People say it was because of a frozen shoulder that Viv stopped but, that was the real reason. He went back to boxing after that though for a while.

Viv didn't need to live up to people he liked to be on his own. We were out in *Julie's* one night and Viv was involved in a fight and there were loads of them. Viv was fighting with these men and everybody that knew Viv had moved away from him over to the other side but Tim Healy hadn't. He come up to Viv to pass by and was clipped but, Viv hadn't realised it was Tim Healy it wasn't until afterwards that they said, 'You've hit Tim Healy!' Viv thought that he was going to get the police involved. There was a joke that Pat Roach would be coming in to get Viv, Roach was a real life professional wrestler that played a part in Auf Weidersehn Pet.

Viv's hero was his dad and his favourite film was Zulu. There was only one man Viv looked up to and that was his dad. I feel that I could help anyone that ever suffered the loss of a loved one. After the loss of Harry my brother-in-law I became stronger again.

My brother's wife died of cancer aged forty-six. Out of the eight of us three of us have lost our partners. Until you lose somebody you just can't advise anybody or understand how he or she feels. Until you've experienced it you would never understand what it's like. Not until you've been there. I helped my brother and my sister through their loss.

My mam's seventy-one and I think if there was anybody else to die in our family I don't think she could cope. So you could imagine on Boxing Day we were just sitting because we never ever bothered with Christmas or New Year, but we have a little party for them (the children) and at five to seven we received a phone call I screamed. The message was that Peter, my brother, had been killed, 'They've pulled his eyes out and his ears off and shoved a knife through his heart.' So I'm sitting listening to that and my other sister's in Tenerife where she goes every Christmas she hadn't been since Viv last took her to the airport, but, she went back this year. I remember when it was that Viv took her she asked, 'Where's that Viv?' I said, 'He's in the shower', she said, 'Do you think he'll take us to the airport?' I said, 'Of course he will.'

Well, Viv did take her; somebody else was supposed to take her that morning but they had collapsed. Funnily enough, you know how you take them there and say, 'There's your case I'm away', he never left until she got on the plane and she said, 'All the way to the terminal I was saying, 'Go on, get yourself away', and he said, 'No!' This was said afterwards and by five past six he had been shot and had died. She received a phone call because Paddy Leonard was in Tenerife and he told my sister about what had happened to Viv. She phoned here as soon as she found out. By then we were back in here from the hospital Viv didn't look like he had died there wasn't a mark on his face. He wasn't fighting he couldn't care a less he knew he was dying because when he put his hand inside of there he could feel the hole on his side.

A taxi driver stopped and Viv was pulling his shirt down and he was saying, 'Get me up, don't let the people see me like this', when he was pulling his shirt he felt the hole and he said, 'Oh! They've done it this time!' Terry Scott and Nicky were there he said to Nicky, 'Just look after Anna, my mother and father and the kids because I'm going.' Viv was very calm even in the ambulance the police were saying to him, 'Viv you seen who it was, they didn't have masks on.' Because the little girl who was the witness who he gave the money to in the shop said she had seen them because she ran after Viv and said, 'Happy New Year.' She described that there were three of them around that corner. The police had said to him, 'Did they have masks on?' He was still alive and it was ten to seven when he died. I had been there at the hospital half an hour and he hadn't even arrived but, when he got there he was still alive then.

The shopkeeper saw Viv crawling by the shop he heard the bang but he thought it was something but, he didn't think it was the gun and that was when he went out he said that Terry Scott chased somebody.

All of this pressure Viv was under I didn't realise until after he had gone. His head must have been done in he wasn't very well it wasn't long since he had the abscess on his buttock and that took the living daylights out of him. He had to go back and his card's still in the draw his next appointment was 25th January (94). He was always sweating cold sweating he just couldn't be bothered with it in the end just sick of it. He just wanted to get it on the books and let somebody else do it and move to a quieter place with chickens and that. I'm smashing now with the kids and that I go out now and have a drink and socialise. When I'm talking to people it's gone from my mind, but, the minute I walk in through that door it's there. Even if I was to drink six bottles of Vodka I only sleep for two hours.

I never went out for the first two years but even if I do go out it's mainly in my brother's bar. I have been going out now in the last year. I don't know if I would ever meet anybody ever again but, my brother, Peter, said 'I don't know if Anna could ever meet anybody else as nobody could take Viv's place.' I mean it's easy to say, but come back in two years time and I could have fallen in love again.

Viv was a real professional he looked after you but, as for himself he only lived for the day. He didn't put anything to one side for a rainy day. If he got older and couldn't do that profession anymore then he might have thought about it. We did once try to save we opened a bank account for a mortgage. He gave me £200 to put into the bank and I asked for a balance, which was given to me as £2.82. I said, 'You had better check it as that's not right!', she said, 'Well, how much?' I replied, 'There's a lot of money in you'd better check it?' So she checked it all and said, 'There's definitely only £2.82 left in the account.' I said, 'Well you'd better get the manager because there's definitely more I know what I put in!' When all came to all Viv had been going in and signing a piece of paper and getting the money out for the bookies. Another woman come and said, 'Your Viv's been coming in and signing the piece of paper and drawing out every week.' I wasn't bothered I went back to the bookies and pulled him he was full of himself laughing he knew when I went in what he had done. I said, 'You're joking there's me going in and them saying there's only £2.82, well that's me finished.' So I let that one go and I never ever tried to save again the book is still upstairs with £2.82 in.

My brother, my sister and her husband loaned me the £12,000 as a deposit on this house. We didn't ever get to pay the mortgage as Viv died. There was an insurance policy that covered it but it wasn't paid out because it was in probate because it was contested by Gillian Lowes (Viv's former girlfriend).

Julie Rutherford among others has also contested Viv's estate. Viv hadn't bothered making any allowance about Julie because he had assumed that his associate who he used to train with had accepted responsibility for the child Viv denied was his. Viv always believed that this man was the father of a child to Julie because he gave her lifts to prison to visit Viv. It was sad because Viv never seen his daughter but, I always gave Alan Rooney money and presents to take up for her. (Alan lived nearby Julie.) Even Gillian Lowes whether it was Mothers Day or even Christmas whoever you get to speak to will tell you if you ever speak to Rob Armstrong he'll tell you. (Rob

Armstrong refused to give an interview in memory of his friend Viv so could not confirm this.) I used to pick the kids clothes and send them to them and pretend they were off their mothers for their birthdays. Then Gillian Lowes contested it she had checked out to see that my name wasn't on the mortgage. The reason for that was because of our lifestyles and that Viv had got a letter from the solicitor asking us to come in and get it signed because the people who owned the house wanted it signed over. I kept the letters and even the solicitor was sick of writing letters and at that time he didn't have his driving licence and that was when Alan Rooney was driving for him. I said, 'Go to the solicitors and get this signed with Alan', he said, 'It had better be the two of us, both our names?' I said, 'No, just put your name as long as it's signed'.

That is honestly and truly the way it was, I didn't think for one minute if he had left me for somebody else that I would not have still had this home. I knew what type of person he was he wouldn't have went, 'That house is mine you get out with your two kids', that wasn't Viv. I didn't think at that time, 'Oh! I better get my name on it before Viv dies or something happens', so when she contested it I just couldn't believe it. She wanted my house so what she decided to do was pal up with Julie Rutherford because she must have thought, 'If there's two of us up against her we'll definitely get it off her.' It didn't matter if there was fifty of them against me they both hated each other and they made friends, got the same solicitor to fight me, but since then I don't know if they are still friends, I think they fell out. She knew how kind I was to her and she knew Viv was here. She knew Viv would have wanted me to have our family home.

His mam and dad thought the world of Gillian Lowes they liked Gillian and had no reason not to like her, even the dad (Viv's) couldn't believe it and he said, 'Gillian that was Anna's.' It was talked about at his parents and with his brother and sister and Viv even said, '...and David's (Anna's brother-in-law) lending me the £12,000'. Because his father knew he wasn't a saver but, when David said, 'I can lend you the money', this thing that I told you that was all going ahead. That was David's taxman money and he had the money put away and David said, 'Viv, I'll lend you this money, I'll lend you the deposit and you can pay it back within six months because it's the taxman's money.' Viv was getting £1,000 a week of this man with a bar in Gateshead he said, 'I'll just leave that for a few weeks until it mounts up and I'll give you that money back in twelve weeks.'

It wasn't written down on paper. He didn't know the score over that he wasn't going to say, 'I hope nothing happens!' I mean Viv's diamond ring was five grand, but Viv had spent the money and David said, 'Here, I'll lend you the money', Viv did a job and maybe got ten and he gave David the five grand straight back. David did a lot of things like that but, Viv always told his mother and father when he went up he said to his father, 'Oh, I've got this diamond ring David's loaned me the money for it and I'll pay it back next week.' He was making more money by this time so he wanted nice things the dad and the mam knew that David had loaned him £12,000. Lately it has been alleged that Gillian Lowes said, 'There's no way David lent him (Viv) £12,000', and she wants to see it on paper. Why would she want to live in my house that Viv and I lived in? So David's been to his solicitor and had to pay £700 out of his money to get this going and David's solicitor said, 'What's the proof?' David didn't even have the money in the bank to prove he got it out and David Says to his solicitor, 'Here, I'm not a liar I'm not gaining anything by saying I lent him that £12,000 I didn't even want it back.'

David didn't want twelve grand off me but when they (Gillian and Julie) started being horrible then David said, 'What about the twelve grand? I want that back.' There was a bit of friction in the family but, all what Viv's dad ever wanted to do was to have Viv's wishes carried out. He said, 'My son said that house was for Anna and the insurance money was for the grandchildren so because he's not here I'm not going to change his wishes.' He only wanted to stand by Viv's wishes he never went on my side and never went against anybody. He never went against his grand children for me or me for them he only wanted to do what his son's wishes were and what Viv had told him.

At the end of the day they want the money and they want this house. What about all the grief my family has suffered? What about my windows being blasted in with a gun and my two children? Have theirs suffered? Their windows have never been blasted in with their children in the house. I've had to put up with it all and them coming to the door and all the staring and them fighting with my brothers none of their brothers have suffered this or any of their sisters.

Why haven't they come across then and got Karen Young? They want the money, Gillian Lowes and Julie Rutherford I confronted Karen Young and bided my time. They don't want to live here because they aren't from here they want it up for sale and they want the eighty-five grand. The last time I saw Julie was when Viv got buried her maiden name was Rutherford then she was Coffel and I think she has another name now.

What happened was Julie Rutherford never knew about any type of insurance but I didn't think it was fair because at the end of the day I didn't know if the second one was his? The girl was though and I thought, 'Well really she should get something because she was Viv's daughter and so was treat the same way as the two sons.' So I, Anna, dozy me goes to my solicitor and said that I would get a loan for £40,000 as my house was paid for as it was worth £80,000. Julie Rutherford knew and joined up with

Gillian Lowes and they didn't even want that offer; they wanted the house.

There are solicitors and three barristers involved the costs are all whittling away the insurance money if it ever gets paid out.

The picture that the press keep using in the newspapers of me wearing that revealing dress was actually stolen. The press came in and wanted to look at photographs and stole that particular photograph. I went to see the police about it and asked for that picture back that was stolen and it's the one that the press is using without my permission. The police did get it back for me but, it was a one that Viv hated because it was that little yellow dress. (Anna was advised of the copyright laws, more of that later on whilst Anna awaits payment from the newspapers that used a stolen photograph to boost newspaper sales.)

I was promised some money from this John Merry who I mentioned earlier, 'I said I don't want money I want the truth', and he said, 'No! I'll give you some', I said, 'Well if you do it it will go in the reward fund in the bank I'll put it in there or if nothing happens I'll give it to charity.' He turned his pocket out and said, 'Look all that I've got is £43 I promise I'll send some more. Promise me you'll not tell any other reporters about this story so as to give me a chance to get it in the papers. His story appeared in a Sunday newspaper under a headline indicating that Viv headed a £2m Drug Empire and protection racket! So from then on I just haven't bothered with journalists. I wouldn't entertain them at all from now on."

By this time I am only on page three of seven pages of questions I had prepared. I am asked if the book is about gangsters? Just then Anna's mother joins us, as we have been there rather longer than planned because what Anna says is so enthralling. It would be too easy to just cover the life of Viv from one standpoint, a gangster's standpoint but you see Viv was not a gangster, as you will find out later.

The Government is more of a gangster than Viv ever was. I will show you how. There is currently an advertising campaign on UK TV about car tax dodgers. To explain for those of you in countries that do not apply car tax it is a tax called Vehicle Excise Duty imposed by the government on motor driven vehicles that use the public roads in the UK. If you are visiting the UK with a car from another country this will not apply to you so do not start worrying, yet. Start and worry when toll roads are introduced like on the continent. The advert shows a worried looking motorist sitting in his smart shiny car. His car gets clamped as a warning because it has no vehicle excise tax disc on it. That is very akin what a gangster would do, give you a first warning. Then the car gets lifted away because still no money is forthcoming from the motorist to pay the evaded duty. So the man is well and truly done when his car eventually gets put in a crushing machine. That is the act of a gangster taking something away from you and smashing it to pieces just because you refuse to pay them money. Rather like the act of a Mafia mobster giving you a choice, so to speak. At the end of the advert the car is dumped in a little crushed heap and a dog cocks its leg and pisses on the pile of crushed metal. Isn't that akin to the scene in the 'Godfather' when a film producer wakes up in bed and turns to see the head of his million-dollar racehorse lying next to him? The Mafia gave him a choice; he made the wrong choice. Isn't that the threat the present labour Government is making to you the motorist? Pay up or your car will be crushed up and not worth anything more than a dog's piss. Since only a fraction of the tax goes on road repairs it really is a case of the Government 'taxing' the motorist in the gangster sense of the word. The biggest piss take is the tax applied to cigarette smokers being used in the arms industry and consequently cigarette smokers are helping to kill non-smokers who die as a result of weapons use that their money has went to. Next time your doctor tells you that you are costing the country a fortune because you are a smoker tell him where to stick his stethoscope. The Government wins hands down when it comes to being the daddy of the gangsters. Viv did not come anywhere near.

Anna Continues, "The man wasn't a gangster as such. The gangsters we know are underground London types where they put people into cement bridges and that sort of thing. He wasn't that type of man he was a boxer and he could handle himself the people that knew him loved him he was an absolute gentleman. The people that hadn't really heard about him thought that he only did nasty things they just thought. 'Ugh! Viv Graham, he's a rotter!', but, if they really knew him they would have felt completely different. I had friends that if you said the wrong word they would run and were terrified of trouble. One of them said she was nervous about going out with us with Viv in the company. When she knew Viv was coming out with us she felt really nervous but when she did come out with us she couldn't believe how gentlemanly he was. He jumped up, got her hand and gave her a chair and to this day she says, 'What a lovely gentleman he was.' My own mother got the same talk from people by them saying, 'He's big, he's trouble and this', but, she said, 'He was nothing like that.' And she went on to say, 'I met him and knew the difference, all those people who don't know him haven't'.

People knew what he was capable of and he didn't use a weapon. They knew he would come face to face with them and what they didn't know was that he would always give them a chance. He wouldn't just run, he would say to them, 'Look don't do that don't be like...', and if he got another phone call about them then they were in bother but he would let them walk away. That's why they kept coming back because they knew really at the bottom of him he was...she knew him (as Anna hods in her mother's direction) to knock a kid out and then give him money.

One Saturday afternoon we were going for a meal and we bumped into a man Viv knew he was called Durant. We were out on a Saturday afternoon shopping and going for a meal he stopped us and took his coat off and said to Viv, 'I can't work anywhere you stopped me from working, I've got a mortgage!' Viv said, 'Me? Not me I wouldn't stop you working anywhere', Durant then said, 'I've had enough', Viv said to his wife, 'Tell your man to put his coat back on.' Viv was on parole he'd just got out of jail Viv didn't want to have a fight and he wouldn't. They had a scuffle the lad fell off the kerb and Viv picked him up and gave him £50 and said, 'I'll give you a job anytime'. It was Rob Armstrong who he had a fight with him and not Viv, but, the rumour was he wouldn't let Durant work on any of the doors in the town. So we bumped into him when he was also out shopping with his wife.

A fight between Durant and Rob Armstrong some time months earlier in *Madison's* nightclub had resulted in some damage being caused to this man's eye. Viv was being blamed for it, but it wasn't him who did it.

Then there was John Jobie from Gateshead. He had started carrying a lot of tales and he came into *Julies* nightclub with his wife Viv went to him and he said to Viv, 'It was a load of lies'. He said to Viv, 'I'll go with you to their doors and prove they are lying.' Viv said to me, 'Anna, what do you think, do you think it's rumours?' I replied, 'They will be rumours because people like to start trouble you know what people are like.' I used to believe them but, the rumour was that John Jobie wanted Viv seeing to. Viv didn't believe it and I didn't believe it either. That's how trouble started but this ended up in a friendly manner and Viv was still friends with John Jobie.

Viv and the Sayer's fell out when he was in jail and they didn't make it up, he also fell out with Rob Armstrong, but, they made it up although they weren't as close. Dodgy Ray was one of Viv's closest friends but they fell out. Terry Scott was a friend of Viv's, but I wouldn't say he was one of his best friends.

I know by when he died that people who I never knew and they wrote saying that they felt safe when Viv was around and that people felt safe when Viv was watching the bars. Some of the TV documentaries shown made Viv seem like that doorman who glassed that woman in Manchester. That was horrible, it made people think Viv was like that. The stories about Viv weren't balanced especially when it showed Viv setting about that club doorman. The reason for the attack was that this man had attacked two ten stone lads and smashed their jaws as far as I was told when we came back off holiday.

At the same time the Sayers' went to *Hobo's* and as far as I knew they had a falling out with Stuart Watson. They come up to Viv because at that time they were friendly with Viv and they said that the doorman wouldn't let them in there. 'Come down with us Viv?' Viv didn't have a clue that Watson was in there (*Hobo's*) or that it was Stuart Watson on the door. Viv had been looking for Watson as the manager had been in and said that Watson had been in and broke one of their jaws and that was the message Viv had been given from the manager of a nightclub. That night the Sayers' went to *Hobo's* nightclub as far as I know they must have had this falling out at that time. Viv was portrayed as being a horrible man savaging that man. You tell the story though of a man who was eighteen and a half stone and little men who were only ten stone and that tells a different story to the one reported on TV and in the press Viv was standing up for the little man but in doing so he was made out to be the bully, which was not so.

Viv sponsored John Davison the world champion boxer. He fought his last fight wearing a robe with Viv's name on the back. Viv saw someone who was coming up through what he had been and offered help, John accepted this."

That is the end of the interview and what has been written is extracted from the interview that Anna Connelly very kindly gave me without any payment at all which adds credibility to what she has said. If Anna had received a big fat cheque then what she had said might be doubted in fact Anna did not ask for a penny. Her hard work is sure to be rewarded one day. Anna has returned to her job of being a carer. Can you imagine what that must be like after shopping in *Peaches & Cream* and having £600 dresses bought for you? She is a woman with indeterminable courage and strength to come through the tragedy her life has given her. Some are not to be rewarded in this life and their job is to serve and be rewarded thereafter. My wish is that Anna will somehow get her reward in this world. A whole book could have been devoted to Anna and indeed this was offered and a share of the book sales was offered to her. She turned it down? Is this the act of someone seeking riches for themselves? All Anna wants is justice and the memory of her late beloved Viv restored to how it really was not the way the press and media twisted it for their own financial gain.

The women who read this might be able to feel an affinity with Anna and her situation and if that is so then let it serve to guide you through your own troubles. Anna would be pleased for anyone who is helped thorough their own pains after reading this it would mean that Viv's death would not have been in vain.

To the men that read this chapter. Let this show you how heroic acts of violence can leave a family suffering the loss of a loved one. Think before you drink. Cry before you die. Say sorry before you lose an eye. Show your love now don't wait to have it carved on a stone. In your heart is a pearl, open up that oyster of a stone and let your love shine through because it is too late when your friends are sitting on a church pew. Viv would have backed all of this up a fighting man who knew that fighting solved nothing.

Anna contacted me and asked if I would add something to her interview. What is covered concerns an article in which Viv was supposed to be a police informant. The article that appeared in the *Evening Chronicle* on September 14th 1998 by the Chief Reporter, Andrew McKegney, caused Anna enough concern so as to raise the matter. Anna says, "A well known villain said that Viv was supposed to be a grass. Viv was never a grass and if he was why won't they stand up. It's easy to say because he's not here why can't they stand up and say their name if they say he was a grass and tell me what was his name and get the police to come forward to say what Viv was supposed to have grassed to them. I don't believe that person exists because it's just too convenient for the comment to target someone who isn't here to defend him or herself. The newspapers are quick to print this sort of thing, but not so quick to admit they used a stolen photograph without my permission."

This chapter is finished off by including a poem written by Dominique, one of Anna' daughters. I suspect her mam helped her just a little with the prose. Poems are inventions of the mind and take you away from life's realities. Wine and poems used to be a man's way of passing time a lot has changed since then. This poem is real, about a real situation. We don't want a mention in *The Times* Literary Columns. That is not what this poem is about. Any prizes for it then send them to the Viv Graham memorial fund care of the publishers.

To My Dad, Viv

**What is goodbye? Just a word that makes us cry;
When a soul-like ship pulls from the shore**

**In a place where I've been just last night in a dream;
Each saying, "Don't cry for me for I am waiting for you"**

**In this world of summer's blue the land of eternity;
When I asked, "Can I stay?" they led me away saying, "It's
not your time; there are songs you must sing and plant seeds
in the spring.**

**Lots of Love
Viv**

Dominique

4

Gillian Lowes – The Dark & Deep Woman

This chapter is not what was originally intended for your eyes that chapter has been binned at the insistence of Miss Lowes' solicitor, Mr A C Baker of Baker & Co Solicitors of Winlaton, Gateshead. We were pursued by a fax from Mr Baker and then a formal letter to one of the management within Mirage Publishing. I can tell you at first hand that Miss Lowes spoke to me and she said that Mr Baker said to her that she could go to prison for what she had said. Since this threat was given to Miss Lowes by her solicitor it seems logical that Miss Lowes is fearful of giving her name to the original. Of course this is debatable if it was actually said to her by a solicitor, such advice seems highly unlikely since Miss Lowes is not in any position of being subject to pursuing any action on her children's behalf.

Miss Lowes was left with a copy of the taped interview for which she specifically asked that it could be left with her so she could let her son, Dean listen to it when he returned from school. This now seems to have been a ploy used by her just to obtain a copy of that interview as after speaking with a third party who has contact with her son, Dean, he has not heard that tape in the six months or so that Gillian Lowes has had the tapes in her possession from the moment I and a female chaperon walked out of her home.

Miss Lowes then asked for a copy of the first book, *Viv (Graham) - Simply the Best* and her reason for asking for it was that her son had been asking to see it. I was asked if I could forward a signed copy to Dean. That I did after I explained that she would get a free copy of the next book, as her chapter would be in that. I have it on good authority that the book was not even shown to her son Dean and that he had to read a copy of the book that another family member had in their possession. I spoke with Miss Lowes some one week after forwarding her the book and I asked if she had given the book to Dean and she confessed that she had not as she felt awkward about her youngest son, Viv Jnr, not having his name in the book. I explained that it may not be right that someone as young as him (eight) should read such a book. Some weeks later Dean has still not been given the book by his mother nor heard the taped interview specifically asked to be left just so he could listen to it. I have this on good authority from someone close to the family in fact Dean did not even know of the existence of the tapes!

Mr Baker the solicitor acting on behalf of Miss Lowes children via Miss Lowes' father John who has been nominated as the legal next friend of the child beneficiaries of the estate. This legal jargon simplified means that Miss Lowes' father is the person fighting to get the money out of Viv's estate for the children of his daughter. Usually it is the mother who is nominated to this role if the father is dead in this case. I have been informed that John George Lowes, the children's grandfather, is the one who is behind all of the court actions and other actions aimed at undermining the stability that has been wrecked in the Graham family.

Mr and Mrs Graham Snr do not have a very good relationship with Miss Lowes as she has fought tooth and nail over the money locked away in insurance policies worth in excess of £150,000 plus the house that Anna Connelly is still living in with an estimated value of over £90,000. The gloves are off in this mammoth fight by the Lowes family to grab some of this wealth. Viv's father had said what Viv's wishes were and Miss Lowes went against this and brought in a legal team, she was urged on by her father and subsequently he has become the legal next friend which obviously indicates his interest in the money and has become motivated. Now both Gillian and her father are chipping away at the base of the money tree. Each trying to out smart the other or so it seems to those I have spoken with.

Miss Anna Connelly raised her concerns in the matter of her home being repossessed from her and her children who Viv accepted as his own and the children equally accepted Viv as their father. Miss Lowes made it known of her anger that Miss Connellys children would have a roof over their head when in fact her children had to live in a council house. What Miss Lowes has forgotten is that Viv's wishes were that her children should get a share of his insurance policy while Anna would get to keep his house for her and the children. That has been ignored here and the whole lot looks to have been thrown into a pot where winner takes all in this real life game of roulette where everything at stake is gambled on one turn of the wheel of life. Gillian along with her father will be happy with the outcome as long as the ball lands on her number and they scoop the loot.

The acting solicitor for Miss Lowes, Mr Baker, telephoned to speak with the author who was unavailable at the time. Mr Baker then forwarded a hand written facsimile for the attention of myself, the author. My secretary contacted Mr Baker who could not give a valid reason for his intervention or unusual method of stalling the publication of Miss Lowes chapter that she had in her possession in audiotape from for some six months+. My secretary asked when he was likely to be seeing Miss Lowes he was not able to give a time or date as he had not spoken with Miss Lowes at all but, only with her father. So here we have a solicitor acting only on a third parties instructions. Basically he did not seem to know his arse from his elbow. His fiddle was really playing a horrible tune and he became a bit stroppy at the end as naturally my secretary wanted to know the reason for his intervention and as to why it was being given this delay. He could not give any answers at all this was due to the fact that he did not have any to give.

We have to go back a number of months when two researchers and I were arrested and certain details the police seized in relation to the first Viv Graham book. I can advise that the computer system and some discs were handed back way past the release date of that book which led to it being released over one month late. The police still had computer discs relating directly to the book with copy letters to people directly concerned with their help in that publication on discs up until early November. The reason for this cannot be explained as the police said to the press that they were not interested in this side of things. If this is the case then why have my Recorded Delivery letters not been answered to date by Superintendent Alan Nichol of Northumbria Police? Why did officers take photographs of the pile of photographs relating to Viv? Rather interestingly I spoke with Miss Lowes very recently about whether she had heard from her solicitor I was told she would call him that day and get back in touch with me. I was told from Miss Lowes that her solicitor was in court and she did not get the opportunity to speak with him. That set alarm bells ringing in my head because I was told from someone that this delaying tactic could have been brought about because of some connection with the police and my research into corruption within Northumbria Police, which is still ongoing and nearly at a conclusion. This has to be seen and obviously not worth pursuing at this stage.

A letter was later received at the address of Mirage for the management and it was from Mr Baker of Baker, Gray & Co Solicitors. The letter was long winded and all that it really boiled down to was that they wanted to check the tapes that Miss Lowes has against the chapter forwarded to her for her approval, but somehow her father managed to get it and take it to Mr Baker. Since the chapter did not have any connection to Mr Lowes. Mr Baker went on to say that he was not aware of Miss Lowes having a tape recorded record of the interview until after he had spoke with her some four days after he faxed his hand written letter. Miss Lowes had even kept this from her solicitor when in fact she could have at any time in the previous six months let him hear the tapes, but, no they wait until the eleventh hour and then kibosh the publication date of this book just like the last book had been held up.

'Miss Lowes wishes me to assist her in its approval and Mr Lowes recognises his important representative capacity in relation to little children in the High Court action.' That is part of Mr Baker's letter to Mirage and that really says it all, big people playing at being little Hitlers and trying to dictate their authority that carries no weight at all. My decision on the chapter has been compromised by the use of children and again they have been brought into play to pull on people's heart strings just like some High Court judge is supposed to feel about poor Viv's children suffering the hardship of the loss of a father when in reality it is all about children being used as pawns in a the game of roulette mentioned earlier. I do not go for that at all and now this whole chapter is being re-written on the instructions of the publisher. The following is an account taken directly from my memory and another person who was present as a chaperon in the interview that Miss Lowes gave full consent to, at the outset. No fee changed hands and maybe this was the reason for her late withdrawal, maybe she thought that if she stalled the consent that she would be offered a sum of money, or was this the father's idea? This really did not surprise me and the thought comes to mind, 'It isn't over until the fat lady sings'. This phrase is very poignant to this particular case as Gillian and her father believe that her chapter will not be enclosed within the pages of the second book, how wrong and misguided they are!

I remember asking Gillian about Blackpool and if she and Viv had ever been to the West Coast Candy Rock Resort. My reason for doing this was that a man called Gary Ward has alleged that he was not guilty of murdering a man on Blackpool beach because in fact he was in a fight further up the beach with Viv at the time the man was murdered. (This is covered in a later chapter.) People I have spoken to have not been able to place Viv in Blackpool when the alleged fight took place. But, I am becoming more sceptical of what people say due to what has happened and how things have been twisted so that people can take full advantage of Viv's death and use him like a moneybox.

Gillian said that she went for a family holiday to Blackpool and that it was in the latter part of the week that Viv joined her. Whilst the interview was going on a female friend of Gillian is present, Tracy Paxton, she at times interjected. Tracy interjected with so much that at one stage it seemed she wanted to take over the chapter and to have it wrote from her point of view as opposed to Gillian's. Gillian recalled to my chaperon and I that Viv took her home and on the way back he spotted a jewellery shop where he picked a ring for her. Gillian said she had previously been engaged to Viv and felt uncomfortable about which finger to put this ring on. Viv's comment was that he wanted them to become engaged again and to marry but Gillian felt uncomfortable at this thought. She felt it was fine being his girlfriend and enjoying the odd holiday and so on but, that was as far as she wanted to take it.

When Gillian had been engaged to Viv everything was fine until she discovered he was seeing Julie Rutherford and she then gave Viv his engagement ring back. This scenario is uncannily like the one in which his latest fiancée, Anna Connelly, gave him his engagement ring back on a prison visit after she discovered Viv was seeing Gillian behind her back and that he was the father of her latest child. This so much incensed Anna that she walked out of the visit and did not go back in fact it was Viv who went cap in hand so to speak back to Anna to beg her forgiveness and dedicate himself to being loyal to her. Gillan said that Viv did not keep anything from her and obviously this then meant that while she and Viv were having their secret meetings continuously right up until the day he died that she knew of Anna's position in all of this.

At the time of Viv's spell in prison he was visited regularly by Gillian and his family they were all friendly way back then and acted like a family. Julie stopped visiting and so had Anna that just left Gillian to receive Viv's attentions she is recalled to have laughed at the memory of her being the only woman out of the three that had visited Viv who was left. During Viv's imprisonment she had given birth to young Viv and a number of people connected to Viv had called at the hospital to see the new born baby. One of the people was a man close to Viv at that time, 'Dodgy' Ray, he took some photographs into prison so as Viv could see his new son.

Gillian knew of Anna Connelly and Julie Rutherford's existence yet she still continued seeing Viv intimately. Anna had thought that Viv was only calling to see the children when he visited Gillian. Both Anna and Julie did not know that Viv was still seeing Gillian behind both of their backs! Viv's affair with Julie resulted in two children one though is having to prove their connection to Viv by undergoing tests to confirm that Viv is their father. Gillian told me that DNA tests were being carried out and that Viv's parents are not co-operating with this as Julie's solicitor has contacted Viv's parents' solicitor. Gillian gave me the history behind Jodie Annie's name, Viv's child to Julie, the name is that of Viv's grandmother. Gillian went on about how she had babysat Jodie Annie and that she was alright but she was pleased to carry that out only occasionally.

Queen of the Castle seems to be where Viv put all the women in his life and if the worse came to the worse he put them in the tower metaphorically speaking that is by making them pregnant thus making them unattractive to

other men so that he could devote his time to others in his life. Gillian felt on
cloud nine by knowing all of his intimate secrets that none of the other two
women knew and obviously this made Viv more attractive to her in the fact
that their relationship was clandestine. Viv was asked not to lie to Gillian
and his favourite saying to Gillian that most of the others' fell for was that he
felt relaxed and that the place was a sanctuary but, that sanctuary only lasted
for a short while as his watch was his master and time made him hurry to his
next appointment in which he would say 'I've got to fly now, bye.' Gillian
accepted that she was one of Viv's harem and she went along with all that he
demanded. Gillian went on to cover the fact that Viv had hurried off more
quickly for the bookies than anything else but he always telephoned her and
Gillian said that Viv was terrible and never off the phone calling at all times
of the day and night.

As for Gillian going out she would disappear and then return to find Viv had
been on the telephone demanding to know where she had been and why she
was not back home by eleven. Viv would be at Anna or Julie's home and it
would not be wise for Gillian to call him, as it would cause problems. Gillian
had somehow turned from being a childhood sweetheart in which Viv
acquired her because of a £5 bet with a fellow pupil that he would kiss her to
her now being the other woman in his life. Somehow though Gillian was not
going to lose her grip on Viv and it would have been easy for her to let him
go and make of her life what she could, but it did not turn out that way. She
wanted him regardless of his lifestyle and commitment to other women in his
life. Somehow Gillian had changed from being Viv's first choice to second
best.

A triangle of love,

Gillian Lowes,

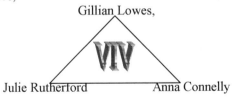

Julie Rutherford   Anna Connelly

Like the King on a chessboard not being able to meet the other King face to
face a confrontation was to happen and all three of Viv's lovers were to meet
at the funeral of the man they all professed to love. Julie met Gillian as
Gillian walked up to her and introduced herself. Julie was quick to raise the
fact that Gillian had lied about getting the services of a solicitor to fight for
the estate of Viv. Check out Julie Rutherford's chapter for further details.

Anna and Gillian did not speak at the funeral but both knew who the other
one was instinctively. I remember asking Gillian if she thought everyone

who was involved in the fight to get at Viv's insurance money would abide by what the court decided and her reply was, 'Yes'. In retrospect I believe that if it did not go her way though she would say 'No!' Of course as Gillian reminded me she is not losing anything as the fight can go on until the oldest child is eighteen, in another five years time. Since She has two parts of the jig-saw in the children that are not being disputed as Viv's children she stands to gain quite a bit and her father as legal next friend will have some say in the use of that money when it gets shared out. That is if there is any money left to share out.

Tracy offered her support to Gillian by saying, "They are Viv's children and should be provided for, Gillian is going to get nothing out of this. If they (the court) said tomorrow, 'Right Dean Graham and Viv Jnr Graham get £100,000', it's not going to help her. It's going to help them when they are older and they will benefit from it, not Gillian. They should come first to be provided for you've got Gillian and her family, you've got Julie and her family and you've got Anna and her family. The outcome was that Anna should get the house because Anna has had no money for her children, but, Viv's own children, both his two children here and his other two to Julie they are in council houses except for Anna. The council provide these houses they haven't been bought." Gillian finalised what Tracy said by saying it was alright for Anna living in that house but the fight was not over the house as it was the newspapers that stirred it all up when they wrote about Anna's children having a home but, Viv's children not having a roof over their heads. Gillian is placing a lot of faith in the judge who decides what families get what. She tries to hide her feelings of a disappointment that Anna is still in her home and she says that the fight is not over the home Anna and her children are living in right now. If that is the case then if Anna is kicked out into the streets by the court Gillian might want to tell her then that the fight is not over the house?

Tracy gave the impression that she knew Gillian for many years and was in close contact but after I had investigated into the matter it came to light that Tracy had only really come onto the scene after Viv's death. This can be taken in a number of ways and I do not wish to sway you, the reader either way, make your own decision. Tracy was rather abrasive with me in terms of the money argument about Viv's estate. I tried to calm the situation by moving off the touchy subject of money. I say to Tracy that it looks like she is getting the clubs out of the draw and tin hats are going on and the barbwire is going around the fence in defence. This seemed to defuse the situation in which we had a laugh at the picture I conjured up of Tracy being like a Dad's Army character marching up and down Gillian's street keeping money grabbers at bay.

However the talk of money still goes on and Tracy seems very involved with the money situation. I wonder if Mr Baker is writing to her telling her she could go to prison for her involvement? Tracy goes on, "Ann has to claim the house and the money is to be split between Anna, Dean & Viv and Jodie Annie & Callum. Fair do's if that's the judges word then that's it it's over it's finished, but, it's just a case of their solicitors working for them to get what they are entitled to that's all it comes down to. To me there wont be any bitter feelings none whatsoever." Tracy says this with a great big omission from her statement about who should get what on the other side of things. It is obvious to me that she has lost sight of who the money was actually to go to from Viv's wishes. Viv's parents were in Viv's wishes, the children were in Viv's wishes for the money side of things and Anna having possession of the house was in Viv's wishes. Viv's father, Jackie (Eric), has confirmed this. There was never ever any mention of Anna being awarded any money nor is Anna interested in that side of things. That is the side of things that Tracy has lost touch with provision was made for Gillian's children yet she is fighting for more and going against Viv's wishes. I cannot see what was wrong with Anna getting the house the children sharing the money and one particular policy being paid out in favour of the parents of Viv? This is examined in another chapter further on.

Gillian told me how Dean had absolutely idolised his father and when Viv was murdered how he had to undergo private counselling sessions to come to terms with this terrible trauma that still continues to this day. As much as Dean idolised his father the same could be said of Viv idolising his father, Jackie, he listened to advice and counsel from him. Gillian went on to tell me how Viv tried to get out of what he was doing but he didn't know how and he wanted somebody to help him achieve this. Viv would often say, 'I wish someone could help'. Gillian told Viv to pack it all in but, he just could not find a way to get off the tiger's back! Remember, 'He who rides the tiger cannot dismount.'

Tracy abruptly interjects, "The day Viv died I think his father died and he's got to walk around with that for the rest of his life, they had a very strong bond." Tracy interjects in an interview that was arranged with Gillian and since Tracy knew of this book covering Viv's life she obviously knew she would be in it, so be it.

Gillian relates how Viv would come back to the little community village of Rowlands Gill and Highfield and have the odd drink in the local bars. People just accepted that he was Viv, one of the locals, but back in Newcastle he was looked on with awe. There seems to be a big difference in how Viv revelled in his new found status and how he would use that in Newcastle compared to how he would use it if bumping into someone in the local bars of his home village. He liked that and he could be himself.

With regard to holidays spent together there was a time when Viv and Gillian had planned to go on a holiday to Cyprus when Viv was nominated as a friend's best man so to thank Viv for carrying out the duty he and Gillian were invited out there where the man had spent time whilst in the army. Viv told Gillian he did not like going abroad so that plan was scrapped. To make up for this Gillian booked a holiday to Corfu, on her own. Viv found out about this and he tried in dissuading her from going and he ended up taking her to the bus station so she could get to the airport. Viv went off on a holiday abroad a few weeks later without Gillian and this prompted her to book her own holiday. Was it spited or was it showing Viv that she was not just there for the ride, so to speak?

A place that Viv seemed to enjoy taking his conquests to was Blackpool, he took Gillian and another couple, as soon as they arrived there Viv took off to the bookies with the other man in town, he did not even stay to help with the suitcases out of the car boot. Gillian told me that Viv must have won a lot of money as the woman they were with out of the other couple whispered to her that Viv had won a lot of money. Viv denied he had won any money at all but, Gillian went on to say that she padded his pockets and then the next day she found it hidden (about £500) in a cushion and she went mad at Viv. This indicates that Gillian was only concerned about where the money was and she eventually found it as she did not believe Viv when he said he had not won any money. Why did Viv withhold this information from her? Obviously he was concerned at her finding out, concerned enough to hide it away from her. This goes against what Gillian had earlier told me about Viv telling her everything. If that was the case then why did he not tell her about this big win and the money? The difference between Viv and Gillian, which she admits, is that he did not value money it was a case of easy come easy go.

Fishing books were a fondness that Viv loved to read. He was a typical countryman who was at one with nature. A book about ferreting was passed on to Dean by Viv's father. Viv did not have the time to carry out his hobby of fishing because of his other commitments.

Viv did though confided in Gillian about a threat he received from London and he said that she had to stop taking the pill if he did receive such a threat. Here it is difficult to tell if this was something Viv had invented just to get Gillian off the pill, as he wanted her to have a baby. As was told to me by someone else he liked it if his women were pregnant as it made them unattractive to other men. His only reason for this was his deep-seated insecurity that somehow came about in his life from a man such as he that had to always look confident on the outside. Maybe that was it, all of the outward machismo had made him feel emotionally stunted within, and whom could he trust? Maybe people had made him empty promises?

74

Again Tracy interjects: "Do you think the type of person they made him out to be in the papers that it was an impossibility for the life that Viv was supposed to lead and still travel here to see Gillian seven days a week? To me that wouldn't even come into his lifestyle if that was the kind of lifestyle that he was leading if that's the type of man he was supposed to be."

What was it like to be involved with a man that could be injured or even dead at any time I enquired of Gillian? She told me it was frightening and that she knew people would always want to have a fight with him but she did not think he would get murdered and maybe one day he would get out of it all. Maybe she was dreaming of what could be? She knew Viv was not invincible, but the way his life suddenly ended shocked her. The problem was that Viv did not carry fear in his dictionary of words, he just did not know the meaning of such a word. Gillian confirmed what a lot of people said that was he did not carry a weapon. It did not bother Viv when he walked around a corner he just walked on the night he was murdered he would not have suspected something like that happening at all.

Gillian was asked about the shooting incident outside of *Manhattan's* in 1989 and her reply to me was that 'yes' he was shocked, completely shocked. Viv mentioned in the press that these people who shot at him should have come out and fought with their hands but this only happens in novels or in films and the hero walks away to his sweetheart, err sorry sweethearts. Gillian said that Viv did not know what that shooting incident was about. It was covered in the previous book *Viv (Graham) – 'Simply the Best* and the man who pulled the trigger were fingered! Gillian said that Viv was the type of person who would have said 'Just put that down!'

Gillian talks of Rob Armstrong and she says that if he was there the night Viv was murdered then Viv would still be here. I say that might be the case but, then Rob might not have been here as he protected Viv in the *Manhattan's* shooting and likewise no doubt he might have took the shots that were intended for Viv on New Year's Eve 1993. Gillian went on to tell me that Viv just did not have any sense to be aware of anything like this happening. He was just like us although he was very fast in his movements if he had been more aware he would not be where he is now. Even the night he was shot he looked at his window that was put out and a car just pulled up and they shot at him. Viv had in Gillian's opinion thought that the window of his car was just smashed and the culprits had been and gone.

Gillian accounts for some of Viv's movements the day he was murdered. At 2 o'clock in the afternoon Viv was outside of Gillians home and he spoke to a friend, Denny Haig, they shook hands then Viv came in and off he went. He then visited a betting shop in Swallwell. Gillian explained that Viv was very friendly with a woman who worked in the bookies and he bought her a dress? (Author's note: this seems rather odd as he would have had to explain

75

himself to Anna about this generous action, was Viv seeing this woman?) That night, Gillian told me, Viv rang her at ten minutes to six and she recalled that little Viv was asleep on the chair and Dean was staying at a friend's. Viv's conversation went along the lines of how were the children keeping and he passed his love on to them saying he would call the following day. Gillian put her son in bed for about nine o'clock and it was recalled that the phone rang but it was ignored when Viv Jnr wanted a story read to him. She awaited a promised telephone call from Viv at midnight, which came and went with no call and Gillian heard a knock on the door. Gillian's sister called with Denny Haig and what was mistaken as laughter coming from the visitors was in fact cries of loss. The first Gillian was told of Viv was from her sister, Eleanor, and she was told that Viv had been shot! Viv's parents and his sister called a few minutes later and passed on the news that Viv was dead. Gillian cannot really recall much after that.

Anger from Gillian has been kept within her even though she was angry that it happened she does not blame anyone as she said Viv was his own man. It was as if he was swept off his feet by the speed that things were happening around him. Gillian passed a message on to those people who have anyone involved in this sort of thing to just get away from it and leave it to the police. Viv was there he was looking after everyone and he did help the police with their inquiries into muggings, murders, knifings and when someone had been shot. Gillian continued to say that after Viv had gone everything just went wild and out of hand.

Gillian has obviously suffered the tragic loss of someone close to her and the consequences of doing what Viv did in his life could surely not have been surprising to anyone from a city but, to someone brought up in a shielded village environment like she has it has been more shocking. What Gillian told me about the effects it had on her are carried forward in what she says about the people who murdered Viv. She said that she hoped that if the person is married or has a family that there family has not ever got to go through what her family went through and that they may not have known the consequences of what they did and she said that she did not know if they wanted to kill Viv or warn him off. Gillian obviously knows more than she is letting on for her to say this however she insists she did not know what he was involved in so that is accepted.

Gillian is rather coy when I ask her if she has been asked out since the passing away of Viv and she does not really answer that with a 'yes' or 'no' just a 'not really'. The activities of Viv's children in the sporting sense are coming on fine and Dean is pursuing a number of sports including rugby, football and swimming.

Gillian recalls at the time of Viv's murder she wanted to take her own life because the real full meaning of the relationship she had with him hit home and she wanted to be with him wherever he was. The children were thrown up at her about what life was all about but she did not want them at that time so early after Viv's death. She overcame grief faster than some and in about six months she realised that she did have the boys and did have to live for them.

Gillian says that Dean wants to be a policeman and he does not want to be a troublemaker. Again we have an interjection from Tracy: "He wants a career doesn't he doesn't want to follow his father's footsteps that way and going into boxing he wants to branch out and make his own decisions. He's sticking in at school to try and do that as well."

Gillian admits that the children's dad was not very bright at English, , but he was good at maths.

Here is something that cannot really be explained. I gave Gillian a signed agreement not to write anything other than what was in the taped interviews. This chapter is not adhering to that because her solicitor does not want any part of that chapter printed. He has not produced a High Court injunction to stop this happening but to save any linger on that chapter has been ditched because no doubt at the eleventh hour he will produce that white A4 sheet that most publishers get slapped on them at times.

What really pisses me off is how Gillian had a similar agreement from a member of the press about four years ago. She took that agreement to the boys' solicitor and he said that it was fine to sign it as it meant that nothing could be written that she did not say! You can imagine how pissed off I was at being told I would have to re-write this chapter because probably the same solicitor gave the all clear for a member of the press to write straight off without having to give or show Gillian a copy of what was written and this signed agreement was her guarantee of correctness. Now we have this plonker of a solicitor acting on a third parties say so using the children as blackmail against my publisher! My publisher has given me guidelines for writing this and all I can say is that this chapter is more interesting especially since Gillian did not like the way I made her sound in terms of how she spoke. I told her I could not make her sound like Prince Charles, as people just would not believe it was her speaking to me.

Gillian went on to tell me that she was happy to sign this journalists agreement some four years ago and she said that it proved it was the only way to offer an interview. Really! If that is the case then why are you reader not now reading that interview? Anyway, let us move on.

Viv used to call Gillian 'Little Lowesy' when they were at school they had pet names for each other. Viv used to call at Gillian's home and she told me that he used to complain of terrible headaches and that was when he came here directly from Anna's. She put it down to the pressure and not the boxing some people thought it to be caused by. Gillian said it was the job that Viv was doing that was the cause of the stress however, how did Gillian know what job Viv was doing when she told me she did not really know what he was up to. For a woman who was in the dark over what he did she certainly knew plenty what he got up to because she went on to tell me that everybody wanted looking after by him and it really got out of hand he could not cope and in the last year of his life he was receiving lots of threats and he was really stressed out.

Gillian told me that Viv did take threats seriously and she assumes for some reason that someone had rung Viv up from London to say they were coming up. Viv asked her to come off the pill and that meant he did receive a certain threat he was waiting for, but Gillian told him he had no chance of her coming off the pill for him. At times Gillian is lost for words to some of the questions I put to her in her neat little bungalow in a cul-de-sac street offering peace and quiet. Gillian asked Viv why he did not want to live with her and the children. Viv put her off by telling her to wait until everything was finished. He used the excuse that the children or her could get hurt, but in reality he was living in Newcastle with another woman and her two children so that argument goes out of the window as there was more chance of something happening in Newcastle than in a little Village with only one main road leading into it. It sounds like Viv was stringing Gillian along in his classic keep them hanging on approach.

At the time Gillian was having Viv's first child he was seeing Julie Rutherford in 1985 really Gillian did not want to become pregnant, but she had come off the pill because she no longer needed to take it with Viv and her being finished. But, although they were not together they started having sex again. The obvious result was that Gillian had a baby, Dean. No baby ever asks to come into the world, but once it is here it must be cared for and Gillian, to her credit has become a good mother to the two boys.

Viv's involvement with Billy Robinson of Gateshead was said by Gillian to have started after Viv became a doorman at the *Hedgefield* in Ryton when a friend phoned him to ask for his help because there was a bit of trouble in a pub at Gateshead. The trouble was not involving Billy Robinson or Paddy Leonard but later on the two of them walked in to a bar called *Wheelers* when Billy and Paddy walked in. Gillian was sitting beside Viv and he sort of writhed a little bit but, he did not let that show to them and he stood his ground. From then on Viv and Billy got on like a house on fire. Gillian blames the couple from a small village nearby called Burnopfield for sending Viv there and ultimately being responsible for his involvement in the club and pub scene that was to lead to his death.

Viv had said to Gillian that he would not live with her but when it was all over he would come home. What though was he waiting for to be over? Gillian did not expand on this and for her to say this she obviously had an idea of what it was that Viv was waiting for to be all over. Viv confessed to Gillian that he did not love Anna the way he loved her and that she would always be his childhood sweetheart. It was recalled by Gillian that Viv came back off one of his holidays and it was about six o'clock in the morning when he called with a suitcase with three bottles of perfume in it. He said that one bottle was for his mother but, his mother did not ever get it so it was obvious he has brought each one of his three loves the same bottle of perfume home from the holiday. A marriage was proposed to Gillian in this early morning visit and she wrote it down on some paper but it was not to be and Gillian was kept hanging on.

Viv went off with Julie while he was still seeing Gillian and she was gutted at the loss of Viv to another woman. Obviously Gillian must have felt second best to Julie as Julie must have felt second best to Anna when Viv moved on to her leaving Gillian third best. Julie was all over Viv like a rash in *Finnigan's* and Gillian noticed this and become very jealous. Viv was thrown out and his eight carrier bags of belongings were handed to him even though Viv only stayed at Gillian's a few nights of the week as he was still living with his parents at that time.

Gillian was asked if she had received any clothing or anything from Anna. Gillian replies, "Well, looking at Anna's taste with that horrible yellow dress, what does she look like in that." Tracy sniggers in the background at this then as Gillian finishes what she has to say she joins in their childish game and laughs along with her. The yellow dress in question here is the one that always crops up in newspaper articles about Viv.

Viv's temperament was questioned and Gillian said that Viv was not easy to get angry and he had to be pushed to the limit before anything happened and he was really soft. Viv was heartbroken when Gillian kicked him out and he would not stop going back to her.

I was told that Gillian thought part of Viv's stress was caused by the fact that he had to be everywhere at once and there just were not enough hours in the day. He just wanted to keep everyone happy. Viv used to call in for a sandwich during the day when the boys were at school and then call to see them during their break time. Too many people from different parts who were bigger and harder than Viv and they wanted to have a go at him, but he did not want that. Viv was seen as a target for people who wanted to set up a fight between him and their man. In fact one of the people lined up for Viv to fight was Lenny McLean (Co-Author of *The Guvnor*) but Viv wanted to see him fight before he would take up the challenge. The alleged man to organise this fight was Kenneth 'Panda' Anderson the original Geordie Mafia. This is covered in another chapter though. It was alleged that a man called Andy Winder from Darlington who had moved on to time share scams in Tenerife had a fight with Viv. This was denied by Gillian , but she did say that later on it started to get really heavy for Viv and he did not know how to get out of it.

Gillian says that she and Rob Armstrong are close and he calls to see how the children are doing. A story is told about how Rob went to see Viv after they had fallen out and he called at the house Viv had just bought when it was being done out and they had a heart to heart but Gillian did not go into detail and she said if I ever got to talk with Rob he would explain it all. I have not been able to talk to Rob and at this late stage it would not matter if he did call as the space has gone but, I can only assume he has his reasons and as always those that do not wish to speak are not pursued.

I ask about something that was said to me regarding a lot of Viv's friends going over to the other side could they have meant to Gillian's side? Tracy says without any prompting, "It's a total breakdown of communication in that half we are here and they are there. We don't cross their line they don't cross ours. You wouldn't send anybody in to talk because they'll never talk." Here Tracy is back to her Dads Army style character with her stern bellowing voice. I go on to mention an insurance policy valued at £150,000. Tracy immediately interjects, "Yes, yes that's the house one." It seems that Tracy is in possession of quite a bit of knowledge about these affairs.

Gillian denied ever hearing of an offer that Anna had passed to her solicitor about the property. I do not wish to go into full detail here but I know Anna is telling the truth because she has stuck by what she said in interview yet Gillian denies all knowledge of that offer. I can only now assume that her solicitor, oops sorry Mr John Lowes' solicitor, did not pass on the offer because he felt he could push for more money.

So there you have the unofficial version of the interview that took place many months ago. We do not need Gillian's permission to publish this or the assistance of her solicitor, oops sorry, her father's solicitor who said he would act swiftly in the matter of approving the draft copy. Since he would have to be a solicitor with publishing knowledge no doubt we will still be waiting until the cows come home, up to now over three and half weeks later we have not heard anything from him. Very swift as swift as a kick up the arse from a one legged man.

Just as a matter of interest it has to be pointed out that the computer discs returned to us from the police turned out to be someone else's discs relating to bakery invoices and so on, obviously relating to some sort of fraud. I hope to be able to say the original discs have been returned and the police have been informed of their mistake. Hopefully it is a genuine mistake as the discs that I await return of (nine) have some very sensitive material on them.

5

Exclusive first time interview – Julie Rutherford

The following interview is brief but very poignant because of the fact that Julie Rutherford has not ever given anyone an interview. The press tried without success and she has been a bit of an enigma through all of this. Some people might have even thought she did not exist. It would be unfair to say that Julie was the other woman because that could be applied to the three women in Viv's love life at some point or another.

Julie was sought for an interview, but Gillian Lowes led me to believe that Julie was not open to being interviewed about her life and times with Viv so although it was known where she was it was felt that her privacy was important to her and her children.

The interview came about because of some things Anna Connelly had said with regard to Gillian Lowes and Julie Rutherford within her interview. I felt that Gillian deserved a chance to refute or accept what Anna had said. The parts of Anna's interview that related to Gillian were forwarded to her, I make no secret of that. Sheer coincidence meant that both Julie and Gillian were attending a solicitor's appointment in connection with the estate of Viv, they briefly spoke with each other. Gillian related some of the things to Julie that were in Anna's interview and as a direct result of that Julie asked Gillian to inform me that she was willing to talk to me.

Julie could not sit comfortably with some things that she heard Gillian relate to her and she needed to put her side of the story. Julie now succinctly tells me the things she wants to have straightened out for the sake of her children and to stop the vicious rumours and innuendo that is hanging over her.

Page nine of Anna Connelly's interview, it is stated by Anna that for Julie to become pregnant by Viv she would have had to have had sex with him on a prison visit, for that to be his child (Julie's second alleged child to Viv), whilst he was serving his three years for his part in the assault on fellow club doorman Stuart Watson. I asked Julie what she had to say to that? "It's true."

Further on in Anna's interview on page ten Anna alleges that Viv knew Julie was seeing someone else; Julie interjects "When?" I continue reading the part of Anna's interview relating to this '...it wasn't a thing that bothered me, I said to him "You did have sex with her and it could be." (Meaning Viv's child.) Julie replied, "She's lying on that I had never to go out never mind seeing any other man."

Anna went on to say, 'It wasn't a thing that bothered me because I hadn't been visiting him and he said "Nah!" for some reason he didn't think it was his he knew Julie was seeing another lad, Viv used to say to her "You want to get your maintenance paid for that bairn". Viv felt the real father was a man he used to train with in a gym who gave Julie a lift to prison to see him. Viv felt out with that man and went to train in another gym, etc.' Have you anything you wish to say about that? "Rubbish, the man was Viv's very good friend. If that's what she insinuated before there used to be two guys one used to take me up, but he used to aggravate because Viv was very, very jealous and he used to say stupid things to wind him up. Anything would wind Viv up, 'I seen her knickers getting into the car' and that was it! So he had said 'I don't want him to bring you in anymore', because he was a wind up and other reasons. He had this other man bring me in as he had Viv's car at times. I know that Viv had been told that the car had been seen outside of my door at 6 o'clock in the morning, which was a load of rubbish as this man was petrified of Viv. The man that Viv's friend had said was at my house whilst Viv was in prison wouldn't even look at me from across the road. Who in their right mind would? Who would do it? Would I do it? Be stupid enough to get pregnant by somebody else and face the wrath? No! I don't think so, that's silly", says Julie as her voice dries up with emotion.

Julie mentioned facing the 'wrath' so it was put to her that Viv was assumed to be a gentleman and had if it was the case...Julie interjects again "I was his girlfriend at the time, Steve, and if I was going with somebody else..." I interject with a scenario for Julie to ponder and answer which is, if Julie went to visit Viv and told him she was pregnant by someone else I am sure Viv would not...Julie again interjects, "I would have emigrated. I wouldn't have done it." It is again put to Julie that surely Viv would not have been as nasty with her as she was suggesting he could be especially if he thought she was pregnant to someone else. "I think it would be a different kettle of fish if I had told him that I was going with somebody behind his back. Viv was a very, very jealous and possessive man. I don't think he would have took it lightly, I don't think so."

Viv fell out with this man and he went to train in another gym…Julie interjects, "I didn't understand why he wasn't at Viv's funeral somebody had said they had fell out, why did they fall out? I've never seen this man from visiting prison and I still don't know why they fell out." (Author's note: it is pointed out here that the man in question is not Rob Armstrong as he also fell out with Viv.)

It is alleged that Viv actually said to the man in question 'You want to get your maintenance paid for that bairn', Julie says, "He would say that! In a joke." What if someone else had said that, would Viv have accepted that as a joke then? "If somebody had went in and told Viv that I was going with somebody else…" Julie has difficulty accepting this scenario and says "No, no it's too stupid for words, nah!"

I quote some more text from Anna's chapter, 'After Viv had came out of jail he came to me and said, "Will you come back to me?" He had sent some letters and cards and that. I said to Viv that he was a single man and he could do whatever he wanted and to go with Gillian or to go with Julie and whoever he wanted, but he didn't want this he wanted me.' (Anna) I asked if that would be right? "Probably, I've heard it all before I've heard the same lines when I was pregnant and Viv liked getting you pregnant, but he didn't like having the responsibility of the pregnancy, certainly not."

Again I quote from Anna's chapter, 'We were going to get married and got engaged on Mother's Day I said that if he came back that would have to be the finish with Julie and Gillian and he couldn't have the one night away here and there because that's not what I want neither, I wanted a proper relationship.' Julie: "I threw him out actually when he went back to Anna." Julie repeats this whilst exhaling and this gives her a voice a husky quiet sound, "I t h r e w h i m o u t r i g h t. We had a fight because my house was nearly burgled and it was because he was late, so of course I went off in a tantrum and ended up falling out. He came back the next day and he got the alarm fitted and then obviously he went back over to Anna's and came back a couple of days later, no! A week or so, no! It was weeks later but then I wasn't interested, but it was all right because I was safely pregnant and you were safe for nine months nobody is going to fancy you in nine months."

Did Viv feel that after the pregnancy he could return to you? Julie: "He came back, yeah." Did Viv feel that Julie was his possession? Gillian: "You are his possession, YOU ARE HIS POSSESSION, you're right that's exactly what you are until he says different. He didn't want to lose anybody, he didn't want to lose Anna and he didn't want to lose Gillian."

Julie was told that Gillian said that Viv was very honest with her and that she knew about Julie and Anna. Julie says of this, "He wouldn't have dared he was obviously open with Gill, but not with me no. Obviously I knew that he was living with Anna. He used to come and confess, but that was like…", Julie changes her words in mid sentence, "…after I had Callum he was

"Anna's because she could have him as far as I was concerned, but it doesn't stop you loving him. And I loved him and I still love the man but I hated him at the same time. I know for a fact that he was living with Anna then but it didn't stop him from coming here."

So Viv had not ever made a decision whereby he said, 'I'm going to live with Anna'? Julie: "Not likely he had every excuse in the book." It was explained that Anna said Viv had no time at all to be able to have these trysts with you or Gillian. Julie: "If she could keep an eye on him then she's a better woman then I am."

I explained that as far as Anna was concerned Viv did not have the time for such flings as he was always on the mobile telephone speaking to her. He would be back from wherever within a short time and he would bring Anna her cigarettes in because he didn't like her going to the shop for them. Julie: "I wasn't allowed to go to the ice cream van, yes." Julie says this with the tones of someone being told off for something they hadn't quite done wrong.

Obviously though when Viv was not with Julie at times when she was not pregnant I asked her if it was a burden for Viv? "I don't know I just know he knew I wouldn't do it. Viv was dead for some time before I considered going out again."

Anna said on page twelve of her chapter, '…because maybe he had been sly with me by going with them (Gillian Lowes and Julie Rutherford) and telling me lies and then when he was sent to jail and he came out he knew I had never been with anyone. So I thought maybe he thought I was going to do back to him what he did to me and is this his insecurity with me.' I asked Julie if she thought that was the insecurity with Viv because he had Julie, Gillian and Anna? Julie: "Probably, yeah he was definitely insecure within." Would Viv give Julie the third degree if she ever went out? Julie: "Yes, often in fact there was one night I went out and he was here 8 o'clock in the morning my female friend and I had been out and we were lying in bed laughing and carrying on when he opened the door. He was just standing there because he knew I had been out the night before, that was when he was with Anna. There was a mutual friend of ours and he used to phone every day even when Viv and I weren't speaking he phoned her every single day. It came to the stage where I stopped going to her house until after he died because she told him everything, what I had on, where I was going and everything."

Julie was told that Viv did the same with Gillian. Julie: "Of course he did, this is what I'm saying, Anna's, like, saying, 'He's my sole property'. Anna is silly (Julie does not mean Anna is silly as in stupid, but that she was deluding herself of the truth) because she knows that's not true", Julie states this again but louder, "**IT'S NOT TRUE.**"

I again quote Julie from Anna's chapter, 'Julie Rutherford has also contested Viv's estate. Viv hadn't bothered making any allowance about

84

Julie because he had assumed that his associate who he used to train with had accepted responsibility for the child that Viv denied was his.' Julie: "Load of rubbish, load of rubbish, that's maybe what he told her."

Why was Viv in a state of denial about this child? Julie: "He just told you what you wanted to hear, he was the same with me. I'm not saying it's the cowards way out, he just didn't answer you he just didn't like to hurt your feelings. If that got him away with it then he would say it." I asked what Anna would have said to Viv it he admitted he was the father? Julie: "Anna would have had a fit wouldn't she? That's probably what he thought anyway."

Julie was asked if the relationship was over with her and Viv after she had Callum? "Well it was over for that time, but it was on and off all the time. That would be it for a couple of weeks then he came back in about the March and I was getting ready to go out and I didn't really see him much after that, but I used to keep in contact with him and he would call occasionally."

A significant question is asked that will become relevant in the Gary Ward Blackpool Beach Murder chapter. Julie is asked if Viv ever took her to Blackpool? "Yeah, it was before he went to prison in about the March or May of 1989 and that was supposed to be a new beginning and we were sitting in a pub called the *Manchester Bar*. He had said, 'Whatever happens in the future doesn't count, doesn't matter.' I said, 'What are you talking about', because I had a few halves and he didn't drink and I asked 'What are you talking about?' He again said, 'Whatever happens in the future doesn't count this is a new beginning from today' and he would go on like that. I was going, 'Yeah, yeah, yeah right.' Little did I know at that time that he been with Gill and obviously she was pregnant and he didn't have the bottle to tell me. I didn't have a clue and then I think we fell out in the September for a while and he was going away on holiday. He said he was going away on business and we ended up having a big huge fight and he went anyway and again my friend was there, she had seen it all. He was on the phone to her from the airport and whinging on and then he was ringing me saying that he had made a mistake and this and the other and he came back it was just before my birthday. In the September it was just before and he was sitting in front of the house looking up, I was in a different house then. I looked out and thought, 'What's the matter with him?'

Because he used to come up and confess I didn't want to hear things and he had come in and confessed, he said he had actually been away with Anna. I went off it, but that was another time. It took him about two hours to tell me I said 'Just tell me', he said 'No, because you'll leave me, tell me you wont leave me?' He wanted me to swear on my bairn's life that I wouldn't leave him I said, 'Come on you obviously have something to tell me and he said, 'You've already just said her name', because I already had just said 'Anna' and he went 'Yeah' and I flipped."

"Then a couple of days later it was my birthday and it was crawly, crawly time. I went out on my birthday and he was locked up the same night on September the 29th and he was actually locked up after twelve that night because we had been out he dropped me off, went to work and was locked up. Then in December he hit me with the news that 'Gill had a baby.' Prison visits are about twenty minutes, half an hour or something I think I made a lot of enemies at that particular time people would come on the visit with me and I didn't want them on the visit because I needed to know what, where, why, how and everything. I think I was nasty to one or two people and after that I stopped going I said, 'That was it'. I wasn't getting anywhere I phoned Rob Armstrong's wife and I said, 'Will you tell Viv I wont be back we're finished' and she went, 'OK'. I literally moved house and everything, but then he started to phone. When I went back he had said that Anna had been visiting and he told her that he wanted me to come back in to see him. By this time it was about March. I had stopped going for weeks and weeks, I used to go about four and five times a week. I know his dad used to go on a Thursday and I would go most other times."

Looking at what Julie says it is quite clear that Viv was replacing the loss of Anna on the prison visits with Julie, as Anna said she had walked out on a visit leaving Viv with the engagement ring and if you remember from Anna's chapter he threatened to smash the prison down, obviously Viv had a rethink and convinced Julie enough to come back in. Something is pointed out here and that is that Anna says she gave Viv the engagement ring back, yet Anna says in her chapter that they got engaged when Viv came out of prison on Mother's Day. Maybe they became re-engaged.

I again continue to quote from what Anna said in her chapter, 'Viv always believed that this man was the father of the child to Julie because he had assumed that his associate who he used to train with had accepted responsibility for the child that Viv had denied was his. ... Viv never seen his daughter (his first child to Julie), but I always gave Alan Rooney money and presents to take up for her.' Julie: "Well I've got a twelve year old daughter who can be asked if she ever seen her dad, of course she seen her dad. If Anna knew Viv how could she possibly be certain of what she says. Alan Rooney bringing me presents and money for my daughter from Anna is not "true". I continue quoting, 'Even Gillian Lowes, whether it was Mother's Day or even Christmas Day whoever you get to speak to you will tell you if you ever speak to Rob Armstrong he'll tell you.' Julie: "Tell you what?" I explain that he could confirm that what Anna had said about the presents and money being sent to her. Julie: "Well I don't know where she was sending them but she wasn't sending them here. Do you think I would accept presents and gifts from Viv's girlfriend? No thank you, I don't think so!"Quotation continues from page twenty-one, 'So when she (Gillian Lowes contested it I just couldn't believe it. She wanted my house, so what she 'decided to do was pal up with Julie Rutherford because she must have thought. "If there's two of us up against her we'll definitely get it off her." It didn't matter if there were fifty of them against me they both hated each other and then they made friends.' Julie: "I didn't hate her I don't hate anybody I didn't know the woman. Gillian might have hated me, I mean fair enough but, I DON'T HATE PEOPLE. Then again Viv told me that they hated each other (Anna and Gillian) and that she (Anna) hated me and obviously she has because she's given me all this grief."

Anna had said that Julie and Gillian had decided to pal up with each other. Julie: "We didn't do anything of the kind." She (Anna) could not believe when 'Julie and Anna contested' and wanted her house. Julie: "Robbie Warton came knocking on my door a few months after it I don't know maybe weeks because there was no talk of any solicitors no talk at all and he had said, 'I've been told to tell you that you have to get a solicitor', I said 'For what?' He replied, 'Because Gill is trying to take everything including the house.' I had no contact with Gill at that time and I didn't really know what was going on about and he had said, 'Just get a solicitor!' Also believe it or not from a very strange source, which I was told came from an area west of Gateshead. I didn't believe the man because I thought 'This is him giving me advice and pretending it's come from up there.' The advice was to get a solicitor and this was within a matter of weeks from my first being told. So I said, 'Right! What the hell's going on.' So I got my friend and I asked her to ring Gill and ask her if she'd got a solicitor and she had said to this woman 'No I haven't.' So my family had said something's going on so 'go anyway' (to a solicitor). And here I discovered that some lies had been told whereby Gillian had said she did not have a solicitor. When I went to a solicitor they said that she (Gillian) did have (a solicitor). So I thought, 'Well what's she lying for?' And then the funeral actually came around and they came and introduced themselves they were very nice to Jodie. They took Jodie to the grave they took her forward and I was with my family at the back of the church in the seats and I was actually talking to Gillian's dad and I said to Gillian, 'You told me you didn't have a solicitor?' She went, 'Well I didn't know where you were coming from I didn't know how to react to you because we had not 'ever spoken before.' That was the first time I was introduced to her, she came up and introduced herself."

Jodie Annie has met her grandparents, did she stay with them from time to time? "Yes, she had been to see them through the day but she had not stayed with them overnight." Obviously then, it was put to Julie, the grandparents accepted Jodie Annie as their granddaughter? "They also said this is my grandson', because his mam (Viv's mam) on the day of the funeral went, 'I know, I know it's our Viv's, Callum Vivian Graham is his name.' What can you say to that?"

Julie is asked that if it is right that property should be fought over? "If Anna wants a house then why doesn't she buy a house the same as what Gillian and I would have to do, it's his children we have to think about. Her children have got their father our children haven't!" Julie feels that her children should be compensated for the loss of their father and who is to argue with that. That is Julie's belief and it does not contradict any loving mother's feelings, however it is only her point of view, not the feelings of a court of law. There is nothing within here that can be termed out of order and the opinions expressed are only those, opinions.

Anna expresses that neither Gillian nor Julie has had to put up with their windows being put in or that neither of them challenged Viv's killers and all the staring and the fighting. Julie: "I wonder why?"

Continuing what Anna says, 'Why haven't they come across then and got Karen Young? They want the money...' Julie: "Sorry, who?" It was explained that Karen Young was arrested for allegedly having some involvement in the murder of Viv and featured in Anna's chapter. Julie: "The reason I..." Julie changes tack mid sentence, "...as far as I was concerned I was out of it and I hadn't spoke to Viv for three months.

He had paid for me to go on holiday, Primrose Valley the four of us (Julie and her three children) in a caravan. I have an older son and two little ones and I went off with my cousin and I never heard from him until the Christmas. Viv had sent the money for us in 1993. He phoned me from hospital (abscess occurrence) I had never been on holiday with the little ones he asked where I was going? 'Caravan', 'Yeah, that's OK.' So he sent me some money over via taxi. When I come back that was it I never rang him, if he wanted me then he knew where I was.

Then he sent Robbie Warton at Christmas. He was gone in December, I had not been seen going out with him in the last two years of his life he said, 'It was too dangerous you wouldn't believe the lifestyle I've got now Julie?' He came here and it seemed he had the world on shoulders he knew it was his sanctuary and he knew he was safe." It is mentioned that Gillian was told the same thing from Viv that he was feared for her safety yet Viv was living just about in the heart of Newcastle with Anna. If he felt threatened then what made him stay in such a place that made him more vulnerable with his fiancée and her two children? He had warned Gillian and Julie of the dangers that his life now carried therefore it did not make sense that he should want to stay living somewhere that would cause harm to those loved. Conjecture in this matter throws up a few answers, one might be that he used this as an excuse to keep Julie and Gillian hanging on a thread for whenever he wanted them thus he could have his cake and eat it so to speak.

Julie quotes directly from one of the many letters that Viv wrote to her whilst he was serving his three year prison sentence, he was concerned then. He said the only way he would get out of it was if he was shot. "But it might "just have been an excuse as the man was full of excuses. The last two years of his life were totally different to the time we spent together, totally different. The exact words Viv wrote down are, 'The job I do, you don't know when the fuck you could be killed...Julie, from what you've heard today you will see I live a dangerous life the only way I can get beat is by getting shot', that was letter number 134 wrote on 11th June 1990. This is what he wrote when he was in prison but his life was different when he left prison. The last two years I don't know what happened?" I explained that people used him. Julie: "Yes, I know they always did though, Steve, he was too nice." I explained that Viv's father said that people used his son as a moneybox. "Yes, that's exactly what they have done."

I ask if any of Viv's supposed friends have given her any support, no one at all? No one has enquired as to how you are? "Oh yes they've asked, 'How are you?' 'Fine'. As I told you before I made a lot of enemies when Viv was in prison they used to think things. This friend of Viv's has a lot to answer far as far as I'm concerned he used to say that it was me, 'She's working herself again.' I used to get letters from Viv and he would say 'I don't want anybody but you to come in', that included his friends. He would say, 'I love my friends but I'll see them when I get out.' That is the way Viv was, his friend would say, 'It's her!' And so, I was the villain of the peace."

Julie is asked if this man's friendship with Viv was coming under threat and he felt his friendship was more important than Julie's? "Definitely. I was the scarlet woman by the sounds of it I think he did the same to Viv's dad I think actually. Viv had said that I couldn't put right or something the damage caused where his dad was concerned. I would say, 'What are you talking about?' I don't know what he said. I hadn't ever spoke with Viv's dad. I was a threat to this man he wanted to be closest to Viv." I remind Julie that somehow this man and Viv had a falling out. "Well exactly, I had said that to Viv's dad at the funeral I said, 'Wouldn't you have thought that after what he had done to you that you would realise the things he had said about me were lies?' He would Say, 'I know, I know.'

Julie took steps to have me informed of her willingness to talk and I believe it is better to talk than to say nothing as even the courts now look at a man's right to no reply as being worn out. The Days of the Magna Carta that King John signed in 1215 are long gone and now silence is deemed to reflect guilt. There are some people who believe the old adage, 'Speech is silver and silence is golden'; I am one of those believers, but in order to silence the wagging tongues Julie has had to talk.

This whole situation boils down to money and property. Julie says about Viv's lack of leaving a will, "Believe me, Viv used to do silly things to spite us and this was probably one of them. My one and only concern is my son and what people have said about him. Viv just wasn't the same guy. He used to always be happy go lucky and couldn't give a monkey's. He didn't "and wouldn't involve me in his private life. I didn't open the door to the press I was just put down as Viv's secret love and I just let them get on with it. They had my name down as Coffell in the papers let them get on with it I couldn't care a less what they said I wasn't reacting so I thought, 'Dead end.' Anna had made me react to this because of what she had said about my children."

I ask with regard to Alan Rooney alleged to have brought presents from Anna because he had at that time lived nearby to Julie. Julie: "He brought the little one's car, a Noddy car and he fixed it up. It was his birthday or something; Robbie Warton brought a big tractor and a couple of buggies it was when Viv was banned from driving. Viv would phone and say he was sending them over, they never came when he didn't tell them to."

Julie was asked if she had seen anything with regard to the money and clothes allegedly sent to her? "Viv did not like me to have money he thought if I had money I would go out. If we weren't speaking then he would not give me money."

Finalising things I ask where she and Viv first met? "*Finnigan's* at Felling in Gateshead. Viv actually nipped my derrière he wasn't as suave as people would believe he wore a pair of crimpelene trousers and a fly away collar shirt, but he had the charm and he had the smile. Apart from that fact he had a lovely bum, he nipped mine so I had a little bit more to drink and then I nipped his. Apparently he was with his girlfriend, Gill, and she had seen it and it had caused an argument that's what I remember from it and from then on that was it. We were an item for years and years as far as I was concerned until he was murdered."

At short notice this chapter was included within the book

6

From School to God

School

The past headmaster of Viv's school has become a Labour Councillor for Chopwell & Rowlands Gill in the Labour controlled GMBC. (Gateshead Metropolitan Borough Council). Many would say that Councillor Henderson has become immortalised as the man who helped bring about the monolithic structure of the Gateshead Angel, but he is a modest man and wishes it to be known that he was part of a team that brought about this sculpture. Councillor Henderson modestly says, "I was only the chairman of the group that oversaw the development of the Angel there were many others as equally involved as I was so I cannot accept that the credit comes down to only one person."

For those of you who do not know what that structure is that we go on about you will see it on the front cover of this book. It is not for the author of this book to babble on about such sculptures. Inanimate objects of this nature are best left for the experts to criticise or favour. Councillor Henderson says, "The Angel has in some way brought fame to the Gateway of Gateshead." The Angel greets those who drive northwards on the A1 towards the now famed Gateshead Metro Centre shopping complex which was a forerunner for most other out of town shopping developments that the rest of the country has took to be the landmark to the future in how shopping complexes should be designed.

The interview is now in full swing and I have to ask if it was right that Councillor Henderson had really given over twenty interviews to the media in one day relating to the Gateshead Angel? "Twenty one interviews in fact "television, radio, Sky you name it, all because I've been involved with the Angel project. If I had not been involved then those interviews would not have come about," says Councillor Sid Henderson.

Moving on to the main question I ask Sid if it was easy to recollect what Viv was like as a youngster especially since Viv was one of many thousands of children that passed through his school? "I can remember Vivian Graham due to my involvement with football and being a qualified FA Coach at the time when Walter Winterbottom was the England Coach as he signed my coaching certificate. So because of that involvement with football I can recollect Viv. I had been involved in schoolboy football and coached the district team with the help of my teaching colleagues. Viv Graham was one of the team members that many other teachers and I devoted a lot of time to. So maybe I knew the footballers a bit more than others did. We used to have football matches on Thursday and Saturday mornings it is a rarity now that you get teachers giving their time in such a way.

That is partly due to government policy where Baker who was Education Minister brought it in where they said you had to do so many extra hours out of school and what happened was that teachers said, 'I've got to do so many hours so I'll do that and do no more and it kills a lot of junior football." Sid has a real passion for the game as he says it with a real sentiment in his voice.

Sid Henderson is the last of a tough breed, he became a qualified FA coach under the guidance of an England coach's techniques, he then gave much of his time, without charge, to the junior game. Sid was asked if this country was far behind the rest of the world in coaching terms? "I think it's moving away from that now, but I mean at the same time what we play football for is not necessarily to win every game in front of you and become a professional, I mean what I call a professional footballer. It was part of the ethos of the school really encouraging young people such as lads that caused bother and so on. I remember a lad that used to come out and play in goal he was a right little horror you know. If there was a threat of him being dropped from the football team he changed his attitude altogether. There were all sorts of things tied up to the football it wasn't just a question of coaching them and getting good results.

I was at Highfield School (Viv's former school) from 1969 and I left in the summer of 1987. I remember Viv Graham because he was part of my football team and I had a particularly good team that year and he was the centre half and a good centre half at that. There wasn't much got past him he was a big lad even at eleven and he was a good team player and he fitted in with everyone else. Certainly we didn't have any bother with him. There were no indications of…I mean he was aggressive like many lads are in a football team sort of go in and out of the wing and get the ball and so on he "could certainly do that. I thought he was a very likeable lad and very, very enthusiastic about his sport not only that his parents were also very supportive too and they used to come to the football matches. As far as ability goes I would have said he was pretty well, of average ability." What is said here about Viv indicates that he was not a type of person to be a school bully or wallow in the glory of being on the team.

Sid was asked if Viv had a team spirit? "He was very much a part of the team, a very commanding player in defence even at eleven but there were some good lads on the team along side him as well and they all played together and did very well."

Do you think Viv would have been better advised to stay within football rather than to go on into boxing? "Well certainly boxing is not quite my scene but I enjoy watching it. I don't know how it took off I'm not sure because when he left our school I lost touch with him and therefore I didn't know where he was developing and how he was developing.

What happened was after I left Mr Hewitson had taken over as the new head at Highfield School and certainly Viv Graham's child was at that school. The letter you showed me earlier from Maureen McLaughlan to Viv who was the nursery teacher verified he was very generous and very helpful towards the school. I mean there was certainly less vandalism when he was about. He used to look after the school in a way when he became a parent."

Gillian Lowes said that when Viv was late in turning up for school he would escape being told off? "He was a very likeable person, very likeable and he was very respected within the community and he was very, very loyal to his family there was no question about it he looked after his parents he made sure they were OK."

Sid has experience of living in the Highfield area, being a councillor and travelling into Gateshead he will see such things as the Gateshead Angel, which to him it is all quite normal. What about those people that live in that area who have not been beyond the boundaries of a rural place was it a daunting task becoming a councillor? "No I don't think so. I did some time on Tyne & Wear County Council before its abolition by Mrs Thatcher (former Prime Minister). I was chairman of the County Council prior to its abolition by Mrs Thatcher before going onto Gateshead Council."

I asked that question because Viv was more at home in Rowlands Gill than he was in Newcastle. I can see the charm that an area such as Rowlands Gill offers people because it is in a sort of self-contained world. Sid says, "It's a small village in itself a village community that has residents associations which are very active, the schools make up the community as well so every body would know Viv. I mean Frank Clark for instance was a Highfield lad that went to the same school just before my time and he became the manager at Notts Forrest he won everything he won an FA Cup Medal the European

"Cup Medal and so on. He's just been sacked from Man City as the manager because they weren't doing too well. It was the same story behind his family they supported him tremendously. So he and Viv came from the same area and went to the same school albeit at different times."

We talk about Sid's background he was born in nearby Greenside not far from where his mother was born in Highfield, Rowlands Gill. So he speaks from first hand experience. Sid had lived for a while in Pelaw (east of Gateshead) when he was first married and he goes on to say, "It was the only place we could get, an upstairs flat we were just kicking off and didn't have much money." Sid has not had everything put on a plate for him and he attributes this to the way he was brought up and which direction you get pointed in.

Is there any guidance he can give to those families who are not, perhaps, paying much attention to their children? "I think that's a very difficult one to answer, really. It's a question of if the community can help. As far as the council goes we've just converted a couple of houses in Whitfield Terrace as a centre for young people in Highfield like a drop in centre and it is open for anyone who lives in the area and for young mothers. There is a nursery school and I think nursery school education is a very important part of people's lives many of the young people don't have that opportunity. What I mean is that Nursery school has compensated for some of the lack of provision that was made within their home. Nursery schools give an opportunity for young people to access books and access materials and so on which they may not be able to in their own home. I think it reflects what teachers believe in, which is trying to help children achieve a standard of citizenship."

Sid is asked if this progressiveness he has is something within him? "No I think there are lots of people like me who give a lot of time for their communities and I think you find it more in rural areas than you do in towns but, that's just a generalisation. I know plenty of people who are similar to me who are involved in community associations so on." This caring attitude that Sid points out has struck a chord because unlike what someone had tried to indicate to me that people like Viv could be portrayed as the loving father and so on because people like that had to love someone anyway and because of that people like I could write that sort of thing saying things like, 'Viv the caring father' or 'Viv the loving son' and so on. Well, here's news for that person, Viv has come from a rural background and he helped out his old school (letter proves it), he bought a whole table of religious ornaments for children at a Holly Communion, he had a heating system fitted into a boxing club those things can be proven! What about those things? That does not indicate that Viv was a man who only loved his children or was just a generous loving son.

Viv's generosity was mentioned and it was suggested to Sid that both he and Viv might have had a similar outlook with regard to the caring side of their natures. Was that because of their rural background? "I think it's because we were brought up in a rural background of a small caring community. That might have been and I would like to think that might be part of it. He had a soft spot for Highfield School I think he had happy times at the school.

Just to summarise, I don't think there was many people who didn't have a high regard for him in our community." With that the interviews comes to an end and Councillor Henderson is thanked for devoting some of his time to what is considered by many to be a touchy subject. After all I lost a university lecturer from Sunderland University to the pressures of having to give comment for the last book. Councillor Henderson did not hesitate when asked to give an interview with regard to the late Viv Graham.

GOD

The cross and the switchblade are not as incompatible as at first it might seem. Those who live in a different sphere of activities to the average person usually take comfort in looking to a higher authority, 'Thank God for that'. How many times must it be said in a day around the world? A near miss in the sky or on a busy motorway makes most raise their eyes upwards whatever their religious beliefs. 'Allah' is a name as much used in different parts of the world as the name 'God' in other parts. 'No matter how big and strong you are there is always somebody better'. Those are the words Viv said to his son, Dean, whoever he meant there is somebody bigger and better than the person he must have thought of. People would argue that the ultimate Daddy of them all is God.

'Nobody fucks with big 'G' because this is his patch, now go and tell them that.' No! You cannot imagine God giving that message somehow, how he works is through the church and a man that has devoted over thirty five years of his life to those in the East End of Newcastle is doing work on behalf of his boss, God. No one could go up to Father Michael Conaty, MBE, and tell him that he has to make way for someone bigger and better than his boss because in Fr Conaty's eyes there is no one bigger and better. So he does not need to be impressed by stories of this one and that one pulling each other's arms off in a fight or pulling someone's head off and shitting in their neck. This would not impress a man who has met death many, many times and walked away from it. A man that has seen the poverty stricken so bad that he helped set up a training firm and open learning centre to help the people of Walker find work and receive a better education. There his achievements do not end. He has also set up the John Boste Youth Centre and a day care centre for the elderly the actions of this modest man speak louder than any words ever could. He spent his first ten years in Newcastle working in the Heaton area. He now has the reins to Saint Anthony of Padua Church and his only wish is to be left alone to get on with his work and not make a fuss over his honorary MBE, which he wont be able to use after his name because he was born outside of Britain. Rather like giving him a chocolate fireguard really, something that he cannot use. What about just giving him £50,000 and forgetting about the title so he could have used that for his flock.

What he has done is something that very few people could emulate, maybe Diana, Princess of Wales, would have surpassed it but since she had a whole team of charities working towards her goals that would have been understandable. Fr Conaty actually met Diana he must have been an inspiration to her when she saw what he had achieved in such an area of industrialised scrap. Piles of people who had given up hope of ever becoming employed again.

Fr Conaty says he has received the honorary MBE on behalf of his parishioners one of them being Anna Connelly. Anna's connection with the Catholic Church were mentioned in her chapter and how Viv had started to turn towards her religion even if it was only in a curious way. Although Viv professed to be an atheist (non-believer in God) his respect for her religion was apparent. Fr Conaty was praised as the 'people's champ' and this is an understatement for what he has achieved. Viv was a benefactor to those in need but he did it under his own flag as opposed to Fr Conaty running under the flag of God.

Pinpointing Fr Conaty down for an interview was a difficult task. I wrote a number of letters and made umpteen telephone calls with messages for to pass on to the Father went unheard. Giving up would have been the thing to spring up in most people's mind, but this was a challenge and this man was important in being able to reveal certain things in fact his message is the most important thing in this book. For that alone it was worth pursuing him I hope some good will come of it for all of you reading this from within a prison cell whether that cell be in your head of your own making or around you for real.

I start by asking a long winded question to help Fr Conaty become relaxed as it is usually a daunting experience giving an interview to someone writing a book about the issues within. "The church here within this Parish is very active." I asked him if he would find that people would automatically turn to the church on those occasions when predominantly heavy job losses had arose and, perhaps, people weren't feeling too happy in a time of need? "It's like every other community some turn to God and some turn against. It doesn't follow any particular pattern." There is a reason for asking the question because in later years in some way in terms of this church, Saint

Antyhony's, in terms of supporting Anna's faith and perhaps in his time of need when he felt pressurised because of all of those other activities that went on within his life and people who demanded his time, perhaps, then... Fr Conaty interjects with, "But I never knew what he did or anything" I can see where Fr Conaty is going as he is not a person to sit in judgement and obviously feels that I am seeking some secret that he holds. On the contrary I seek to know how the area is and how it reflects its character from within Fr Conaty.

Did you notice if Viv had a willingness to speak with you on things and to give support to those that came here? "Well he certainly did want to see them come here he seemed to be an awful friendly bloke and he seemed to be the type of fellow that would do anything for anybody that was the way I found him. But I had no idea of what his life was, I'm just speaking as I found." Did he offer any support to the church? "I think he used to get himself involved in the school where the kids were and as far as I remember he helped organise things." There were missionaries that stayed at Anna's Connelly's home do you recall that? "Well they would have been connected with Saint Francis." Fr Conaty confirmed that he remembered them staying at Anna's home. This confirms what Anna had told me that both her and Viv looked after them when they stayed at their home. "These were people who come up to work they were from down south. There was some generosity there I thought."

In times of someone's needs such as the parents of Viv Graham what could you say to someone who has lost a son, but is not a believer in God and what sort of support is there for someone like that from someone who has a direct line with God so to speak? "The meaning of faith is a person's faith that I would have felt is a gift of faith powers that walk along with people who haven't got faith you don't impose faith on people who don't want it imposed you walk along side these to help them because that's what your faith drives you to do. Faith doesn't give you an insight into another person's atheism or why they disbelieve or anything else because that's not what it's about."

It was put to Fr Conaty that he could accept what they believe in? "Yes, am I making sense what I say? What I'm saying is the reason why a person of faith walks along with all people is because that's what your faith drives you to do. That's what being a missionary really is." So was it like being a tool? "Yes, yes but they can't decide, this again is a misnomer (wrongly applied) you see. Christ said, 'You have not chosen me I have chosen you, God has called you.' All of these people around them that have faith will have an influence, but it's God who calls."

Would you say there are different levels of being a believer? "There is only one reason and it is because God loves you we all we are all the same in his eyes his love for us was expressed through the son who was his image he laid down his life for our salvation and that's the great thing when he died for all people without exception. Faith is knowing that we are part of the life, you and I, of living and knowing God."

It seems that Fr Conaty can empathise with people even non-believers. Fr Conaty could accept Viv in a non-judgemental way I asked if that was critical in his position? "Yes, that's absolutely critical." What about if someone came to confess about killing someone could Fr Conaty's non-judgemental role still stand? "In a confessional they would receive the absolution, it's called the absolute forgiveness of God. Which I could be an instrument in giving absolute forgiveness." The reason this is asked is because the way Viv died and very tragically, the person responsible must be carrying a tremendous weight. Is Fr Conaty saying that the Church and God could forgive this sin? Should that sin not be repented and forgiveness not sought then could it be in the eyes of God that the doors to heaven would be closed to them? "I couldn't make a judgement on that, the mercy of God is boundless we don't like to discriminate or be selective. You see we can't play God, this is what you are asking."

In terms of revenge and those who have no faith and have to carry the weight of a tragedy that has happened within the family and not to feel vindictive and not to carry out revenge perhaps there have been people who wished to carry out revenge and still do. What would you say to those who are still seeking revenge? "Revenge, retribution are very much Old Testament concepts we are in the new covenant we are much more towards spirituality, punishment and retribution and revenge are progresses by forgiveness and that forgiveness is total and that takes a great leap in spiritual maturity to cope." It was asked that if someone was contemplating revenge and was not a Catholic then would Fr Conaty still help them? "Yes. There is no other road unless we come to terms with this."

That is the end of the interview and I ask Fr Conaty if he has anything he would like to ask or say? "How are you producing the book, is it from cuttings?" In retrospect at this question it reminds me of an article by a local paper in which they condemned the first book (*Viv (Graham) – Simply the Best*) as a 'rehash' of hundreds of column inches. So when I listen to the taped interview it brings a smile to my face. I laugh in fact, because a book that is worshipped by most within the criminal fraternity that has been out for a number of years is made up completely of newspaper cuttings, yet it received a very good write up from the Evening Standard, who buys the Evening Standard? The difference is I pull no punches about the press and do not arse lick my way up to the top. That first book in this two book series you will now understand was simply an introduction to this book. There were accusations that 'the 241 pages were struggled to be filled'. I thought they said I struggled to fill the 241 pages for a minute there!

When someone calls a housing estate the Bronx then you would not be blamed for conjuring up all sorts of hostile pictures in your head, people peering out of cracks in the wall whilst aiming guns at defenceless victims, muggers working in threes and so on. That is the picture painted of the Pendower Estate in Newcastle's West End. Where does the church come into this? Reverend Richard Taylor was in the midst of offering £18,000 out of the Church Urban Fund. Reverend Taylor runs Saint James' Church in Benwell, Newcastle nearby to the place where the infamous Mary Bell lived as a child.

The actual payment is about £100 per week for a family to run a drop in centre the rest of the money goes on other expenses for community work in the area. Here the church as usual has had to step in a pick up the pieces that the city cannot. The scheme is hoped to pave the way for other similar schemes if this pilot project works. Rev Taylor says that non-church goers would be just as welcome and this bears out what Fr Conaty said about acceptance of those who did not believe. Residents on the estate were withdrawn about what would really help and did not think it would be a success. If Rev Taylor is half the man Fr Conaty is, it will work 'for sure' as the Irish say.

The residents have had past problems in getting the city council to carry out repairs and maybe this area should have been looked at first since you cannot run such a scheme from crumbling buildings.

7

John Davison – World Champ

I first started boxing as an amateur actually when I was 25, I had nothing else to do, I had just got married I was living in a flat at Throckley in Newcastle and I had bought an MFI unit. I had noting to put on it, a couple of lads said, 'Come to the gym in the West End.' Phil Fowler was the coach there, I said, 'It's a mug's game' they persisted and said, come down, come down.' So I went down punching the bag and Phil Fowler said, 'Who do you box for?' I told him I hadn't boxed and he said, 'You have!' I replied, 'No I haven't.' I did some sparring with the lads and knocked three of them out. They just went crazy and I was told I should be a boxer, again I said it was a mug's game. Then again I had this MFI unit with nothing on I thought, 'I might as well box just to get a few trophies for the unit.' I wasn't working so I might as well box and get some trophies and that is why I said I would box.

After the first year I fought the world rated number one a boxer called Paul Hodgkinson, an amateur, a great lad. My first nine fights, I had nine knockouts and I fought him. They stuck me in the ABA, which is the national championship at featherweight. I knocked Paul out in the first round and then I went on to Captain England 17 times all over the world.

Then I had been picked for the Olympics and I trained for two years. Politics started to come into it though. I had already fought a boxer called Michael Delaney and I beat him twice, but they sent him instead of me. There is a long story behind that they just thought I was too aggressive, I'm more of an aggressive style more of a professional style. When you box for England they like a tippy-tappy boxer, jab and move. They don't go a lot for aggression and I was a very aggressive style so they didn't go along with that, as amateurs don't really like that. I had travelled all over the world and boxed the world number one, the world number two and the world number three. I won a silver medal against the world number two, Yurri Alexandrov, from Russia, so I naturally thought I was going to the Olympics and I wouldn't have turned pro. I was never at home, I was always at Crystal Palace every week-end training. It creased the wife when I was overlooked and Delaney was chosen instead, a man I had beaten twice!

Delaney got beat in his first fight at the Olympics, he didn't really seem to try, his heart wasn't in it by the look of it. I thought, 'I'm not going to box amateur anymore.' Kevin the national coach kept phoning me up asking me to stay as an amateur, but it didn't change my mind.

How Viv come into it was that when I turned professional I was looking for a sponsor and I was looking all over and somebody mentioned Viv's name. I asked him if he knew anybody who would sponsor me, he offered to sponsor me to the tune of £1,000, which helped me get all my gym equipment and other items. I had a proper gumshield, gloves, boots, headguard and a gown. Our sparring friendship grew, he used to come into the gym and spar with me. He couldn't believe how strong I was for a featherweight.

Viv must have been around eighteen or 20 stone at the time and he could punch, really punch, his hand speed was very fast, he was tremendously fast for a big fellow. Your hand speed is a lot different from your body speed and it was a natural thing he was doing when he was boxing. You train all the time with your hands, that's how you get your hand speed, but your top half speed you go with the flow. Hand speed doesn't mean the rest of your body is fast. (Author's note: this obviously accounts for Viv's ability to be able to sort two or three men out within seconds.)

Personally speaking I thought Viv was a great kid, a real nice gentleman. I didn't know anything about his lifestyle he helped me out, he started me off in the boxing, him and Rob Armstrong they were the ones that gave me the money.

When Viv was an amateur boxer he thought about going professional when we were sparring I said that with his size and strength he could probably beat half the professionals in the country at that time. I used to say to him, 'You want to turn professional.' I had Viv's name on my gown in the last fight I had when he was alive and for him giving me that £1,000 I said I would get '*John Davison, Sponsored by Viv Graham*' put on my gown, but the cameras avoided that area and it was covered over. It was just a friendly sort of thing to do as he gave me the money to get me started off. I suppose he started my career. It might have seemed that I was advertising thuggery, but it was simply returning the favour. The first gloves that I won the World International title with I'm sure I gave Viv those gloves.

I was boxing in a booth on the town moor in Newcastle for a while at the beginning of my boxing career. I still have the same mates and when I won

101

my first major title I was car booting on the following Sunday. People were walking past and they couldn't understand why I was selling junk at a car boot sale. I said I'm not going to change just because I've won the title. People automatically thought because I was the champion I should change my personality.

At the end of the day your friends are more important than anybody else, you stick with the ones who you know. Some that are trying to be your friend are going behind your back calling you names, they're not your mates. So I've never changed I've still got the same mates I had years ago and I still drink with the same mates.

I remember when I was boxing in Manchester as a professional. I stopped my opponent and this little kid come up to me and he said, 'I'm going to be a champion one day.' I patted him on the head and said, 'Good lad.' It was the first time I met Naseem Hamed! We met years later in the Metro Centre when he made it big and he was fighting up here. I went along to see him and I said, 'Can you remember?' And he said, 'Yes, I remember, c'mon lets have our photograph taken together.' He's a good kid. The reason he isn't liked on television is because of the way he acts. It's all hype and that's what it's all about now. In real life he's not that person as appears on the television.

I have an interest in training people who want to box. Boxing training is the best fitness training in the world. Nobody has ever done what I have from Newcastle. The last man that won the British title from Newcastle was called Thomas Watson, sixty years ago. It was a job to me and that's it. I still do what I did al those years ago, antiques, car boot sales, shopping and wheeling & dealing. When I was brought up there were tin baths and outside toilets and that wasn't that long ago. Viv and I were brought together with a common bond and his background was not of any concern to me, we came together as sparring partners and that was my life at that time.

My neighbours accept me a normal and no different to anyone else and that is the way I like it although people do still come and shake my hand because it was only about five years ago that I retired.

Amateur boxing now seems a waste of time because if you get a head shot now you get a standing count its so strict now because of dangers involved. As for women boxers I trained Audrey Godfrey who was the first woman ever to fight in the ring up here. That is another piece of history I made. I do train quite a few women who do it for keep fit purpose it's great if you want extra stamina, keep fit or you want to lose weight. Athletes should do more boxing training because it's the best training, I help women who want to lose weight and feel good about themselves.

Fifteen years ago it all started and I was pleased of his help. I was pleased to present his kids with my gown so that his and Anna's kids could say, 'My dad sponsored John Davison the first man to win two World International titles and a British title in sixty years from Newcastle.'

I have sparred with Billy Hardy from Sunderland. Most of my later opponents were from Korea/Thailand I couldn't get many UK boxers to take me on because I was a big hitter. I tried managing a few boxers about five, but it is a cut-throat game.

To finish off this chapter it is only right that a piece be wrote about Aryee Jackson who came to this country from Ghana in 1956, before I was born. The book is dedicated to Aryee (sounds like Harry, but without the 'H' although most called him 'Harry') who became known as the Gold Coast Champion when he beat Andy Marty in a non-title bout. This young 18-year-old featherweight was once described as the perfect boxer. His jabs were immaculate, his footwork was simply amazing and he fought like a seasoned campaigner.

This is what one critic had to say about him, "Only since the days of Roy Ankrah have I seen a boxer endowed with such limitless stamina and capable of throwing punches at such non-stop amazing rapididty as that exhibited by Jackson. The fame of this young firebrand spread and managers from the UK were desperate to sign him up, even wiring him his full travel fare from the Gold Coast to the UK.

The fare was returned and Jackson arrived in Newport to begin his new career under the guidance of a man called Joe Carr. Jackson trained in the dock area and so many people wanted to watch his lightening footwork and rapid punching that it was 'members only'. A sparring partner of Jackson's was Terry Jenkins from Griffithstown who helped him prepare for his contention for the Empire featherweight title.

Ronnie Morgan of Llanbidy, Wales was the man to go down in less than 160 seconds in Jackson's debut bout at Carmarthen. Morgan was not in the same class as Jackson.

The headlines of newspapers told the story of man on a mission: 'Jackson again', 'One of the best wins of an excellent evening's boxing...Aryee Jackson who gave height and reach to the tall London flyweight Ernie Fossey won over eight hard rounds. Jackson the nearest thing to perpetual motion...' 'Jackson stops Lawrence...Ken Lawrence who retired at the end of the fourth round...' 'Denny Dawson retired at the end of the fourth round with an injured hand...Jackson a non-stop little battler hustled Dawson...'

'Bowes is beaten...Geordie Bows the County Durham featherweight was outpointed by Cardiff based Aryee Jackson. It was only Bowes third defeat as a featherweight for the ex-North East pit lad who was a star in the bantamweight division. The only other two to get the better of Bowes have been Phil Lundgren and Howard Winstone. It seemed that jackson MUST tire as the fight went on, but to everyone's surprise he didn't.'

Promoter, Mickey Duff had arranged for a fight between Howard Winstone and Jackson at Liverpool Stadium. Winstone was having his first contest since becoming champion by beating Terry Spinks. The now 22 year old Jackson was experienced enough to take on such class opposition as Winstone and this would be a crucial fight for him, tonight. Jackson proved a difficult opponent. Winstone took the first three rounds by the narrowest of margins.

Jackson's unorthodox approach was not mastered by Winstone, the fourth was a slugging match in which Jackson came off the better. Winstone threw a right upper cut after Jackson had been warned twice for leaning, the punch had little effect. Jackson grew in strength and had Winstone all over the ring and in the ninth drove Winstone from one side of the ring to the other. The referee asked both men to make a fight of it, but in the tenth the fight petered out and the prolonged boos of the fans showed their dissatisfaction. Winstone won on points, but was booed out of the ring.

Jackson beat a mixture of opponents including the Belgian champ, Aime Devisch at Nottingham ice rink. He was hailed as a world-beater, when he learnt how to punch directly. Jackson said of himself, "When I see myself in the gymnasium mirror I try and hate myself. As I shadow box in front of that mirror I try and think it's my opponent. I always try and build a hate up on my opponents when I fight."

Jackson stopped former Australian featherweight champ, Max Murphy, in the fifth round in Sydney, Australia. Jackson was contracted for three fights in Australia and was much sought after and a crowd pleaser with his special non-stop punching style.

What becomes of former boxers of such style and calibre? At present, some 30 years on, Aryee is in a nursing home that is in Wales, the only visitors he gets are close friends from the North East of England. They are fighting to have him moved to a nursing home in the North East so that they can visit him more regularly, but there has been an objection from the nursing home that he is currently resident at. Ayree is friends with former boxer Daniel Lartey. Daniel's son, Dez, regularly makes the trip to Wales to see his adopted uncle.

Many thanks to Dez Lartey for archives and photographs relating to Aryee. A man that would have given any current day featherweight/flyweight a hard time. Naseem Hamed would certainly have had a hard time if Aryee were around now with the entire up to date training methods and improved techniques of boxing.

Quickly covering the unlicensed bouts and bare knuckle fighting it is hoped that in a future release possibly entitled: *Goosey, Goosey Gander* (or a similar sounding title) you will be able to read of many prize fights from the past and present. That book really will cover the violent side of life that goes on under the very noses of those who object to such things. No pissing about in that one, the gloves are off!

8

Spiritualist Reveals Killers Identities

For those of you with a weak constitution or nervous disposition it is advised that you seek medical approval before reading any further. What follows is a direct result of the author's determination to seek the assistance of a spiritualist medium. Many cranks and fakes are about ready and willing to take your money. You would be better advised to give the money to charity rather than take up some of their services. How do I know? Because I am a qualified clinical hypnotherapist. I trained with the Academy of Curative Hypnotherapists at Peacock Hall in Newcastle's Royal Victoria Infirmary. Why I mention this is because we are bound to get some arsehole from the local press saying I am talking rubbish when I write the following details.

During the course of my hypnotheric travels I would book a space at Mind, Body & Spirit events to promote my particular type of Groverian therapy adopted from a man called David Grove. No doubt he will be surprised to get a mention in a 'gangster' book. There would be about half a dozen so called clairvoyants/mediums/spiritualists in attendance sitting waiting for the gullible or hopeful punter who quite willingly parted with £10 for a five or ten minute reading and a further tenner to prolong the agony. I would hear the same mediums hour after hour use the same ploy on the willing punters, "There's something connected with your hands dear, (Oh! Really, your hands) let me see have you had some joint trouble?" Reply: "No." "Well has there been someone in your family who has had hand trouble, maybe they were left handed or something like that?" "No." "Well has there been someone you know who has had hand trouble?" And so it went like that all day, yawn, yawn. By the end of the day's session I felt ready to take any fare paying punter on board for a five minute tour of there Great Auntie May's rendition of 'Knee's up mother Brown' for a tenner of course.

I must point out that obviously there are some very genuine mediums about but in all honesty they are as rare as rocking horse shit. From reading Sharon Tate's and Anna Connelly's chapters you will be aware that they sought solace in visiting mediums and the like. They ended full circle back to their church. Had they have had the services of the lady I sought out then I am sure they would have still returned to their Catholic faith but in a much better frame of mind.

Spiritualists are reviled and hated by the church because they are seen to be incompatible with them and as having direct contact with the devil. This belief is not just the belief of one church but a whole array of faiths. The Bible forbids the practice of spiritualism, why? Because there must be some truth in spiritualists having gifts and powers to contact the other side. Why is the church so keen to advise against this type of activity? It is said that God forbids his people to consult mediums and if this is to be believed as being true then there must be some truth in what they can reveal. One of Jesus' disciples met a medium and on meeting her he cast out the evil spirit that supposedly controlled her. The occult can work in two ways for good and for bad. In this investigation the good side was called on.

The spirits of the dead are supposedly called up and contact is made with them, you the reader can make your own mind up after reading this chapter. I for one kept an open mind to this type of gift being used in such a serious investigation. What transpired swayed me to believe that there was something in this type of thing? The New Testament condemns the practice of spiritualism. Authority from the dead is apparently withheld from contacting the living but the argument could continue in that Jesus rose from the dead and appeared to his disciples? This was surely contact with the living from a man that was dead. I do not intend to get involved in religious arguments but simply wish to advise of what has been said of this activity. You are well worth being advised to the hidden dangers as well as the comfort and solace such type of thing can bring those in distress and hopeful of contact being made.

How do you go about seeking the services of someone with such a gift? Well it is not as easy as you would think. The mention of Viv Graham sorted out the chaff from the wheat. That left nobody willing to come forward from Newcastle! One medium wanted £500 and to be anonymous with no contact allowed from anyone who sought her services via the publisher. This could leave us open to accusations of inventing the person so that was thrown out.

After all it would not do to invent such a person because unlike the press we actually like to use real people in this sort of situation. We do not use anonymous people wishing to hide behind a veil of words created by some Joey journalist from a Fish & Chip wrapper paper. It was actually easier finding a hitman as featured in *Viv (Graham)* – *'Simply the Best* than it was finding a spiritualist for this remit.

The police in some forces in the UK have used the services of spiritualists USA is awash with them. The lady who I found shall be called Crystal the name is obviously not her own as she asked that it be changed, why? Because the contact she made revealed one hell of a lot, to pardon the pun. What can be said here is that Crystal asked for no fee or free publicity? Crystal did not know who Viv Graham was and had no prior knowledge of his activities throughout the North East's clubland circuit. That concludes that she was not in it for the money or free publicity, but Crystal did say when asked that if anyone wished to contact her that they could do through the publisher's PO Box address whereby their telephone number, full name and address would be passed on. That surely proves she is for real, oh by the way! No press masquerading as Joe public, please; as happened with Anna Connelly being pursued by a journalist over the telephone and only when pushed on the matter did they confirm they were from the *Sunday Sun* (Newcastle). An article then appeared about how Anna had made contact with her beloved Viv via a spiritualist.

On with the interview that took place at the murder site, the site where the killers dumped their blue Ford Escort getaway car and then on to Anna's home. Articles belonging to Viv were given to Crystal, which she held close to her while she sat in the rear of our spacious car in the course of visiting these sites on a quiet Sunday afternoon. The event was taped from start to finish with my trusty recorder and specially adapted mike lead. This recorder that had never let me down in the past had decided to develop some faults when it was replayed and taped to a master tape. Those results were eerie to say the least. Batteries were always replaced with new ones before any interview. They could last up to eight hours if need be but were replaced after every interview of every four hours if the interview took longer. This system meant no interview was lost. What was listened to on the original tape whilst transferring over to the master tape had one of our female researchers in a state of shock for a number of days. I do not wish to reveal what it was because some member of the journalistic brigade would start taking the piss. I am not easily shocked or moved by things that at first appear strange, as I believed that everything could be explained. I listened to that particular part of the tape over one hundred times, at least and I have reached my own conclusion. This is for real, not a spoof story. I do not need some scientific geezer wearing an ice cream man's coat to examine the tape and tell me they cannot prove anything conclusive. I do not wish to reveal something that the press can pick up on and make this serious investigation into a mockery because they simply wish to sell newspapers. They can piss off and find some other sucker for their headlines. To prove this is no wind up I will now stop going on about it and safely put the master tape away intact out of harm's way where no one can meddle with it to try to advance their own cause. I would ask anyone who might get the privilege of reviewing this book not to raise this point as it is a serious investigation not a club for tyre kickers wanting to jump on for their own advancement and making money for old rope of sensationalism. We are talking about a man who has family who love and miss Viv immensely therefore a circus of mediums and spiritualist coming out of the woodwork is not intended. Genuine ones do not advertise in the press or Yellow Pages mentioning 'As seen on TV', 'As consulted by XXXXX' or 'Madam XXXXX as heard on radio.' Right straight into the revelation.

We are sitting in Border Road, Wallsend only a matter of feet from where Viv was gunned down, nearby to 'Head Hunters' barber shop! Crystal says, "He wasn't the least bit surprised by who murdered him. He didn't give it a second thought about who the people were as he actually expected the people to behave like that, so instead of telling anybody he assumed that people would have known. He was definitely thick headed the night he died from some cause." (What Crystal says here fits in with what Anna Connelly had told me some weeks before about her suspecting that Viv was spiked to slow him down.)

"In some form it was affecting his concentration and annoying him, irritating him. Could he have had any premonition that this was going to happen?" Crystal asks. She was told that Viv said he would die before he was forty; he just lived for the day.

Crystal was right in what she said about Viv knowing who his killers were because, when he talked with his nearly to be brother-in-law, Peter Connelly, about who he thought was most likely to kill him, Viv actually named the people who were responsible and Peter named someone who was responsible in some way for putting it together. Crystal was correct about that and confirmed what had been found out.

Crystal asks, "Had he had a previous head/neck injury at the back of his head?" Viv's frozen shoulder was the only known injury near to his head/neck although he did suffer from pounding headaches. Crystal: "That would affect his neck. I get a very great impact from his boxing on his thought processes. He could be very quick witted and also could be very thick, a very funny combination," says Crystal with an outburst of breath in between her words. This shows she is focused on the event. "I think the glass was already gone in the car and that was supposed to be something to disguise something." This ties in with the fact that Viv was warned about the consequences of him coming back to his car and finding a popped window or flat tyre and dilly dallying too long. "That was absolutely deliberate and it was something to do with how to fire the gun as well something to do with not worrying about windows going up and down or something it was a mechanical aspect of firing the gun so it was necessary, it doesn't completely make sense to me."

I put this to Crystal; "So if someone was to shoot from that back lane if he had got into the car they would have had to shoot at the window and the bullet may have deflected so do you think it may have been the concern of the killers?" Crystal: "The window was already out it was quite deliberate and I would say it was almost out in a particular position as well. Going back to Viv I'm very intrigued by how he thought because it's like he...well he certainly wasn't your average guy in terms of his thought processes at all."

I put it to Crystal that Viv was made into what he became and wanted to get out of it but couldn't and those people who made him into what he became left him to get on with it and left him all on his own. Crystal: "He was carrying an enormous amount of tension around as well. And I would say he could be very soft and sentimental and also very aggressive as well; really a very peculiar mixture. People around him wouldn't necessarily know when and which was to come out. He would be more scared than he would be willing to admit to anybody. Also he was pretty careful, he really did tip toe in some groups. It didn't appear to those outside the group that he was tip toeing around, but he did pussy foot around people. He would come up as not very nasty and abrasive, but was also very careful."

"So he did it in a nice way?" I ask. Crystal: "No! I wouldn't say so! He could be charming, but he could also be ruthless he knew how to play things. He knew which way things would swing and yet in some ways he wasn't that intelligent, on mundane things he wasn't that intelligent. Very, very peculiar mixture. Is this sounding right?" Crystal asks. I do not verify or confirm what she says I simply say, "That sounds like a general description of that man.

I think his body was quite a struggle to him. I think he needed to keep it very functional and yet it used to bother him a lot, particularly his shoulder and neck. He was very aware of his body being powerful and yet he didn't feel very comfortable with it either. He wanted it to be supreme, he wanted to really be powerful, to be well built, to be on form to be like an athlete's body and yet a lot of the time to him even though it looked good it didn't feel good at times. He was very aware, ...he almost felt disabled with it at times. The image of himself was, he wanted to be bigger but he wasn't comfortable with what he had." Viv was trapped in the typical body his builder's syndrome; not ever becoming as big as the mental picture he had in head.

Crystal is shown some photographs of Viv after she has said this and that confirms to her what she has said is correct. It would have been far too easy to show Crystal some photographs prior to us starting, but that would have made this contact doubtful with her description of him. "He needed that image, but it didn't feel comfortable for him. He actually felt more comfortable with his body when it wasn't like that. I think that affected his thinking as well – perhaps that was the steroids?

He got sloppy in terms of how he looked after his life towards the end. I would say his thinking processes deteriorated and took more risks and in a way he was 'asking for it'." Crystal is asked if these risks were new risks? Crystal: "He couldn't keep being 'on guard' - it was so exhausting. Which meant that he let his guard down more in the last couple of years of his life. His thinking processes were quite seriously affected by the time he died. He wasn't as rational, he wasn't as sensible, he wasn't as clear headed, he wasn't even thinking things through so he was more of a target."

She is asked about the people who did the harm and did he know where it came from? Crystal: "Yes he knew. Was one of them quite thin with quite a small jaw? I've got a vision, the top half of the person's face was bigger than the bottom with probably larger ears than should be, proportionately larger ears. Someone who didn't make total sense in terms of what he had achieved in life - a weasel like person. Someone who was very, very confident and very, very quick witted and very ruthless and very talented."

Crystal is asked if the person she is describing could retort with a fast answer such as a witticism that could fit the remark that Crystal had made? Crystal: "Yes, yes, yes, that would fit. This person didn't control anything with his body, he controlled with his mind and his cynicism. I would say he was between thirty and forty and very thin in his youth. He was very, very capable of ruling people. He certainly had no concerns for other people. That puzzle's me clairvoyantly how with those looks he could command the position that he got to. A powerful man with a lot of luck on his side to get to that position, with a lot of shrewdness. Someone who completely understands how to play people off against one another, without getting caught."

Crystal can actually read my mind; thought processes would be a better description of it. This helps out very well as it cuts down the need to explain things in detail to her. Crystal says to me without any prompting, "It doesn't fit what you're thinking." What has confused me here is that I am wondering who Crystal is describing because I have something else on my mind. Usually this doesn't show and I can think bi-laterally whilst listening. Crystal knew my thoughts did not match what she had been saying and let me know. This was my first indication that Crystal was more than what met the eye and I was beginning to wonder if what she was saying could be right.

My views were now changing at this point.

I go on to say, "Now wait a minute! You've got something right there, it fits the party who I believe gave the money and other payment for the killing..." Crystal interjects and says emphatically, "Yes, yes, yes", I continue "...that's who it fits that's right, that's right it does fit. I thought you meant the actual person responsible, the perpetrator of the crime. You are right because the face and the features you describe..." Crystal again interjects, "I'm describing the person that ordered it. (Read the Murder Scenarios Chapter for more in depth coverage.) Even before I arrived here I've got the person and if you showed me a photograph of them I could say 'yes' or 'no'. If someone gave me an identikit I could do it. He wasn't always well shaven and he had his hair pretty short at the time and it was brownie mousy coloured. He had a very black and white outlook and wouldn't wear colourful clothing and I don't know why but you wouldn't catch him out wearing bright types of clothing.

Two people were told to do the hit. If they hadn't of succeeded they would have been very thoroughly tripped up and left flat on their faces. I think something would happen to their feet or their ankles I don't know why, it's not knees it's lower; ankles. They would have had their faces damaged if they didn't succeed they would have had their faces smashed in first. These people were terrified, absolutely petrified and very similar in terms of how they dealt with it. They thought in a very similar way, were they brothers?" My reply was that they were very close but not brothers. It is explained that the people responsible and a few others had got wind that people had wanted Viv out of the way..." Without warning Crystal says, "I think we need to move away from here", I said "Do you think?" Crystal: "Yeah! We can't continue here, sorry I just feel like we do." I get my seat belt on faster than normal and speed off in the seven series BMW with a feeling of uncertainty as to what Crystal meant. I believe she had felt something or spotted something in one of her mind pictures and I wasn't hanging around to find out what it was, because at this stage the atmosphere was becoming a bit discharged, the area around Crystal had become very steamed up yet my windows were clear. This gave the look that Crystal was surrounded in a mist, although that was not the case.

We then headed towards Anna Connelly's home and parked nearby. Crystal Says, "You were talking, weren't you?" My reply: " I was actually then you just said...do you think somebody phoned the police and said..." Crystal: "I don't know I just... somebody phoned somebody I'm not sure if it was the police I just didn't want to be..." Crystal fails to finish what she started to say and I feel it was something more sinister but I do not wish to add things that were not said. "...anyway I needed to comment on something you were saying. Oh! Yes it was about were they brothers? They certainly think in the same way."

I ask if they were frightened of failure? Crystal: "Horrified! They had been given some specific instructions but the rest they had to workout for themselves, they were petrified. I would say the specific instructions were in terms of weapon, window down, what they yelled at Viv." She is asked that there was something particular they had to yell to Viv? "Yep! Something very derisory. They were also told locations not to risk and, areas that were safe. This was a second or third time they wondered about doing it. They had one firm try and one other one that they aborted and then this was the third attempt."

Did Viv have any awareness of this and what made them abort the second attempt? "They aborted after a police presence. Not a police presence that was actually relevant, but they aborted." The police higher up the chain of events but there was a reason why they didn't do this themselves? "Yeah! They would have been linked too strongly they would have been too obvious so this one had to be delegated even if it had to be delegated to a buffoon. In a way they were actually expecting these two to get caught but the person that ordered it would have been quite happy for them to be caught. He actually thought they were such idiots that they would actually get caught and these two thought they would get caught too. Somehow they managed not to. I think they were very lucky not to. They were terrified because they were caught between the devil and the deep blue sea.

The people involved in the killing had a meeting with those that wanted it done and when they were approached they would have looked foolish if they had of backed out. They weren't approached, but told. They were allocated the job. Like in social strata or hierarchy they were in a lower level. The hitmen responded to orders. They weren't on an equal footing with the man I described as a weasel." Crystal is uncannily close to the description of the main person responsible. The description she has given as a 'weasel' will probably stick and time will tell if this is the correct person. (A photograph was forwarded to Crystal of this man and she confirmed that it was indeed the picture she had in her head of the man who gave the instructions to the two killers.

Crystal is trying to get a picture of those in the car she says, "One of them had quite curly hair, dark brown. These two have a sense of humour. They could mix sociably better; the weasel had a sarcastic sense of humour but no real proper sense of humour, a very nasty sense of humour, a very bitter sense of humour as well. On the personality side the weasel guy is far more psychopathic and the other two were very much in denial like, 'I don't think I did it so I didn't do it'. Believing that if they didn't think about it then they hadn't actually done it - they were kidding themselves.

There is some dodgy stuff in the police around here!" I ask, "In terms of what?" Crystal: "Being paid?" It is pointed out that there are links between police and big time criminals, which is proven by anti-corruption ploys within certain police forces. At this point and previously on the master tape something has happened that sent the hairs on my neck and back standing on end I knew by what was and is still on the tape after Crystal's comments that something else was present with us in the car apart from the three of us.

Even when I listen to it again and again now it still sends shivers up my back. I did say that it would not be mentioned again but I cannot deny what I heard on the tape. I do not wish to be labelled a crank or another Glen Hoddle dabbling in things that are untested. I was not frightened by what I heard on the tape as it did not concern me directly but because of what is on the tape I know something is being done from somewhere far more powerful than here on earth. I know that something will happen because of this incident. One person has the answer to all of this and he will understand what I am writing here because of something that happened in his life.

"The police are quite happy with the scenario now because it means they've got some degree of power here that they can control. They know that they could pull these people. The power balance has changed, the balance of power goes to the police." Crystal mentions a police officer although not by name that is quite high ranking and is sort of thin. Crystal: "Quite high up but not at the top. He's quite a solitary person. Aged in his fifties with connections with the weasel. There are lots more people involved in this than the ones we are talking about. The death was used as an excuse to change the power balance and didn't particularly look for an outcome but when things happen they act accordingly. The police know the full scenario but haven't pursued it heavily because that means they can pursue other things. The police trade both ways they trade the catch them out, trip them up, lock them away. There's three ways they play, they play that way and put different levels of pressure on to keep certain levels of violence and certain levels of crime under control.

Dodgier all the way, as well different levels of strata here, they are certainly not clean." Did Viv know his killers? "I would say he knew both of them he would have recognised them more as messengers rather than as paid to do it rather than ordered to do it, rather than they deciding to do it themselves. He had dealings on and off with them but he knew of a lot of people."

Crystal is asked that if she were given the initials of the killers would she be able to communicate and confirm the initials were correct? Crystal: "I think it would be better if I try to describe them. We'll start with the one with curly hair. One has got curly hair that has at sometimes been curlier than at other times. Brown to black with hands that are quite grazed and rubbed on the knuckles and rings on the middle fingers but not on the outside fingers. Aged late twenties to early thirties when it happened. Someone who could be very rough with a girlfriend, he threatened to strangle her. Not carrying a lot of flesh and wearing quite scruffy clothing. If there was a woman involved she could have had blonde hair but dyed brown."

When Viv crawled along that street after being shot did he notice anything? Crystal: "Only his pain and the weight of his body which gave him some difficulty in moving his arms because of the weight of his body. He was far more concerned with the state of his body than who had done it."

Viv had come to rely on his body over the years and this shooting had took any dignity away from him in terms of him having to drag himself by his arms along a main road in full view of the passing public. Not just a death whereby he died instantly but a drawn out event where his dignity was unseated and he was left to crawl with his last remaining ebbing energy. He knew he was about to die but his concern was for those around him so that they would not have the indignity of seeing him die in such a state. Right up to the end his concern was for those lesser mortals around him. Viv was concerned that no one should see him in the gutter with this wound and he tried gallantly to pull his shirt over it as well as asking to be helped up so he didn't look as bad.

Crystal: "I think he felt very cold as well with the shock." What was Viv thinking when this happened? "His only thought was to get away. He didn't care who'd done it. He hurt; it was physical..." Crystal makes a sound which indicates a deep seated pain.

Did Viv get the peace he craved for while he was alive? "I'll try and get him now. Yeah, in a way it's a relief. Also I think he was aware he was hurting people a lot and there was apart of him that just wanted out of that. So in a way it was like, 'I'm not doing anything to hurt anyone.' Yeah! I've got him on the other side now! He's more concerned at what he's done than what others have done. Viv would be tickled pink at what you are doing. He has a nice gentle sense of humour as well you know. He's such a chameleon. I would say in spirit he's more concerned about his kids not going the wrong when they grow up. But he really wanted better things for them." It was pointed out that Viv had a number of children and that he visited them at all times. He gave them lots of things he didn't have. We have a set of his trainers with us and I point at them explaining that Viv was happy with cheap 'Dunlop' trainers compared to those we had with us but in the end it was only the best of everything, £90 trainers, £90 shirts it was literally the best of everything which only started when he came to live in Newcastle.

Was Viv concerned about what people thought of him in terms of money? Crystal: "I think he was more concerned about his body than anything else. You get things like that when you're clairvoyant people we perceive ourselves completely differently than others perceive you.

We then move on and visit Anna Connelly's home but I point out that it was at my instigation and not Anna's that this move can be put down to. Anna explains to Crystal about how the other clairvoyants had took her for a ride and how it had first helped but then 'a lot of them were telling lies by what they had seen in the papers and they just started to make it up.' The talk is small and there is not much time as Anna is hurrying to go out so we cannot make an appraisal here. Anna asks how we know we have things right and it is briefly explained to her that because of Crystal's help we know the whole story because of parts of the jig-saw being pieced together with Crystal's help. I am at odds to be able to disclose certain things due to awaiting certain evidence coming to my attention.

Anna asks if Crystal can sense Viv in her home at which Crystal replies, "I've had quite a strong sense of him and he worries about his kids and he worries about you and the people around you. He struggled with his life and his body and in a way it's a release not to be doing that any more. There's a tremendous amount of grief at being separated from you and an incredible amount of tears and unhappiness, almost like he'd lost part of his soul. He was particularly fond of your daughters as well. His spirit feels very resolved compared to some people I see. I think he was always aware that he was going to go and that helped him prepare to some degree. So when it happened it wasn't like, 'Oh! My God this wasn't supposed to happen.' So in that way I think it helped him resolve things more easily." Anna says, "You're right there he knew it was going to happen and he wanted to go, and it was a relief to him; he had constant headaches all the time." Crystal: "Does it come from the back of his neck the headaches?" Anna: "Yes, he always had tension across on his shoulder. He had a bad shoulder as well." Crystal: "I know he tried to carry more weight. (Extra body weight.) Did it feel uncomfortable as well?" Anna gives a conflicting reply but later on it is shown to be out of context in one way. "No, he liked carrying weight the more the better." Crystal: "I think it was good for him that he looked like that I think he didn't actually like the feel of that much maybe he hadn't told you." Anna: "He didn't because he liked running and he couldn't run with that weight on him, so yeah maybe it could be right, maybe he never told me that bit. What else, is he happy?" Crystal: "I certainly get a much happier feeling than the two years before he passed over because he struggled with himself in the last two years a lot. I get a strong sense of resolution around it. I've had people that come through to me and have told relatives to 'F' off because they're not resolved, he's not in that category. He's looked at himself and he's worked through it but he's still very concerned about the people he loved very, very concerned and you haven't coped very well and he's struggled with that." Anna: "I have now, these last nine months I have, but not before I didn't. I think he's moving on anyway because that's the feeling I get. He's happier now." Crystal: "There are different stages up there. He worries about you." Anna: "I'm just glad he's happier, in a happier place than where I am, I'm telling you." Crystal: "I've had a good link with Viv today."

What is a very good quality tape, recorded on my Panasonic recorder, has shown signs of slowing down the play speed and then increasing play speed for no apparent reason this was discovered on playback. There is also a lot of electrical interference and static on the tape, which has not happened before. The tape speed returns to normal with no explanation, make of that what you will, again the master tape has been kept for reference purposes.

We are now off to visit the site where the killers dumped their getaway car. The place in Simonside Terrace, Heaton, Newcastle now has houses built on what was once a strip of waste land. So we are parked as close to it as we can get. On re-playing the tape it is found that the tape has recorded only at about three-quarters speed, again this is for no apparent reason. No doubt some university professor will come along and give a million explanations such as flat batteries, power surges, poor quality tapes, electric current in the atmosphere, etc. All I would have to say to that then why has the same tape been used time and time again afterwards, nothing similar happened?

This could be looked upon as some scientific experiment but I do not go in for that sort of thing as it is above me. What I do go in for though is something called a sixth sense like when you know who it is that is calling when your telephone rings and you pick the receiver up and say, 'Hello, XXXXX' they get a surprise that you know who it is before they even speak, but you do not know how it happened, let science explain that one? The tape is so full of static interference and poor sound quality that I can only interpret snippets so you have to bear with me on this what follows.

No one spotted the killers leaving the car or go to another vehicle. It was reported though that a female was nearly knocked over by the car as it sped around the corner towards here. Crystal: "I haven't really described the other guy." Crystal describes something intimate about this man that is withheld on her advice. I say, "Is there a woman, erm...", Crystal finishes what I was about to say, "...in common, no but I think you might think there is." This woman is just incredible! She has taken the thought right out of my head and that has sent my sixth sense off because I have not had this happen to me before so I say, "I do think they did actually, yeah! That's right. It's uncanny I'm starting to get tingles."

Crystal is laughing and she is on full power at this site. I start to think to myself that there are certain things I have not to think about in this woman's presence. This is not some stage show. It is for real, we are really doing something and I cannot help but feel what Crystal is saying is direct from a connection she has made with Viv. My guess was that I had indications that Viv had warned one of this lot off from his areas of Wallsend, Shieldfield and Byker over a woman. I embroider on this with the full details so that Crystal has a background to my thoughts. She says, "It's not true, they didn't have a woman in common. One of the men still has a score to settle." We now have a pinging sound like an echo finder on a submarine interfering with the sound quality. An electrical whirring sound is heard but that is from the electric window being lowered. Now we sound like the Smurfs talking. Interpreting what has been said is now difficult but to give you the gist of it Crystal intimates that the killers had left the car quickly but within a short time they had decided to set fire to it although this was not a specific plan of theirs. Now the sound quality is returning to normal and the Smurfs have left us.

There was a story that one of the killers had arrived at a local drug dealer's house and asked for an alibi. Crystal: "I query when the car was set alight? I think the killers came back later to do it." I ask about the gun? "The gun is a bit of a talking point and is still around."

Crystal says something that is very important for her and I, but over the top of that I hear a sound on the tape recording that I know is wailing. Crystal says: "I'm clear that one of the killers is presently free, so I don't particularly want to describe him in any further detail for my own safety." There is a third person, Crystal says, and quite audibly a howling sound is heard but much more clearly than the previous wailing. I can sense a whole pack of animals listening in the background with the howling and wailing sounds spasmodically littered in the background.

The same recorder, same tape and same batteries were used after this and there were no 'special effects' on the tape, it was quite clear. No doubt we will get some member of the press saying we are all potty and therefore pre-empting this we are not giving any interviews relating to this subject either now or in the future so please do not contact us asking for an interview.

Crystal has not asked for any fee, she does not advertise and does not need the work from any publicity as she has enough to keep her going. Should anyone wish to pursue her services in a genuine way then please forward your full details name, address and telephone number to the publisher who in turn will pass them on to her, as mentioned previously definitely no journalists posing as the public.

Terri - The woman allegedly with Viv on the
night of Blackpool murder

Viv & Gillian Lowes - Mistaken by Gary Ward
as the woman Terri

Viv and friends in celebratory mood

Gateshead Metropolitan Borough Council

Education Department - Highfield Primary School
Highfield Road, Rowlands Gill, Tyne and Wear, NE39 2LX
Head Teacher Mr R. Hewitson B.Ed. (Hons.) - Telephone: (0207) 542086

25 · 11 · 93

Dear Viv,

Thank you very much for the toys you sent for us yesterday. We appreciate your generosity and look forward to playing with them. It really is most kind of you. Thank you again.

Yours sincerely,

M. M°Laughlan.

Letter of thanks to Viv from his son's school.

John Davison with Sunderland's Billy Hardy

Ayree Jackson rowing to victory in the late 1950's.

Building where Viv used to train - a place of torture for those who indulge in weight training

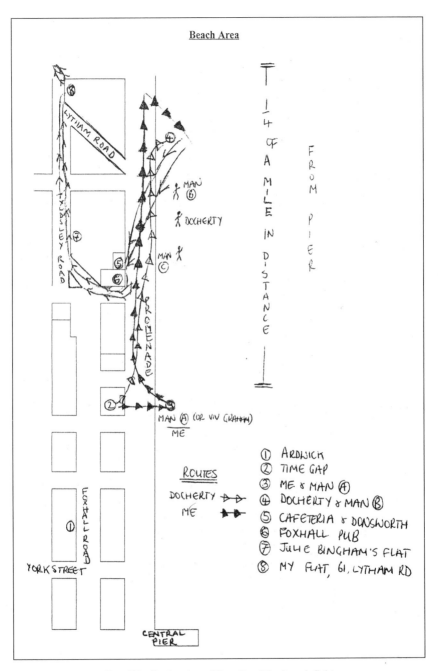

Gary Ward's drawing of the site of the beach fight.

9

Hazel & Jack of Hearts

Eric and Hazel Graham are the parents of Viv. Eric prefers to be called Jack and from now on that is how he will be referred to. Asking to interview the parents of Viv was not an easy thing to do. Journalists had pursued them in the midst of their grief at all hours. There had been a big bust up as a direct consequence of the 'Cook Report', I was, after all, only another one of those to request a comment, who was I after all; only another areshole out to contort and twist the words of those wanting to tell it like it was. I had to prove myself somehow, how? There was no cut and dried way to get through the red tape in my way. Promises would not get me anywhere, as that was not something that many people had kept to. After many weeks to consider my plea I was granted an interview although a limited one, but none the less it was a start and for me just to be able to talk to the parents of Viv would be a great honour.

That might sound like I am dedicating this chapter to Viv. That is not the case it is a dedication to the two people who brought their little baby into this world with all the hopes that nearly all parents have for their children. Everyone's little Johnny is going to play football for England, learn to play the piano, become a great painter and anything else they thought he was good at. Viv's parents got to see their little Viv become big Viv. On the achievement side of things he made his parents proud, not just because of the boxing medals and cups he won or the football talent he possessed as a schoolboy, but because of his kind and gentle nature! If any parent can bring their child up with a kind and gentle nature then they have achieved something far more in excess of a World Cup winner's medal. Jack and

Hazel Graham achieved the success of being able to instil into Viv something that not many people could learn in two life times; manners. The old fashioned way of bringing up their son, Viv, and their other children have shown that the old qualities have not completely died away. Modern living, fast talking, fast food, while-U-wait services, processed in one hour, 24 hour supermarkets, all day drinking, 0891 premium rate numbers, express services, next day delivery, take now pay tomorrow, therapy sessions, pay to view channels and the like have to some extent killed off what was left of traditional upbringing.

Smaller communities can still impress the rest of us by showing the true grit style spirit. Viv would see his parents just about everyday and who can blame him, when you read this chapter it will give a different perspective to how Viv is seen.

Accompanied by a female chaperon I called at the village home of Mr & Mrs Graham. Surrounded by fields this could have been in any rural area of England. There was one difference here though and that was there was no snotty atmosphere of plastic card dwellers or curtain twitchers, this was a down to earth rural village council estate where just about everyone knows everyone; a working class 'Emerdale'. (UK TV Soap.)

On entering Mr & Mrs Graham's home the atmosphere was strained, Karen, Viv's sister and her husband Martin were present in the living room lit by a table lamp. Mrs Graham escorted us in, but there was one noticeable absentee, conspicuous by his absence, Viv's father. Jack Graham had not spoken with anyone about his son's death and sure as hell he did not want to talk to another interested party; me.

I had brought a list of questions and I showed them to Mrs Graham and had I of known her I would have loved to put my arms around her and comfort her from the noticeable fear I was causing within her. "Why do you want to ask these questions?" Mrs Graham asked. It seemed they thought I was having an inquisition into the secret background of Viv. I stated my case as best I could and that briefly was, Viv had been badly done by from the press and the rest of the media. I had been asked to write the story of it all some two years prior to this interview, but I felt it was too soon after Viv's death to delve into his past and to ask the questions I would be asking now.

We were talking away and my chaperon asked if she could use the ladies room before we got started. Upstairs she went, where I had heard the floorboards creaking for the past few minutes and I could tell someone was walking around. That someone of course was Mr Graham, Mrs Graham went upstairs to show my chaperon the way when she heard Mrs Graham talking to her husband, something about me asking questions and so on. Jack did not come down though and I progressed with my point of view and just getting into the swing of things when the stairs were heard to creak, someone was coming downstairs. Everybody just stopped talking and all eyes were cast on

119

the living room door. The silence had created an expectancy that something was about to happen. Like when the camera zooms in on the bomb and hold for a few seconds, everyone expects it to blow up, but the bomb does not blow up and the suspense increases. It was as though everything had slowed down and things were moving in slow motion. Everyone looking at the door like frightened little puppies awaiting the outcome. We were all siting in a dimly lit room and the door opened and all that I could see was a silhouette that seemed to fill the whole doorframe.

It was the eyes that I noticed at first, dark and powerful, a nod and a wink and you were shifted out of the way, sort of thing. The light just caught the shaven head of Mr Graham. The darkness that came from behind him exaggerated everything making it seem that he was looming larger than life. What was I to do? I stood up and walked across with my hand gestured out in the handshake position. "How do you do, Mr Graham Sir, pleased to meet you?" The hand that met mine seemed to be twice as big as my own size eleven hand.

The ice was broken and the best interviewee I have interviewed throughout all of this took centre stage. Jack is a natural orator, but Hazel keeps him supported throughout the interview, which is an exclusive, as he has not spoken to anyone at length over this matter and I can understand why. Jack is a man's man and, although he has seen better years, he still has an aura of power, physical power. Even though he has suffered some illness he is still a man to be reckoned with by virtue of his worldly-wise wisdom.

Right, on with the interview. Jack is prompted into talking about the *Hobo's* incident. For those of you who do not know what the *Hobo's* incident was it is best to read *Viv (Graham) – 'Simply the Best'*. "Our Viv was at the court case there was the two Sayers', Davie Lancaster and Fish Tams and there was a sixth lad and they were looking for him. He was going into Durham jail every week visiting them. I don't know if somebody must have tumbled, but it was weeks after because they chased him, busies in their cars and they caught him outside of Durham, but the QC for the prosecution, Williamson, and you know in a court when they keep having little recesses he was standing their and his words were, 'I don't know what the effing (fucking) hell I'm wasting my time here for? A fight between two bloody doorman' and they were his words. The busies had got the lot and fetched it in as affray. If you seen the tape, from them going through the door to them coming out it was only minutes. Three minutes, it took three minutes. Now then, there were two busies in *Hobo's* and they were on surveillance for drugs. They were from Tadcaster, they were Yorkshire busies, they weren't from here. The policeman said he had never seen a fight like it in his ten years on the police force. He said that our Viv started on Stuey Watson, moved off, two attacked him kicking and punching, they come and the other three went in kicking and punching. So that's six blokes kicking and punching one man and if you look at the video Stuey Watson comes out and he's hardly got a mark on him. How they can tell me…I mean six old pensioners should have put him in hospital. You've got six blokes kicking hell out of him. They said to the busy, 'Why didn't you show your warrant card?' They said, 'We were on surveillance.' They were asked, 'What would happen if a lass was getting raped, would you have just sat back and watched it, like?' He got three years for it in the end.

There's another thing about your stinking journalists, John Merry. Sitting in Anna's on the Thursday night and the reason he was there he said he was going to try and get a story together to see if he could sell it to the papers to put the money into the reward fund. He even threw £43 on the table, he said, 'Here, that's all I've got on me. Now listen, please don't approach the press and if you're approached by the press don't say a word because I'm going to get the best deal I can here.' On the Sunday morning in the *Sunday Sun*, £2m bloody Drug Baron, that was it. There was a photo that was stolen, the one where Anna is wearing that yellow dress the one that was in the papers, it's always in.

The thing is there's been that much written and said about Viv Graham, whatever happens to whoever or a friend of Viv Graham it's in the papers. I think the photo's have stopped now because Doctor Dawson got on about it. It's been four years, why can't the papers leave him alone." The press is discussed for some while and particularly about how Viv was portrayed as a Drug Baron.

To signify how the newspapers had got it wrong Jack says, "And I had to pay his car off. Me like a silly bugger had to go and put my name down." Jack says it's not so as to go against his son, but to show how that if his son was making so much money from his alleged drug empire then why was he having to guarantee his son's car and now he had to take over the payments." Hazel interjects, "The bailiffs came here twice to take furniture out for this car money owed. He said, 'There isn't sufficient in here to cover it so I'll just tell them you haven't got nothing', he was brilliant." In a way Hazel was right, what could the bailiff have taken to cover the £000s still owed on Viv's Ford Sierra Cosworth? After all this was a humble home, clean and comfortable with all the items needed to make life bearable, but with nothing that could repay such a debt. Any bailiff taking items out of Jack and Hazel's home would have to have a heart of stone.

It is asked what of Viv's friends, could they have helped out? Jack says with a certain amount of anger in his voice that sums up his feelings about those who were the supposed friends of Viv, "I'll tell you and you can put this in the bloody book as well, they weren't friends they were hangers on; he was a money box for them." Jack says this with conviction in his voice and is so sincere about what he says that the sadness of the situation cannot be relayed by this book and the writings within it. You would have to hear the sincerity in Jack's voice to know what he says comes from his heart. Jack continues with the same frame of mind when he says with sadness in his voice, "And he was a minder for them! That's what he was." Jack is speaking for a lot of people when he says this, "When they were with Viv Graham they were ten foot tall, 'Oh, I know Viv Graham, good friend of mine', so people back off."

What Jack says is so important here because he says in a few words that others would be fearful of saying. I am pleased that Jack had the courage, which surely it took, to come down those stairs. Jack strikes me as the type of person who would give you his last, the typical Geordie man from the past, hands as big as shovels and shoulders broad enough to carry the world on. Nothing could ever beat such a man that was, until his son was murdered in cold blood with the best part of his life ahead of him, how could any man bear such a loss, no matter how wide his shoulders are? Showing open grief went against tradition for Northern men to be able to show their feelings, it was not the done thing to breakdown and cry because the man had to be the pillar for his family to look up to. These men had to carry their grief in secret.

Jack relates an incident in which his son exercised his right as a private citizen to carry out some late night security work. "At the top end of the village a lot of old people live and they were forever getting robbed. So he went up and sat in an old woman's house all night, sat in the chair all night waiting, and nothing turned up so he went to a certain party and said, 'Look if another one of those houses gets done I'm coming for you, even if you haven't done it I'm coming for you, I'm going to make a job of you, so spread the word, you're the one that's going to get it', it stopped. Christmas, before he died when he was shopping with Anna and an old lady wanted a turkey he said to Anna, 'Keep her occupied', he went into a butcher's shop and came back and said, 'There you are, mother, there's your Christmas dinner.' They don't know about them things and when he sponsored the footballers and the boxing, things like that."

Everything what Jack says is said with sincerity and sentiment Jack's son-in-law, Martin, asked that when the book was published would it be riding on the back of violence? In answer to that there is enough violence which is fact and does not need to be sensationalised to promote the book. It has been harder finding things such as what Jack says compared to violence while-U-wait, sort of thing. Violence is all around us; the quietest street can become a blood bath within seconds. There you are, sitting all comfortable with your mug of cocoa and all of a suddenly the street is awash with busies (police), helicopter floodlights and the Armed Response Team (ART). That sort of thing would have once made headlines in the national newspapers, now it's lucky if it ends up in the tittle-tattle column of the Sunday Bugle. Now it is humanistic everyday things that attract publicity, fly-on-the wall documentaries, Animal Hospital and that sort of thing attracts far bigger audiences than the Jerry Springer show. Anyone can set up that type of show; every area has its resident loony willing to try anything for their fifteen minutes of fame. Look for a real life hero though and you're fucked!

Jack continues, "He gave a kid £500 the week before Christmas, he hadn't a penny he couldn't get the kids anything for Christmas, Viv said 'There's no kid should get up on Christmas morning without presents, give me it back when you've got it.' (Author's note: Pip Wright was the man who Viv gave the money to.)

Hazel: "He saved Rob Bell's life", Jack takes it up, "If Rob knew that we were here he would...wor Viv bumped into him (Peter Donnelly) in the Green, he was crying to wor Viv saying, 'Di'vent hit me', Viv said 'I'm not going to hit you, don't worry.' You see the trouble is..." Jack takes a breath before saying the next part of his sentence as if it is releasing a great burden from him to be able to say this to someone, maybe for the first time, "...he couldn't be a bloody gangster at all, he was too soft. You get these that lend you money and if you don't pay it, it's doubled and then a good thumping and then you get a leg broken the next time, he was too soft. Mind when he kicked off, if he had a fight he could go, there's nobody ever done it yet..." Jack reminds himself of the present situation of his son's absence by saying, "...well they'll never do it now. He was hard that way it was good, but the other way he was as soft as claggy taffy (claggy toffee?). He was as easy for a hard luck story..." Hazel adds, "He could cry like any other man", Jack continues "...he was as soft as clarts that way."

We talk some while about police corruption and what really went on within a certain situation, but alas legal reasons stop this being written within here although it is logged and at the right time, if there ever is a one, it will be revealed.

Jack continues with the interview changing the above subject matter and he talks of Inspector Peter Durham, "He tried all ways to get our Viv. When Viv come out of prison they were following him in the car and taking photographs of him. They went around the town (Newcastle) and followed him all over and he just used to go, 'All right lads', but the surprising thing is what a hell of a lot got on with him. From what I've heard all the jumpy jacks are back in the town now and people won't go back into the town. On the happy baccy and the stuff." This lends support to what I was told about Jack being anti-drug and obviously this was passed on to his son, Viv. "People are just petrified where at one time you could go and sit and have a good night with nothing to worry about."

Hazel gives her account of meeting one of the Sayers family and on this occasion they receive praise, "I met Stephen Sayers when our young Viv (their grandson) was poorly in hospital, he was a gentleman. I couldn't get over him he was at the hospital at 8.00 o'clock in the morning when I walked into the general. He said, 'I'm sorry I've met you under these circumstances', Viv was still in prison and they'd let him out, so he come to see little Viv." Jack clarifies how Stephen Sayers was out of prison before his son, "They got two years and our Viv got three. So they were out, but he was at the hospital to see the bairn. They were all friends then." I explain that Viv was used as their ammunition then so that they çould say, 'Well, this is our guy.' Karen, Viv's sister, throws up something that says it more succinctly, "Using him as a minder."

After his prison sentence Viv went his own way, Jack explains, "Wor Viv was always a loner though, I mean if somebody said, 'I'll fettle Viv Graham!' He would jump in the car and he would go to that place where this bloke had said what he was going to do, 'Where's so and so, I'm here?' 'He's not in." "Well I'll be back tomorrow night." Where they take teams now he didn't need that sort of back-up. He would go in and he'd never been to that place in his life and wouldn't know the bloke from Adam, he had no fear."

The name Lee Duffy is brought up and Jack speaks candidly about this man, "Duffy said wor Viv wouldn't meet him, wouldn't have anything to do with him." Background information for those of you wondering whom Lee Duffy is. A full chapter is devoted to him in *Viv (Graham)* – *'Simply the Best'*. Duffy came to Newcastle from his manor of Middlesbrough in Teesside a few times looking for Viv so as to have a fight. On one occasion he was allegedly wearing his shorts and went to a club and beat some doormen up so as to flush Viv out of hiding. He arrived in the back of a van, jumped out, kicked a few doormen about and the word got back to Viv whereby he decided to stay at home, which is hard to believe. Assuming these doormen would allow Duffy to do that, then doormen would come in from the surrounding pubs to help out. Viv felt awkward about meeting this man, so it goes. Jack feels strongly about this and offers up this explanation, "Not likely, he couldn't brae wor missus. What a load of bloody tripe." It is explained that people wanted Duffy to settle their scores with Viv, but that is only hearsay.

Viv got on with people and Manny Burgo is mentioned as an example, Jack says, "They had a fight (boxing bout as amateurs) and Viv braed bloody hell out of him, because his old man said to Viv, You did that to my son.' There was two of the judges sacked through that fight because they gave it to Manny Burgo because he was English Amateur champion. Viv never boxed for years and he was finished with the boxing, but he still had the fight with Manny. Viv had not fought for years, he won the Northern ABA championships in 1977, and he had three fights in the one night down South Shields to win it. He then went to Denmark to fight, he was in Liverpool and he got a frozen shoulder and he got beat. He just concentrated on weight training and running, but you know what happens once you start hanging about with lasses, training's out the window." I interject with, "You get skint", we all laugh at this. Jack mimics a woman speaking, "You think more of bloody football than you do of me. You know what they are like. So he just pursued weight training." Hazel says something very worthy of being mentioned, "He never was in trouble with the police as a teenager, never. He (Jack) used to say to Viv 'Burgle anybody or rob them and me and you are finished', you know." Jack confirms this, "I said if you ever come in here and have been doing a house or drugs, that's me and you done."

Jack is a down to earth guy and calls a spade a spade, Viv used to seek advice and looked up to his dad, I now know why after speaking with Jack for some time. Jack is the sort of man who speaks with a matter of faculty manner and immediately puts you at ease with his baritone Geordie twang. You may wonder, at the way he speaks, why I have not tidied this dialogue up (as demanded by some of those interviewed), I prefer to listen to people with dialects as opposed to speaking the Queen's English. The reason being that it has took as long for regional dialects to be built up, as the human race is old, why waste this culture, which has been around longer than any Queen's English.

On the advice side of things Hazel says, "He used to come here on a Sunday morning after he'd been to the nightclub. We used to always have loads of company and he used to say to everybody, 'Right, I want to talk to my father, everybody out!', it didn't matter who was in." Hazel says this in a nice way and it does not come across very well, giving the impression that Viv was abrupt with everyone, that was not the case or intended to come across that way. Hazel continues, "In fact when this came out about Viv I didn't even know anything existed, we can't say." Jack helps out and is quite honest in what he says, "We didn't know half that went on, that was his business he was a man for himself, you make your bed you can lie in it. What ye de is your business, but as I say drugging and out dodgy like that I don't agree with, I've never agreed with it. As I say he's a man for himself and we don't know half nor quarter of what he did or didn't do down there." (Newcastle)

Karen offers her support in this, "I always thought he had two separate lives because me and Martin started socialising with Anna and him. We started going to the town and night clubbing, we used to get the feeling he didn't want us down there." Martin takes up on what Karen says; "obviously anything could kick off at anytime where he was so obviously it was for our safety as well." Jack speaks with wisdom when he interjects with, "It's a different ball game doon the toon. They can buy you at one end of the street and sell you at the other end."

What about when Viv wanted to relax? Jack: "We used to go shooting at Haydon Bridge, everything just seemed to lift off him, I don't know how you explain it, but it was like waking up on a Sunday morning." Hazel: "He delivered a ferret he sent it by taxi! 'I love you dad, here's a present for you', it was a live ferret. The poor man." (The taxi driver.) Jack tells of how Viv

125

came to send the ferret to him, "There were some kids knocking a ferret around the street and he gave them £2 he said, 'Here's £2, I'll buy that ferret off you.' He then said to the taxi driver, 'Here take that, here's the address, give that to my father.' The brother-in-law's still got it yet. He sent it all the way from Wallsend." Hazel confirms Viv's love of animals, "He always had hens we've still got his two dogs you know here, Steve. We've got his Alsation, Max, and the Labrador. I bought it in 1989 when he went inside. I had got him a pup." Jack adds, "She didn't know what to buy him so I said 'Why don't you get him a Labrador to go shooting'. I said I know who'll have to look after it and to feed it. My Alsation died, when he got Buster he got the Alsation. He said, 'I'll give the Alsation to my father, I've still got the two down the garden. There were lads with pigeon lofts out the back and when he was young he used to get squealers, little 'uns, off the lads. He had about a dozen or more. We used to put them in a cardboard box and put them in the wagon and get away over to Whitehaven and I would let them out. Viv would say that they had got back at such and such a time. They were just pets, eh man." Jack is full of these sorts of nostalgic stories and I can picture all of the things he describes and the sentiment that is expressed in jack's voice, what pictures were flying through Jack's mind when he said 'eh man.'

Karen is Viv's younger sister and Eric is the older brother, now 40. Viv was a middle child, which might explain his caring ways, but that is not for me to delve into. We talk of how Jack has an aversion to reporters and he says, "That fettled me with television and reporters when he did that on the Thursday night and on the Sunday morning I saw the headline, '£2m Drug Baron' I said they are not worth a bottle of pop. And then the Cook report they tried to make wor Viv out as bad as them that done that manageress up in Manchester. I said it wouldn't have been as bad as if that's what it was about it had nowt to do with security, protection, drugs, drinking it was just a sham. It made him look like..."

The trouble the 'Cook Report' caused for the Graham household is nobody's business. It is not for me to bandy about publicly the private arguments the Graham's have had with certain other people over the items raised in the 'Cook Report', but I will say it has a lot to answer for in terms of misrepresentation of people's opinions. TV documentaries can cause innocent parties severe trouble. A Cook Report researcher telephoned Gillian Lowes asking her if there were any changes to her circumstances only a matter of months ago. They wanted to ascertain any new developments. Had they known the trouble that was caused by their show, well... Jack expresses his anger, "If I had been a stranger and I had seen that on television I would say, 'He must be a wicked pig, him!' People that didn't know Viv would say he was nasty, but it had nothing to do with the programme, but the buggers stuck it in about protection. So when I seen the Cook Report and I knew that things were wrong within it I then wondered how many more Cook Reports are wrong and have been twisted to make them look worse than what they are. If I was walking along the Quayside and a little bairn fell in the Tyne and I dived in and got it out there would be a little bit like that. But if I walked down the Quayside and picked a kid up and hoyed (threw) him in the river there would be headlines this big. I mean murder, rape and anything like that they make as gruesome as possible to sell papers." I was told from a publican, Peter Connelly, that a Cook Report researcher had called into a pub he had and said he wanted to put cameras in the corners of the bar. Peter asked 'why' and the researcher said, 'Because you're going to have some trouble in here.' Peter said 'Not in this bar I'm not'. He told them where to go. This stage-managed TV documentary seems to be a little bit based on the Jerry Springer show. Hype and sensationalism create TV audiences and prime time TV is big money. No doubt Roger Cook has balls as big as King Kong's in respect of him having courage to pursue those that he was asked to, but his team are the ones that are responsible for putting him in these positions and ultimately he has been used as a means to them getting what they want, TV viewers.

Jack is asked about Viv's apprenticeship days as a doorman. Jack: "He was as green as grass when he started at the *Hedgefield*." Hazel disputes this and says, "It was in Burnhopefield, the *Travellers Rest*." Jack continues: "He started working in a number of pubs as the person owned three and he went through to Whitemare Pool (South Tyneside) and he ended up at *Finnigan's* in Gateshead. That was where Viv had the fight with Paul Ashton. The fight went on up the road for about twenty minutes. They reckon Billy Robinson stepped back to see what wor Viv could perform like. He played with Ashy for twenty minutes around the car park and Ashy was shouting and bawling at him to stand still so he could hit him. Viv was just bop, bopping he was like greased lightening. Then he went to work at Wheelers on the Gateshead side of the Tyne Bridge, just before you go over on the left-hand side, it's closed down now. He was with Billy Robinson then. The problem was Viv was from the sticks and the townies didn't like this. They would say, 'Where's he from? WHAT!' A lot of them had the idea that no one was going to come in from the sticks and do anything to them sort of thing."

Jack is asked where the turning point came of changing Viv to a 'Viv of the town' compared to 'Viv from the sticks'. The bit in between point 'A' and point 'B'? Martin offers his view, "As things progressed he just became more popular." Jack: "More and more tried to down him, he won and he won and he got his name more known and more known in the pubs and the nightclubs. The more that had a go at him the more he beat. His name just spread like that, you know." Hazel talks of Viv's childhood about when he had run-ins with his peers, "I used to fight his battles, Viv wouldn't fight." Jack offers up a story about Viv's childhood, "He fought out there with young Stubsy and Stubsy was knocking hell out of him. I said, 'I'll bloody murder you, lad, for letting him do that to you, give him some back.' I used to take him to boxing and he took to it like a duck to water. He had four things going for him that very few fighters have got, I mean street fighting. He had speed, he had the wind, the stamina and he had the hitting power. Put them on that street or a football field and phew. They just couldn't put it together, they don't know how to use their hands, and they depend on just strength and weight. You can be as strong as a bull, but if you're not fit once you start puffing and panting you're finished. You're fighting some bugger and you start puffing and panting and he's still! It's time for you to reverse because you're going to get a tousing. Viv knew how to hit and the weight training gave him the strength. He put four down in less than four seconds. Four blokes in the bar, Anna's dad come up to Viv and said, 'I was just going to give you a hand there, Viv.' Bump, bump, four left hookers and they didn't get up mind you. I'm not just saying that because he was my lad."

What were Viv's fears? Hazel: "You know something he was the most scared person of the dark. He was petrified, petrified." Jack says with laughter in his voice, "He would come in through the night, to go out the room he would open that door, put that light on and there's a switch to the top of the landing he would put that light on. He would fly up the stairs and get a hold of his bedroom door and hoy it wide open. Then he'd knock the switch on and go in. One night I said, 'Oh, Viv feed them dogs, son'; 'Aye, right you are father.' He would go out the back and I would sneak out of the front door and sneak down the garden, it was pitch black. He would shout at the dogs, 'Howay!' I would go 'Urghhh!' The tins and the food would go up a height and he's in here like a shot." We all break out into spontaneous laughter at the thought of this and luckily for us we are all on the same wavelength to be able to enjoy a moment of nostalgia.

Jack talks of when he and Viv went shooting and how good of a shot Viv was. I know what you will all be thinking or generally thinking, but do not. Viv was from the country side and there way of life is different a double barrelled shotgun does not hold the same fear for these people as it would for a city dweller looking down the barrels of a sawn off. Game pie and salmon were things that people took for granted in rural areas so for them shooting and fishing was a way of life.

Hazel describes how when Viv passed a pub called the Golden Lion he would say, 'I'm home' to all his mates that brought him up in the car. She met him a few days before he died, didn't you, Karen? She said, 'What's wrong with your face today?' He said, 'Oh, I'm just fed up, Karen, I'm on my way home I'm sick of paying bills. Viv had just bought a house at the time."

We talk of the Gateshead Angel (the Angel of the North) and about an article that appeared in the *Telegraph*, which depicted the people of Gateshead as being thick for having the Angel. This sort of bombastic approach unseats all what the Northerners have fought against for many years. Hazel says, "It's horrible" and Jack adds, "I think it's a waste of space myself. The people of Gateshead had no bloody choice in the matter. It was the council that made the decision."

Viv's artistic ability is enquired of and Jack is not full of himself or self centred because he can criticise himself, which is the mark of a man at ease with himself he says, "I think he was a bit thicker than me when he was at school, wasn't he?" Bear in mind the tone of voice jack has when he says this, he is not condescending or patronising himself or Viv. It is not said in a disparaging way, but simply to show lack of artistic ability. Jack: "it was only in my last three years at school that I picked up and I think Viv did the same. Viv was obsessed with strength. He started with a bullworker and when he was working he would put six more bricks in a hod than anyone else and it just went on from there." Martin: "He always covered his body with a big shirt, he didn't go around with his chest hanging out." Jack: "He looked far bigger stripped than he did with his shirt on."

I use the opportunity to go off at a tangent on the subject of Viv without a top on. It was alleged that Viv had a fight on the Quayside with one of the Conroy's and he tore his shirt off like the hulk. It was allegedly Michael Conroy (Paddy's brother) he was fighting with. Jack: "The way I put it down to is like you've seen these old cowboy films, the gunslinger, there's always somebody wants to take your reputation. Well as he went on his reputation just grew and grew and more blokes tried to take it off him. He wasn't like a bully."

Viv used to hold his head and say to himself, 'Why is that man trying to have a go at me?' Jack: "Viv would say to me, 'I was sitting there having a quiet drink and another one kicked off.' I would ask him if he won and Viv would reply, oh, aye I've knacked him, you can't even go for a quiet drink there's always somebody wanting to have a go at you, man.' He used to go out with Anna and they would say, 'He's on his own we'll get him while he's on his own.' He just got the reputation as a fighter and you've always got somebody to tell you what they think of you."

Viv bought a house just before he died and Hazel says, "He bought this house because he said Anna had not had anything. That house was for Anna, nobody else, I mean all the conspiracies all the nastiness about the money, it was for Anna that house." This is where Viv's wishes have been ignored and Jack confirms what his son told him, "All of this trouble that's been on about the money Viv sat here, not once, he said it a few times in front of Karen he said, 'Father, if ever anything happened to me he says the house is Anna's the money is for the two bairns. This is where all the trouble started as it was put to me that everything was for Anna to hell with the bairns. The are my two grandbairns and I told him (solicitor) I said it was my son's wishes that if ever anything happened to him the house had to go for Anna and all the money to his two lads and I said that's what I stick by because he never made a will. If you haven't got a will everything goes to your children. Anna wouldn't sign the thing to joint the house with Viv when the house was bought, she said she didn't want anything to do with that. Now all the bickering and the carry on, nastiness and people stopped speaking we are all the baddies and it just went on from there."

From what Jack says it seems that money has been the key issue for a number of people and it has cut through Jack's heart so much so that he says, "I'm only pleased the grandbairns stayed with us on a Friday and Saturday night long before all of this happened, I've done it for donkey's years, otherwise the buggers would be would be saying 'They're just getting the grandbairns in to see if they can get into any money'. But they cannot say that because the bairns have been staying." Jack is not favourable as to which of his many grandchildren stay sometimes they have had five or six there on a Friday night. Hazel says something that could be the answer to what has kept there spirits alive, "It is our grandchildren that have kept us going, we look after Karen's and Martin's because they work, our Viv's two boys come down and Eric's oldest boy doesn't come down because he's too big, he says. But we always have five of them, don't we?" Hazel looks to Jack for his confirmation to which he says, "Wey aye. We wouldn't have it any other way. Viv and Dean used to live only a stone's throw away, but now they've moved further away they come on a weekend."

We talk of Viv's commitments to others and how he had to be in a number of different places at one time. Jack: "Viv passed his test first time and he was a Cracker Jack he wanted to be here before he got there." Jack says this in the best possible way with no malice intended, Jack expresses everything succinctly and he has a sense of humour that comes across without him even realising how enthralling it is to listen to him. I get the feeling he could call the Royal family to their face without offending them, as it is not within his nature to hurt or offend anyone. Jack: "If he was going along the road he would say, 'I've got to get past him he's to slow' pheeeeee, pheeeee." Jack makes a sound like cutting through the wind to indicate how fast Viv drove. Adding, "Not doing out daft, no, not stupid risks, but he had to be away and that bloody thing he had like, it would catch pigeons, man." We discuss the car and Jack says matter of factly, "It wasn't a big old Mercedes or a fancy BMW it was just a Sierra Cosworth. It had a 2.9 injection engine in it. It was a flying machine there was nowt swanky about it."

Viv's heroes? Hazel: "Just his dad, he worshipped his dad, nobody else." Jack is overcome with embarrassment and says in a low tone, "I never heard him." What he means by this is that Viv did not openly say soft mamsy pamsy things. But the point is taken about who Viv looked up to. Jack continues, "He like the film bloody 'Zulu' he watched over and over again, it's a cracking picture like." Hazel says, "He loved home cooking you know and he used to get me to do a spotted dick pudding, put it in the cloth and dish and he used to say to me, 'Now mother how long does this take to cook,' and he used to take it back with him to Daisy Hill in Newcastle with him and cook it down there. Christmas cake, I think everybody in Daisy Hill had a Christmas cake off me, scones, pork pies I think I kept Daisy Hill in them. The minute they came out of the oven he would pinch them."

Viv's grandmother stayed at Jack and Hazel's home for about five years, after her husband died, and eventually she got a little place nearby to her son's home. Viv had obviously gained his reverence of older people through his grandmother and when he knocked an old lady down through the most smallest of accidents it must have brought it all back as I have it from a good source that Viv cried over this incident. Who can blame him for shedding a few tears in such a set of circumstances? Karen moved in with her grandmother and stayed with her for about ten years after this. Hazel: "Viv's was obsessed with his nanny, wasn't he?" Jack: "Viv would take her all over in the car up to the damn and down the coast, of course my mother would sit on a clothes line gannin' from here, she would go to hell and back if it was a ride out. I used to say to her I'm going to Keswick tomorrow with the wagon, well her parents belonged over there in Maryport. I used to go over, take her up and get her in the wagon."

How did Martin get on with Viv? Martin: "Viv did little pranks on me like throwing buckets of water out of the window. It must have been when I threatened him," he says jokingly. Martin used to train at a place called 'The Hut'. Jack says the place, "It's just a hut, there's no running water or nowt like that, just up the steps, a door in, benches and weights and all the local lads go in there and train. You would just come home and have a bath or a shower. It's like a brick foundation with wood sides. When it first started off it was St Johns Ambulance Brigade. When they started the weight training away, they asked if they could use the bottom end of the hut this other end was all stretchers and that sort of thing then the St Johns Ambulance just sort of seemed to die out, nobody went to it and the lads took it over and paid the council a rate. It's been there for twenty odd years now."

Indeed 'The Hut' is still there and an unbelievable sight, the sort of place that those seeking the eye of the tiger would train, if they were hungry enough for that sort of thing. It is full of menacing looking weight training machines and other machines of self-inflicting torture. The facilities are few and it is the sort of place you would expect to see a regiment of SAS officers queuing up to get out of.

I am sitting looking at a family that is issuing forth all sorts of stories about Viv. The fear that was first there upon my arrival had been long gone and here the barriers had been broken down, I see them all in my minds eye and my recollection is of a warm friendly family that had been short changed by the media and had not been given a fair crack of the whip. Here is hoping that this chapter has restored some dignity to that side of things. I find it such a great shame that so much pain has been caused to such a huge amount of people have been hurt because the desires of other people to murder Viv were fulfilled.

Hazel: "Our Dean (one of Viv's sons) and I have a great understanding we confide in each other and we talk for hours, he tells me everything. If he's got problems he tells me." It is mentioned that Dean had private counselling, would it have been just as good for a sit down with his grandma' and granddad? Jack: "Yes!" We talk of personal things that are not meant for such a book and therefore are not included. York University in studies discovered that counselling was a waste of time. I am a qualified counsellor and hypnotherapist I have professional qualifications to substantiate this. I speak from experience and would say that Jack and York University are right in what they say. Counselling makes a person re-live their experiences and the main thing is that counsellors have to drag it out of you. What better way to soothe a problem than to talk about it with a close family member who has the wisdom of age on their side?

Reverend Mark Jackson who officiated at Viv's funeral said, 'Things have been said that maybe shouldn't have been' he tried to resolve those things. Hazel: "He was a marvellous little man." Jack intervenes: "Do you like vicars do you, do you like churches?" This question takes me aback slightly, as it is not easy to answer someone who has been through so much pain as Jack has. I mention I know a priest who goes to see Newcastle United play and he has a pint of beer at times, Jack: "He'll be a Catholic is he?" I reply that he is and jack says, "I knew bloody fine well he was!" Everybody laughs at this but Jack stays seriously, "I'm an atheist me, I'll tell you bloody well straight, but the Protestants they are two faced, the vicars. But the old Catholic father when I was at Saint Joseph's he use to go down everyday to the *Townley Arms* and have two pints."

The talk of religion changes the subject matter within that to the matter of Harry Thompson who died from a stabbing incident. Hazel breaks our laughter when she strikes a serious note and says, "You know Father Conaty brought our Viv's name up in Harry's sermon." Jack relents and says, "Aye he did." The tragedy that struck the Connelly family is to some extent nearly as bad as that what the Graham family suffered at the loss of Viv. The lives of Viv and Harry were lost to needless violent acts. Harry was killed whilst pursuing the recovery of items stolen from his home in a burglary. He went to the home of those he suspected and a fight ensued in which he was stabbed and died from his injuries. This is not the chapter to continually talk of tragedy especially since I know Jack will at some time read this and therefore out of respect to Mr Graham we will continue on a better note.

What advice could the Graham's give to anyone considering pursuing making places safer for others, like Viv had tried? Jack: "Leave it alone because now it's a gun in life, it's not like me and you going outside and that's the end of it. They'll stab you or shoot you or get a team up or baseball bat you. There's nowt like that now, you cross somebody and there's a team out the next bloody day looking for you or they cross you and you get a team out looking for them. I think a lad now far better mind his own business because he's not going to win no battles there's too many druggies. This bloody druggie business, I mean they're out there mind they'll stab you in the night and wake up in the morning and they wouldn't know they'd done it. You haven't got to be a big bloke, you can be six stone nowt, but you can put a knife in somebody or shoot somebody just the same as somebody seventeen stone can do it. You see a lot of these bouncers, just look at a man I know (name withheld) he's married and got a baby, he says 'Jacky, it's bloody crackers man, you don't know when you're going to get a knife in you or…'"

What drives people on to become a doorman and a troubleshooter of other people's problems? Jack: "Well the doorman, the majority of them, have got back up in a club and when they leave a club most people don't know where they come from. At the same time it beats working for a living. If somebody said they were going to do something to wor Viv he wouldn't get a team together, he would go and sort it out himself. He never went with teams all over the place. That's just the way he was, he had no fear of anybody, he never carried a weapon. He never had a gun, a baseball bat or a knife he just had his fists. If anyone had pulled a gun out on Viv he would have stood his ground and tried to talk." Karen confirms this by saying the same.

Jack is asked about Viv consulting over an offer of work that came from Tenerife. "I told him to keep away from it I said, 'just stay clear of it'. Viv was wanted to do the fighting." The man who allegedly made Viv the offer I am told from another source was Paddy Leonard. Jack continues, "Not only that I says there was bloody guns and all sorts over there. I said it's not worth it 'you stop home.' I mean when you're twenty odd or thirty you never think you'll get to sixty and your afraid of nobody you never think what's going to come off. I didn't want him to go and he never went."

This is a poignant moment to take a quick look at timeshare operations. One particular incident involved a man called Mick Cook, Essex boy tried to make it big, sort of style. He is now serving some 19 years for the murder of Rachel Charles, 9. Portugal is home to thousands of ex-pat Brits and out of those thousands there are many who live in the world of gangsters all doing shady deals.

In November of 1990 Rachel went missing as she walked home from school. It was four days later that her body was found under a pine tree only a few miles along the coast. It was alleged that Cook, then 38, had abducted her, tried to have sex with her and when she fought back he strangled her in his car. The conviction of Cook is unsafe since speculation about who really did murder Rachel goes on. Rachel's stepfather is thought to have known more than he ever admitted to knowing.

Vale Navio, where it all happened is on the edge of the Algarve coast in Portugal. Some twenty years ago the place was only of use for scrubland farmers. Now though it is home to timeshare touts who have turned this idyllic place into one of the biggest complexes in Europe where timeshare developers have created villas, apartments, shops, clubs, pubs and bars. Somebody earned a lot of dosh from this scam. The first lot to cream off the top of this money pile were gangsters from Portugal.

The result was that the timeshare properties were not worth the contract paper they were drawn up on. Scams had rendered the properties worthless, that was if they were even built as many were not. Banks had given loans secured on the properties and people found that they did not own any interest in the apartments they had just bought a one or two week share in it. News travels fast and a bunch of Brit gangsters arrived on the scene like vultures in the early 1980s. Not being able to break into the timeshare scene some used the word 'protection' in their vocabulary more than Durex ever did in their advertising. They had a special protection. They would protect the timeshare salesmen from falling down and breaking their legs for a grand a week. It is stated here that Viv would have ended in this somehow.

Drug dealing, counterfeit money and travellers cheques, murders, prostitution, protection rackets (classical style), thefts, burglary and more have been seen by the residents in Vale Navio. Two men had tried to organise meetings to object to this sort of thing happening. Tony Madden from Luton was shot at when he tried to put a stop to it. Brian Morgan a businessman from Manchester had two steel balls fired at him. They became embedded into his car. He was there to expose who was ripping the people off. The local police did not want to know about.

The Algarve had now become an open gate to criminals entering Portugal, which is one of the main sources of drugs, which outsells to the rest of Europe. On the face of it to any tourist everything seems normal, but gangsters are not tourists as such.

Mick Cook, knee high to a grasshopper, was the typical Southern (Cockney) wheeler-dealer. It has been said of him, 'He is a ducker and diver, a strictly cash-only man, born to fiddle. If he buys a car he fiddles the paperwork. If he makes a profit he fiddles the tax. If he tells you it's raining, it's because he's selling umbrellas. His family are law-abiding, hard working people and Mick had a good trade as a car sprayer and panel beater. But he always had one eye on the wrong side of the law. Still for all that, he was a small player, no great intelligence, no big front, no gun and no chance with the big boys.'

Cook ventured into business with a bit of private enterprise in Portugal after moving there in 1989 and starting panel beating at a garage. It is said he went there with a suitcase containing just over £60,000 in cash. The private enterprise bit was when he started running unlicensed tours for tourists. During his socialising he spent time with other Brits in a pub that was given the nickname 'Wonkey Donkey' (*Nags Head*). He split up from his wife and moved to Albufeira and that is all there is to know about Mick Cook's private life, or so it seemed!

The last anyone saw of little Rachel was when she got off her school bus that took her from the International school at Vilamoura, eight miles away, to her home at Vale Navio. She was spotted holding hands with a fellow female pupil and then seen to leave her and disappeared around a corner. The local police (GNR) did not seem too fussed over her disappearance and a search party of some 30+ Brits looked for her that night. (19th November, 1990).

Cook had a red unregistered Triumph TR7. The following day a gardener said he spotted someone of Rachel's description getting into a red car with foreign number plates, he knew Rachel well and was positive it was her.

A ransom demand of some £300,000 was demanded for the safe return of Rachel. Now the police were interested and the Policia Judiclaria were called in. Cook was questioned, as was everyone else who owned a red car with foreign plates. Cook denied being in Vale Navio at the time of Rachel's disappearance. Rachel's stepfather told police he had seen Cook touching up little girls and he was sure he was capable of the crime. Rachel's mother said she was sure Cook was one of very few people whose car that Rachel would have got into. Coupled with a knife, some hair and a coil of rope found in Cook's car and the fact that a local riding instructor said he had seen a man in a red sports car that could have been Cook up near the area where Rachel's body was found.

Cook was arrested a few days later and allegedly he confessed to killing Rachel within an hour of abducting her. His past record was sent from Interpol and the police said he had a history of indecent assault. (Read the Paddy Conroy chapter in which the UK police said to the Spanish authorities that Conroy had used pliers to torture a woman he went on to rape, just so they could have him held. Conroy was lucky to escape with his life in the Spanish jail where he was held because of these lies.)

People though had made their own minds up at Vale Navio who they suspected of the killing of Rachel. The suspect that just about every Brit had in their mind was Rachel's stepfather Ray Charles. He was a big fumbling man who knew no manners and lied about his past, saying he owned land and had thousands of pounds. He too drank in the Wonkey Donkey and during a drinking spree prior to when Rachel's body was found he was talking incoherently saying he had seen Rachel in a vision and he knew she was dead and 'her time was up.' Funnily enough he also had a red car with foreign plates. Later on, a rope and blanket covered in pine needles were found in Charles' car boot by several men. A medium was called in and she told them to search further afield. Charles disappeared for four hours and returned covered in scratches. Had he gone to move the body, when the search closed in on the area where eventually Rachel's body was found he gave up looking!

Bill Taylor managed the timeshare touts who worked the streets and after Rachel's body was found he confronted Charles in the Wonkey Donkey. Charles asked whom he thought had done it and Bill Taylor told him straight out that he was the main suspect. 'I think you did it.' 'Why, Ray? Why a nine year old child?' Charles shook his head and said, 'I don't know.' Few doubted that Charles had killed his stepdaughter who he hated and used to shout at her regularly some believed the motive was so he could have his wife all to himself. Others believed that gangsters were involved to some extent and that she had been murdered in front of Charles to teach him a lesson. Another line of thought was that Charles was planning a scam and Rachel knew of it and could drop him in it so he killed her in case she spoke of his plans.

Cook denied ever signing a police confession and that he was beaten until he agreed verbally that he had killed Rachel. Five police worked him over and in that time he had a gun thrust into his mouth. He wrote from prison that in the end he just wanted it to stop and he said 'If you say that's how it was, then that's how it must have been.' Although he had been to Vale Navio that day it was only to buy a phonecard and he had forgotten in the first interview that police gave him.

There was no evidence to convict Cook. None of the scientific tests had proved a single link between Rachel and Cook. (*Gary Ward – The Blackpool Beach Murder* chapter later on has to be compared to this lack of scientific evidence also. Ward was convicted on his own confession that he made mistakenly.) The tyre tracks found near the body did not match his tyre tread. The hair they found was from a dog! The only thing the police had was Cook's confession the body had been cremated and blood under Rachel's fingernails was not examined due to archaic laboratory facilities. The gardener could not identify Cook when he spotted him the day after the abduction! Cook was picked up in a set-up ID parade in which he was pointed out by a police officer saying to the riding instructor witness 'Is this him?' before and after each pass.

The trial was a farce and should have been written by Noel Coward, had he been alive. Cook did not stand a cat in hell's chance. There was no evidence against him so his defence could not really refute much. It was said to have been a sex crime. But all in all Cook was a patsy taking the fall for some gangster who had paid £40,000 to get out of it or so a source claimed in an affidavit he made to his English solicitor. He claimed that three Algarve businessmen had paid a bribe of £40,000 to ensure that Cook went to jail. The man who told the source was the go-between who paid the bribe.

Cook's past convictions that Interpol had sent the Portuguese police via fax showed he did not have any convictions for sexual assault as was said by the

Portuguese police. His record as shown on that fax is six convictions for theft, receiving stolen goods and causing bodily harm.

It is likely that what really happened was connected to timeshare scams. The resort centre was contacted by phone and the £300,000 was agreed to be paid so as to keep everything hush hush and not frighten off prospective timeshare buyers. Cook may have been involved in picking up Rachel with her stepfather's permission. Gangsters could have found out and compromised Cook and Charles by killing Rachel thus nullifying their game. The £40,000 paid to get Cook convicted was to get him off the streets, that meant that neither Cook nor Charles could spill the beans about what really happened. Cook always living in hope of being released and Charles' only release was when he died from cancer in 1992.

That for you is what goes on in such places that Viv was asked to get involved in. Andy Winder was from Darlington and he ran a modelling agency, but decided that he wanted a piece of the cake. He went into timeshare in Tenerife and he paid dearly for it, with his life when he was involved in a knife fight. (Read more of him in the Scenarios to a Murder chapter.) Jack was right to advise Viv to stay away from such things that Paddy Leonard asked him to get involved in.

Higgins Security is mentioned and Jack says of them, "Higgins Security, they were from Birmingham they wanted Viv to go and see them I told Viv to let them come to him." This is covered in Anna's chapter so rather than go over old ground I will leave it at that. What can be said though and it is common knowledge is that recently all of *Legend's* security staff have been sacked and 'bouncers' employed by a company run by ex-Olympic shot-putter, ex-policeman and budgie breeder, Geoff Capes have been brought in to the Newcastle city centre nightclub. Capes stands at 6'-5" tall and weighs in at 22 stone. He is not a great fan of being flown and therefore for that reason he travelled to his last Olympic event by sea and air, avoiding the air like the plague. The reason for the dismissal of the door staff at *Legend's* has been suggested to be is because of their lack of regard for patrons, preferring to fight them rather than keep the peace. Higgin's Security came in from Birmingham in the past to take over the role of local doormen and Viv got involved. Doormen begged Viv to sort it out for them; he obliged and saved them their jobs. Viv is not around to sort this one out now though; will it end up with reprisals?

We broach the subject once more about who has helped the family after Viv's death. Hazel is quick to say, "I wouldn't want anyone's help", but I think this is more out of old-fashioned pride than anything else. All of those people that Viv helped and made money for are described by Jack, "They weren't friends they were hangers on, he was a money box for them and a minder for them he got the money from the doors on different jobs and that's all he was. What I mean by that he got them jobs is he looked after their jobs for them. That's the way I mean he was a moneybox because if anybody wanted a lend of money he would lend them it. Any trouble and he would go and sort it out for them. That's all he was to them, a moneybox." Hazel says about Viv's genuine friends, "Viv had two genuine friends Robbie Warton and Rob Bell they both keep in touch, they come up here every so often, they are genuine people. Rob Bell treats us like Viv treat Joy, we buy them presents and he buys us presents."

It seems from talking to Jack that he seems more worldlier wise than most people in Newcastle are, it is asked how he acquired it? "I was as thick as a chip at school me, lad." Hazel interjects, "You did the doors though when you were younger, you did the local dances." Jack plays it down by saying, "It was just the local dances there were no nightclubs then! Chains out of the collar and that sort of thing. It was not as bad as now, you had broken bottles, chains and flick knives, but this drug business set it all off. Then you were hoyed out of the pub at ten o'clock. And you come out of the dances drunk. Now you can get some in a right state drinking all day and night and they are on this bloody stuff. It's a different ball game in the town."

Hazel may well have pinpointed something that attracted Viv into his profession, "He did it for the money, there was no money here for him. He hated going out at the finish though. He would sometimes just stay in." Jack defends Viv about people calling him a doorman or bouncer, "He wouldn't stand at doors it got to the point that if he looked after a place he didn't need to be on the door, 'Mind, Viv Graham looks after this place, kick off somewhere else, like.' Viv suffered migraine, which he got from his mother she suffers terrible with it. He used to take paracetamol like taking smarties."

Was it stress that caused these headaches as well? Hazel: "Definitely, stress brought it all on. Eh, I mean at times it was terrible. When he got that abscess and they said he was filled with steroids, what a load of cod's wallop there wasn't a bit of steroid in his body. They said that about the steroid thing around about the time of his funeral." Jack: "I said to Viv, 'Why do you need that for, I'd rather be fifteen stone or fourteen stone or ten stone of muscle and bone rather than be eighteen stone of bloody water, it's like carrying two stone of bloody taties on your back. One minute they're sixteen stone then they're nineteen stone." "There was a time he had no neck, his stomach hung over his trousers and you ribbed him something rotten", says Hazel looking at Jack. He takes the story up, "He stopped doing the running he was just concentrating on the weight training. I used to say, 'Bloody weight training aren't you? You want to get on that field outside the house and get running again', 'Aye, father, I'm going to, get some of this off', 'Well you want to then, you'll meet a young Viv Graham mind."

It was mentioned that Viv always used to say that he would meet someone bigger and stronger. Hazel: "That's his dad's saying." Jack: "I used to say to him that there's always somebody that's going to be bigger and stronger than him or younger than him. Bigger, stronger, better. I used to say, 'It doesn't matter if you live to be sixty, you cannot beat twenty year old or a thirty year old. Sometimes there's always somebody coming up, if you're never defeated there's a time in your life when there's a young 'un is good enough and fit enough to beat you because you're getting too old.' So I say's, 'You either beat somebody that's better than you, there's always somebody in the world that's better than you somewhere, it doesn't matter who you are. Just look at your boxing. The best in the world can get beat. If you keep on with it then the older you get there's a young 'un coming up and he beats you.' It's a fact of life."

There are some points raised that Jack wants me to air. "How can the press prove he was a £2m drug baron? Another thing they had in, that he was going over to Amsterdam every weekend for drugs, he only went there once when he went with Mary, Anna's Sister. The reason was that Harry, Mary's husband, worked on oil rigs and he had two weeks on and one off or something like that and the oil rig was near a holiday resort. Harry said, 'Instead of me keep coming back home have a weekend in Amsterdam.' She went over with our Viv. Harry his wife and Viv spent the weekend in Amsterdam, that was all there was to it.' I mean where's the proof of it that he was active in drug dealing? A solicitor said you can anything you like about a dead man, he's dead he cannot argue the fact." The saying 'dead men tell no lies' is a poignant thing to mention here. Jack talks about stories in the papers of bent vicars, which we all break out into laughter over, everyone will recall seeing a story sometime in their life about such a thing on the front pages of national tabloids.

Jack: "Another thing, I don't know how these film stars when they go in and out of places and they're sticking cameras in their faces, I don't know how they don't kick off. It's bloody serious the way that they hound people, like coming out of courts, I would stop all of that." Hazel: "We had letters put through the door saying, 'We wrote nice things about Viv, if you'd only talk to us' and things like that. I went to the graveyard and photographers were following me to the graveyard. I used to go before 8.00 o'clock in the morning to keep out of their road. I used to do all sorts to keep away from them." Jack: "I opened the door one day and they were there, the television that was. I had to go to the inquest and two of them were in the street and they took my photograph, it was too late to stop them." Hazel: "Anna's had them sitting at her table and she just thought they were loads of friends coming in. They asked her had she found somebody new."

Jack talks more on the ecclesiastical side of things, "If I had my way I would sack every vicar, Catholic father, rabbi, mothers, every religion and sack them all. There's been more bloodshed and murder, bloody religion, in this world than anything else. My second wish I would fetch Guy Fawkes back and give him all the bloody gunpowder he wanted. My third wish would be that Britain would have a ruler that would stand up to the rest of Europe, we don't want to be told by them what we can and what we cannot eat. What we can do and what we cannot do. See what I mean. On top of that all of those asylum seekers, as soon as the boat come in I would turn it around and say, 'Back to where you belong.' Some of them are parasites living off us. If there were no religion then there wouldn't be any Catholics and no Protestants so there would not be Catholics and Protestants fighting in Northern Ireland. You wouldn't have Moslems and Sikhs fighting, everybody would be one, everybody would be the same." Hazel says to Jack with surprise in her voice, "Do you know something, I've never heard you talk as much in months, I'm pleased Steve and his chaperon have come tonight. It's done you the world of good."

What Hazel says here has shown me that Jack has been withdrawn in the past over the tragic loss. I see before me now a man that could run for election in any office of the local council or parliament, subject to Guy Fawkes not turning up. His orations are comparable with speeches given by most good talkers and dare I compare him to the late great Sir Winston Churchill in the way he can hit the chord of things. I say to Hazel that Jack must have been an attraction to her because he was (and still is) the big strong man who gave her protection. Hazel says, "He did what?" I repeat that which I had said as there were others talking; it masked some of what was said. Hazel: "I thought you said 'painted the kitchen' for a minute." We all burst out laughing, you would not have thought that possible only a few hours ago. In response to what Hazel said Jack replies jokingly, "That's women's work, that!"

During our time there Hazel has kept us supplied in tea and biscuits all the questions have been answered without pressure from me in any way.

We talk of the insurance policy side of things, which was covered in more detail in the unofficial chapter on Gillian Lowes that you might have read earlier. Jack tells me that Hazel does everything, paying the rent, the poll tax and other bills he says, "Letters come through the door, she reads them, she sorts them out I have nowt to do with it. The only thing I was saying is that if the insurance pays this other money out then how can they not pay me out. If the insurance company says something's not right then nobody should get paid out although I don't begrudge the grandbairns their money. They should either pay everything or nowt out." "The next legal friends have applied for a grant for the children, but Anna has not had anything" says Hazel. She finishes off by saying, "I mean, he lived there." The situation must be terrible for Jack and Hazel being in the middle of it all while those around them are fighting for the money. It is not a case of the state helping Jack and Hazel fight for their rightful share they have paid out considerable legal fees that they can little afford. Jack: "They took his bloody money and the lads that made it all out who signed the forms and all that, they were the people that gave him the thing and everything. They signed forms to say they knew everything he was doing. He's got payslips and tax forms to say he was working. I'm just sorry for the situation, the way it has went, because if Viv had said 'Mind, that house is for the two bairns' then I would have said so, but he didn't say that. I would not betray the trust of my son and what he wanted. He said she (Anna) had to have the house and the two bairns had to have the money. I know he didn't make a will, but it's what he said. That's what my son wanted and that's what my son will get if I get my way. Viv was like a father to Anna's two bairns." Hazel shows me a copy of the paperwork that Viv signed and annotated for the insurance side of things." The insurance policy, that Viv wished his mother and father to receive a payout from should anything happen to him, was valued at £60,000. Viv had signed a hand written authorisation on the insurance proposal form 'Along with parents I would like to share out along with my two children.' It meant that this particular policy was to be shared between his two sons to Gillian and his parents. That could mean a number of things, 50/50, half to each pair or 1/3 to each of his sons and the third share going to his parents. They've got a statement from Rob Armstrong, Joe Blackey and two others. The three who worked for the company have all since left.

Viv had signed the following statement for this particular insurance policy in question, 'I would like my children to have a good start in life and I would also like to have my money instead of wasting it. I would like to leave £20,000 to my parents and £40,000 for my children.' I have it on good authority that the insurance company in question, Providence Capitol (formerly Old Mutual), immediately withdrew insurance cover for one of those who made a statement against them – Rob Armstrong. This is covered in more detail in a later chapter whereby I wrote to the insurance company concerned with the permission of the Graham's and I had a meeting with Tim Gray of Sinton and Co Solicitors representing the interests of the Graham's. There are other outstanding payouts on other policies that are part of the legal argument. Jack: "All these doormen in the town, any town, that means any of them getting murdered, then all of their insurance policies would be void." Hazel: "They have paid two small ones out as far as I know. Anna paid her mortgage for months and months and it is a good job she had a big family. The house was full every night. We still have a talk on the phone (Anna)."

We talk about Terry Scott an associate of Viv's who was there just seconds after Viv was shot. Jack says, "When it happened Terry said, 'I'm your son.' I've never seen him from that day to this. He just started to move in Viv's circles in the latter part of Viv's life and wasn't a mate of Viv's for years and years and years."

Jack: "When I went into that house I just had to get out. (Anna's home) Seeing that picture on the wall of the little girl having her communion, that did it for me." Hazel: "Viv could have a fight with someone and then shake hands, even with Stuey Watson, he made friends and he was invited to his birthday party, but he wasn't a party lad. He was dead old fashioned." Jack: "On a Saturday night he would got to the *Railway* pub in Walker, quiet, he would have a nice drink." This indicates Viv was not a party animal and he much preferred the quietness of what could be considered old men's bars. We talk of a whole mish mash of things and as they come they are here for you to look over. We talk of Michael Sayers and Jack says, "He did say he had some trouble with Michael Sayers. Hazel: "But no word of a lie that Michael Sayers pulled into the yard one Christmas and gave us a Christmas card and £100 when Viv was in jail." Jack: "Everybody's all friends, but if you fall out you can fall out, can't you? So you're not friends anymore"

What about Viv enjoying the odd bet or two on the horses? Jack: "I said you're crackers man, put it away and salt it away I used to say, 'Have you ever heard about the grasshopper and the squirrel?' He said 'No what's that, father?' 'The squirrel gathers all the nuts it hides them all over the grasshopper just jumps about and enjoys itself. The winter comes, the grasshopper has got nowt to eat, but the squirrel's got all it's nuts to eat. You're not going to be thirty all your life; you're going to get to forty, fifty and sixty. You can't keep this game up at that age.' He would say, 'Aye man, father I'm not bothered about when I get to that age I'm living now, man.' When Viv used to go the boxing matches with Rob Owen, 'Red Corner, blue corner? £25 on the red corner.' He didn't know what that kid was like he hadn't a clue what they were like. He was just laughing and couldn't care-a-less about what happened tomorrow; live for today let tomorrow worry about itself. Well yer bugger he was 34, but he had a good life. He had a good last ten or so years. Well, see when I think back as well, I worked all my life and an insurance bloke came around and he said, 'Get a pension out for when you retire?' I said 'Get away I could be dead next week, lad, what good's that to me?' We won the pools at work in a syndicate. They said 'Buy a wagon man', I said 'When I park this wagon up tonight I forget about it until tomorrow morning and if there's out goes wrong with it he's got to fix it. I want none of that I could be dead in five years time.' It's come and it's just went as the years went on, it was all spent, but when I was older it's like what I said to wor Viv, I mean maybe if I had invested that money or joined a pension scheme I would have had a good pension. I said the same as Viv and he was just doing the same stroke."

Hazel told me that as long as Viv's dad was around that he would not have married anyone as his relationship with his father was more important to him. I can see this, as it was his father he worshipped and loved it was him that he confided in and asked his opinion on certain matters. Viv did not leave it to chance for anyone else to advise him.

Many thanks go to Mr & Mrs Graham and family for this contribution.

10

AFTER VIV's DEATH

The death of one man did not diminish the continuing occurrences of drug related crime in the North East. But the killers had certainly shot themselves in the foot, metaphorically speaking, because it brought everything on top in the way the police came down heavy on drug dealing in pubs and clubs. In March 1998 early morning raids by police officers from three forces across the region resulted in twenty four arrests and the seizure of over two hundred and fifty cannabis plants in Operation Antarctic. Two months spent gathering intelligence by drug squad officers in County Durham. Houses in Darlington, Shildon, Bishop Auckland, Spennymoor, and from premises in Gateshead and Billingham. When you consider that the harvest from one cultivated plant can give a return of over a thousand pounds in cash it's not small time crime, as the haul would have yielded a cool quarter of a million quid. Drug users need to get the cash from somewhere to buy the drugs and this has a direct impact on crime figures. Drug users are committing crime to further their drug habit. Thus the police feel that to attack the area of drug supply will have an effect on reducing crime.

Allegations came flying thick and fast about this being a 'gangland murder'. The media wrote of Viv, 'Gangland Murder Victim Viv Graham led a secret double life as one of the North's biggest drug barons...' Ask yourself this, how did the media know it was a gangland assassination? Where was the proof that Viv was a drug baron? Some junkie makes a few allegations and the press accept their word as if it was the messiah speaking. Yet by the same token the press would have shot down any such remark if Viv were still alive. The press only use the material they see fit in their, sometimes, distorted representation of the truth.

Rival thugs were reported to be bracing themselves for a spate of tit-for-tat shootings. What rival thugs were these? No names were used but what it really meant was that any associate or friend of Viv had better watch out. One former close associate of Viv had made contingency plans by having a reserve car parked at the end of his street in case he should need it to get away fast. Assuming he could run faster than a bullet to get to the car if any pot shots were taken at him!

So called friends had come forward and told the press that Viv had got involved in the drug scene in a big way and that he was blown away because he stopped taking supplies from heavy criminals in London. Viv had allegedly found cheaper drugs abroad! Really? How clever of the press to realise those drugs can be brought abroad much cheaper. Anyone with half a brain knows that the drug cartels of South America offer big discounts for bulk purchase. Where do they think the drugs originate from? Apart from what is home grown in this country in sodium lit gardens, in people's attics and lofts the majority of drugs come from South America.

The same fictitious friends of Viv no doubt knew the names of these London based gangsters and helped the police out as much as possible when they made their inquiries into the murder of Viv? That I can assure you the readers was not the case and that is direct from the police themselves and my inside source of information who has been helpful up to now by declaring that scenario not even to be fit for the bin it was so full of holes it could have been used to sieve flour.

The tension that hung around those associates of Viv in the wake of his death was measurable by their scarcity. Viv had become the unsung hero to many in the area he come to adopt as his second home. A plaque was quickly put up declaring: 'Uncle Viv: Our Hero you will always be in our hearts.' Surely not! The youngsters of the area were honouring this drug baron. Maybe the honorary title of 'Uncle' was given because he was the best drug supplier. The reality of it all was that Viv had indeed been an uncle type figure to the many children who needed such a man to look up to for hope. Everyone has their hero and Viv was theirs their very own local hero. Children are a good judge of character they have not lost their belief in hope that all things are possible.

Accusations that Viv had been a police informer were now starting to do the tours. Read Anna's chapter relating to the latest most up to date news about these unfounded allegations. Allegations that he had informed on rival crime families were widely reported and started to be accepted by those in opposition to what Viv stood for. Let us just assume then that Viv had been a police informer and he was passing information to the police, then why were the press so keen to put this point across as if they were a rival standing in judgement against Viv? The press who are allegedly supporters of the law actually turned it in to some kind of evil thing that he had been an informer meeting regularly in cloak and dagger locations with senior police officers so as to pass on information of the highest level.

What is odd about this accusation is that Viv had served his three-year prison sentence for his part in the attack on at that time fellow club doorman Stuart Watson. Do high ranking police informers receive three-year prison sentences for committing violence that 'six old age pensioners' could have bettered? OK that was back in the early 90s maybe Viv had changed his tune since breaking away from crime families and going it alone. Maybe he needed to survive by hook or crook. If that was the case then he was not alone since just about most high-ranking criminals always use the Ace card when the chips are on the table.

Viv was not party to any police covert operations against him and this suggests that if he was informing then it was not on a basis of passing top quality information. How likely was it that Viv would not have top-notch information at his hand to pass on the police? The Karen Young chapter relates that someone saw Viv meeting with a police Inspector and the third party who spotted Viv, believing him to be informing. During inquiries it came to light that Viv was seen in Gateshead Police Station, but bearing in mind that his car was parked in the main car park for all and sundry to see it seems unlikely that he would be advertising his whereabouts if he was up to no good.

Dog eats dog. Five per cent of arrests for crime come about because the police officer just happens to be about at that time but 95% of arrests for crime come about because the general public informs the police. Make of that what you will. Every person has the ability to become an informer. What if you were walking along the road and you witnessed someone bashing a granny over the head with a weapon and they grabbed her bag. The last bit of pension she had was in that bag and she was going to the shop to buy her only friend, a cat, some food. You can identify the young hoodlum and get justice for the old woman. What do you do? 'Lock the bastard up' I hear you say.

Northumbria Police spoke highly of Viv after his death. I only came across one police officer who had a bad word against Viv and I detected something deeper than the normal hatred that jealousy brings. That is not for me to go into here, as this book is not about personal grudges. It was suggested that Viv would still be alive if he had of stuck to minding jobs and stayed out of other people's business and behaved himself like a good little boy. Bollocks! What about the Late Lenny McLean who only did minding jobs. He was shot in the back twice on separate occasions and stabbed in the back umpteen more times.

Viv did stick to minding jobs because that is all that he knew but that is not what got him murdered.

When I was arrested along with two researchers into allegations of fraud connected to another book that is being written about how big companies rip you the public off by short changing you with short measures and fobbing you off with poor quality the subject of this book came up a few times. One particular instance was when a certain CID officer who will be unnamed asked me if some of the people in the Viv book had been sought for their permission to be included within. I thought this a rather strange question to ask since the press do not go around asking permission for the lies they print about people. Can you imagine them, 'Err, excuse me Mr So and so will you give us permission to write this lot of lies about you?' If that were the case there would hardly be any news at all. In defence of that question asked I say this. The truth is sought and no man is bigger than the truth. Corruption is exposed because the truth is stronger. The truth is connected to good, lies connected to bad. The truth is endeavoured to be exposed regardless of the pain. For those who cannot take the truth then maybe that is why you need to take drugs, to shroud reality.

March 1995 the peace in Wallsend was once again shattered by the sound of gunfire. Shotgun blasts rocked the already nerve wracked area and an innocent man fell to the ground dead. Murdered in cold blood. Joe Clarke, 42, was returning home after a night out accompanied by his son, Robert, 17. They had been for a game of pool. A game that was once blamed for the cause of a misspent youth could now be looked upon as a bond between father and son.

Two men had got out of a taxi nearby to where Joe and his son where walking by. Robert Clarke's only crime was to have glanced at one of the men for which he was rewarded with the butt of a gun being smashed indiscriminately into his face knocking him to the ground. Joe shouted, 'Leave him alone, he's only a kid.' Mr Clarke was slashed repeatedly across the face with a knife by one of the men while the other one used the shotgun as a club to hit him with. One of the men said 'Load up.' By this time Robert was up off the ground when he was lunged at by one of the men holding a knife. Robert swiftly kicked the man in between the legs, that made the man back off.

What was described as a 'bomb going off' was actually the sound of a shotgun being discharged at Mr Clarke's buttock. The sight that must have been there for Robert to witness words just could not describe the pain that he must have been going through to see his hero father who defended him from two drugs crazed junkies in such a horrific state. Robert ran up the street and his father tried his best to hobble after him to little avail. Robert turned to his father when a second shot was fired mortally wounding Mr Clarke. The murderers ran off into the protection of darkness from their drug-fuelled killing. Joe's brother, Billy, was a serving police officer in the East End of Newcastle. With words of calmness he spoke of how his brother, Joe, had been the most caring and thoughtful out of all the family. He could not understand why so much violence was used on a man who hated aggression.

Joe left a wife, Joyce, and three sons. He worked hard as a bus driver to support his family he was no lout or trouble maker in fact he was a very modest man and would have hated the publicity surrounding this incident. Only the publicity surrounding this incident was needed to help capture the two moronic thugs who were to eventually blame drug abuse for not knowing what had happened. They were not so troubled by the drugs so as to not know how to operate a gun or wield a knife yet all other cognitive thought processes are lost?

The two supposed drug crazed killers had just committed a burglary that night and unfortunately for Mr Clarke and his son they happened by in a taxi. Colin Moore, 22, and Ian Widdowson, 20, were hounded down by Detective Chief Inspector Keith Felton (now Superintendent at North Shields Police Station). DCI Keith Felton was second in command of the Viv murder inquiry and therefore was no stranger to this sort of gruesome bloodshed. Only this time the press would not be able to say it was gangland or drug related. Anyone walking past these two at that time would have suffered the same serious mortal injuries as Mr Clarke needlessly suffered.

The second gunshot went into Mr Clarke's chest, as he was moving away from the duo that had at first attacked his son. John Milford QC was prosecuting when the case went to court. He said, "Widdowson was heard to shout 'Go on Colin shoot him.' Mr Clarke was judged by a firearms expert to have been shot from no more than three feet away from a single barrelled shotgun! A witness gave evidence and said that after the shot put Mr Clarke down his head was stamped on and only ended when his partner pulled him away. A further attempt was made by the gunman to shoot Mr Clarke as he lay bleeding but again he was pulled away by his partner.

Moore said he was high on Temazepam (wobbly eggs) when he was arrested by police and could only remember fighting with Mr Clarke when he heard two bangs. His co-accused too had a similar story of being high on drugs that night.

Previous to this court appearance Moore appeared in a lesser court and whilst in the dock passed banter with those in the public gallery as if everything was just fine. Just fine for him that was, not Mr Clarke or his son.

Robert Clarke blamed himself for the loss of his father. These two junkies had not succeeded in destroying one person's life, but in fact a whole families life. Joe's brothers, Jim, George and Billy his sisters, Martha and Angela his wife Joyce and his three sons will not forget the man who was a friend to all who knew him. Bringing this on a par with the murder of Viv is meant to show how life is so precious and must be enjoyed to the full as Viv said, 'Life is too short to worry.'

Billy put the feeling of such a loss when he said, "This was a gross mindless killing...Even in this job when you see all sorts of tragic things you can't begin to understand what others are feeling until it happens to one of your family. When something like this happens men are just big softies.' Comparing this to what Peter Connelly said in an earlier chapter it might hammer home the everlasting pain caused by such a senseless act of violence committed by two people so high on drugs that they did not really accept what they were doing. Comparisons to the Viv murder are very close as will be seen later on in that particular chapter. A dark Wallsend street, two men in a car one with a gun both off their trolleys from the effects of drugs, does that sound familiar?

A night out on the town was to end in tragedy. Newcastle's Bigg Market was the setting for this particular murder. The place to be! The place where the buzz is! (£15,000 was awarded to a man who discovered what made the Bigg Market buzz! I could have told anyone that, for a fiver.) One of the best places on earth to spend a night out. Called the 'Bigg Market' not because of its size but because it used to be a market where Bigg was sold. That was a particular type of Barley that had four rows of grain to every ear. It was at one time called the 'Oat Market' naturally oats were sold there. Now people still go there to get their oats, so to speak.

April 1995 was to be the last year in Brian Anderson's, 21, life. A year that had already been filled with tragedy with the loss of a son due to cot death syndrome. Brian was paying his first visit to the notorious Bigg Market area of Newcastle after coming to terms with the loss of his first son. His life was full of tragedy from an early age of seven when his father died, this loss caused him to need professional help. That tragedy was put behind him when he had a steady relationship which gave him a daughter. Life was just starting to go right for Brian so why not have a lad's night out on the town (toon).

Brian and three friends were enjoying a drink in *Macey's* and decided to move on. On leaving they were confronted by a pack that had only just been thrown out of the same place by the bouncers because they were harassing other customers. One group leaving peacefully the other much larger group, of about ten was headed by David Morrison, 19, were leaving forcibly. A melee developed between the two groups but it ended as quickly as it started and the two groups dispersed.

What was thought to have been a minor skirmish developed into something much more and the group headed by Morrison attacked again? What could have been a typical act of bravado with a bit of argy-bargy was to end up with Brian being chased after he was hunted by the other pack. There is no wish to cause any further pain or suffering to Brian's family by seeming to belittle the gang, that chased Brian, to that of a pack of animals, but it was exactly like that. They chased Brian through the narrow Pudding Chare off the Bigg Market and the minute Brian lost his footing and fell they were on him like a pack of seething dogs. Kicking, punching and stabbing their prey. (Pudding Chare - derived from a corruption of the word Pow Dene then called Pudding for short. Also thought to come from the name of a northern delicacy; Black Pudding.)

Morrison carried a knife, which he says was needed to defend himself from a criminal near to the home of his grandparent. He carried the knife in a specially concealed pocket he had cut into his jeans; this was a pre-meditated thing to carry the knife around with him. It was not a case that he just came across it and used it by chance. The knife was thrust into Brian's back it then went on to pierce his heart and the result was what you would expect from such an injury; death!

All the excuses were given under the sun as to why it happened, but the word 'why' is an emotional one. It was suggested that Morrison had a bullied upbringing and that he was singled out because of his grammar school education. It is usual for the defence to say the defendant had no chance in life as mitigation, yet here was Morrison's defence using his advantage in life as a negative point! Morrison was lifed up 'and showed no emotion as he was led away.

May 1995 was to see one particular gun siege that was to cause turmoil in a woman's life for years to come. James Thear of Gateshead considered himself one of the Geordie Mafia, but by virtue of his lack of kudos and respect for women folk he is ousted from that infamous role of honour. Thear had previously been involved in an armed siege when he was with others. He was shot at by a police marksman and received a wound to his arm whilst he was reloading. The gang were counting money from robbery proceeds in a house that was in darkness and used torchlight to do their counting by. This attracted attention and that is when the police arrived on the scene in that particular incident. What do you think his prison sentence was for this crime? The answer is further on.

This incident though was far more depraved than robbing people of money. Thear robed a woman of her dignity, then he raped her. He waited for her to go to bed and then used an excuse to be allowed in, as he knew her estranged boyfriend. After he had horrifically carried out the rape within hearing distance of the woman's two children he left.

For the first siege that Thear was involved in, December 1991, he received a paltry three and a half-year prison sentence. He was cornered and had hoped to blast his way out of a cul-de-sac house with a shotgun. People had to take cover. It was only when he was shot in the arm by a police marksman did he surrender. He had made threats to kill and possessed a shotgun. He received a three and a half years prison sentence for this? Yet Paddy Conroy receives three times this time for allegedly abducting and assaulting someone who desecrated his father's grave! (More on this in the Paddy Conroy chapter.)

Thear had a history of perversion as he used to talk openly to children about explicit sexual matters. He would ask them if he had seen their sister or mother naked in the bathroom. That information is first hand from a very good source. After the rape he took a taxi to a nearby housing estate and holed up once more, it took armed officers to get him out. He was also to face charges of being a troublemaker on a tourist air flight returning from good old Tenerife. What is it about Tenerife?

Thear received a ten-year prison sentence for this whole escapade. He rapes a woman in earshot of her children then starts a gun siege. It makes you wonder what the fucking judges do on an afternoon when they assess their sentencing policy on the golf course. One judge was known as the domino king because of the way he would sentence offenders. 'I have decided to give you three years, but since you have shown remorse it has been reduced to two years although the severity of the crime is worth five years you have been let off lightly and could have received seven years.' Ha, bloody, ha.

Thear's family insisted he had not raped anyone prior to the trial and when it all came out they did not know what to say. Because of his crime he will serve only a maximum of 6 years and 4 months with time off for good behaviour, the woman will receive a life sentence that she will never recover from. Flashbacks do not go away!

September 1995 another pub shooting! Derek Lee had a hit carried out on him; he was stabbed in the chest and blasted in the legs with by a shotgun. He left the *Coxlodge* pub at 11.00 p.m. A fight took place inside the bar and one of the attackers left the pub and concealed himself behind a car. As Viv's father Jack has already pointed out these arguments and fights usually lead to those on the wrong end or losing end using tools or coming team handed. This is exactly what happened here.

When Derek left the pub he was followed by one of the attackers who was still in the pub. The man who hid behind the car jumped Derek; the other attacker had a gun, which he clumsily dropped on the way out of the pub. This was used to heroically shoot Derek in the legs when he was down on the ground. Derek had suffered a stab wound to his chest and it was this that killed him although a gunshot wound to the leg can still kill by virtue of the shock so either one of his attackers had the same to face, in this typical pub ambush, in terms of the murder.

Another pub shooting on Tyneside took place in The Grainger pub in which the publican was blasted in the leg with a shotgun. William Thompson lost his leg as a direct result of the shooting, which took place near to closing time in front of regulars inside the bar. The gunman made no attempt to hide his identity and was known to most of the people in the pub.

More pub shootings! October 1995 three men were shot at in front of other pub regulars in the *Star Inn* in the centre of Newcastle. The attack happened at 8.30 p.m. Three gunmen blasted the men in their legs as they stood at the bar. The men were regulars and it was not a protection racket or take-over bid, but at least one of the men was a Geordie Mafia member involved in criminal activities. The three shot men were lying on the floor covered in blood in this multiple kneecapping with claret everywhere. The attack was aimed at one man specifically and although it looked like a war zone it did not result in any of the men dying from their leg injuries. The barmaids though had to be treated for shock at the sight of the men's gory injuries. The pub was not known for such violence, but the men involved had no qualms about going in and carrying out there duties, which they did in a casual manner before racing off in a waiting car.

Club doorman Kevin Nightingale, 33, was gunned down outside of his South Tyneside home in February 1996. Kevin died from gunshot wounds in the doorway of his home that he shared with his wife and two children. Superintendent John May who headed the Viv murder inquiry headed this inquiry, it must have seemed like the Viv murder all over again to him. A club doorman murdered in such a cold callous way within earshot of his sleeping family.

Kevin worked on the doors of the *Boulevard Wine Bar* and the *Oz* nightclub. This was a conspiracy to murder wrap for those people involved; Viv was 34 when he died, nearly the same age as Kevin.

We move on to the end of February 1996 when tragedy was to strike the Connelly family again. Harry Thompson, 46, the brother-in-law of Anna Connelly was to die violently whilst pursuing those he thought had burgled his home in the Wallsend area of Newcastle. His search for those involved took him to the Walker area of Newcastle, in the East End.

Harry went to the home of William Waugh, 25, and a fight developed after it was suggested that Harry had provoked Waugh. Anna told me she was there when this incident took place and it is difficult to think how the Connelly's can come to terms with these types of tragedies in their lives. Waugh received three years imprisonment for manslaughter.

June 1996 was to see another shotgun attack on Tyneside. Lee Harman, 25, from North Tyneside received horrific injuries in a shotgun attack that was designed to kill him. The attack happened outside the Longbenton Boxing Club late afternoon. The gunman lay in wait inside a boilerhouse, but Lee became suspicious when he noticed some cars around the back of the club. He looked inside of a nearby empty building, nothing.

As he went into the club the boilerhouse door flew open and he was shot in the stomach at just about point blank range. That shot ripped into Lee's bowels and intestines catapulting Lee backwards, he did not have time to know what hit him. The gunman ran over to him and put his foot on Lee's chest, pointed the shotgun at his head and pulled the trigger. Nothing! The cartridge was dud. The likelihood of coming so close to death and living to tell the tale is unbelievable. Lee managed to get up, but was shot in the legs ripping his muscle away from the bone. Many a person would have died from such serious gunshot wounds, not Lee. He accused his would be killer of being a coward and said he had nothing to fear he had hopes of pursuing his boxing career after this attack just like boxer Howard Mills wanted to when his leg was blasted off in a shotgun attack.

Staying in June 1996 John Lubdbrook, 38, a nightclub owner became involved with three men in a confrontation outside of *BJ's* nightclub in Blyth, just outside of Newcastle. One of the three men pulled out a handgun and aimed it directly at John's head, blamh! The bullet struck him in the head, but again as luckily as Lee Harman had been to stay alive because of a dud cartridge John was equally as lucky when the bullet travelled under his skin and out of the side of John's head causing little injury. Drug dealing was thought to have a connection to this incident although it is not suggested John had any involvement in such an activity it may have been he was trying to stop this sort of activity. The gunman escaped and John was left wondering if he would survive until he realised how lucky he had been.

Moving away from guns and onto drugs for a little while it was discovered that Sunderland had half of its crime committed by those on drugs. Nothing new, these research figures, just walk down any city street on a night time and that will give you the answers to it all. The link between crime and drugs has been around for the last two decades and has steadily increased until eventually saturation point will be reached. The most popular drug used by those committing crime in Sunderland is? Have you guessed, cannabis! Second was heroin, third amphetamines and coming up last was cocaine. The trend nationally though was higher than that of Sunderland's at 61%.

The Government in power at present, Labour, plan to bring in legislation that will mean offenders will be given Drug Treatment Orders or face jail. Drug seizures were up last year, this year and next year are not expected to be any different, new records are being set all the time in drug values seized in pounds Sterling. Cheap heroin has been available for some time and this is blamed on the increase in usage, especially by young people. Most heroin comes from the Balkan's via Turkey. Turks are into this type of drug smuggling operation in a big way.

It was hoped to be able to give you an update on the case of the Cumbrian man, Paul Harrison, 31, boss of a pub and club security firm. He was allegedly involved with a number of Geordies, some of whom are considered to be members of the Geordie Mafia. Since the case is sub judice it cannot be fully covered, apologies given. Harrison from Flimby is denying all charges as are the rest of the men charged with drug offences connected with Class, A, B and C drugs.

Home Office research has shown that the Club Doorman Registration Scheme being run on Tyneside is not up to scratch and that club doormen are

are turning a blind eye on the instructions of their bosses. Some are threatened with violence by crime families if they do not tow the line. This report called *Clubs Drugs and Doormen* gives comparisons between Newcastle doormen and those from Liverpool. Northumbria Police helped compile the report by Sheridan Morris. For anyone wishing to get himself or herself a copy it is under the Crime Detection and Prevention Series paper 86. Available from the Home Office, Police Research Group, 50 Queen Anne's Gate, London, SW1H 9AT. Just say I recommended it and I might get one of those fancy one off payments to come up with a report on one of the topics of the day, so long as it is connected with crime I do not mind banking a fat cheque for such work.

I will not begin by taking the piss out of such a publication as they might take the piss out of this book, but I will quote you a bit from the foreword by S W Boys Smith, Director of Police Policy. 'The concentration of large numbers of young people at dance venues...' hold on a minute, did he say dance venues? I thought he said 'dance venues' for a minute there. Because that is what the old *Oxford Ballroom* was used for about X amount of years ago. Continue '...nightclubs, pubs or large warehouses – provides an attractive lure to drug dealers who see these venues as potentially lucrative market places. This report shows how such venues can become the target of organised crime seeking to operate there through a strategy of control the doors, control the floors.' Unquote. Well, I never! They have actually discovered that crime goes on in pubs and clubs! How many grand do these people get for writing such things?

The main theme of the report is to consider the links between dance venue door supervision and drug dealing. Merseyside and Tyneside are pitted against each other. Tyneside has a Club Doorman Registration Scheme whilst Merseyside has not. A survey by release showed that 90% of clubbers patronising dance venues in London and the South East had planned to take an illegal drug that evening. Cannabis was among the top drug thought of being used and that was ahead of Es, speed and LSD.

Liverpool's doors are mainly run by registered security companies, which of course means nothing. Look at Sabre Security in the *Gary Ward – Blackpool Beach Murder* chapter. A door security firm took control of a large chunk of doors by various methods of intimidation and back handers. That meant they were getting paid to run the doors and cream off their drug money. One team was convicted of drug offences, but within a short space of time they were bang at it again, but using a different company name.

Registered doormen run Newcastle's doors, which really means they are on a register and have had to pass security checks and go on a course. What though is suggested by the report is that North East criminals do not have the 'inclination and commercial acumen to develop a significant door security business.' It is a euphemism (an inoffensive word for one considered to be offensive) for the word thick by the sound of it? Oh, fucking really, thick! A lack of criminal grouping is thought also to be the case for this so do not start writing to your MP just yet. It is estimated that only 10% of Newcastle doormen are under the control of criminals or working under their own influence of taxation. The police put this down to the absence of criminal groupings (gangs). The report went on to say that since the introduction of the door supervisor registration scheme in 1990 it has prohibited a number of key criminals from continuing as door supervisors in the city area. (One was meant to have been Viv.)

The measures recommended for disrupting criminal activity within door teams in venues briefly is:

Police – Keep doing what they have been doing, basically. Test purchasing, awareness, detainment teams put into place prior to raids, uniformed police and CID to work together?, train door staff in procedures of arrest and police, constantly, weak areas.

Councils – Introduce and enforce registration schemes and enforce health & safety regulations?

Club owners – Use only registered staff, More training for staff, search patrons suspected of drug dealing more vigorously and finally employ a split security team, with door supervisors from outside the area alongside local staff. (As happened recently at *Legend's* in Newcastle.)

Organised crime was unable to be defined by the Home Affairs Committee on Organised Crime. I can describe it in a nutshell: 'The ability of a group of criminals to act to together to obtain their goal.' That is my definition of organised crime, "charmed I'm sure."

A door supervisor has been defined by the Home Office as a 'person employed on premises which have a music and dancing licence (PEL – Public Entertainment Licence) in operation with authority from the owner or landlord, exclusively or mainly to decide upon the suitability of customers to be allowed on those premises; and/or to maintain order on those premises.' That role though does not define what the role of the supervisor is in relation to policing the area in question for drug dealers. I do not intend to overly quote from statistics as some readers of *Viv (Graham) – 'Simply the Best'* thought I had gone over the top with that sort of thing, I agree.

The report does go on to explain about unstable relationships within crime groups. That is of particular interest as it can be compared to the Viv murder. These networks of private figures and individuals and groups may have power within certain cliques. Many of these relationships are unstable. It is said that group, sub group or individual interest's clash creating violent conflict, resulting in groups fragmenting, shifting allegiance and consequential new coalitions. This is from Merseyside Police, 1997. What it means is simply that gangs can fall out and those within the gang can change their loyalty after violence has occurred.

A review of police operations against pub and club venues over a two-year period took place on Merseyside and Tyneside. (A sure cocktail for a headache for law enforcers if ever there was a one. A better comparison would have been between Glasgow and Newcastle as opposed to Liverpool v Newcastle.) The operation was over a two-year period and considered the extent of club doormen's involvement in drug dealing and violence along with other organised crime.

January 1995 – December 1996 six large-scale raids by police on nightclubs took place on Merseyside. Some examples of the success include 20 floor dealers identified in a nine-month period, a head of door security charged with conspiracy to supply and one doorman found guilty along with thirteen others of drug offences.

A second operation exposed an Es manufacturing laboratory above a pub, which resulted in five drug people being convicted on conspiracy to supply charges.

A third operation resulted in ten floor dealers being arrested and each receiving a prison sentence.

The fourth case figures revealed that 11 doormen were charged with violent disorder and a few grand's worth of drugs were recovered in the raid.

Liverpool does not have a club doorman registration scheme, yet four surrounding areas do: Knowsley, Sefton, St Helens and Wirral, in early 1996 there were 531 registered doormen in these areas.

The doormen of Merseyside were monitored and it was found that no less than 49 of them were of interest to the police. Nine of them had previous drug convictions, six of the nine had been found guilty of drug offences and some repeat offenders with trials pending. One had been convicted of manufacturing drugs another one convicted of conspiracy and so on. No doubt you get the picture. It is saying that without a registration scheme it is in effect a drug baron's kingdom on the club and pub circuit. Twenty-eight of the 49 had convictions for violence on their records. A further 27 charges of violence were pending between all of them. Three attempted murders and two murders were charges pending!

During the late 80s and early 90s there had been continued low level violence between door supervisors on Merseyside. No single group had control over the supply of club doormen at that time, which meant the drug scene was still anyone's for the taking, that was if they had the muscle to do it. There was a lose clustering of door supervisors in Liverpool city centre, Kirby, St Helens and so on. Each team stayed in their respective areas.

In December 1993 (Same time Viv was murdered on Tyneside) a security company operating in Liverpool City centre began taking over the running of club doors all over the city. The company had previously only covered construction sites and retail outlets, but now it was moving into the big time. The company had previous run-ins with the police. Other door security firms had to be ousted and this was done via cash payments to doormen already in place. Not surprisingly violence and threats were used against those that did not co-operate. Licensees were threatened with planned trouble on their premises if they did not take on the company's services.

There were two main players running the company, both were considered knowledgeable about drugs and racketeering. Brother A was considered along with brother B and C to be involved in drug dealing.

Once the company had secured enough doors in its take-over operation its doormen got to work in selling drugs or taxing dealers working on their premises. Drug selling and protection rackets went hand in hand as doormen were paid cash on top of their wages. The company to cover these enforced payments would issue an invoice for services. It all came out of the venue proprietor's pocket.

Operation Aladdin put the company under 24 hour electronic and physical surveillance as it was now considered more than just a local supplier of drugs and the Serious Crime Squad was drafted in. An eight-month surveillance operation took place, but it was hampered to some extent because suspects were wise to the techniques of surveillance.

Brother A who was a director of the company was arrested after making drug purchases from an associate in Sunderland! Brother A was found to have 250 Es in his car after the deal took place. The man was bailed (a ploy often used by the police to allow the offender time to commit further offences, thus compounding his or her situation when appearing in court for the offences) and in a later incident he was found to have some 2,000 Es in his car and a further 1,000 at his home, the bail ploy had worked. The man later received eight years imprisonment and the Sunderland based supplier only received four years for possession and supply of the drugs! Very lenient sentences? When you consider how Tyneside's Stevie 'Hammer' had received a five year prison sentence for having possession of only 50 Es you begin to wonder how the big players get off so lightly.

Conveniently, a fire broke out at the company's business premises, which were under surveillance. The fire was started deliberately to destroy business records for VAT transactions as the company was avoiding VAT duty. The fire could be blamed for loss of all records and disrupt a VAT fraud investigation. The investigation was started by HM Customs and Excise because of the information the Serious Crime Squad had passed on to them. The fraud amounted to an estimated cool £¼M. The matter was finalised by the police when brother B and two other doormen were sentenced, quite leniently, to three years imprisonment for arson. Brother C had acted as a drug courier and only £12,000 was found in his loft for which he received a nine-month prison sentence for concealment of drug money in his loft. The money and his car were confiscated under the 1986 Drug Trafficking Offences Act.

Considering their prison sentences they all got off very lightly compared to some of Tyneside, Wearside and Teesside's drug criminals. The company now removed from its position as top dog in Merseyside left a 'power vacuum' (Chief Inspector Keith Felton – Northumbria Police Force) and rivalry for the vacant doormen positions. A new company emerged as top dog some 12 months after the demise of company A. It was tun by those who had connection with company A and a number of other areas were within the new company's manor including Warrington, Manchester and Southport. The company developed rapidly and Euro'96 is accredited with this as the company provided door cover for worried publicans expecting and getting trouble from drunken football yobs.

Doormen from company B have had run-ins with other teams of doormen which has resulted in drive-by shootings (as happened to Viv) and another security firm's partner being stabbed allegedly by a doorman working for company B.

The whole scenario is similar to how Tyneside used to be, in terms of shootings and take-over bids with no one particularly taking over the mantle of Viv on Tyneside, so it has became jig-sawed up once more to groups and sub-groups with major crime families being taken out of circulation as happened in Liverpool. Unlike Liverpool though no main company in Newcastle has declared an interest in running the doors and it is believed the murder of Viv has acted as a deterrent to many would be Viv wannabes.

When you look at how many registered doormen Newcastle has it seems to match the figures given for areas around Liverpool: In 1997 it had some 507 whilst the force area as a whole had around some 1,200! Thirty-eight doormen were identified as being of interest to the Northumbria Police Force. Out of them a total of 29 had a total of 54 convictions for violence, including murder and manslaughter. Three of them had firearm-related convictions, six had convictions relating to offensive weapons. Other convictions included arson, threats to kill, kidnap and false imprisonment. The list goes on and on and it seems to belittle the Liverpool list of offences recorded against Merseyside's 'doormen of interest.' Even bootlegging was recorded against one of the Newcastle doormen.

The difference between Liverpool and Tyneside's club doormen was that Liverpool had a more organised company running things whilst Newcastle's doors were looked after by individuals or informal teams. Only the largest of clubs had registered companies operating door security, no one has a particularly significant stake in, and control of, the door business within the Northumbria Force area, although a handful of individuals were considered key players.

Drug dealing in Newcastle's nightspots did exist, but was less organised and more indirect on a smaller scale than that found in Merseyside. Violence is still a threat to doormen on Tyneside if they do not let certain drug sellers into the venue. Few doormen are provided directly from criminal groups on Tyneside so existing doormen have to co-operate via intimidation and threats of extreme violence against them or their families is usual. The doorman is then told to let 'their' man in to the venue to sell drugs and taxation is applied to the door supervisors for running a door on their pitch. It is estimated that only 10% of club doormen were on the take or involved in drug selling on premises in Newcastle.

What was said in the report to be an illustration of the aggressive tactics used by criminal groups who ran club doors on Tyneside was in fact a strike by doormen in Newcastle. If memory serve me correct it was a legitimate strike, but criminal groups put it down here as an organised strike. The local newspaper was informed and word of mouth indicated the chosen night that the strike would take place. It was meant to show club owners, the police and other door teams – of a powerful unregistered doorman, allied with a violent drugs – orientated crime family. Those who ignored the strike were threatened with violent retaliation. Numerous door supervisors did not work that evening and many larger venues were forced to bring in security teams from outside the area.

It is also mentioned in the report that the introduction of a doormen registration scheme in Newcastle brought in, in 1990, prohibited a number of key criminals from continuing as door supervisors in the city area. (This does not mention Viv by name, but he is one of those who they mean, as well as some of his associates at that time.) Because there is no specific company run by 'villains' in the door security business in Newcastle it has made it more difficult for the police to be able to identify the particular criminals who are involved in the drug business. This lack of a registered company allows organised criminals and violent individuals to remain involved in 'legitimate' door supervision. The operations that police carry out against key criminals is in the hope that they can be took off the scene and custodial sentences given to these individuals will break their influence on the relatively clean registered door supervisors and teams.

The report goes on to make a number of recommendations, all academic. What can be said is: that if it were not for Liverpool's unregistered doormen the police might not have been able keep surveillance on company A. Consequently the entire drug, arson, VAT fraud and drug money laundering charges might not have been able to be brought against all of those eventually charged. Tyneside's club and pub guide shows that some nightspots employed doormen that were lacking in the basic elements of what was expected of them.

The difficulty in having registered doormen is that for the same amount of registered doormen who are monitored there is a larger amount of unregistered doormen working the doors of pubs. Small villages are becoming regular places that drug dealers set up shop in the village local. It would be easy for me to flick through the local newspapers of every village in the North East of England to reveal a catalogue of drug crime. Acklington in Northumberland is a known place to buy drugs, Blyth in Northumberland has had more than its fair share of methadone related overdose deaths, Alnwick, Amble, Ashington, Morpeth, Hexham, Durham, Richmond, York, Guisborough, Whitby, Scarborough and so on are places within the North East that have experienced drug crime. For every person convicted of a drug offence there must be at least ten others that are connected either directly or indirectly with that crime. How can that be policed?

Drugs are the staple diet of most organised criminals; powdered courage beats having to drink pints and pints of beer to prove you are a man/woman. The move away from drugs in some quarters is seen as a shrewd move because there are other commodities worth a lot more in the long run. You might trade in drugs and eventually get caught, depending on what class of drug it is, say, A, B or C you could be looking at anything from a slap on the wrist to life imprisonment, unless of course you deal in Es and run a security company in Liverpool, then you get off with three years.

The changeover from drugs to bootlegging is seen as a safer bet by many. It is not a bad thing for the British economy either because people buy fuel in this country, which is heavily taxed by the Government so they gain on that side of things. Vehicles need insurance cover so the insurance companies get more business. People buying cheap booze will buy associated items from their local shops such as mixers, additional drinks they could not get to complement what they have got. Cheap booze encourages people to have an impromptu party in the summer, a barbecue for instance. How many people have been to a barbecue where bootlegged booze has been available? This has encouraged people to buy items with the money they have saved on the cost of the cheap booze. I could go on and on, but I am sure you get the message.

It beats the wrap that a serving soldier along with others had to take when convicted of drug smuggling charges. Kevin Jones, 31, a serving soldier with the Royal Artillery 39 Regiment based in Newcastle decided to become involved in the illegal importation of heroin, Es and cocaine. He had been involved with Dale Mills, 26, another serving soldier from Kingsheath, Northampton, Jason Foster, 25, from Wigan and Paul Bromley from Preston all serving soldiers as well. Others involved in the crime were former soldiers, Paul Wright, 28, from Liverpool, James Bull, 29, from Skelmersdale and Peter O'Toole, 26, from Liverpool.

The trial took place at Liverpool Crown Court because that was the area in which some of the £1m consignment of drugs was seized from a car after they had been smuggled in from Amsterdam.

Jason Foster was cleared of any involvement by a jury and walked free. This seemed like a bit of private enterprise and the dignity of the Royal

Artillary 39 Regiment has been dishonoured. The Liverpool connection is endorsed because of the connections mentioned here. The drugs would have been destined for other soldiers in the UK. Considering those soldiers have access to arms it is of a concern that should the influence of drugs make anyone of them become unstable the consequences are frightening.

Arsonists in the West End of Newcastle murdered Lisa Dodgson, 25, her two children and her babysitter Emma Cater, 16, when they set Lisa's home alight by deliberately pouring petrol through the letterbox and igniting it. It was thought to have been a revenge attack when the murderers struck in the early hours on 14th May 1998. The four had no chance of escaping and the intentions were to murder those in the house by the perpetrators of this unbalanced mindless act.

All four were found huddled together in an upstairs bedroom, which filled up with poisonous smoke very quickly. Although three men were arrested weeks later they were released without charge. The wall of silence once again hampered police investigations into this emotional matter. People feared crossing the traditional 'them-and-us' line. West End criminals vowed to find out who was responsible for this warped attack. In the end it has resulted in charges been brought against a number of people.

The twist in the tail is that the mother, June Richardson, of one of the victims of notorious Geordie child killer Mary Bell has supported a campaign to release Maureen Dodgson, 42, from jail.

Maureen was told of the tragic loss of her pregnant daughter, Lisa, and two grandchildren whilst in prison serving 4 ½ years for drug dealing. She was found guilty of supplying cocaine, amphetamines and cannabis from he home in the West End of Newcastle. Her sentence has just less than four years to run, just over two years with remission for good behaviour.

June Richardson knows what it is like to have suffered tragedy in her life as she lost her own son, Martin Brown, to the evil hands of a child murderess, Mary Bell. That case is not an issue here as it has been addressed so much, what is an issue though is the fact that an appeal failed to win Maureen early release from her torment within prison. The Home Secretary can show clemency and intervene in this matter.

The appeal court decided that the sentence should stand as it is! Her original plea of guilty, it is said, was not taken into consideration at her trial. What I say to that is, if Maureen was running a club doorman security firm in Liverpool and had evaded £¼M in VAT duty and had decided to burn her premises down and have 3,000 Es in her possession then she would probably be considered for release!

A precedent for Maureen's early release is the case of another tragic fire death in which another West Ender, Jimmy Boag, lost his children in a house fire whilst he was serving a four year prison sentence. Mr Boag was released on compassionate parole in the early 80s when tragedy struck his family in an accidental house fire. Apologies are given to Mr Boag if this should get back to him, but he is sure to understand the pain that Maureen must be going through just as much as he suffered whilst awaiting the decision on his release. June Richardson a family friend has put her tragedy behind her to help support Maureen's quest for an early release. Surely compassionate parole could not hurt. Parole is exactly that, parole. It means that if Maureen re-offended whilst on parole and she was convicted she would have her original sentence to serve on top of that which would be dished out.

Michael McMenemy was jailed for perverting the course of justice. Brother of ex-Guardsman and ex-England football assistant coach Lawrie McMenemy received a three month prison sentence when he appeared before Newcastle Crown Court in July of this year, 1998. McMenemy was arrested after he admitted smuggling cannabis and tranquillisers into his eldest son who was on remand in prison. He later withdrew his statement in which he confessed to the offence saying he was told to say, by a female who visited his son with him, that it was him who smuggled the drugs in.

Prison staff spotted the drugs being passed over on the visit; McMenemy was in the company of his youngest son and the female. The trio was told to reveal whom it was amongst them that had smuggled the drugs in. His defence barrister, Chris Prince, said McMenemy was terrified about his court appearance. The three month prison sentence was reasonably lenient for such a serious charge and it was only due to the mitigation that Chris Prince gave to the court as to the reason behind it that McMenemy's sentence was lenient.

Kenneth Togher from Scotland was a lieutenant of Brian Doran a real drug baron. When Viv was murdered in December 1993 Togher was holed up in a hotel counting money for a month until January 1994. During this time Customs and Excise applied to the hotel management to bug Togher's room, they obliged and the resultant evidence on audiotape helped them gain a conviction of 13 men who were jailed for a total of 167 years. Togher is currently serving life imprisonment for his part in a drug smuggling ring that imported drugs from South America. The amounts of money involved in such operations are unbelievable. It is estimated that the particular operation aimed at Doran and Co netted some £57M worth of cocaine and nearly £10M worth of cannabis in Operation Stealer.

What brought this matter to light is that I was told by a source that Togher was suing the hotel chain that allowed Customs and Excise to bug his room. Putting the fact that Togher is a convicted drug baron (a title once given to Viv) for one moment, he has a point. There you are on a long weekend with your beloved in a hotel wherever you have decided to stay. You become intimate and the stud of the year award could be yours tonight. Just imagine, HM servants are taping that! What you are paying for when you go into a hotel is privacy, the same privacy you would expect at home. The right to bear arms is one of the USA's fundamental rights. The right to privacy has to be something this country holds dear to its heart. What few rights have you left? The police can enter your home, on any old lame excuse, with a warrant granted by a magistrate that does not know half nor quarter of it. The police can take items away on the basis that a crime has been committed even if you are not charged, ever. You need not even be told who has brought the complaint. Togher is pursuing his rights as a citizen and anyone that knocks it may as well give up their own rights, what few they have left.

The Mafia, has apparently, had connections with a multi-million pound international tobacco smuggling racket. The racket masterminded by Mafia bosses has been foiled when cigarettes with a duty of £3M were seized in two West Yorkshire locations. A total of 30 million cigarettes were seized when they were smuggled from Montenegro a former state of Yugoslavia and then on into Italy via Naples via Milan and finally into the UK. The Mafia buys cigarettes for next to nothing a pack and then markets them to the country that uses that brand. There have been reports though that there is a batch of counterfeit Regal King Size cigarettes made in the former Yugoslavia. The packets are almost identical, but the product has inferior materials, the tips fall off, the smell is terrible and the goods are dangerous as anything could be in the smoking material used to bulk up the tobacco.

Operation Octave was successful in waging war against drug pushers in Northumberland and it helped net heroin, cannabis, amphetamines and other drugs, whereby 200 people were arrested over a period in connection with drug offences. Six of those arrested received a total of 25 years imprisonment when a new system of police intelligence was used. 'Ibase' is an analytical computer that was used over a six-month period to help police detect crime patterns.

It was discovered that Hazel Brown was part of a group, all played different roles, in the distribution and selling of drugs in the Blyth area. Blyth is so well known for its drug problem that if anyone were going to do a study of the cause and effect of drugs on our society then this would be the place to start.

Ma Baker style boss, Hazel Brown, 40, ran a drug supply business from her home in Blyth, which she shared with her son Edward Brown, 21. Their arrest led to them being sent to prison earlier this year. They received five and four years' imprisonment respectively. Jonathan Walton, 23; four years imprisonment, Jason Scott, 27; four years, Donna Farrington, 28; three and a half years and Malcolm Stappard, 26; five years.

Hazel Brown had been described as having led a very lonely life by her defence barrister, Glen Gatland, he said, 'She became an addict herself.' I have spoken with a number of people from the Blyth area and they say the area has been tarnished by this sort of thing and that it only adds to the tag attached to Blyth as being the most boring town in the whole of the United Kingdom. Maybe that is the reason people need to rely heavily on drugs, to help them get away from the boredom.

Just imagine for one minute that you are a bootlegger and you open your door to what seems to be the Customs and Excise men. They all have clipboards and everything seems above board. You are issued with a search warrant, they search you house and take your entire life savings of over £50,000! What can you do about it because they have discovered tobacco worth £130 that is from the continent and it has not had duty paid on it?

A further raid took place and the victim had the threat of handcuffs being put on him if he did not behave. The man had become suspicious and the bogus Customs men were getting jittery. The final raid they did really took liberties as the woman of the house was threatened that her children would be taken off her and put into care if she did not co-operate. An amount of cash (£10,000) was taken as usual.

This made the real Customs and Excise people's job more difficult as people were refusing to co-operate with them, believing that they were impostors. A total of five raids were carried out on commercial and domestic premises between March and June 1997. Regional Crime Squad were brought in and traced Joseph Varey, 32, Neil Wilde, 31 and Shaun Elliot, 27. They were arrested for the bogus raids in the Sunderland and Durham areas.

Elliot from Hexham in Northumberland received a three-year prison sentence and Varey from the Cowgate area of Newcastle received a five-year prison sentence for his part in the bogus raids.

Finally Wilde also of Newcastle received two prison sentences, the first for the bogus raids he received three years imprisonment, the second prison sentence was a one of five years, which was for an unconnected incident. Wilde's home was found to have two Jif lemon squirty bottles that contained ammonia and some ammunition. It was discovered via DNA testing that Wilde had took part in an attempted kidnap of a wagon driver who was in charge of a goods wagon containing a lot of Cadbury's chocolate.

Wilde had squirted the driver in the face with the ammonia! Wilde did not get his own way when the driver stood his ground causing Wilde to run off. The bogus scam was a clever idea, but the ammonia was a bit of a let down for someone who could carry off such a scam. The bootleggers were getting a taste of their own medicine when they were raided, what were people doing with such large amounts of cash lying about their homes? How did Wilde & Co know of the whereabouts of such large sums and of those who bought booze and fags? Could the people concerned account for the money to show how they had come about it? Anyone can say they have amassed life savings of a considerable amount, but as for leaving £50,000 lying around!

The police made a veiled threat to one of my researcher's, when they raided her home, they told her she had her children to think about? Any mother could crack under the strain of having threats made against her, that her children should be; thought about. That could induce anyone to admit to saying anything to ensure the welfare of their children.

What is the equal opposite of a drugs baron? Answer: A drugs czar. Keith Hellawell has been appointed as the first drugs buster ever in the UK. His past stems from the mining industry right to the very top as Chief Constable of the West Yorkshire Police Force. His role is that of Anti-Drugs co-ordinator and with the help of the Government's ten-year anti-drugs plan he intends to change people's view of how they have come to accept drugs as part of their culture. It would be wrong to say that he can stop drug users because it is the suppliers that are targeted.

The statistics are an indictment on our modern day society, as much as drugs were scorned on only a matter of twenty years ago they are as equally loved by the drug taking culture of this 20th century and as we go towards the 21st century it is doubtful if the drug culture can be halted. Hellawell is an older version of Ray Mallon (currently suspended head of Middlesbrough CID) and has the same confident gait about him. Time will tell!

Operation Antarctic (1998) was carried out in County Durham and this resulted in the arrest of 24 people and 250 cannabis plants being seized from houses in Darlington Shildon, Bishop Auckland and Spennymoor and property in Gateshead and Billingham. The value of one plant is about £1,000 = £¼M for the 25 plants! Commercial cannabis cultivation has an impact on crime because people have to get the money to buy the drugs.

Taking a quick look at Manchester in terms of the drug wars that were supposedly finished there we round off this chapter. The police have not won back certain areas. In a drive by shooting incident a man was shot by a machine pistol when innocently caught him up in an inner-city gang feud. Seven shoots were fired one hitting Ocatavius Jarrett in the leg. The 9mm bullet had travelled straight through the victim's leg grazing a bone on the way through. The bullets were aimed at a mountain bike-pedalling rival. The rivalry that exists between gangs from Moss Side and Longsight is legendary and has been long running. Several tit for tat shootings have taken place in the daylight; increased police patrols have not deterred the gangs. Even Longsight police station has been fired on when youths from the Moss Side area were nearby and a shot shattered one of the windows in the station.

The shootings are said to have started in 1997 when a young man was shot and murdered. This caused the tit for tat attacks until so many shootings had taken place that it would have taken a mathematician to work out which side was ahead on points.

Martin Hanley, a 16 year old, was shot and seriously wounded in Moss Side in February this year. Prior to that, gangs from both sides, Moss Side v Longsight, met on grassland in Bold Street and were shooting at each other regardless of the consequences.

Julian Wagaba was murdered in Longsight in March of this year. A reprisal attack led to Adam Thomas being shot in the leg days later in Moss Side.

The problem now seems to be that police have come down heavy and that sort of high profile policing has resulted in some heavy handed arrests of people who have not had anything to do with this long running feud. The 'guilty until proven innocent' attitude has brought a number of complaints against the police.

Every area has the potential to become a powder keg of trouble, in the right circumstances. It would be too easy to say 'leave it alone', but just as what happened in the East End of Newcastle when rival gangs started shooting at each other and setting fore to each other's premises it had to be stopped for the sake of public safety. Quite a few crime families ended up with very long prison sentences so as to get them off the streets. This is surely something that will happen in Manchester too, given time.

Drug wars always end in bloodshed and the consequences are usually that innocent people get hurt by being drawn into trouble that is not of their own making. The public has a right to be on the street and free right of passage throughout this country, but when drug induced loonies start shooting willy-nilly it hinders that safe passage in a modern society. On with the next chapter!

11

Karen Young – Murder Suspect

It is not very often that a suspect in a murder inquiry is willing to give their point of view. After more than two months of asking and being promised an answer from Karen's family I eventually succeeded in securing a promise from Karen of an interview. The interview was arranged at the office of my publisher. About one hour away from the appointed time Karen called to say that she did not have transport and would not be able to find the office very easily. She asked if another time could be arranged? I had to rearrange the chaperon's times and secure authorisation for extra time for my chaperon, etc. So because of this the interview took place at Karen's parent's home. We were left to it and both of Karen's parent's took no part, Mrs Young was the perfect hostess in arranging drinks before the interview started.

Karen's photograph adorned the wall; one of those makeover shots with soft edges to the photograph. It gave the impression that Karen was thought highly of by her parents. Karen is a head turner, not of classical beauty, but more the gorgeous beach babe. The décor and furnishings in this house on a private estate gave it a feel of one of those show houses you view on a new housing estate, only this was a real lived in home.

The interview starts with talk of a fight that Karen had between herself and Mary and Anna Connelly. "I've had fights with the two of them on two occasions. The first fight was when Viv was still alive I was on Wallsend High Street where I drink and where I lived, my local bars; *The Queens Head*, *The Anchor* and *Chadwicks*. It was a Bank Holiday Monday; I was in company with David Roache who played for Newcastle. Viv saw that I was in company and sent a drink over for me, vodka. Viv used to always send me a drink over and I think them two (Anna and Mary Connelly) got wind of that and weren't happy about it obviously as there was a twelve/thirteen year age gap between Anna and me. That was all there was to it, bitchiness. Mary was making her mouth go like a Yorkshire terrier like normal and then I went to the toilet and the next thing was I was fighting in there with her. Viv stood at the door and it continued Mary just happened to come off worse, he came in and it just stopped.

The second occasion when a fight took place was after Viv had died I was in the town, I'd been to a christening and been Godmother for my friend. There were a lot of us from the East End that had been to the christening and we were out enjoying ourselves. The two Connelly sisters came in with two Regional Crime Squad, they were drinking with them and others, they drink with them regularly, I think I know the name of one of them. Rumour has it that Anna is having a relationship with a police officer who was on the Viv case from what I can gather. He was, allegedly, from Clifford Street police station originally.

Anna and I had the fight in the bar, Anna like gave up and she went back to her company and then I heard Mary's mouth, she had her hair cut and dyed. After that I got a message through Mary Connelly from a friend of mine saying that they had the tape of the fight. The message was, 'Tell Karen Young we're two steps ahead of her, it's cut off its her fighting with Anna not Anna approaching her. What I did was to telephone my solicitor and have it put on record especially with the Viv murder inquiry still going on. Two of my friends who were with me on the night went and gave affidavits in case there was any backlash.

They (Anna and Mary) have habits of saying things that were not true and trying to tie it in with the Viv murder and changing things. They were making things up, but I was protecting my own interests and covering my back."

Allegations were flying around that Karen had been refused entry to one particular nightclub and Karen had said to the doorman, 'Do you know who I am? I'm Karen young and I had involvement with the killing of Viv Graham.' It is stressed that this is only an allegation and Karen answers that: "They are talking utter rubbish and to name a nightclub in Newcastle that I can't go in? There is not a nightclub in Newcastle that I can't get into." I put it to Karen that if this allegation was allowed to go free? Karen answers with a dry sense of humour; "I would have been re-arrested, wouldn't I." Karen is quick witted here and catches me unawares; her looks belie her intelligence.

Hearsay and so on are mentioned and she mentions that it was hearsay that got them arrested in the murder inquiry. Karen had previously told me over the telephone that she had spoken with people and they had said to her, 'Oh, you're Karen Young.' They felt ok (okay) over that and she has had some sympathy. "I initially spoke to Rob Armstrong who was one of Viv's best friends. I had heard rumours that he was meant to be going to do this, that and the other. So I went up to Rob and said, 'Right, what's happening?' and he said, 'It depends how friendly you were with the guy, it had nothing to do with me and I've got nothing against you.' That was it"

Karen was told that we had found that most of the people around Viv were all hangers on and that we had found no one...Karen interjects with, "Who is prepared to come forward." They were prepared to come forward, but no one who we could say 'yes' they were effected, we found family, but no one who was prepared to stand up to the press, who belittled Viv.

Karen was asked what the connection was and how it came about when she was arrested. "It was through shear allegations of the Connelly family." What then was it that made the Connelly's believe that Karen had an involvement in the murder? Karen: "I don't know this is what I can't understand. I've got no faith in the British police at all. If, say, my fiancé had been gunned down the police shouldn't be listening to me (meaning Anna Connelly), I'd be hurt, upset, distraught and not thinking straight, so they shouldn't have been taking much notice of her."

Karen was told that the police looked at all possible leads in terms of who could have been responsible even down to hitmen sent across from Italy and searching for guns from Ireland. Karen: "It's been too far-fetched it was just like a big charade! I was sent letters from Ireland, meant to be from the IRA saying 'We're bigger than you, you'll be dead soon.' It was a practical joke the whole lot of it was." The whole arrest would have been a shock, but the consequences of the arrest that was reported in the press, not then, but later...Karen interjects, "It was on Teletext and the news on the telly and everything. I remember thinking...I had to pinch myself thinking 'This isn't real.' It wasn't real."

Karen was sent wreaths and dolls with their eyes poked out, how did Karen take this? "I was annoyed at first and totally bitter and thought, 'Well these people are cowards.' They knew where I lived, they are sending the things here, but wouldn't come to my door. I think it was from someone who was bitter and twisted probably more towards the Connelly family."

Mrs Young had told me previously that the family had been through an awful lot and the pressure was immense on them during the immediate time after Viv was murdered. Karen was asked about her father being arrested in connection with the police inquiry? "My father was arrested the same morning as me, they came with guns. I was held for 72 hours, everybody else was released after 36. The lad I lived with, Alan Jackson, was kept in for that length of time."

Alan Wheat, the man from Northwich in Cheshire was also arrested and Karen is asked what she thought his connection could be? "I think they were suggesting he was some kind of hit man." Alan had a tie in with the group that were arrested and for that reason it was suggested that he had been brought in to kill another retired boxer. Alan was let go pretty quickly and was not mentioned much to Karen by the police. The first time we were all arrested it was thought of as a conspiracy as I knew he (Alan Wheat) was brought up then the second time it was murder, but they were saying Darren Arnold and Brian (William) Tait, they changed their story, they went from one extreme to another."

A stun gun was found in Mr Young's home and it was asked of Karen what her father would need that type of thing for? "He just came back from America on holiday and brought it back with him, it wasn't a high voltage one just a low voltage one, it was more a fun thing actually, new fangled as nobody had heard of them", Karen says with a wry laugh. It is pointed out that they were used in Glasgow discos long before that to rob people with, you would be dancing away and suddenly you would get one in your back, you'd drop and they would take things off you in a dark corner. So for that particular reason were quite popular.

When Karen was waiting in the police cells what was her line of thought on the questioning? "It was no reply. (That was the time when 'No reply' was still accepted as a person's right to silence.) I think they believed that I was in it and knew something about it or had organised something. I was astonished and amazed. I told Chief Inspector Keith Felton that it was a complete waste of police time. I remember we were taken to magistrates' court for a further detention after 36 hours and Keith Felton swore my life away he said, 'He was an inch away from solving the Viv Graham murder' and he hasn't. The two final people he wanted kept in custody and we were supposed to get charged! I was actually shouting across the court, 'You're talking utter, utter rubbish.'

Some of the anguish that Karen went through during this time is summed up by her, "In a little town when someone is murdered it doesn't happen every week, so obviously it was the talk of the place it was headline news. To think, your daughter and your sister are caught up in some sort of gangland, it's not very nice is it?"

Witness statements put Karen near the scene of Viv's murder and what is suggested is that because Karen was already within that area and within the pub scene could it not be a mistaken case that, yes she was seen but it may not have been that particular day. "Yes there were suggestions that I was the blonde woman who was supposed to work the car alarm or something. They changed it that many times, it was meant to be that stood and watched him die over his body, there was that much said that I don't really know what the story was really supposed to be."

Alright then, I ask what Karen was doing that day? "Actually this was the problem, I couldn't answer that because I was sitting at home on a New Year's Eve, I had a sunbed, was painting my nails and was going out. The only thing I had, to say I was in the house, was a BT itemised phone bill. They had in effect said that I had rang people and left the phone off the hook, went out, committed whatever and came back." How long was the phone off the hook? "Ten minutes/fifteen minutes." How far was it from your home to the murder scene? "Five minutes by car." So, it was suggested that Karen would know the exact time that Viv was to leave the pub (6.05 p.m.) dashed there and left the phone off the hook and with the help of her friends she would be covered with that alibi of being at home using the phone? "They just tried every angle possible and even said people were paid £500 to say things like that."

A likeness of Karen was identified as being near Viv's body as he dragged himself out of Border Road back to *The Queens Head* pub he had left only moments earlier. What can Karen say to that? "I went to go on an ID (Identity) parade, I got there and was told it wasn't taking place then. The police took a secret video of me, without my knowledge. They got ten other girls, blonde, and they made them do exactly the same in the video and they were showing it to the witnesses regardless. They asked for my consent, I went, 'Just do it', because they would do it anyway." The police asked for your consent? "I don't know if they did, they just took it that they were going ahead and they did." So did you give your consent for that? "No, No." When they took this secret video recording how did it come about? "Because they were asking and asking 'Why didn't you sign on at the dole with Mr Jackson?) (Karen's boyfriend at that time.) Alan Jackson did and they got him outside the dole and they got me subsequently with him, he knew they were going to do it because I wouldn't consent. They were secretly going to do it; they took one of Mr Jackson and Darren Arnold.

What had happened was they had done it the wrong way about, they had took them (the video recording) and my solicitor went along whilst they were getting played to the witnesses to view it and they had called the meeting off, saying he had his dates mixed up. He subsequently went on holiday and they did it in his absence. I was down the country and I had rang up my solicitor and he said, 'Oh, yes the ID was done when I wasn't there.' He should have been there, but wasn't!" This video ID seems to have been mishandled by the police from Karen's accounts.

"From that they came to re-arrest me at my flat, they kicked the door in with a warrant and said we arrest you for murder with Darren Arnold and Brian Tait. They were in prison, they removed them from prison and took them to a local police station. I wasn't here, I rang my father the next day and they (Arnold and Tait) had been in custody for 24 hours he said the police wanted to speak to me again. I came back up the country and met my solicitor at the police station. I was held again for 72 hours!" Karen had travelled back up North to hand herself in. She gave an account of her movements, voluntarily, and had nothing more to say, based on legal advice.

The Tait and Arnold situation was raised and it was put to Karen that Viv had warned Tait to stay out of his patch? "I used to see Brian around and he was in the bars. I'm not 100% sure but Brian was seen around the bars in the same company." Was there any rivalry between him and Viv? "Viv was a bully, Viv only picked on people he knew he could get away with it."

Do you think maybe then, Viv in that situation where you were in the pub, Tait was in the pub everybody being able to live with each other, 'He isn't a threat', 'She isn't a threat' sort of thing that was the case? "Yes." Karen is asked outright if she had seen Viv intimidate anyone or threaten them or even bully them, bearing in mind Karen had said Viv was a bully? "No, I've heard various stories of him hitting people, only little lads and things at Walker. I've never actually seen him intimidate anyone or bully anyone. Although I've heard allegations."

My researchers and I have pursued all of these allegations, that Viv was a bully, but nothing has been substantiated and here was the perfect opportunity for me to find out the truth from someone who knew Viv reasonably well. Yet, Karen did not see any bullying from Viv. Viv had confronted Richard 'Fago' Dodd, when he was pointed out to him walking around the Metro Centre (convicted ramraider), because he had heard that Fago was going to run him down with a car. Fago was no match for Viv, but he did not run away and said to Viv, 'I'm not going to run away from you because I know that would be no use, you're a big guy and I know you could hurt me.' Viv said, 'I'm not going to touch you, don't worry, but is it true that you were going to run me down?' Of course, it was not true and they parted in a friendly manner, but this would have been a perfect opportunity for Viv to assert himself on someone much smaller and weaker. Viv would have to have a very good reason to pursue someone in such a way that many people thought he went on.

"I think he got in with the wrong company that caused a lot of trouble because he did actually used to try and say to some of us, 'Come out the bar, when I'm in show me a little bit of respect.' Everybody just sat together and wouldn't move. I'd been brought up here, he wasn't from here." What do you think he wanted you out of the bar for? "I used to think that it was because Anna and Mary were on their way to meet him. He was always wanting us out of the bar." He was saying 'out' though to the whole group and not specifically to you, Karen, was it that some of those people were dealing in drugs, was that the reason? "No, I think also Viv dealt in drugs, I've never been involved in the drugs side of things!" It is not suggested that you are involved in drugs in any way, for me to do that I would have to pursue and prove that, but I am not. I am more interested in that pub and that there was some dealing going on there that Viv did not like. There are allegations that Viv was dealing in drugs in Wallsend and that police raided a pub and got £14,000 worth of drugs and money that belonged to Viv, but that cannot be proven, but what you are suggesting now is that Viv, as far as you are aware, did Viv have some dealing with drugs? "Maybe and maybe some of the people in my company were drug dealers, I mean that type of thing they would keep to themselves." Would you think then that he (Viv) would see it differently, it could be seen as two ways, one: he dealt in his own drugs and wanted them off his patch, Karen interjects, "More so." Two: they were dealing in drugs and he did not want them in that pub? Karen: "More so, it was his patch and he didn't want anybody stepping on his toes. He had his followers and saw others as rivalries and threats to his little drugs empire, that he so-called had, according to the press." I tell Karen that it is plain to see that she is holding an awful lot back. If I was to go into a pub I could immediately identify where the drugs are coming from, 'Drug dealer, drug dealer, buyer, buyer.' You are pretty worldly-wise and if someone within your group was dealing drugs you could identify the source pretty quickly. Karen: "It's a thing I tend to stay out of, because it's really none of my business is it." Without you naming names some people in that group would have had some drug involvement. I know people who smoke happy baccy and if they want to smoke it, that is their decision and if you are in a group then who are you to tell them to stop. You might like the character of the person and the personality of the person so you can overlook certain aspects. Karen: "What you see is what you get. Maybe there was people at the bar smoking the odd happy baccy." I know of people who are not particularly cared about being caught in the act of smoking drugs and some actually brag about it openly, I cannot rule their lives. You have an opportunity, Karen, to say 'I'm a girl of the world and if I'm in a group and some people deal in drugs I can walk away from that' or I may say 'I didn't see that.' There is no way it can hurt you, Karen: "Can't incriminate me. If people are going to do that, good luck to them." What is being said is that when you were in that group and Viv said, 'I want this group out of this pub', you are in a group and not naming names, Viv continues to say, 'I want you out, even though you Karen aren't dealing in drugs, I want this group out of this pub, show me some respect.' Now when that did not happen and that group did not move out of that pub? Karen: "He used to stamp his feet, like a big spoilt child. He just seemed to hold back he didn't want to hold back." Because he liked you, maybe? "No, he cannot go around bullying people. There's a saying 'What goes around comes around'. He cannot go telling people what to do all the time, especially in the villain world. He was what I would put as an amateur trying to get mixed up in the professional world. He thought he was number one and he was proved wrong, I mean look where he is now; he's dead. It did him no good. He had no brains, he was all brawn obviously he had his following, his run-arounds, we called them. We used to make stories up in front of them so they would run to him. And we would see him charging up and down the High Street." When you say he was all brawn and no brain obviously he had some thinking capacity, he loved old ladies and children and that sort of thing, do you think he was genuinely trying to make pubs into a safer place for anyone to bring their families and friends? Karen: "No, he was trying to make a buck or two." On what do you base that answer? "By what I've seen, a lot of his followers deal in drugs, obviously I'm not going to name names. Obviously he was protecting somebody's interests, maybe his own, maybe somebody else's. I think he was trying to make some money." No one ever seen Viv with a bag of drugs going up to a dealer saying, 'That's my £500 tonight, old son, there's your bag of white doves, go out and sell more.' Karen: "No, I certainly haven't seen that. I just think he wanted certain people out of the bar and certain of his followers in, for what reason I don't know."

Karen says of Viv when he first arrived in Newcastle, "When he first arrived on Shields Road he used to buy me drinks. That was a lot of years ago, around the *Hobo's* carry on. Then later on a bit more hostility came into it when drugs came into it. After Viv came out of prison he changed his tune. It was alleged that he was a police informer and I've actually witnessed him myself when I was driving along the High Street and a bust was going on in the *Queens* I got a Chinese, I was putting it in my car and he was standing talking to the Regional Drug Squad with their dogs." (Author's note: yes a raid did take place and Viv was present when that raid took place, but it was his local pub and he did not have any drugs on him.)

Karen: "Why wasn't he stopped and searched, he came along from the Anchor." (Author's note: This is true, Viv looked along from The Anchor pub to where the raid was taking place in The Queens Head pub and he and a certain senior officer eyed each other up. Although there was nothing to incriminate Viv it seems that people do not think there is no smoke without fire, as Karen has thought.) Karen again pursues her line of thought: "Why wasn't he stopped and searched, other criminals were taking out the back and stripped, why wasn't he. Why did he come out of the other bar and not stay in there drinking his drink? He was untouchable that was the impression I got."

The group that Karen spent time with in The Queens Head often had Darren Arnold and Brian Tait in it, which Karen has admitted although there were plenty of others too and this was common knowledge. It was put to Karen that allegedly Viv caught her selling drugs and told her to stop it and grabbed her. She was living with Alan Jackson at that time and it was also alleged that she was having an affair with someone else in the group. Someone then said to Karen that she should not let Viv push her around like that. Karen: "Viv never ever laid a hand on me. And as for selling drugs on his patch!"

Karen was a shoe shop manageress at that time and still works within the retail industry getting up at 7.30 a.m., she must surely feel very angry? Karen: "Where would I have got the time and I certainly wouldn't be getting out of bed early in the morning. I don't know how these people can actually sleep in their beds and warrant their jobs and getting job satisfaction from going out and upsetting people's lives, turning them upside down and not taking any notice of what I say. Wagging tongues come from an empty head."

The media portrayed Karen in such a way that they suggested she had a conniving way about her. Karen: "The police actually said I was a 'very clever very highly intelligence minded person. I'd just like to know where they get it from, I haven't got a GCSE to my name." Karen underestimates her intelligence here, as I can vouch from talking to her that she is a good looking, head turning clever woman, which I tell her. She was on bail and awaited a CPS decision that hung over her and her family for a long time when she was on bail. She had to report to the police station twice a day then once a day and it became more relaxed as time went on.

Surely the harassment over the time could be classed as emotional torture: "They were constantly outside my house walking dogs, taking rubbish away, etc. My solicitor actually told me that my phone was bugged, Mr Grant from Samuel Phillips & Co was my solicitor at the time. They seemed to know everything I was doing before I went out and did it. My mail was also being tampered with. What had happened was things would go missing such as a bank statement, I would ring the bank and they told me that a statement had been sent out. I would ring the insurance company for a cover note and they would send a one out, but that did not turn up either, yet they had insisted they sent one out. The police said that someone was going to get in touch with their lawyer and drop a subtle part of the jigsaw to them. What was going on in their heads I don't really know."

Darren Arnold and Brian Tait were on remand at that time for other offences, Karen's boyfriend was the cousin of Darren Arnold. Karen is asked if she knew the West End family by the name of 'Sayers'? "Yes, yes, we all drank in nightclubs and knew each other and Darren knew them as well." Karen was asked if she knew of a confrontation that allegedly took place between Viv and Michael Sayers. Viv had grabbed Michael Sayers in a nightclub and was going to set about him. Viv chased him out of the club, did you hear anything about that? "Actually it was Madison's nightclub and the week before I think it was when I was in there and Michael Sayers came in with someone from the West End. He had a bottle of champagne he gave me a glass and people in the company I think he also sent a glass over for Viv to be quiet honest. Viv never chased Michael out of any nightclub from what I've seen.

There is what you would call North East crime families in this town and I think Viv would have been very dubious of confronting any of those families." We have a witness that seen Viv confront Michael Sayers? Karen: "That was meant to be the week after, the Saturday after some incident, but I never seen it. I heard that they had a fight, Michael and Viv, after the nightclub shut." Michael though surely would not have stood up to someone like Viv? Karen: "Rumour has it that he did stand up to him. I don't think he's the type to run away either." It was put to Karen that Viv would not have considered anyone a match for him physically in such a situation? Karen: "Probably, yes, but there would have been reprisals!"

Karen is told of an allegation that was thought to be the run up to Viv's murder and the reason that a number of suspects in the Viv murder inquiry were arrested. Here is how I put the allegation to Karen and it must be remembered that it is only an allegation based on what the CPS had to consider. The person you were living with at that time being the cousin of Darren Arnold who in turn was a good friend of a well-known West End crime family was ordered or told to assist in the murder of Viv. The crime family said about the alleged Viv and Karen incident, 'You aren't going to let him walk all over you like that, are you, he should be done in?' Two were selected to carry out the hit and it may well be this is as mysterious as, the two hitmen from Italy, just allegations. Karen: "It is, purely alleged."

The other point is this, which is put to Karen for her opinion, Darren Arnold knew of a stripper called Sascha who worked out at a gym in Birtley, apparently the blue Ford Escort used in the Viv murder was stolen from nearby to that gym. Karen: "Darren was arrested the first time from her home." Was he having a relationship with her? Karen: "Yes, yes." That is the allegation as to how the getaway car was come across on the day Viv was murdered. Karen: "That was never mentioned to me."

Karen cannot speak on behalf of Darren Arnold and she says of him, "He's getting on with his life, obviously he suffered tremendously as well because in a court case the Viv allegation came into it. I think that is why he was so harshly sentenced." Was that for an attack on an off duty club doorman in the Heaton area of Newcastle? Karen: "Yes, but the doorman had previously attacked Darren. The Viv Graham thing came up in his court case and I think that's what swayed the judge to sentence him so heavily to eight years in prison. He had never been in trouble before in his life."

When arrested Alan Jackson was charged with being in possession of drugs! A cannabis plant? Well, the police had to get them on something to justify the manpower going into this. Darren Arnold had no previous convictions prior to that, here he is though after the Viv Graham murder on Tyneside, a nightclub doorman he had a confrontation with bumps into him in Heaton, Newcastle. They have a fight and it so happens the club doorman is seriously injured. Arnold had to hear the Viv allegations again in court and although he was not on trial for Viv's murder the prosecution were not prepared to let it go unheard that he was one of the main suspects along with Brian Tait. Although it must be pointed out that he had no connection to Arnold's attack on the doorman.

It was put to Karen that Tait doesn't seem like the type of person that would let any person walk over him no matter who he was, Karen says, "Yes." There was an allegation that Tait was up and down Wallsend and Shields Road after Viv's death? Karen: "Yes, there he was on that New Year's Day." Up and down there clearing the tills out of pubs, are you with me at the end of the day…Karen: "Yes, but technically he didn't have a rick with Viv, Brian." But once Viv was gone? Karen: "He thought it was free run."

Tait had a confrontation with Peter Connelly, was there a reason for that? Karen: "He emptied the bar I know that, yes. Peter Connelly had been making his mouth go all over to the police. The police said they were inundated with phone calls about us and that Peter Connelly was constantly at the police station in connection with the murder. I would ask why they were pursuing these allegations. They said they had to because of Peter Connelly, so Brian went down to the bar to ask why. Peter was living at the premises with a woman who had children. He got attacked with umbrellas and all sorts so he just left because Peter was upstairs and wouldn't come down, what could Brian do, he wouldn't hit women so he just left it at that time. I heard there was another occasion."

Do you think Peter was afraid of Brian Tait? Karen: "Yes, definitely. Brian went to see Peter because he wanted to know why he was getting everybody arrested." Surely, Brian might have thought that people thought it was him because he was running up and down Shields Road doing things which gave a degree of weight against him? Karen: "That was only allegedly, though." Which is not a point that is wanted to be pursued by us since that is not the matter at hand, regardless of what I have been told by others. Whatever evidence I have been given it is not for me to pursue.

What could Viv have done to remain alive? Karen: "Maybe stayed out of the company of the Connelly's, that spoilt him. They enticed him, 'Do him, Viv, do him Viv, do this, do that' and Viv wasn't very bright. I always said, you could wind him up very easy. He thought he was indestructible, invincible and he could do whatever he wanted, but for what reason?" Viv predicted that he would be dead before he was forty. Karen: "Obviously he knew he was making enemies of the wrong people. There were a lot of rumours that he would be dead in X amount of years. There was one thing, Viv no more for '94. * It was allegedly said in the pubs before. It was said in the underworld for about 18 months before Viv was murdered." (*Before he was murdered. This was the New Year's toast after Viv was murdered.)

Karen is asked if she knows Margy Denene (Deneen). Karen: "Yes, I had actually heard that you had phoned her up and that she wasn't speaking. I had mentioned you and somebody said that you had been in touch with Margy. From what I can gather there was a few attempts on him and allegedly there was eight masked men from the town went to his home when he lived in Daisy Hill with pick axe handles, bats and smashed all the windows. Anna and the kids were in, Viv wasn't, and she ran upstairs, he never followed up that."

We talk about police informers and about high-ranking criminals turning informers, Karen says, "Viv was spotted in Cramlington meeting with a police Chief Inspector. David Glover was the last person you would ever think of being a police informer. All what I will say is if you are a villain and you take that path you would end up dead, it's as simple as that. It's a very serious gamble to take."

We talk about the Sayers' for some time and of John who is serving some fifteen years for Robbery, the Geordie McVicar. He was charged with one crime and it was very heavily denied although proven in court. John is due out soon and it can be said that he is a tactician and a thinker, no doubt these past years have been etched heavily into him and he has re-run the case through his head time and time again. Hopefully we can cover some of his case within this book.

Karen says that the police said to her, 'We can come into your life, we can wreck it and can turn it upside down and we will walk out' Karen went on to say, "That is certainly what they did. I just can't believe it can happen, I'm very bitter to Northumbria Police. I came back because home is where the heart is. I've agreed to speak to you because it's in the public eye and a public thing, people that know me, know I'm not a vindictive, conniving powerful thing like this and wouldn't get involved in a thing like that."

I ask Karen straight out if she and Viv had a relationship? "All I will say is that there were rumours that Viv wanted to take me out for a meal and that was really it and I never ever went." Viv wanted to take you out, how did Alan, your boyfriend feel? "He was in prison at the time, but it was never ever mentioned never talked about. He was (Viv) a police informer I wouldn't be seen with people like that, it was my general feeling. Over the years it turned a bit bitter. I don't think he felt anyone would have the cheek to do it. He couldn't understand why he couldn't get his own way. People were using his name, who has to hide behind anyone because you always get what you deserve."

Karen says the same as some members of his family have said about those that used him. "I think Viv was very reasonable at first, but eventually it was a knockout. Viv had any amount of fools running around after him. Maybe they were using his name to line their own pockets. I think he warned people first, he stayed away from big crime families, he feared them."

The conversation goes on to a man covered heavily in *Viv (Graham) – 'Simply the Best'*, Lee Paul Duffy. Karen met him when he came to Newcastle to allegedly fight with Viv, Karen Says, "It was a Sunday night in the town. It used to be a place in a basement by the Station. Viv didn't turn up so Lee went to the Bigg Market and knocked some doormen out. Lee was often in Newcastle drinking. I've seen him on a few occasions in *Walker's* nightclub, *Rockshots*, *Ritzy* and *Madison's*." The fight that was arranged between Duffy and Viv was to have been a case of winner takes all. Whatever 'all' was, is left to the imagination.

Karen: "I take my hat off to Lee, I mean I remember when I first met Lee everyone said he was No 1 in Middlesbrough. I said, 'Get your shirt off, give me a look at your muscles.' He did come that night and he was game. I think he stood a chance from what I could pick up. He was tall and broad. I think on that night he knocked about ten out."

I have to agree with Karen here because Duffy was a boxer not a steroid freak. He could last more than thirty seconds because of his training. He tried to anger Viv by knocking out other club doormen, but Viv kept away because there was some underlying threat from somewhere else. Karen: "I think Lee wanted to come over and establish himself here and he wanted to fight Viv."

Karen has the tan and the blonde hair to go with it so I ask her if she felt powerful because she was the blonde stereotype? "I used to think how did I get in all of this trouble, I can see it now looking back, but I wouldn't change it. When I first came back I was new fangled with everything. But now I wonder why I came back because it's the same old Newcastle. When I was in Manchester I didn't like it, but I can see what I miss now. The people from Manchester are more laid back and the Geordies are in there fast." Would she prefer the Manchester or Newcastle area? "Newcastle."

A lot of people said that Karen is a younger version of Anna Connelly. Karen says of Viv, "I remember his smile and when I first met him he was like a big silver back then. He was massive, 'I remember saying to him, 'How did you fit through that door?' And that was that, we got on from then on." Viv seems to have come to Newcastle rather like Charles Dickens going to London and looking for the streets paved with gold. The promise of something brought Viv to the city of plenty away from his little village community.

With all the best intentions in the world Viv became tainted by the city life and tried to mix, but he was not accepted. Karen has previously mentioned she was not going to be told to get out of a pub by Viv who was not from the area. Viv thought differently to city folk, quite naturally he thought his charm would win the day. Maybe in Rowlands Gill it would have worked, a place that you could up to a few years ago have left a telephone directory in a telephone box without it being vandalised.

We had small talk at the end of the interview and Karen spoke of some other big names in the criminal world on Tyneside, Teesside and Tenerife. She knew them all and spoke of Ernie Bewick from Sunderland allegedly attacking another well-known name who she was an associate of. We can not go into detail with reference to this incident as it is presently Sub judice. The man attacked was not the type of person that would let anyone walk all over him, he was allegedly a tenacious terrier like person who would stand his ground even if he was out number or over powered, he would show no fear. It is alleged that up to three people were involved in the attack, which resulted in the man dying. Ernie Bewick is currently remanded in custody awaiting trial. The Ernie Bewick v Billy Robinson fight is covered further on.

12

Murder Scenarios

One year prior to the Viv murder, 23rd December 1993, Paul Logan, 25, was murdered when he was sent to deliver a takeaway to an isolated farmhouse near to Shotley Bridge in Northumberland. Blue House Farm was at the end of a track off a country road, earlier an order had been placed by telephone to the Golden Flower takeaway a few miles away, only the call had been made from a telephone kiosk ½ a mile away from the takeaway. Paul called the number back to confirm the location of the farmhouse some half-hour after the order was placed.

At 9.55 p.m. Paul arrived at the farmhouse in the midst of a snowstorm, but the occupants did not recall placing the order, he left. At 10.30 p.m. the occupants of the farmhouse had noticed the delivery driver's car was still at the end of the track, with its headlights illuminating the area. Paul was nowhere to be found until just after 2.15 a.m. his battered body was discovered in the snow.

The murder weapon was not found, obviously a weapon had been used to inflict such injuries on the local hard man from Shotley Bridge. When someone of Logan's status is murdered in such a way it always creates fear within the local community, people fear that if such a man can be murdered so callously then they fear of what might happen to them? People were not going to talk for fear of a reprisal from an unseen, unknown source.

Logan's family put up a £10,000 reward for the conviction of the killers, but if fell on deaf ears. The difficulty with any such reward, as I have previously written, is that no one is sure how they would be paid such a sum or even if the money existed. This was the difficulty in the Viv reward of

£100,000 being offered for information leading to the conviction of the killers. That money was not administered through a solicitor and therefore any credibility was lost. How could it be claimed was also a mystery, who would own up to writing a cheque out if it came to that? People are not stupid and unless the money was 100% guaranteed to be there for them at the end of it, it might as well have been a £1M reward offer, because no one was going to come forward until they knew for certain the money was going to be paid out.

£10,000 is a lot of money to offer people in such a small community, but again the money was not visible or guaranteed via a legal authority. This is where these sorts of rewards fall flat on their faces. The same is said of the Gary Ward reward offer of £10,000 if evidence was found leading to him being granted bail from his life imprisonment sentence. Anyone can talk about these sorts of amounts, but when it comes to putting their hands in their pockets they can have short arms with deep pockets.

I have not pursued any reward from any of these cases as I am not interested in such money, but for those people in the know with hard evidence to get a conviction for the two murder cases, they would be more than willing to spill the beans for such money. I know that for a fact, but unless the people they fingered were convicted and put away then the informants' lives would not be worth living. That is the reason no one comes forward to claim such unreliable rewards with only a verbal guarantee of a pay out.

Fifty detectives were working on the Logan murder inquiry from Consett police station. Five men were 'helping' police with their inquiries and an identikit picture was issued showing a man they wanted to interview in connection with the murder. The mystery man had been seen in the village on the night of the murder and a few days earlier. Earlier in the month two men were spotted sitting in a blue Bedford van outside of the *King's Arms* in Shotley Bridge, they were seemingly watching delivery drivers at the nearby Golden Flower takeaway where Paul worked on occasions.

On the night of the murder the identikit man was seen with another man in a red Ford Fiesta between 8.30 and 10.00 p.m. Paul's past was chequered and he had connections with criminal activities and criminals. But like every unsolved murder case this had one thing in common: one piece of the jigsaw was missing to complete the overall picture the police had built up in the course of their inquiries.

No one was saying anything publicly, but the police had a lot of information to work on. The difficulty of going in and out of such a small place like Shotley Bridge is the service roads. It would be easy to be spotted coming and going and the chance of bumping into a police patrol vehicle would always be a risk. The murderers were more than likely local because they had knowledge of the farmhouse and they knew the routine of ordering and how they might be called back. When Paul called back, one of them was waiting by the telephone so as not to raise suspicion of a bogus call. He was on his way and it would be easy to just wait for Paul to go to the end of the track. They could follow on and then lie in wait for him in the cover of darkness and swirling snow. The attack was not sudden because Paul had run some way before being caught, he knew that an attack was to take place so he ran. He was the local hard man, but something told him he was in for a good hiding and his status was not going to help stop what was about to happen. The 'fight or flight' mechanism had kicked in. It took more than one though to see this through and as a hitman based in Manchester told me the more involved in the crime then the odds go from evens to one million to one in favour of being caught.

Just like the Viv case later on, a number of people had been 'helpful' with the police inquiries. The murder was carried out under the cover of darkness, a telephone call had been made from the killers although no direct threat had been made. More than one person was involved in this attack. The reward did not have any effect in helping people come forward and Paul, like Viv, but on a lesser scale had a reputation as a hard man. This reputation may have contributed to the brutality of the murder, as the killers knew that if they did not do the job fully then they were in the shit. Paul could have identified them and reprisals would have been forthcoming from his associates in this close knit community.

Some six years on one has been charged with the murder and just like any other unsolved crime in this country there is no statute of limitations, the murder hunt is always on going.

Consett, a town not far from Shotley Bridge, was once a hive of industrial activity until British Steel shut down over twenty years ago. There were some big payoffs for those that had been there most of their working lives. Many were rich for a short period of time and then the money just whittled away or was spent as fast as it was got due to people's lack of ability to save or invest such large sums, some as much as £20,000+. It was and still is the first place in the North East to have temperatures that fall below zero and is always usually snowed in at times during the winter months. That sort of past coupled with the weather conditions makes the people pretty tough.

Pretty Rachel Tough, 18, was a childcare student at the Chester-le-Street Action Community College. Auburn haired Rachel helped out at a local school as part of her ongoing training. Rachel was found with head injuries believed to have been from hammer blows, she was dead, lying in a pool of blood. This was the gory sight that was found in the kitchen of the council home that John Thompson, 27, his wife Michele and their three children. Rachel lived three doors away with her mother and three other family members.

Thompson was in the house with Rachel while his wife had gone out. Michele Thompson returned home to find the grisly scene and she knew that if her husband had anything to do with it he would not be able to live with it. She told murder hunt detectives of her thoughts on the matter, but they continued a nation-wide lookout for Thompson.

Thompson was found by a woman walking her dog in woods about two miles away from his home; hanging from the end of a rope! Thompson had done as his wife suggested he would do if he were guilty of the murder. The fire brigade had to be called in with special equipment to lift the body down from a secluded place. Whatever the reason was for Rachel's murder it will always be left to gossips to talk about. Thompson was mentioned in the previous book and his connection with the criminal underworld in Consett is well known.

Consett being Consett you would not think that it could have a reputation like it is starting to achieve. As well as Thompson being thought to have had connections with the Paul Logan murder it was suggested that he had connections with another unsolved Consett murder! Julie Smailes, 27, was strangled and then stabbed to death in her home which was set on fire to try to burn evidence of the deed in October 1996. Julie was a computer sales manager who dabbled in lonely-hearts column romances often meeting strangers for sex. The murder of Julie was thought to have had no connection to her liaisons with lonely-hearts friends. My own inquiries reveal that the police have been told from a number of sources that the person who murdered Julie was a female. Whether this is idle gossip or not, the police have questioned some 6,000 people and a number of females have also been questioned. As of yet no one has been charged. Thompson can be ruled out as a suspect from what has been revealed to me by those in the area.

The person who murdered Julie has a cunning mind and thinks quickly sort of like leaving things to the last minute because they are lazy, it is only their quick thinking mind that masks this laziness. Strangling and stabbing her made it look like a sex game gone wrong, was that deliberate by this quick thinking killer? Strangle and stab sounds like a double tap, which is a thing that professionals use to ensure the person they want dead, ends up dead - a shot to the head and then one to the heart. This person who carried out the murder though is not a professional, they kill only because of anger within themselves. The anger within was caused by Julie and I would guess the killer now regrets the killing because the anger has gone and a sort of sadness is left within them, that has changed that person's life very much. They will no doubt eventually read this and recognise those traits within.

All manner and form by way of conjecture was alleged about Thompson who had been in prison. He was said to have been a convicted drug dealer (similarly to Viv being branded a drug baron, after he was dead) and had been quizzed in two previous murder cases. The second of the two unsolved murders he was quizzed over was that of takeaway deliveryman Paul Logan. Thompson was said to have been in prison at the time of Paul's murder.

You would think that a small community like Consett could take no more, but there is more to come because as much as Thompson was thought to have connections with two unsolved murders he was also accused of having a connection to the street fight murder of father of two Malcolm Hester, 28, from nearby Briardale. Malcolm was attacked in the Delves Lane area of Consett and this was attributed to one of the local hard men, Thompson. His wife points out though that at that time they were all away on holiday. Gossips being gossips though will not let such an opportunity drop, which is sure to have the community talking over it for the next 20 years at least.

Again the gossips were wrong and charges of murder have been brought against Stephen Richard Parker, 23, Paul Phillips, 18, John Baron, 24, Kevin Strike, 18 and three boys under the age of 17. They and two others await trial for this and therefore it cannot be gone into in too much detail because it is sub judice.

Consett is starting to get frayed at the edges and could become another Blyth if it does not clamp down on recent events. Employment prospects for the younger generation is limited and urban regeneration programmes are needed within this community, that is plain to see. There are employment advisor services and British Coal did have advisory services for those wishing to start up in business. Drugs play an important role in the lives of teenagers and certain areas have it worse than others do. The hard man role is dying out; barrel chests are being taken over by a more subtle approach. The size of a man's biceps used to be the measure of his strength, which is now being replaced by brainpower. Although we will never quite get away from the occasional need for some immediate muscle power.

The final scenario is nearly ready to be looked at. It was suggested that Viv was murdered as a direct result of his involvement with people from Tenerife. A man called Andy Winder was originally from Darlington; he ran a modelling agency prior to leaving for the Tenerifian time-share racket. It has been alleged that a man called Paddy Leonard originally from the North East of England had a run in with Winder and for his troubles winder was threatened by Leonard with Viv's name. It was about that time Viv was asked to go out to Tenerife, but Viv was advised not to by his father and told to stay out of it. Winder however told Leonard that if anything happened to him then there was money left for a hit to take place on Viv. Winder unfortunately died as a result of violence and the rest is self-explanatory.

Interestingly enough a bar owner in Tenerife hired some hitmen to take out her lover. Coincidentally the woman, Jacqui Ambler, 33, is originally from Durham, which is not to far from Darlington. The supposed hitmen were actually two doormen that worked in the bar. They confessed that she hired them and for their trouble they each received 29 years imprisonment. Michael O'Hara Jacqui's lover was crudely murdered, but a twist in the tale was that her son allegedly held the key to proving her innocence. Although he travelled to Tenerife with his grandmother it did not stop his mother being found guilty and receiving a 27 year prison sentence. Information has been awaited on this case for some time and up to now it has not arrived therefore it must be put to one side. There was some doubt though as to Jacqui's guilt and therefore until the matter is resolved there is always doubt, but have you ever tried to get off a wrap in a foreign country. The minute they see a Brit they think a number of things and one of those is money. Break something and find out how quickly they will call the polizei for that 'British Lout.'

The penultimate (One before the last) scenario is a new murder case in the North east and up to now is an unsolved one at that. The difficulty is that there are so many twists and turns in this case that it could take up half a book on its own. For that reason a lot of the translation of the importance of this case is lost in such a small space allocated for it.

Stephen Sweeney, 45, was sitting behind his desk in his factory unit in Felling, Gateshead, he was alone in the building, all the workers had left and it seemed that the killer picked their time precisely when they entered the building. Maybe even a dummy run was carried out, but video cameras on other factory units could have caught the killer on video as police are checking footage to see if it reveals anything suspicious.

Twenty-five staff at the factory were about to be put on to short time because of a shortage of orders for furniture that was manufactured there. Workers had a genuine fear of losing their jobs because of lack of work and many felt the firm would be closing down soon due to this. Many thought that Stephen was director of the company, but in fact he had been banned from holding a directorship.

Carol Taylor, 38, had been the common law wife of Stephen for the past eight years she had become a director and recently Richard Caddick of Humshaugh became a director. Stephen was less than 5½ feet tall and he kept fit so he would have been pretty quick on his feet compared to someone taller and heavier, that indicates he did not go to make a move before being shot by a handgun. He was either kept sitting at gunpoint or he knew the person, which is an easy enough 50/50 assumption.

8th July 1998 and between 4 p.m. and 9.10 p.m. when Carol and their daughter went into the Cascade furniture factory they made the discovery that Stephen had been shot at his desk. Blood was coming from his eyes, the sight that it must have been for their daughter is nobody's business!

The factory had a £1M turnover, but in spite of that it only had a credit rating of less than £1,000. Further to that it was discovered that the firms accounts had not been filed with Companies House as per rules of a limited company. The whole financial picture was bleak what with a VAT bill of £25,000 going unpaid, an overdraft of £11,000 and creditors being owed an estimated amount in excess of £70,000. Profits were down to £153,000, which left only £200+ in the firm's coffers after the wage role was paid out.

Both Stephen and Carol held a £1 share in the business. That would have been the limit of their liability in the company that was incorporated in 1994. The police revealed that Stephen was of previous good character, which is of no use in determining who the killer is. It only tells us that Stephen had not been convicted of any offence it does not mean he did not commit any offence. That is always the difficulty in this sort of situation because the moment a clean sheet is shown it seems to indicate that nothing untoward was going on. It is not being suggested for one minute that his was the case with Stephen, but it can side-track the police as suddenly the go off the criminal side of things and start looking at other motives.

It came out in the wash, as most things eventually do, that Stephen owed creditors some £400,000 when one of his companies, CAS Upholstery Ltd went bust. One particular creditor was owed £150,000, the value of Stephen's luxury home at Hebburn, a few miles East of the suite factory. The police were pursuing what was said to be some 800 lines of inquiry and had interviewed just about everyone they could think of.

The factory was not kept open and needless to say the workforce of 25 lost their jobs. Carol could not keep the factory open because of cash problems. What was kept being mentioned was the now familiar term 'hallmarks of a gangland execution'. The factory did open for a short while after the murder, but it could not continue with cash flow problems, it closed two weeks on.

Cascade was set up six weeks prior to Stephen's old company CAS Upholstery going into liquidation. Carol's role in the new company was to act as Company Secretary, which is required by law to have a one if limited. Stephen was given a six-year ban from holding any directorships. Martin Duffy was a director of Cascade from 1996 until February 1998. The reason for Stephen being banned from holding any directorships for six years was that he had allowed CAS to trade whilst insolvent. The Department of Trade and Industry took him to County Court. The company had £6,000 in the bank yet owed a total of £402,000 to over 60 creditors throughout the country. The taxman was owed £42,000, and numerous other bills that go with running a company, NI, and so on. It was found that £142,000 of cash sales had not been recorded!

Stephen had not told anyone other than those close to him that he had been disqualified from being a director, not even Mr Duffy who took over as a director. It was said of Stephen that he was 'hard but fair.' Someone close to him thought, by the way he was found in his chair, that Stephen might have known his killer so as to allow him or her to get close enough to shoot him in the head with a hand gun. It was not uncommon for him to still be in the factory up to 8.00 p.m. and it was common knowledge. His social activities were pretty thin on the ground apart from his training although he was a member of the Rotarians and Professional Masons.

Stephen was use to the good life having had a private education although he was brought up in South Shields. Richard Caddick, 54, resigned as company director only three months into his job?

An anonymous letter was sent to the police saying that two cars were parked near to the premises at about the time of the murder. A man in his 40s was seen twice at the factory premises the day before Stephen was murdered and an identikit picture of the man has been issued without any success of a lead. No murder weapon and no motive with 800 lines of inquiry and up to 60 police were working on the case that has been scaled own to some extent due to the cost.

Richard Caddick is also a partner in Richard Johns' Outfitters in Hexham, Northumberland. The premises quite conveniently caught fire last year when the place was nearly gutted. A big insurance payout was made and the shop was refitted and restocked. Since then charges have been brought for insurance fraud, again because the case is sub judice not much can be said. The fire was said to have been an unfortunate accident prior to charges being brought.

What could the motive be for killing such man as Stephen Sweeney? What if he had an insurance policy out on his own life with his family named as beneficiaries and he just could not face the loss of his business? Assuming that was the case and he knew the right people to do the job it could be a possibility although there is not wish to cause distress to his family it is a possibility. The debts that his old company had were never paid off and were not likely to be either. The £152,000 debt was to one creditor. Stephen had opened up another company and that had started trading the minute the old one ceased trading. There would be a lot of unhappy people out there regardless of how unfortunate the loss was to Stephen. The fact was he was still trading and had suffered no visible loss to himself, he was still living in a luxury house. It was sure to cause some anger to at least some of those his company owed money to.

It can be put to down to love or money; usually killing in a crime of passion ends up in the murder being botched up. The skills of being a lady-killer are not necessarily the same skills needed to literally kill someone. On the surface it seemed that Stephen was the doting father and loyal lover. He spent time in the gym, what was going on at home, was his life as secure as it seemed? The money his firm owed had a big chunk of it owed into Manchester from what I hear, if so it could be looked at as a gangland hit. What sort of hit was it? Was it a double tap? Did anyone hear any shots being fired? If not then could it have been a gun with silencer fitted? Not an easy type of thing to mess about with. Stephen had some idea of what it was about because of his position describes as one hand on the window ledge and one arm across his desk. That does not sound like someone about to run away from a killer. If there was an insurance policy then who stood to gain from it?

Viv had been threatened that many times that he just accepted it and got on with his job. He had become desensitised to the fear that he initially had over such things. One suggestion was that a man called Big John had brought over the murder weapon from Ireland. The ballistics experts checked this out and there was not a cross match between bullets fired in Irish killings by the same type of weapon.

Two Italian hitmen had been sent from Italy by Gazza was another story, which was so outrageous that it hardly warrants my effort in the writing of it. The thought behind it was that it was a reprisal for the attack Viv had allegedly made against Gazza while he was drinking in the town. What does emerge from this story is the sense of humour that people still have in the North East of England.

It has been alleged that Viv was present when a deal was done with counterfeit money in Blackpool. £25,000 of counterfeit money was handed over and it is said in the *Gary Ward – Blackpool Beach Murder* chapter that the people concerned would not let Viv off lightly with this sot of thing and thus he was found and murdered. Sabre Security in Blackpool was run by a shady characters particularly John Herd and John Barratt. A man called James Docherty had alleged connections with some very shady characters and in a letter to Gary Ward Docherty mentions some details about Viv. Gary Ward is suggesting that a hit was placed on Viv because of his shady dealing against certain directors of a security firm he worked for before being sentenced to life imprisonment. He suggests that Viv should have stuck to his own patch instead of trying to take over cities such as Manchester and Blackpool.

Viv use to frequent the bars on Wallsend High Street particularly *The Queen's Head* and the *Anchor Hotel*. There was even talk that Viv had some sort of business interest in the *Queens* how true this is of course is anyone's guess as Viv's business affairs are so muddled up. There was even talk that Viv had a number of other business interests in other pubs around the North East. Whatever you believe it can be said he liked to get into the *Queens*.

When Viv firsts started going in it was fine and everyone accepted everyone. A group of regulars used to be in and Viv wanted to stamp his authority on a certain group because he felt he was not getting the respect he deserved. Some say that Viv wanted the group out because it was stopping his drug dealers from dealing others say he had his favourites and wanted them in regardless of the drug dealing. Whatever way you look at it he just wanted a certain clique out of the pub.

Within that group was Karen Young, Darren Arnold, Brian William Tait, Alan Jackson, 'little legs' and a few others. Admittedly some of the men smoke the odd joint now and again and this seemed to ruffle Viv's feathers, so it is alleged. One week prior to New Year's Eve 1993 there was a confrontation and in that it is said that Viv turned on little legs causing him to suffer an injured rib. It was said that little legs was standing up for Karen Young as Viv had said something to her. Karen admits that Viv had not hit a woman and he was a gentleman always offering to buy her a drink and he even asked to take her out for a meal, but as Karen said she felt uncomfortable in his company because people within her group suspected he was a police informer and it was not the done thing to become involved or seen with someone if they had even the slightest hint of being an informer, even if it was not true.

There was certainly ill feeling between the group and Viv, but as Karen said she was there first and that was her local so why should she have to socialise elsewhere? Viv was concentrating more on the East End of Newcastle in terms of his services being taken up by publicans. He travelled around in his easily recognisable car and most people had his telephone number so checking around on his movements was very easy. He had let his guard drop over the years and was not very security conscious, maybe believing that it would never happen to him even though he said he would not live to see 40.

Guns are reasonably easily available, but even more so back then in '93. Viv left *The Queen's Head* public house on New Year's Eve 1993 and within minutes he was callously gunned down. Just prior to Viv leaving the pub little legs left. The group that Viv had a conflict of interest with was not in.

Viv died later that evening from gunshot wounds and the word got around Newcastle that he was dead. In certain quarters champagne bottles popped their corks and the celebration was a dry sense of humour, 'Viv no more '94.' Doormen refused to work, as they feared that they would be next on the hit list. The whole city of Newcastle's nightlife came to an abrupt stop as doormen walked out in fear or sympathy.

The police made a number of key arrests, Darren Arnold, Karen Young and her father, Brian William Tait, Alan Jackson, Alan Wheat, Michael Sayers and Lee Watson.

Karen Young had to move out of the area because the hate mail and smear campaigners disrupted her life. Her role was alleged to have been a distraction to Viv somehow and that was the reason she was arrested, because police believed they had witnesses strong enough to testify in court that she had some involvement. Karen was kept in custody on two occasions for stringent questioning, but she stood her ground and used her right of 'no reply' that was applicable then.

THE chaff was sorted from the wheat, Alan Wheat was no longer wanted for further questioning, Watson, Sayers and Mr Young were also considered to have been fully questioned.

That left, KarenYoung, Darren Arnold, Alan Jackson and Brian William Tait to await the outcome of the CPS decision as to whether they should be charged, the wait was many months and eventually the case against them was dropped. The charges talked about were conspiracy to murder to just plain murder. The Crown Prosecution Service had to consider the following. The car used in the drive by shooting had been stolen from Birtley and the area it was stolen from was beside a gym that was allegedly used by a female stripper that Darren Arnold was having a relationship with. That was the connection they were trying to prove. It seemed too coincidental and too convenient that the car was stolen from Birtley nearby to a gym. A witness had given a description to the police and that description matched one of those arrested, but because of fear of reprisals the witness suffered from nerves and could not go witness if called on. There were other witnesses, but they were considered to have too much of a criminal record to be able to stand cross-examination. One alleged witness was to have been David Glover Jnr. He was to stand trial on a kidnap/torture charge along with Paddy Conroy form the West End of Newcastle. It was alleged that in return for the police speaking up for Glover he would go witness in the Viv Graham murder trail against some he had named. Unluckily for him and luckily for those he was to have gone witness against he was found guilty and received a 10½-year prison sentence and for that reason and that reason alone he refused to go as a witness for the police.

Glover had previously said to the police that he knew of a safe house that was used which formerly belonged to Stephen Craven's (Serving life for the Penny Laing murder) father. Someone had gone to view the flat and had a key cut, so the story goes. It made an ideal hideout as the place that the car was dumped and burnt out at Simonside Terrace, Heaton, Newcastle was just across a field from this bungalow. It meant that the bungalow could be used to hide in, Glover had mentioned that the car had hit a wall and left a scrape of blue paint on it and allegedly the police found this so it made what Glover was saying sound plausible.

A Heaton woman, Margy Denene, was asked by a man if he could come into her home and stay a while, she was too keen to move him on as she became suspicious of what he had done. Later that night champagne corks were popping and the toast was 'Viv no more '94.'

The payment allegedly for the hit was a bag of cocaine! Viv was no longer around and what the police had to consider was who would be trying to make a take-over bid because they initially thought that it was another heavy outfit vying for power of night club doors. That was not the case and the power vacuum could not be filled although a feeble try was made.

The killers of Viv have not been caught and a lot of turmoil has happened in people's lives because of his death. Allegations have flown around thick and fast and fingers have pointed and chins wagged an awful lot over the last five years. Viv's death was not necessary and the matter is for the authorities to pursue. Many people have had to readjust their lives because of all of the hearsay and rumours that have been going around. Karen Young gives her account of what happened in the previous chapter and there is no reason to disbelieve what she has said. She was good enough to grant an interview and her co-operation is appreciated even down to her candidness about the atmosphere inside the pub.

Many thanks to all of you with your letters of support and stories especially from those of you who wrote from within prison offering me your support after I was arrested and the Viv book documents were seized by the police.

Should any of you wish to write letters of support to Mr & Mrs Graham (as many have already done) you can address those letters of support to the publisher and they will be passed on to them.

13

Clubs 'n' Pubs guide

Here it is your free guide to Tyneside's clubs and pubs. Obviously it has not been possible to cover all of the establishments in the Tyneside area, but you can be assured that most of those covered are reasonably well known. If you are visiting or intending to visit Tyneside it is hoped that you can pick from the establishments covered those that suit your needs.

To start with though we take a general look at the social scene. Pubs in England at present time of writing are allowed to open between the hours of 11.00 a.m. to 11.00 p.m. from Monday to Saturday and 12.00 noon on Sunday to 10.30 p.m. Certain pubs though do apply for extensions when applying to renew their liquor licence. Some establishment that are only open late in the week can apply for Special Hours Certificates. The stipulation is that the venue must provide other entertainment apart from drinking, such as music or food. Some of the food in certain establishments can be said to be entertainment, so beware as that side of things can be a ploy to apply for the certificate.

Tyneside, Teeside and Wearside are set to go continental, although not many people know it. Who would think that the once smoke filled skies from the effect of industrial toil in the North East would eventually be host to the smell of international cuisine? Most cities in England have relaxed their licensing laws to accommodate what has become the norm in the capital, London. The North East is last as usual to follow suite in considering longer opening hours, 24 hours while you wait drinking!

The title '6th Best place in the world to party' that was once said of Newcastle seems a little out of date considering that the 'town' (toon) closes at 2.00 a.m. while in other cities such as Manchester, Leeds and some other Northern cities the partying continues long after the toon has shut down for the night. (Early morning.) Comparing Manchester to Newcastle it is found that pubs, clubs and cafes in Manchester has grown from 250 to nearly double that, 450, since licensing laws were changed. The fear that licensing authorities have is that later, longer opening hours could lead to an increase in violence or drunkenness. This has been proven to be just a fear that people have when drink is looked at in terms of creating madmen out of mice. Yes, booze is responsible for making people more aggressive and that if it were not for booze the amount of violent offences would be halved, that is accepted. But consider this, what if booze had never existed, what would the alternative be? A snort of cocaine perhaps just like the days when snuff was the 'addiction' of the day. Booze is more controllable because it is legal and therefore it can be monitored with stricter controls applied.

That is what makes all these working committees that look into the effects of booze on communities is so laughable. The drug that causes the least damage in terms of knock on effects has the biggest of hurdles to get over when licensing is considered. That is why Newcastle and Middlesbrough have working parties looking at the consequences of longer opening hours. Northumbria and Cleveland Police are the ones who will have the last say in this matter. The problem is that when nightclubs close at 2.00 a.m. there is one almighty exodus from city centres throughout the North East. That is when police are on standby because for the next hour or so trouble could happen.

Extending the closing time would stagger the amount of people leaving the city centre. One thing to think about is that how come Scotland has later opening times than England when there are fewer people living there? It is not for this book to be a lever for licensees to get their own way, but looking at it from a neutral point of view it must be said that there would be a lot of advantages to the community in longer opening hours. Extra jobs, more money for the local economy, more regular police patrols thus maintaining high profile policing in a highly volumised retailing area.

Drug dealing is a problem no matter what time of day or night venues are open. Laws are in place to protect the innocent, but what of those who are not innocent, how much protection should the law give them? David Mowbray, 31, of Blyth was charged with allowing premises to be used for supply and use of heroin when David Kenneth Birch of Eslington Mews, Ashington collapsed and died in a Blyth Street. Birch was old enough to know what he wanted out of life, what can you do about a forty year old man who wants to make his own decisions?

A South Tyneside nightclub, *After Dark 11*, was closed down after a teenager collapsed and died outside. Thomas Skillcorn, 16, collapsed and died in September 1998 in what is thought to have been a drug connected death. The club was inspected and found to be running with a defective fire alarm system. When you consider that premises of such venues have to comply with Health & Safety laws, which are in place for the safety of everyone who patronises the venue.

What is the use of having fire escape doors if, say, for instance they were to be padlocked or it the premises became overcrowded breaching the safe amount of people allowed as per its fire certificate? That in effect would make its insurance policy void and if a claim was made who would pay up, the owner!

What if you were the brother of an ex-school teacher turned world famous rock star, would it help you out of a jam? Philip Sumner, 42, brother of Sting, (Gordon) ran the promenade situated *Dunes Bar* in the coastal area of North Tyneside. Some 70 police officers raided the bar in November 1997 and under aged drinkers were found to be on the licensed premises. Chief Inspector Allan Curry of Tynemouth area command oversaw operation Red Light. The place had become a meeting place for school children who later gave evidence in court. It was stated by one 17 year old that she and her friends regularly patronised *Scott's Bar*, the *Olive Grove, Pier 39 and Rio's Wine Bar*. *Whisky Bends* though was said to have acted more firmly when she was turned away because she could not prove that she was 18 or over.

Dunes was an accepted place to go because more than likely no questions would be asked of anyone's age. The *Rex Hotel* was also raided and the operation revealed a contemptuous breach of the laws. Philip Sumner applied to have the licence of *Dunes* renewed, but his application was turned down even though he said the age limit for entry would be increased to 21 and over. Whitley Bay and Tynemouth are places geared up for tourism, but every so often there will always be trouble in the quietest of places. Look at Scarborough and Whitby, once a haunt of the Scottish looking for a week away from it. Whitley Bay is no different, people visit the place from all over the world. Groups travel from place such as Manchester and Merseyside just for a weekend away from it all. Just as any coastal resort has to contend with drunks that cannot hold their drink it is no different on Tyneside, which Whitley Bay and Tynemouth are parts of.

Scouser's (Merseyside's locals) visiting for a stag weekend ended up in trouble when they caused trouble outside of *Rio's Bar* on the Promenade at Whitley Bay. Victims were head butted, stamped on and hit over the head with weapons. Prior to that in May 1998 thugs travelled from Birmingham to chance their arm in battle with locals. It resulted in Anthony Coughlan, 26, being jailed for nine months and his pal, Dean Wheeler, 30, receiving a Community Service order of 200 hours. Youths from all over the country have been involved in incidents of violence, Viv would not have stood for any of this and it would have been nipped in the bud.

Newcastle are planning a Hogmanay party in the run up to New Year, 1998.

That will see a relaxation in licensing laws although it is in Newcastle's own interests as this is a dummy run for the millennium celebrations the following year. Someone who has considered the real aspects of late licensing is Newcastle's Councillor Norman Povey who is the Public Protection chairman. Councillor Povey is more interested in making Newcastle more attractive to visitors from a cross section of the community, not just those looking to fill their tank. He is right of course because boozers can spend a lot, but it is the catering trade who really offers the punter a good night out. There are many people who would love to visit Newcastle and then have a meal and a drink after attending some early evening entertainment.

Publicans across Tyneside have formed Licensees Against Public Disorder (LAPD). The scheme was created by publicans from Whitley Bay just as similarly as the Pub Watch Scheme was originally started by publicans from North Yorkshire. It sometimes takes those in trouble to come up with their own remedy to the problem that is specific to their problem – teeny drinkers. Over 18s can go into a police station with proof of age and are issued with an ID card. Venues operating this in the first instance were Idols, *The Rex Hotel, Whiskey Bends* and *Rio's Bar*, all favourite places along the sea front. With this in place it assures, to some extent, that under aged drinkers who cannot hold their booze will not cause trouble for those seeking a good night out. 250 licensees have been written to in North Tyneside by the police to let them know about the ID cards being in use. As Chief Inspector Allan Curry said, 'Young people and alcohol don't mix.' *Idols* manager Alison Elliot, is chairperson of LAPD, which shows that the licensed trade is helping to police itself.

Newcastle city centre is to be revamped, but an area that really has seen a change is the previously Dickensian looking Quayside area. What was planned to be Newcastle's biggest hotel had to be scaled down to please planners. There is a shortage of hotel rooms in Newcastle and this to some extent will help although it is still some way behind the facilities that Manchester can offer. Maybe planners need to take their blinkers off. Architects, Mackellar Scwerdt Partenrship (a good old Geordie name) worked their balls off to get this to the build stage, they had to burn the night oil to please planners. The project is to straddle Tuthill Stairs and the Hanging Gardens on the Quayside.

Out of sight out of mind, so they say. Especially if the place is underground. Consent was given for a £65M development that will include a casino, multiplex cinema, pub, club in the heart of Newcastle. At present time of writing it has not been buitl, but if you get an A-Z and look for Neville Street, in the future that is where you will find this complex. The nightclub going underground is planned to be built under a disused furniture store, up from the Bigg Market? Enough of the history lesson let us move to the cruisin' for a boozin' guide.

Clubs 'n' pubs Guide
Researcher: Neil Morris

Name of venue: NEWCASTLE	Chase	Flynn's	Waterside	Akenside Traders	Jimmyz	Hanrahan's
Safety/Overcrowded	NO	Very cramped	NO	YES	Very busy	YES
Price of drinks high/low	Very high	High	Average	Average	OK	High
Entertainment	Music	Ditto	<	<	<	<
Trouble: yes/no	None witnessed	No	Ditto	<	<	<
Décor: 1(bad) - 10 (good)	10	7	9	7	7	8
Doormen's attitudes 1-10	9	6	7	7	8	7
Atmosphere 1 - 10	9	7	7	6	8	8
Too hot/cold	Just right	hot	cool	hot	Just right	Cool
Pleasure or pain	Pleasure	OK	Pleasure	Ditto	<	<
Age range	25-35	18-40	20-45	18-45	18-45	25+
Staff friendly 1-10	10	8	9	9	10	9
Service: fast/slow (F/S)	F	S	F	F	F	S
Toilets: clean/dirty 1-10	10	5	6	8	8	7
Glasses: clean/dirty	Clean	Ditto	<	<	<	<
Choice of drinks	Very good	Good	Yes	Yes	Yes	Good
Dress: smart/casual	S	S	S	S/C	S	S
Place to be: Y/N	Y	Y	Y	N	Y	Not so much
Drinker: rich/poor	Student/ Business	Mainly student	Upper crust	Mainly business	Student	Older person
Disabled access: Y/N	NO	Ditto	<	<	<	<
Staff attitude: 1-10	Good	Good	Good	OK	Good	Good
Doormen hurry you?	N/A	N/A	No	N/A	N/A	N/A
Parking	No	Ditto	<	<	<	<
Drug dealing	No	Ditto	<	<	<	<
Gay bar	No	Ditto	<	<	<	<
ANY OTHER COMMENTS	This is the place to be at present	Very narrow, crammed	-	-	-	-

196

Researcher: Neil Morris

Name of venue: NEWCASTLE	Quilted Camel	'Offshore 44'	Martha's	Waterline	Red House	Bob Trollops
Safety/Overcrowded	Very busy	Yes	Yes	No	Yes	Yes
Price of drinks high/low	Very high	High	Average	High	Quite high	High
Entertainment	Music	Ditto	<	<	<	<
Trouble: yes/no	No	Ditto	<	<	<	<
Décor: 1(bad) - 10 (good)	10	5	8	8	4	4
Doormen's attitudes 1-10	6	7	7	7	4	5
Atmosphere 1 - 10	9	5	7	6	3	5
Too hot/cold	Hot	Hot	Cool	Cool	Hot	Hot
Pleasure or pain	Pleasure	Ditto	<	<	<	Pain!
Age range	18-30	18-35	18-40	18-40	1835	18-35
Staff friendly 1-10	9	8	10	9	7	6
Service: fast/slow (F/S)	S	S	F	F	S	S
Toilets: clean/dirty 1-10	8	7	7	7	4	6
Glasses: clean/dirty	Clean	Ditto	<	<	<	<
Choice of drinks	Very good	OK	Yes	Yes	Good	Good
Dress: smart/casual	Smart	Casual	Smart	Ditto	<	<
Place to be: Y/N	Yes, now	N	Y	Ditto	<	<
Drinker: rich/poor	Millionaire 'B' class	Student	<	Business/ Student	Student	<
Disabled access: Y/N	No	Ditto	<	<	<	<
Staff attitude:	Good	OK	Good	Good	OK	OK
Doormen hurry you?	N/A	Ditto	<	<	<	<
Parking	No	Ditto	<	<	<	<
Drug dealing	No	Ditto	<	<	<	<
Gay bar	No	Ditto	<	<	<	<
ANY OTHER COMMENTS	Very nice G/Atmos V/G Decor	-	-	-	Old hat	-

Clubs 'n' Pubs Guide
Researcher: Neil Morris

Name of venue: NEWCASTLE	Dobson's	Bliss	Ikon	Pump House	The Quayside	Legends
Safety/Overcrowded	Yes	No	No	No	No	Yes
Price of drinks high/low	High	High	High	High	Very High	High
Entertainment	Music	Ditto	<	<	<	<
Trouble: yes/no	No	Ditto	<	<	<	<
Décor: 1(bad) - 10 (good)	5	8	9	5	8	9
Doormen's attitudes 1-10	4	4	4	7	6	3
Atmosphere 1 - 10	5	7	9	5	8	8
Too hot/cold	Hot	Warm	Cool	Cool	Cool	Very Hot
Pleasure or pain	Pleasure	Ditto	<	<	<	<
Age range	18-40	18-40	18-30	18-30	18-30	16-30
Staff friendly 1-10	6	8	8	7	9	10
Service: fast/slow (F/S)	S	S	F	F	F	S
Toilets: clean/dirty 1-10	6	8	8	8	8	7
Glasses: clean/dirty	Clean	Cracked glass	Clean	Ditto	<	<
Choice of drinks	Good	Good	Very good	OK	OK	Very, very good
Dress: smart/casual	Smart	Dress up	Smart	Smart	Smart	Smart
Place to be: Y/N	Y	Y	Y	N	Y	Y
Drinker: rich/poor	Student	Anyone	Anyone	Student	Student/ Business	Younger Drinker
Disabled access: Y/N	No	Ditto	<	<	<	<
Staff attitude:	Good	Goo	OK	Good	Good	Not bad
Doormen hurry you?	N/A	Ditto	<	<	<	<
Parking	No	Ditto	<	<	<	<
Drug dealing	No	No	<	<	<	Yes
Gay bar	No	Ditto	<	<	<	<
ANY OTHER COMMENTS	Old, but popular	Very good club	Very hot club	-	Nice on a hot night	Place to be Good all round

198

Name of venue: NEWCASTLE	Julie's	Cooperage	Lennon's	Ram - Jams	Head of Steam	Chambers
Safety/Overcrowded	Yes	Quite busy	No	No	No	Yes
Price of drinks high/low	Average	Average	High	Average	Low	Average
Entertainment	Music	Ditto	<	<	<	<
Trouble: yes/no	No	Ditto	<	<	<	<
Décor: 1(bad) - 10 (good)	6	5	5	5	6	1
Doormen's attitudes 1-10	5	6	8	6	6	3
Atmosphere 1 - 10	7	4	Average	Quiet	Quiet	Rough
Too hot/cold	Very hot	Hot	Warm	OK	OK	Hot
Pleasure or pain	-	Good	OK	Pain	Pleasure	Pain
Age range	18-30	18-35	18-30	18-40	18-40	16-50
Staff friendly 1-10	7	6	6	6	6	5
Service: fast/slow (F/S)	S	S	F	F	S	F
Toilets: clean/dirty 1-10	6	6	7	6	5	3
Glasses: clean/dirty	Clean	Ditto	<	<	<	<
Choice of drinks	Good	Ditto	<	<	<	<
Dress: smart/casual	Smart	Smart	Smart	Casual	Smart	Anything
Place to be: Y/N	Sort of	No way	N	Y	N	N
Drinker: rich/poor	Anyone	Student/ Business	Student	Student/ Business	Student/ Business	Rough folk
Disabled access: Y/N	No	Ditto	<	<	<	<
Staff attitude:	Bad	Bad	7	7	5	2
Doormen hurry you?	N/A	Ditto	<	<	<	<
Parking	No	Ditto	<	<	<	<
Drug dealing	No	No	-	-	-	-
Gay bar	No	Ditto	<	<	<	<
ANY OTHER COMMENTS	Full of footballers	Not a place to be	Tends to play 80s music	Off beaten track	Off beaten track	Very low class, gets worse

Clubs 'n' Pubs Guide
Researcher: Neil Morris

Name of venue: NEWCASTLE	Kiss	Circus-Circus	Idols	The Vaults	Macey's	Robinson's
Safety/Overcrowded	Yes	At times	Yes	Quite long narrow	Yes	Very busy
Price of drinks high/low	High	High	Cheap before 8.30	High	Ditto	<
Entertainment	Music	Ditto	<	<	<	Best music Bigg M/ket
Trouble: yes/no	N	Y	N	N	N	N
Décor: 1(bad) - 10 (good)	6	7	6	5	5	6
Doormen's attitudes 1-10	4	2*	6	6	5	3
Atmosphere 1 - 10	Rough	Rough	Good	Good	Average	Excellent
Too hot/cold	Hot	Warm	Air condition	Hot	Hot	Very hot
Pleasure or pain	Pleasure	Pain	Occasional Wet T/shirt	Good music	OK	Pleasure
Age range	18-35	16-30	17+	17-30	Caters for young	17-35
Staff friendly 1-10	5	6	6	7	8	7
Service: fast/slow (F/S)	Slow	Fast	Slow	Fast	Slow	Slow
Toilets: clean/dirty 1-10	5	3	2	5	4	2
Glasses: clean/dirty	Clean	Ditto	<	<	<	<
Choice of drinks	Good	Ditto	<	<	<	<
Dress: smart/casual	Smart	Casual	Smart	Smart	Not too strict	OK
Place to be: Y/N	Y	N	Y	Y	Y	Y
Drinker: rich/poor	Anything anybody	A rough lot	All round	Ditto	<	<
Disabled access: Y/N	No	Ditto	<	<	<	<
Staff attitude:	5	2	OK	Friendly	Friendly	OK
Doormen hurry you?	N/A	Yes	No	No	No	Yes
Parking	No	Ditto	<	<	<	<
Drug dealing	-	-	-	-	-	-
Gay bar	No	Ditto	<	<	<	<
ANY OTHER COMMENTS	Good bar gets crammed	Rough, but good has lasers	Same every week sound worth a visit	-	-	Loud dance music!

Researcher: Neal Morris

Name of Venue: Newcastle	Pig & Whistle	Yell
Safety/Overcrowded	6	7
Price of drinks high/low	Average	Average
Entertainment	Y	Y
Trouble Yes/No	N	N
Décor: 1-10	7	8
Doormen's attitudes: 1-10	6	7
Atmosphere: 1-10	Excellent	Very good
Too hot/cold	Average	Very hot
Pleasure or pain	OK	-
Age range	17-35	17-40
Staff friendly 1-10	7	8
Service: fast/slow	Slow	Slow
Toilets: clean/dirty 1-10	5	6
Glasses: clean/dirty	Clean	Clean
Choice of drinks	Good	Good
Dress: smart/casual	OK	Smart turn out
Place to be: Y/N	Yes	Yes
Drinker: rich/poor	All round	All round
Disabled access: Y/N	No	No
Staff attitude	Very friendly	Very friendly
Doormen hurry you?	No	No
Parking	No	No
Drug Dealing	-	-
Gay Bar	No	No
ANY OTHER COMMENTS		80s bar good DJs, crowd, participate, Value.

The areas in the squares marked with a dash '-' indicate that nothing of this nature was sought out at that time.

* Circus –Circus is indicated here because in a rather petty manner one of the doormen spotted my researcher writing a young lady's details down, he came across and took the jotted down phone number off him and tore it up. Doormen are there to ensure patrons do not get molested in this sort of way, the offenders would be ejected. There was an incident in the bar, which was taken seriously enough to warrant me calling the club's management. A young woman had been spotted running out of the bar with blood pouring from her. I asked if they had recorded this incident and what had been done to ensure she was not seriously injured. They could not help me in this and nothing was recorded. Particularly after the Penny Laing incident it would have been nice to see venues being more vigilant and caring about such matters.

Parking facilities are available nearby, but not directly outside of the venues concerned. Disabled access is non-existent. Make of that what you will. Neil is in his mid 20s, straight and single.

Clubs 'n' Pubs Guide
Researcher: Glen Miller (that is his real name)

Name of venue: NEWCASTLE	Waterline	Flynn's	Chase	Jimmyz	Quilted Camel	Mather's
Safety/Overcrowded	No	Yes	No	No	Yes	No
Price of drinks high/low	High	High	High	Normal	High	High
Entertainment	Music	Ditto	<	<		
Trouble: yes/no	No	Yes	No	Ditto	<	<
Décor: 1(bad) - 10 (good)	8	5	Very good 10	8	6	8
Doormen's attitudes 1-10	8	5	8	7	7	8
Atmosphere 1 - 10	5	6	7	7	6	8
Too hot/cold	Norm	Hot	Cool	Cool	Hot	Cool
Pleasure or pain	Pleasure	Pain	Pleasure	Pleasure	Pain	Pleasure
Age range	20-50	20-40	18-40	18-50	17-35	18-50+
Staff friendly 1-10	8	10	10	10	8	10
Service: fast/slow (F/S)	Norm	Fast	Fast	Fast	Norm	Fast
Toilets: clean/dirty 1-10	7	3	Very Clean 10	8	7	9
Glasses: clean/dirty	Clean	Clean	Clean	Clean	Clean	Clean
Choice of drinks	Good choice	Norm	Very good	good	norm	Good
Dress: smart/casual	Smart	Ditto	<	<	<	<
Place to be: Y/N	Y	N	Y	Ditto	<	<
Drinker: rich/poor	Student/ Business	Students	Student/ Business	Ditto	<	<
Disabled access: Y/N	No	Ditto	<	<	<	<
Staff attitude:	Good	OK	Good	Good	Norm	Good
Doormen hurry you?	No	No	N/A	Ditto	<	<
Parking	No	No	No	Yes!	No	Yes
Drug dealing	No	Ditto	<	<	<	<
Gay bar	No	Ditto	<	<	<	<
ANY OTHER COMMENTS	You can drink out-side	Upstairs bar	Best bar on the Quayside	Good Music	2 floors	Big bar

Viv – and the Geordie Mafia
Researcher: Glen Miller

Name of venue: NEWCASTLE	Hanrahan's	Water Side	Akinside Traders	'Off Shore 44'	Pump House	The Quayside
Safety/Overcrowded	Yes	No	No	Yes	No	No
Price of drinks high/low	Low	Norm	OK	High	High	Very High
Entertainment	Music	Ditto	<	<	<	<
Trouble: yes/no	No	Ditto	No	<	<	<
Décor: 1(bad) - 10 (good)	7	8	7	5	3	7
Doormen's attitudes 1-10	6	7	6	7	8	8
Atmosphere 1 - 10	7	8	7	4	5	8
Too hot/cold	Cool	Cool	Hot	Hot	Cool	Cool
Pleasure or pain	Pleasure	Pleasure	OK	Pain	Pleasure	Very Good
Age range	17-40	18-40	18-50	18-45	19-50	20-50
Staff friendly 1-10	-	8	9	6	7	9
Service: fast/slow (F/S)	F	Norm	F	S	-	-
Toilets: clean/dirty 1-10	8	7	7	5	6	8
Glasses: clean/dirty	Clean	Ditto	<	<	<	<
Choice of drinks	Norm	Good	Good	Norm	Norm	Good
Dress: smart/casual	Smart	Smart	Smart	Casual	Smart	Smart
Place to be: Y/N	N	Y	N	N	N	Y
Drinker: rich/poor	Mixed	Business	Business	Students	Students	Student/ Business
Disabled access: Y/N	No	Ditto	<	<	<	<
Staff attitude:	Good	Good	Good	OK	Good	Very Good
Doormen hurry you?	N/A	N/A	No	N/A	N/A	N/A
Parking	At the back	No	No?	No	No	No
Drug dealing	No	Ditto	<	<	<	<
Gay bar	No	Ditto	<	<	<	<
ANY OTHER COMMENTS	View of the river from inside.	Good bar on water-side	Parking for about 7 cars	Needs refit	Nice bar	Very good Drink outside

203

Clubs 'n' Pubs Guide
Researcher: Glen Miller

Name of venue: NEWCASTLE	Legends Nightclub	Julie's Nightclub	Cooperage Nightclub	Idols	Vaults	Macey's
Safety/Overcrowded	Yes	Yes	No	Yes	Yes	No
Price of drinks high/low	Norm	Low	Low	Cheap in happyhour	High	OK
Entertainment	Music	Ditto	<	<	<	<
Trouble: yes/no	No	Ditto	<	<	<	<
Décor: 1(bad) - 10 (good)	9	2	1	5	7	7
Doormen's attitudes 1-10	4	7	4	6	8	5
Atmosphere 1 - 10	9	7	5	Good	Good	Good
Too hot/cold	Hot	Very hot	Norm	Air condition	Hot	Hot
Pleasure or pain	Pleasure	Pain	Pain	_	_	_
Age range	16-30	21-50+	18-40	17-45	19-40	17-30
Staff friendly 1-10	10	7	4	18	10	8
Service: fast/slow (F/S)	Slow	Norm	Norm	Y	F	N
Toilets: clean/dirty 1-10	8	4	4	2	5	5
Glasses: clean/dirty	Clean	Ditto	<	<	<	<
Choice of drinks	Very good	Norm	Norm	Good	Good	Good
Dress: smart/casual	Smart	Ditto	<	<	<	<
Place to be: Y/N	Y	Y	No!	N	Y	Y
Drinker: rich/poor	Young	All round bar	Students	Young	Mixed, all round bar	Students
Disabled access: Y/N	No	Ditto	<	<	<	<
Staff attitude:	Norm	OK	Bad!	Good	Good	Good
Doormen hurry you?	N/A	N/A	No	<	<	No
Parking	No	Ditto	<	<	<	<
Drug dealing	Yes?	No	No	_	_	_
Gay bar	No	Ditto	<	<	<	<
ANY OTHER COMMENTS	Best music in town	70s & 80s played all the time	Needs a refit	Bar staff wear bra & knickers	_	_

Viv – and the Geordie Mafia
Researcher: Glen Miller

Name of venue: NEWCASTLE	Lennon's	Ram-Jams	Head of Steam	Chambers	Kiss	Circus-Circus
Safety/Overcrowded	No	No	No	Yes	Yes	Yes
Price of drinks high/low	High	Low	Low	Low	OK	High
Entertainment	Music	Ditto	<	<	<	<
Trouble: yes/no	N	N	N	N	N	Yes
Décor: 1(bad) - 10 (good)	7	4	5	1-2	4	8
Doormen's attitudes 1-10	3	6	6	2	5	2
Atmosphere 1 - 10	Norm	Dead	Dead	Bad	Good	_
Too hot/cold	Cold	Cool	Hot	Hot	Hot	Very hot
Pleasure or pain	Pleasure	Pleasure	Pleasure	Pain	OK	Pain
Age range	20-50	20-50	20-45	16-35	18-40	16-30
Staff friendly 1-10	7	4	5	2	5	6
Service: fast/slow (F/S)	F	F	F	Norm	F	Norm
Toilets: clean/dirty 1-10	7	6	6	4	6	4
Glasses: clean/dirty	Clean	Clean	Clean	Dirty	Clean	Clean
Choice of drinks	Good	Good	Good	Bad	Good	Good
Dress: smart/casual	Smart	Smart	Smart	?	Smart	Casual
Place to be: Y/N	_	_	_	_	_	_
Drinker: rich/poor	Student/ Business	Students	Students	?	Mixed	Poor
Disabled access: Y/N	No	Ditto	<	?	?	No
Staff attitude:	7	6	7	3	5	4
Doormen hurry you?	N/A	Ditto	<	<	<	Yes
Parking	None	Ditto	<	<	<	<
Drug dealing	_	_	_	_	_	_
Gay bar	No	Ditto	<	<	<	<
ANY OTHER COMMENTS	Nice place for a quiet drink	Too quiet	Too quiet	Very rough bar	Thin long bar-nice	A lot of drunks dancing

205

Researcher: Glen Miller

Name of venue: NEWCASTLE	Red House	Bob Trollops	Dobson's	Bliss	Ikon
Safety/Overcrowded	Yes	Yes	Yes	No	No
Price of drinks high/low	High	Ditto	<	<	<
Entertainment	Music	Ditto	<	<	<
Trouble: yes/no	No	Ditto	<	<	<
Décor: 1(bad) - 10 (good)	3	2	4	6	9
Doormen's attitudes 1-10	4	4	3	4	4
Atmosphere 1 - 10	3	2	6	7	9
Too hot/cold	Hot	Hot	Very hot	Cool	Cool
Pleasure or pain	Pain	Pain	Pain	Pleasure	Pleasure
Age range	18-40	18-40	16-50	16-30	16-30
Staff friendly 1-10	8	7	7	9	10
Service: fast/slow (F/S)	S	S	Norm	F	F
Toilets: clean/dirty 1-10	4	5	4	7	9
Glasses: clean/dirty	Clean	Ditto	<	<	<
Choice of drinks	Good	Norm	Norm	Very good	Very good
Dress: smart/casual	Smart	Smart	Smart	Very Smart	Very Smart
Place to be: Y/N	Y	Y	Y	Y	Y
Drinker: rich/poor	Student	Student	Student	All sorts	All sorts
Disabled access: Y/N	No	Ditto	<	<	<
Staff attitude:	Good	Good	Good	Very Good	The BEST
Doormen hurry you?	N/A	Ditto	<	<	<
Parking	No	Ditto	<	<	<
Drug dealing	No	Ditto	<	<	<
Gay bar	No	Ditto	<	<	<
ANY OTHER COMMENTS	Bar looks like a shed from	Ditto	Needs a refit	90s club	One of the best clubs

206

Glen covered the same clubs and pubs as Neil, some were researched at different times to when the other was out and about. The research was carried out in August/September 1998. At times both Neil and Glen covered the same premises together. It was important to have both of their viewpoints as Glen is slightly older than Neil and is engaged. Both like a good time and are fairly easy going typical Geordie lads. Typical is defined as level-headed, but not over the top lager louts - more middle of the road. Neither of them are gay, but were asked to check if gays were catered for in the venues they attended.

Since none of the premises were noticeably frequented by gays it was decided to include a guide to gay clubs and pubs in Newcastle. I am not anti or pro gay, but we are bound to get somebody saying we should have covered these venues. The gay community on Tyneside spends equally as much money as you or I would if we went out and for that reason licensees do cater for them. In fact I know of quiet a few straight people who prefer to go to a gay club because there is so little trouble. Many thanks to Ken for his assistance in compiling the following guide.

Researcher: Ken

The Village	Rockshots	The Courtyard	Heavens Above	Rockies Bar	Barking Dog	Frog & Nightgown	The Powerhouse Nightclub
Toilets are bad	Gay/ Straight nights	More for older gays	Only open in evening	Disco bar	Upstairs and downstairs	Upstairs only	100% gay although straights do go
Waterloo St	Through the week it is gay	Situated at Marl- -borough	Above the Courtyard	South side Red- -hough Bridge	Sunday: Women only upstairs	Drag shows and karaoke nights	Waterloo Street
Has Gay information	Waterloo Street					Has gay information	Has Gay information
STRINGS 11 situated in Middlesbro -ugh and is visited by those from Newcastle	**PARADIS** is **-E CLUB** Middlesbr- ough, Teesside	Cassidy's Teesside	**State 52** Teesside			Waterloo St	

Just to finish off this chapter I have selected my own sort of pub come club for those of you visiting Tyneside. Whenever I make a return visit I usually always try to make a point of calling in to Harry Ramsden's although there is a one in Manchester I much prefer the one in Tyneside. For those of you from across the waters you will be familiar with the name since it is in just about most countries, except USA, they would not know what Fish & Chips were. American accent saying, "Here Chuck, here's your fries and er, erm?" "Oh, come on mom haven't you heard of Harry's fish and chips?"

The reason for me recommending Harry Ramseden's for those of you visiting Tyneside is that it caters for everyone's taste. I did not get a free meal for writing this. I was sitting there waiting for my Cod Fillet, which I have fought to get on their menu for the last couple of years and have succeeded in doing. The main excuse was that cod was a "dirty fish", said the waiter, when I enquired as to why it was not on the menu. The other excuse was something connected to vegetarians or something like that. Anyway it is on the menu, maybe thanks to me!

Whilst looking at the salmon coloured paintwork and the crystal chandeliers I realised that some kids were being entertained by a giant Postman Pat cartoon character. There was face painting for them as well. I can tell you on a Sunday when it is pissing down and your kids want to have some fun it is no laughing matter. OK you need a bit of money to take them there, but so what you only live to see them young once. There are specially designed seats for babies, yes I know they are called high chairs. For those of you who do not drive then you can have a beer or two at the bar or with your meal. If you smoke then that is no problem either, just go into the bar area.

The children's lay area has a door leading from the bar, which is a sore point as why should children have to go through the bar area which has cigarette/cigar smoke and as well as that why entice them to get familiar with the smell of booze. That is my first of two gripes gripe.

The toilets are so clean you could eat your Fish & Chips from the floor. They are checked, the toilets that is not the Fish & Chips, every few hours. The cleaner has to sign a form to say they have checked and cleaned it. There are disabled toilets although my second and final compliant is that the large door to the hallway that leads to those facilities would not be easy to open by someone sitting in a wheelchair.

There is a toffs section for those of you who want to sit a few feet higher than most on a raised dias. That section is surrounded by wrought ironwork with light oak handrails. It gives the impression of a ship's veranda. So while the kids are enjoying being entertained you can chomp through whatever you fancy, the staff are very friendly and genuinely happy to work there. I asked one of the staff right out if they would take a job somewhere else for more money, she replied "No." Because, "I enjoy working here and meeting different people."

Harry's place (plaice) have 'Opera & Chips' nights in their function room or you might want to go to a 'Murder & Chips' night with an all inclusive 3 course menu for £15.00. There is also a Harry Ramsden's 'Sing-a-long' every Tuesday afternoon (subject to change) and it is not just for senior citizens either. The resident entertainers sing the old favourites accompanied by a grand piano. The murder mystery evening might appeal to some of you who play that type of game, which you can buy in kit form I am told. The murder squad takes you through it all while the public can still enjoy their meal as normal in the main restaurant. Car parking facilities are right on the doorstep and if you do not want to get out of your vehicle they have a drive in for you to order from.

The Sounds of Frank Sinatra and the likes are regular ploys the staff use to attract customers, although what usually happens is that the public demand certain shows are put back on the menu for them if they were popular. Harry Ramsden's, Gateshead, Metro Park West, The Metro Centre, Gateshead. Worth calling to on a rainy day.

A new venture is soon to be seen at the Quayside, permission has been granted for a continental style open-air café with 18 tables. *Chase*, one of Newcastle's newest nightspots is to run the café which will open from lunchtime to 8.00 p.m. It is said that the council wishes to change the image of Newcastle so that it can become a regional capital in Europe. The venture is to be directly underneath the Tyne Bridge at Sandhill opposite Newcastle's Guildhall, which incidentally used to be the main courthouse. If you ever get the chance to look at the old dock you will see it looks different to modern ones as spikes surround this one!

Also in the Quayside area is the Live Theatre at Broad Chare. Children get in free on Sundays the reason being you are going to buy a brunch. For the opera buffs amongst you there is t he Opera Café in Market Street West, right next door to the God Father restaurant. The Opera stays open until 1.45 a.m., early finish by the sound of it.

Writers workshops do not fall into the category of clubs and pub, but what the hell, I have mentioned it now. Blackfriars Hall is supposed offers what is called a stimulating series of events at Morden Tower, New Bridge Street, Newcastle. I have not been there, but I am sure for those amongst you that need the stimulation of other writers then this is the place for you.

There are some real fancy named places where you can have a meal and a drink, but I only ever went to about four places in Newcastle and they were surprisingly cheap and the best I ever ate at. That is my opinion, but you have so much of a choice now that I would not like to recommend anyone particularly until I had them researched, which might be carried out for next year to be included in another book as a freebie for you. Any restaurant wishing to specifically have their premises checked out can get in touch with the publishers otherwise if that guide does come out an you are not in then do not complain. Also the same with any pub or club that has been left out and would like to be included in any forthcoming guide then please drop a letter to: care of (C/O) the publisher. Finally, *The Tuxedo Royale* on the Gateshead side of the Swing Bridge caters for all tastes. Our researcher was not allowed on board,T-shirt and jeans,"see I told to dress smart",him,"It's only the boat."

14

Paddy Conroy - Trial or Fiction

Paddy Conroy is from the West End of Newcastle, but his place of abode at present is in one of HM Prisons. He is serving an 11½ custodial sentence for kidnap, torture, false imprisonment and escaping from custody. He was once classed as one of Britain's most wanted men while he was on the run in the Cost Del Sol. On the face of it many people accepted that Paddy was just another West End hard man and he deserved his time just because his name happened to be 'Paddy Conroy.'

How did it all start, a feud existed between rival families in the West End of Newcastle, it had been going on for three years. The violence was escalating out of all proportions to a point where shootouts were happening as regular as clockwork. The law of the gun was the word on the street and there was no less than 20 shooting incidents between 1993 and 1995 in the Wild West End. Tit for tat actions were applied, as one family would do something the other would act in a more outlandish way. Some say it was a war of drugs, but the reason that seems to be true is a lack of respect for one another. David Glover (junior) was classed as an enforcer acting for Paddy.

David Glover was signed up as a fully qualified police informer in 1992. It came about because Glover had been arrested for an assault he made on Philip Abadom of South Shields. The attack on Abadom took place outside of the Oz nightclub in Shields, which resulted in him being left unconscious. Detective Sergeant Ian Smith of South Shields police contacted the then Detective Inspector Keith Felton (second in command to the Viv murder inquiry) who was attached to the Northumbria Police Drugs Squad. When Glover had been arrested for the assault on Abadom he had obviously lost his bottle and decided to 'grass' his way out of it. DCI Felton then met and signed up Glover as a registered police informer, which meant he could receive payment for passing on information to the police about the goings on

within the West End of Newcastle and any other related matter. From then
on Glover thought he was a law unto himself because of his new-found status
as a police informer, he thought he had a licence to commit crime.

Glover gave information to the police alleging drug dealing within the
Conroy family. He then became part of a police operation and was to deliver
some drugs to an address on Tyneside; permission had to be obtained by DCI
Felton to be able to put Glover on an undercover operation. That is the
beginning of Glover's relationship when he joined the other side. Karen
Young (suspect in the Viv murder) told me that Glover was one of the last
ones that she thought would have turned informer. That shows the instability
within crime groups and how unreliable it would be for anyone to think that
any member of their group would not change sides. That is the way it has
been through history and will continue to be, there is always someone who
will turn up out of the blue. Now the fun was only just beginning!

The Harrison family was considered to be one of the main antagonists of the
Conroy family. In February 1995 Alan John Harrison, 20 and his brother
Charles, 18, were out walking their Rottweiler dog in Rye Hill in the West
End of Newcastle. A man approached them; they argued, he pulled out a
gun, shot the dog dead and then proceeded to shot each of the brothers in
their legs. The wound to one of them, Charles, had been severe enough to put
him in intensive care on a ventilator.

A number of other members within the Harrison family had been shot at and
injured over the time, but none of them would make statements to the police
or give any indication as to what it was about. The man thought to have been
involved in the shootings of the Harrison's was said to be David Glover. He
had become feared because no one would make a police statement against
him therefore the law of the gun ruled. An alleged incident was that the
Harrison's family caravan had been set alight and in retaliation for this.
Glover was heard to have said that he would not be happy until he had done
as much time as his father, David Glover Snr.

The Harrison's had become a little bit pissed off at having their caravan
(trailer) set on fire and shot at, so they decided to make a reprisal attack.
They thought it was the Conroy family who were responsible so they were
intent on setting alight to Paddy's 'Happy House' lodgings on Newcastle's
Westmorland Road. James, 25, Joseph, 23 and Andrew Harrison, 21, all
from Elswick in Newcastle's West End donned hoods and were armed to the
teeth with firearms. This was really it; they were on the warpath and on a
mission. Nothing was going to stop them this time. Joseph went up to the
letterbox of the 'Happy House' lodgings that Paddy owned and was starting
to pour petrol through the letterbox, blamh! A shot was fired at his face
through the door. A resulting gun battle took place in the street; their guns
were blazing regardless of who got in the way. An innocent motorist had his
car sprayed with shotgun pellets, he crawled to safety. A child was forced to

run for cover. You may recall in an earlier chapter it was related how petrol had been poured through the letterbox of a pregnant mum of two in which she was murdered alongside her two children and babysitter as a direct result of petrol being poured through her letterbox and then set alight! All caution was thrown to the wind. One of those arrested alongside the Harrison's was a man called Billy Collier, 25. He was released because of insufficient evidence against him to tie him in to the shootings.

Collier had previously received a three year prison sentence for 'granny bashing' a 74 year old widow in 1988. The then 17-year-old Collier had robbed the frail pensioner as she walked home in the November darkness in 1987. She carried a torch and a hand held alarm. Collier saw his chance and pushed the woman to the ground and made a grab for her bag, the alarm was set off and Collier decided he was going to get that bag off her no matter what. He pulled and ripped the bag so viciously that the old lady was so badly injured causing her pelvis and arm to be broken, as direct result of Collier's attack on her. This caused the lady to have to sell her home so as to move nearer to her family. Can you imagine your dear old mother being set on by someone like Collier, his compassion was zero?

On top of this Collier had also been involved in burglary, going equipped for theft, attempted theft, TWOC, driving whilst banned and then on top of all of that he asked for a further eight offences to lie on file. What sort of a prison sentence do you think Collier received for all of these offences to which he offered a guilty plea? Whilst Collier was on bail he stole a car and went joyriding with a pal and two girls. He could not control the car in snow and crashed it. He was chased by a Sergeant from Albermarle Barracks and eventually caught after four miles of running. Collier received a three-year prison sentence and was banned from driving for 12 months for the lot. This is an important feature to remember for when we look at the prison sentence Paddy received for alleged kidnap and torture of Collier some years later.

Collier was not a clean-cut church going God fearing man. He was in the employ of the Harrison's and what incensed the Conroy family so much will be understood by quite a few of you reading this when you learn that the gravestone of Paddy's father was smashed and pieces of it were passed around those in the West End. What sort of lot were these people, doing such things like that! Consecrated ground was defiled and I learned from Paddy that there had even been an attempt to dig the body of his father out of the ground! The Conroy's believed that Collier was on a contract to dig up the remains. When you consider how cold and callous he was in robbing the old lady and breaking her bones, anything is possible. Collier denied attempting to do this.

Paddy said during the trail that it was not for them to inform the police and this sort of thing (grudges) was sorted out man to man. People were scared to come forward even after arrests were made, five people appeared in court as witnesses for the prosecution and all of them had to be given new addresses under the witness protection plan.

Collier was up to no good, being part of the Harrison's set up and as Paddy told me, "I spoke to one of the Bridgwater four who had taken a truth drug and passed with flying colours once he did this then everyone believed him and then (and only then) started to fight for him! I was hoping the same, as then the people representing me would listen to me, not the bollocks the police fill them with behind the scenes.

You're right about the newspapers, but they can only print what the police tell them and you can't sue them once you're dead, can you? Anything, as long as it sells newspapers. I've had the same treatment over the years and one thing I've never been is a gangster or ever portrayed myself as one. Of course once you've had this treatment everybody believes it. Judges read newspapers as well and it always guarantees you double the sentence you would have got if you ever end up in front of them and the police have won again.

My case speaks for itself. Collier has dug my dad's grave up, I'm convicted of torturing him, his only injury is a chipped tooth and I end up with 11½ years, ha, ha, joke ain't it, eh? They had to get me for something I didn't do though, so where's the glory in that. Sir Paul Condon is uncovering corruption within the South London Crime Squad dating back to the 70s and 80s and he's coming to Newcastle next to see what that lot have been up to. I bet that's got them worried, eh!"

Paddy says something about why he thinks Ray Mallon has really been suspended from Middlesbrough CID. The press gives one reason and Paddy suggests another reason. He believes that officers under the command of Ray Mallon, although without Ray Mallon's knowledge, are under what he says, "Serious investigation by HM Customs & Excise. They tried to fit me up with 4 tons of cannabis when I was on the run, customs were on to them straight away and they didn't get away with it." More of this is covered later on for the moment we go back to the Collier grave-digging incident.

The Harrisons' had their trial at York so as to avoid being treat unfairly by those with knowledge of them. They all denied being involved in the arson attack on the Happy Hostel lodging house, but were all found guilty. The charge was conspiracy to cause arson with intent to endanger life and two offences of possessing firearms. The prison sentences were dished out like there was no tomorrow and they were jailed for a total of 30 years, ten years each. It was said that they all broke down in tears upon hearing their sentences. Their trial preceded that of Paddy and Glover, the police allege that the following incident of torture took place.

Paddy and Glover kidnapped Collier, took him to a backyard and beat him up; a gas canister was then used to further beat up Collier. He was then taken to an address and accordingly tortured with a pair of pliers, which were used to snap one of his teeth. That is the police side of things, which on the face of it sounds reasonably plausible, a straight forward kidnap and torture wrap for a man they classed as West End's bad boy, Patrick James Conroy. That would be it, a cut and dried case... but hang on a minute, something stinks to the high heavens about this particular case! How come Glover, a registered police informer of the highest calibre goes down with Paddy. Surely this type of informer gets to walk off into the sunset as the camera zooms in on his smiling face?

Paddy told me, "I have never denied that I got Collier into my car that day and gave him a beating for what he had done to my family's graves, but that is all I done. Collier did get one of his teeth broken, but that happened after I had left. The beating I gave him wasn't a bad one, but it was enough to make him admit that he was being paid £3,000 to commit further attacks on the grave with a shovel and commit a much more serious act this time!!

It was then that I told him he would not be hurt anymore and to go home. I wanted him to explain to one of my brothers exactly what he had just admitted to me who was putting the money up for this to be done. Collier agreed to this so I then dropped him off at a friend's flat whilst I went to fetch my brother. It was then that a further attack on Collier took place whilst I was gone. I am the first person to agree that this should not have happened and I made it perfectly clear to the people responsible for it that it shouldn't have happened. Collier was there when I went mad with those who had carried out the second assault on him. I had left Collier with Glover and his mate.

When I had returned only Glover's mate was there, the owner of the flat (who took no part in the attack) and Collier. I dragged Glover's mate out of the flat and asked 'Why the fuck' had they done this, he said 'It wasn't intended and we had only intended to frighten him by putting the pliers on his tooth, but it had crumbled.' Collier is a smack head and did have rotten teeth as smack does rot your teeth, so I believe what is being said here is the truth. While I was being told this from Glover's mate, (unbeknown to me) somebody was phoning the police. Telling them Collier had his tooth snapped somebody that had been present when it had happened, considering it had only just happened a few minutes prior to my return it could only have been this. (Who was it that had called the police and knew of the attack and intimate details about it?)

It was then and only then that a police car drove past the end of the car park, looked in, spotted me sitting in the car shouting at Glover's mate and then drove on out of sight. The car came back parking up at the end of the car park to watch me. I then started up my car and intended to drive away out of the car park, past the police car and away. I was on my way out of the car park, about half way along it, when Glover came driving in, he past the police car on the way in to the car park. I pulled up next to him and wound down my window, he told me about the copper at the end of the car park and I replied 'I know' and I pulled away driving past the police car and away. Glover had to drive further into the car park to turn around before he could leave it. After I had left the car park and was driving up the bank away from it I spotted Glover in my rear view mirror leaving the car park. He past the police car and went the opposite way to me, down the bank. When I left the car park there were no other vehicles with me.

In evidence PC Noble said he spotted my car and a 4 X 4 Sierra parked outside this flat and he decided to sit and watch them. After a few minutes had passed he said that Davy Glover drove past him into the car park and drove up to my car and the 4 X 4 then turned around and drove back out giving him the thumbs up sign as he passed him, and away. PC Noble then said he sat a couple of more minutes waiting when he spotted me and three other men leave the flat and get into our cars. We are then supposed to have driven past him leaving the car park and went separate ways.

He then says he followed me. This is all lies and the radio transmissions prove it. As I drove up the bank away from the car park the 4 X 4 was going down the bank. This was just as Glover was driving out. The 4 X 4 had not left that car park with me like PC Noble says. In his evidence Glover said he worked for the police and his job was to collect information on me.

Glover said that at the time Collier was taken out of the shop (where he was kidnapped from) he was driving around the West End collecting information on me. He then went on to say that whilst he was doing this he was listening to a scanner and heard a transmission from PC Noble saying 'Conroy's car is in Brunel Walk' (the car park) and he (being it was his job to collect info on Conroy) decided to investigate.

Glover says he drove to the car park and on entering it passed PC Noble at the entrance he then drove to the end of the car park where my car and the 4 X 4 was parked outside the flat (where the torture of Collier took place) he said he knew he couldn't do much as PC Noble was already there, so he decided to just leave it to him and when passing PC Nobel on the way out of the car park acknowledged him and the situation by giving the 'thumb's up' sign."

Paddy claims that Glover lied for PC Noble by backing him up. Right then the best thing we can do is take a look at one of the police transmissions that took place on that day. Bear in mind Glover said he had nothing to do with the kidnap and torture and that he just so happened, conveniently, to be listening to a scanner transmission in which PC Noble mentioned Paddy. Glover says he went to investigate, Sherlock Holmes style no doubt, what was happening. Paddy is saying that PC Noble confirms what Glover alleged. I now leave it to you the reader to assess what was said in the police transmission that Glover says he heard and then decide if what Paddy says is fact or fiction.

In evidence given by Sergeant John Rochester (2909) of Northumbria Police Force who was stationed at the Central Area Operations room at Byker, Newcastle he attests that the following is a taped extract from F.W.I.N 920 of the 13ᵗʰ March 1994. Consul No: 12 attended to by Control Room Operator No: 9005, Mr Wallace.

Control Room
Q. Hello, police emergency.

Operator
Q. Newcastle connecting Tyneside

Control Room
Q. Thank you. Police emergency can I help you.
A. Hello, em, there's some people beating up somebody at Chesterfield road.

Q. Chesterfield Road,
A. Yeah.

Q. At the West End.
A. Yeah, the corner house.

Q. Ah, ha.
A. It's in the back yard. They've got a big canister and they're beating somebody with it and somebody's screaming.

Q. In the corner house at the top.
A. Yeah, on Chesterfield Road, it's right into the corner.

Q. What's your name please?
A. I don't really want to give my name.

Q. Right, so it's the top house,
A. On the corner in the back lane.

Q. Opposite the pub, opposite the pub is it.
A. No, Chesterfield Road end.

Q. Chesterfield Road
A. It goes from about the top of James Street,

Q. Um hm

216

A. You know where I mean, it's across from the top of James Street, sort of the house there, but it's in the back, by that little park.

Q. Right, OK, we'll get somebody out there.
A. OK, bye.

That was the end of that 999 emergency call and it was received at 12.15 Hrs and 57 seconds. The following 999 call was made by Mrs Collier only a minute earlier at 12.14 Hrs and 46 seconds. This shows that from what Mrs Collier says that Glover was there and what he says about running around the West End working for the police at that time was pure fabrication.

Control Room consul No: 9 PC1621 Trapp
Q. Hello, police Control Room
A. Aye, Mrs Collier here (address withheld). Em, my son, Billy Collier

Q. Um hm.
A. Er, a lad called Davy Glover and his mates have just took him away in a red Suzuki van.

Q. A red Suzuki van,
A. Ah ha.

Q. Any registration number love.
A. I don't know, but they're heading towards Benwell.

Further on in the call...

Q. Right, do you know where they're taking him.
A. They're taking him to do him over; I don't know where they're taking him.
Further on...

Q. Right, and it's Davy Glover and mates. OK.
A. Right, thanks very much now.

Mrs Collier was doing what any mother would do and who could blame her under the circumstances she as a mother must have felt at a loss to what she could do to help her son. For all she knew he could have been murdered by time anyone had acted.

The next entry given in evidence was a radio transmission made on City West Frequency. Timed at 13.09 Hrs and 30 seconds.

217

1113   LB

2792   Stand by, 1113

1310.21
Yeah, I've got the red Range Rover travelling west on Buddle Road, sorry, Westmorland Road, towards Buddle Road.

West on Westmorland Road, Roger.

PC 1113
Carring on west Buddle Road.

Reception hopeless, try again.

PC 1744
Yeah, I understand we have somebody following something on Westmorland Road.

1310.45
Yeah, treble one three is following a red Range Rover, at the moment travelling West on Westmorland Road, towards Buddle Road.

1310.54 (PC 1113)
1310.55 Yeah, he's following me at the minute, I think it's Mr Conroy.

PC 1744
Coming down from Benwell Lane, I'll stay in the area.

Roger, 1744

1311.07 (PC113)
Yeah, he's turned into violet close.

Some unconnected transmissions are covered in the evidence; we skip that part and continue with the Collier event...

1312.40 (PC113)
Yeah 1113's got the Rang Rover making off, Atkinson Road towards Adelaide Terrace.

Roger, 1113 2366

DC 2366
Talk through off quickly

Yes go ahead.

DC 2366
See if you can find an ARV (Armed Response Vehicle) in the area of Foxtrot, Foxtrot Tango, believed driven by the Conroy crew, well worth a stop and check out, possibly in company with a white Montego, over.

Continued...

1313.37 PC 3129
Yes, I'm following Patrick Conroy in a Range Rover, he's failing to stop on Benwell Lane in a Range Rover, Hotel 707 Whisky, Romeo Sierra.

A red Range Rover, Hotel 707, Whisky, Romeo, Sierra, what's his location now.

1313.53
Benwell Lane, towards Whickham View and he's gone through a red light on Adelaide Terrace.

Benwell Lane towards Whickham View, failing to stop, going through red lights, any traffic resource.

1314.06
Yes, he's wrong side of the road now, wrong side of the road, overtaking two cars.

Wrong side of the road overtaking cars, Tango 2680

Yeah go ahead, Armstrong Road now, making our way towards, keep us updated.

3129

1314.21
Yeah, were approaching Whickham View, and he's continuing west bound.

West Whickham View, traffic's coming up behind you, keep us updated.

3129

1314.28
Yeah, going to his home address which is Denton Road, Denton Road. Negative he's taken a left, left, onto Broadmead Way, he's travelling South on Broadmead Way.

Left on the Broadmead Way travelling south. Received.

1314.43
Continuing Broadmead Way, middle of the road down Broadmead Way and he's going left, left, left, onto Woodstock Road.

Left onto Woodstock Road.

1315.01
Travelling towards Armstrong Road.

1315.08
The rear door's open and he's continuing middle of the road, Woodstock Road approaching Armstrong Road now.

Approaching Armstrong, traffic's attending the scene if you keep us updated.

1315.23
Aye, he's Armstrong Road, approaching Roundabout with Deleval Road, Armstrong Road now.

1315.47
And he's now left, left, left onto Deleval Road.

Left onto Deleval Road, heading north Deleval Road.

1316.01
Travelling once more towards Whickham View, Benwell Lane Sorry, Benwell Lane, approaching Benwell Lane now.

1316.13
Straight out, failed to stop at the give way, he's right onto Benwell Lane, Travelling east bound.

Right, Benwell Lane, heading east Benwell Lane.

1316.24
Continuing East

Not wanting to bore you too much we move on to India 99 (Police helicopter).

India 99

1318.39
Yeah, travelling to this detail, keep the locations coming please.

Continued...

1319.15
From India 99, ETA (Estimated Time of Arrival) about a minute or so.

3129
1319.20
And we're off road now, we're travelling on the, on a path towards the industrial estate

Continued...

1319.59
He's practising his four wheel driving.

Continued...

1744
1320.28
I'm behind the vehicle, west bound Scotswood Road, by the Hydraulic (pub). Through a red light, west bound, Scotswood Road.

Continued...

Traffic behind the vehicle. Received.

1321.40
Now wrong side of the road.
..........................Dead end.

Continued...

1744
1322.20
Aye, he's going up the road again down towards the BMX track.

Continued...

1322.43
Yeah vehicle stopped.

Vehicle location, stopped.

1322.48
Woolsington Walk, straight off Woolsington Walk.

Vehicle stopped Woolsington Walk.

LB Can we confirm we've got him?

1113 Have you got him, the driver?

1113
1323.03
Yeah, confirmed

Driver detained, received, take it there's nobody else.

India 99.

India 99,

India 99
1323.12
Vehicle stopped, no runners, three units in attendance, I'll give you a better update shortly.

That's received 99.

DC2366 said that the 'Conroy crew' drove the vehicle. In fact as you will now note, when the vehicle was eventually stopped there was only one occupant! PC1113 had earlier requested a vehicle check on Paddy's vehicle and also a one on the vehicle Glover was driving. Why would a police constable be checking the vehicle of a known informer if he felt he was not involved? Ten pages of intelligence came up on the Range Rover.

The police backed Glover up to the hilt in the trial, saying he was seen driving around the West End of Newcastle like he says he was. It meant he could not have been involved in the torture if you are to take the police side of events. What though of Mrs Collier, surely her word must mean something, she feared for the life of her son and had to go against the grain by calling the police. In a moment of stress she had to act fast, which she did it would be in her son's interest to tell the truth of what had happened so the police could extract her son from the position he was in.

Whilst awaiting trial both Glover and Paddy escaped from custody whilst being taken from prison to Magistrates' Court in a taxi minibus. The minibus travelled along Gateshead's Felling bypass when the handbrake was pulled on and the vehicle slewed to a sudden stop. Glover later admitted in his trial that he instigated the escape.

What you have to consider here is the lack of police security around the vehicle taking the pair to court. Such a high profile case would attract a lot of attention and security would be stepped upped as a matter of course, yet here we have the pair going to court in a taxi! Paddy sat on his seat in the min-bus being egged on by Glover to make a move and it was only by Glover's cajoling did Paddy make the effort to escape. Paddy told me, "At one point in Glover's trial he changed his plea and plead not guilty to 'escaping', on the grounds that the police had been involved in it, but he changed his plea to guilty after a conference (ordered by the judge after the not guilty plea by us) with his barrister. Answer me this if you can, Steve, Glover has a much bigger criminal record than I do. He has served a lot more prison sentences than me, this escape was instigated by him and not me! It was his fifth escape, this was my first and last. He admitted under oath that he would escape again if the opportunity arose although he received twelve months less than me he had more charges than me, i.e. assaults on screws, section 18 wounding with intent on a copper, how is it considering all of this that I am a double category 'A' prisoner and he, glover, is a category 'B'??????????????

If you read the prison officers statements who were involved in guarding us when we escaped you will find that I had no intention of even leaving my seat on that bus, until Glover egged me on. Glover is being rewarded for his actions with a cat 'B' jail while I'm given the status of a terrorist!"

Paddy went on to tell me that he was due to have his category 'A' status reviewed, but the main objection to keep him high risk is violence used against a prison officer although it was Glover who assaulted a prison officer during their escape, yet Paddy gets punished for that. That surely stinks to you the reader? Paddy went on to tell me that he felt every solicitor and barrister he has had have been out to stop the truth coming out, he excludes his present solicitor from this. Whatever Paddy thinks of his legal teams is his opinion, I always look for the truth and no matter what will always bring you as close to that as possible. I do not take the piss out of you the reader and pay you homage by buttering up your toast with a load of lies that some of you might want to read. For those of you who like to unravel things then you will know what I am on about here.

Paddy says he has good cause for his opinions and he says, "What went on between Glover and the police cannot be changed if it can ever be proved about certain things that went on between Glover and the police then they're in trouble in more ways than one. They can never allow Glover's evidence to be discredited because they have not finished with him yet. And they need him as reliable-a-witness as possible in my opinion. I've got good cause for this opinion.

When our co-accused and I were speaking to Glover at court he told us everything that had went on between him and the police. One of the conversations we had was about our escape. He told us that the police knew about the escape because he had notified them four days before it happened. Prison officers overheard the conversation and immediately notified Holme House (HM Prison Holme House) the prison from whose officers we had escaped custody from. An investigation into the escape was to take place and as far as I'm aware I heard they weren't happy about one of their officers getting hurt. Since then I have acquired evidence that proves that the authorities knew the escape was taking place and the evidence actually points towards them for actually instigating it."

What Paddy says here has been somewhat edited to cut out libellous remarks although had I the actual evidence that Paddy spoke of then I would without hesitation have included that herein. The difficulty is that all of Paddy's actions have to be overseen of by the police, who he sees, who he writes to. He says he has 100% proof of certain things and he mentions Ray Mallon's suspension, if you are not familiar with whom Ray Mallon is by now, tough shit! He thinks Ray's suspension is connected to his plight and the escape, as Glover was captured in Middlesbrough. No, he does not mean that Ray Mallon organised his escape, so put the telephone down, no need to call your solicitor yet, Ray. Paddy says he could be wrong here about his guesswork of what Ray's suspension was over, what leads him to this conjecture. Funnily enough when I was corresponding with Paddy and he wrote saying all coppers are bent I mentioned Ray Mallon and how he stood for righteousness amongst the police, Paddy wrote back and said I could be right. For Paddy to write that of a police officer shows how even the criminals look up to Mallon and, although begrudgingly, they admire him, somewhat from afar.

Paddy says, "Two officers directly under his command have already been suspended from duty by a trial judge over certain goings-on and he was their boss. The evidence available is a transcript of an audiotape that was sneaked into an interview room at Belmarsh high security unit by Phil Berriman and that transcript proves they got Glover to organise that escape and get me out because they wanted me to frame with further charges. The conversation recorded is with Berriman, his police handler and another officer."

Paddy suggests that a letter from Tyne Bridge Labour MP, David Clelland, is the key to why the police went to town on him and tried to have him locked up for as long as possible? Paddy says, "By hook or by crook." I have that original letter that Paddy refers to. Paddy: "A major internal investigation took place into police activities just prior to my arrest for this, although the outcome of that investigation came to nothing, as always, because the Chief Constable conducting it claimed he could not take the word of a minor officer against a very senior officer. It still resulted in a lot of officers concerned in that inquiry taking retirement. Some of these officers were of the highest rank and the police hold me personally responsible for instigating this inquiry! And rightly so."

The letter signed by David Clelland Labour MP goes as follows:

13 February 1997

Dear Denise

Following your visit to my advice surgery on Saturday 8th February. I have made some enquiries about the issues we discussed.

As I suspected the police will not discuss the details of who are or who are not assisting them now, or who have assisted them in the past and I have no power to insist on this information being provided to me. However, it has been suggested to me that it may have been stated in open court during the trial that Mr Conroy was not a police informer and I have asked for extracts from the transcript to look into this.

I have passed on the correspondence you gave me to the Home Office together with your concerns. As you know my colleague Mr Mudie MP has referred Mr Kelly" letter to the Lord Chancellor" office for investigation of it" contents.

Yours sincerely

David Clelland MP

Paddy told me that he found it an impossibility to explain fully what went on in his trail because it was so "full of twists and turns" and he would doubt I would be able to grasp it, therefore he would "like to speak to me face to face because he knows he could explain it properly. All of Paddy's mail is photocopied and forwarded to the police. All of his visits are listened to and watched. All of the moments of intimacy with his personal visitors are lost on a thick screen between them. His family has had to bear up to it as best they can. What a shame some of you may say, especially since Paddy is a convicted prisoner. I say, what of Paddy's children? They are not criminals, what of his wife as well?

Paddy's plight was brought to my attention by one of the researchers working on the *Viv (Graham) – 'Simply the Best'* book. I started writing to him and as always mail was sent via Recorded Delivery with Advice of Delivery. That way mail could be kept a watch on and so it became a bit of a difficulty for Paddy to get mail directly from me because some of it was withheld because of the circumstances of his incarceration and the fact he was double category 'AA'. The prison authorities were a crafty lot because you see they asked Paddy to sign for Recorded Delivery mail and once he had done this they would not let him see the contents of the letter. On paper it looked like he had actually received the mail, but in actual fact he had not! The prison regime had covered their arses by having his signature on their documents. Paddy got wise to their sneaky ways and he refused to sign for any letters sent this way, in fact I have an unopened letter that was returned to me from HM Prison at Full Sutton, when he was an inmate there. I have proof of this in still having the unopened, returned letter that was sent back with a covering letter from Full Sutton prison

I wrote to a number of high-ranking people concerning this breach of basic human rights. I was not writing to Paddy to ascertain what his crimes were, that was common knowledge, just go into any pub on Tyneside and mention his name; people will raise an eyebrow in acknowledgement of having heard his name. I wrote to the Director General of prisons, Richard Tilt and he very kindly intervened as well as the then Minister for Prisons, Joyce Quin MP. Richard Tilt explained that certain rules applied to prisoners, but after careful and further consideration it has been agreed to allow Mr Conroy to correspond and to receive correspondence from me. Every letter I forward to Paddy contains a reference to the Richard Tilt consideration letter.

To further hamper Paddy he has been moved from HM Prison Full Sutton to Whitemoor and again to his current prison after he was attacked in HM Prison Whitemoor. I wrote directly to the Chief Constable of Northumbria Police Force to be allowed to visit Paddy in mid October 1998. I received a reply saying I would have to apply in the first instance directly to the prison governor of the prison that Paddy was in. I did so immediately, it is now nearly one calendar month since I wrote directly to the prison governor of Paddy's prison, up to now I have not received even an acknowledgement. That is not of a surprise to me and now confirms what I suspected. It is too late to include anything he could tell me face to face into my investigation into police corruption, but not too late for inclusion of certain things in future books connected with crime. I am allowed to correspond with Paddy because this matter concerns serious representation about his unfair treatment at his trial and his unsafe conviction, the process of justice, the penal systems intervention into meddling with inmates' mail and their rights. Correspondence was withheld on eight occasions under the terms of the standing order in force governing Paddy's mail. Paddy tried to Record his outgoing mail to me, the excuse given to him for that failure was the post office had ran out of recorded delivery slips. I have not checked that one out yet as I have not any post office that has ran out of such slips?

Incidentally after Paddy was attacked in HM Prison Whitemoor rumour had gone around that Paddy was on a life support machine and worse, even that he was dead. Paddy is still here and his constant life of harassment by being moved about and held in such secure conditions must be classed as mental torture. Regardless of that he has a strong resolve to see this matter through because he says he has such lovely children.

When Paddy escaped from the mini bus in Gateshead it was said that he made his way to the Quyaside in Newcastle whilst Glover was alleged to have laid low in a caravan at Whitley Bay. Two vehicles were involved in assisting them to get away from the scene of the breakout, if you could call stepping from a mini bus a 'breakout'? Paddy is though by police to have left the country after obtaining a false passport, using someone else's birth certificate and a switched photograph. He travelled to France by Ferry and then on to Spain where he had contacts in the holiday resort of Benalmedena. A number of sightings in Spain soon got detectives on his tail like bloodhounds. This lot was certainly crying for his blood after what had happened back in blighty. The Costa Del Crime is a hotbed of criminals on the run from all around the world and Paddy was no different, he had to keep on the move.

Four months after an international arrest warrant was issued Paddy was captured in an armed police operation at Malaga Airport. Glover was still on the run for some two months after Paddy was detained in a Spanish prison whilst extradition proceedings were going on. It was not just a case of him being whisked back to his cosy prison cell in the UK; formalities had to be entered into.

Paddy tells me what the police did to him in Spain; "They didn't want me hanging around over there fighting the extradition as I was holding the trial up. All the media (radio, newspapers, television, etc.) made it big news, how Britain's No: 1 most wanted criminal had been arrested. The it was said that I was wanted for back in Britain, 'He's a rapist, who, when finished with his victims pulls their teeth out with pliers.' So because of these lies I wasn't a beast, I was a bad beast! The trouble that caused for me whilst awaiting extradition in a Spanish prison is nobody's business, I barely got back to Britain alive." But he did, in spite of this.

227

Remember Phil Berriman mentioned previously (page 224), he was accused of masterminding Britain's biggest cannabis haul, at that time, he accused Paddy of forcing him into it when he appeared in court charged with drug trafficking. Berriman, 36, a scrap dealer from Stockton, Cleveland told the court that Paddy threatened to kill him and his children if he did not do the trip from North Africa.

Customs officers seized £11M worth of cannabis; a big fuck off block that weighed 3.7 tonnes was found on board Berriman's 42-foot schooner the *Melanie* in September 1994. Paddy was the man Berriman identified in court as the man that threatened him. Paddy told me what went on, "When the captain of that boat secretly taped two Teesside detectives in HM Prison Belmarsh SSU (Special Secure Unit) the taped conversation made it perfectly clear that I was supposed to have been fitted up with those drugs, it also made it perfectly clear that the police concerned in that fit up had organised (through Glover) my escape in order to do that fit up. The tape proves it." Paddy then goes on to say it could have been about the time that Ray Mallon was in charge of things, but in defence of 'Robo Cop' I have dug out his antecedents from *Viv (Graham) – 'Simply the Best'* and the extract after this shows where Ray was stationed and so it could not have been down to the time he was boss of Middlesbrough CID.

'Ray Mallon's presence from 1977-78. Cleveland, though, drew back Mallon like a salmon back up the river it was spawned from and he served in the Regional Crime Squad. His talents were passed on to cadets in the Cadet Training Department for a short while and then he joined the CID (Criminal Investigation Department) at South Bank, Langbaugh and served as a detective inspector from 1989-1992. House burglaries had dropped by thirty three per cent in a two-year period when Mallon's strategies were employed there.

Mallon's talents were used in his next appointment, which was as head of Crime Strategy at Hartlepool where he would apply more skills than any water polo match had ever seen. Since he took his post in October 1996 as Detective Superintendent at Middlesbrough the crime figures had their arses...' So, again I must ask Ray to put the phone down as he has no need to call his solicitor with regard to any of the above. I know Ray is a whiter than white character, but as for his junior officers there is no doubt that some of them could have had an involvement prior to him taking over as their boss. Paddy went on to say, "It was two detectives that had been secretly taped and later suspended from duty by the trial judge (at Berriman's drug trial) after the tape was produced during their evidence in that drugs trial and I believe it's quite possible that this is the true reason that Robo Cop has been suspended and not the bollocks of a reason the newspapers are giving."

That is a very interesting story, but it does not tie in with Ray Malon and as Paddy says it is only 'possible' that this is the real reason Ray has been suspended, over the actions of his junior officers. That could have been true had Ray of been in charge in 1995, but that was not so. Although Paddy would not have known this and therefore would be right to believe that the suspension could have been linked to what he says. Bear in mind though that Ray was brought in after all of this had taken place, what happened to Ray's predecessor? Someone had to be in charge of those officers in the case that Paddy mentions. (Read Charrington case near the end of this chapter.)

A formal complaint by Paddy was lodged with the Police Complaints Authority (PCA) against Northumbria Police Force (NPF). The complaint alleged corruption within NPF. When this sort of serious complaint is lodged then you would expect another force area to look into the complaint, especially since it is the police who investigate the police. Two officers from, yes you have guessed, Northumbria Police were sent to sort the matter out, Paddy, not surprisingly, refused to see the officers he says, "I didn't waste my breath on them and refused the visit." Here Paddy is, with what he says is 100% proof that there is corruption within NPF and they send officers from within that force to interview him, can you blame him for refusing the interview?

Whilst Paddy was at his trial he says, "He (Glover) asked me downstairs if I would admit I was in the flat when Collier got his tooth snapped, he told me I could say that Collier's tooth got broke by a punch and not pliers, he says to me 'You've admitted beating him up anyway, so you've nowt to lose?' I told him the rope was found there that he and his mate had used it to tie Collier up with, forensics prove it. The pliers were lying next to the rope and bits of his tooth were found on the floor '…and you want me to put myself in that flat when I had nothing to do with it, fuck off!' Glover then said 'Well, I've already said what I've said and have to stick to it.'

We then had to go our separate ways, Steve. I can't go into some of the things regarding Viv's murder as you're basically investigating it. My only hope now of proving that Glover helped fit me up is if the police charge people with his (Viv) murder and I'm called as a witness to explain what went on between the police and Glover. It may spread some light on my own plight as all this dealing went on at the very same time that Glover told me and our co-accused everything! Right down to the small details and my guess is that charges will be laid before Glover's parole date comes up. Glover says he was to be charged with accessory to murder and go QE (Queen's Evidence) on others. He was also telling us what he was going to spend the reward money on he was getting, funny fucker ain't he?"

In Paddy's trial certain evidence was not presented to the jury. The judge under PII (Public Immunity Interest) withdrew certain evidence. Paddy's defence team has not seen this evidence which is a transcript of a police transmission. I have two transcripts, but as Paddy says it is a one that was in the middle of these two that was withdrawn on the orders of the trial judge.

I have tried to ascertain what is on that transcript with regards to what was said that was so top secret that the trial judge ordered it to be taken out. How then, if a judge suppresses evidence and the defendant says it is the crux of his plea of innocence can the trial be classed as above board? Can anyone remember Asil Nadir of 'Polypeck' fame? He was charged with a multi £M fraud, he gave an MP by the surname of 'Mates' a watch with the inscription, 'Don't let the buggers get you down', engraved on it. He was on bail, guaranteed by a few million quid's worth of sureties when he pissed off to Southern Cyprus, I believe. What was the reason for him fleeing the country, it was because the police had seized all of his defence evidence in raids on his premises. He said that he could not expect a fair trial because the prosecution now had advance details of his defence and he did not stand a chance to clear his name. That is the basis of my pursuing Paddy's case as it seemed the man did not stand a chance whatever action he took to clear his name the prosecution were always one step ahead, Glover was the common denominator.

In Paddy's own words, "Janet Anderson was not interviewed regarding the inquiry." What Paddy refers to here is covered in more detail later on, but it is included because it will make what he says after this seems out of context. It is with reference to an inquiry the Court of Criminal Appeal ruled must be conducted into claims of jury-rigging. "It was her second affidavit that contained all the details that went missing. The solicitor acting for me at that time was Paul Robinson of Goldkorns Solicitors, London. I wasn't happy about the affidavit going missing and believed he was involved in it going missing so got rid of him after the appeal. He told my family at the appeal who were at the appeal that he had only ever seen three people get blatantly shafted by the appeal courts in the whole of his career and mine was one of those three.

At trial my barrister told me 'You do realise you're getting shafted', but what I didn't realise then was that he was in on it. One of my co-accused's barristers told me, 'Paddy you're not at court today for Collier, you're here for your reputation.' That was Glen Gatland, I said to him, 'I'm being railroaded again', and he replied 'I see you've noticed.' I doubt he would admit this now, but it was said in front of all my co-accused. This is what goes on though, Steve, and your everyday people don't realise it, wouldn't want to believe it; good old British justice and all that, ha, ha.

Collier never got charged with the gravestones because my family never made a complaint about it so no charges were possible, even if Collier had admitted it, he denied it in court anyway. The police were holding charges concerning the firebomb attack on the Happy House against him until he gave that evidence against me. Once the prosecution was finished with him he was notified he was not to be charged with it before he left the court building. The police denied that the 'Happy House' was being used to pressurise Collier, but if this wasn't the case then why did they wait until he had given his evidence before he was told he wasn't to be charged?" What Paddy says here does seem surprising especially since the Harrison brothers had been weighed off some time earlier and all received ten year prison sentences. It is not usual for a potential co-accused to await the ending of a trial he is a witness in for the police.

Paddy: "Collier's wife was with him at the shop (where he was kidnapped from) when we drove away with him and she only knew Glover. She knew what he had done and was worried so she ran to his mam's telling her that we had took him away, she could only name Glover though as she didn't know me. Collier's mam then rang the police, now think about it, the only name the police have is Glover's so why did PC Noble come after me and let Glover leave? (The car park.) Glover was not only collecting information in on me he was also out to set me up for them! Glover was the person who had done this and I believe it Was Glover who then, after doing this, then made that phone call tot he police telling them Collier's tooth had been done, it couldn't have been anyone else. This phone call was made before even I had found out what had happened. And I think on, those radio transmissions? It could also be found, a message telling PC Noble not to arrest Glover? That could well be another reason why they will not hand them over. (The transcripts withdrawn under rule PII by the trial judge.)

Collier and his girlfriend had made statements saying Glover had done this. Glover and Collier hated each other and the police couldn't do anything about these statements because they had been made!"

Hang on a minute, Paddy is saying that Collier and his girlfriend made statements that name Glover as one of the kidnappers and as the pliers torturer! Let me get this right for a minute...Collier is the one who is tortured and he identifies the perpetrator as Glover, the statements stand and therefore Glover has to be arrested for the crime and charged, the police are powerless to get Glover off the hook by virtue of theses statements. If that is not some sort of grounds for a re-trial I do not know what else is, I take that back as I do actually know some more reasons, which we will go into, soon.

Paddy continues, "What the police did though was produce information that Glover had given them concerning Collier prior to this incident and it was Glover's defence that Collier and his Girlfriend had lied against him because they knew Glover had been grassing on Collier." Paddy is claiming here that this information had been concocted by the police to help Glover.

Paddy: "The PII will prove that I had only just drove into that car park and could not of been present when Collier got his tooth snapped, like the CPS claimed. They said I was rolling about the floor laughing when it was happening, giving out orders for it to be done. This is bollocks and they know fine well it is. Would I be prepared to take a truth drug if I were in anyway connected in that act, either before or after the fact? Of course I wouldn't! They know this and could not afford to let me take any truth tests because then people will believe me. And they can't have that can they?"

Paddy was advised to secure appeal court rulings whereby people who have been provoked beyond what is accepted as reasonable. Paddy says that since he is not guilty of snapping Collier's tooth and had they said to him that he was guilty because he was there at the start of the caper that extended on to Collier being the victim, trussed up for torture, whether Paddy was aware of it or not then he would have accepted that. But that was not the case he tells me. On that basis he is correct not to pursue what I had actually earlier advised him, apologies given. The prosecution's case was that Paddy was present, giving the orders out for it to be done, which of course is not true. In his own words he says, "They would have to string me up by the neck before I would admit to something I haven't done. It is a out of time for me to appeal against sentence, so that's out of the window." Paddy is right here though; he has no reason to wish to appeal against sentence, as it is against conviction and conviction alone that Paddy seeks a whole new trial.

One thing is for sure, Paddy is right about it being full of twists and turns, but I am here to unravel it all out for you and I to comprehend. After reading all of the evidence I have been forwarded and other documents I know that Paddy should not be in prison under the conviction he received. Had he been pursued on the kidnap and assault charges then, yes that would have been fair dos and no one could argue with that. There is so much conflicting material within this chapter that you would not be blamed for becoming confused at times and I could be accused of all sorts of things by the press, but one thing is for sure you always get the truth here.

With regard to the fact of another matter I was pursuing, Paddy was able to confirm that Viv had been to Blackpool and had a fight in which he took second prize! This ties in with what Gary Ward alleges. The difficulty is that I am hampered by red tape and at this stage I can only leave it to those who are professional enough to handle such things, although I will still pursue the matter privately for Gary Ward. With regards the pursual of corruption within Northumbria Police Paddy says, "If you are pursuing corruption in Northumbria Police and are wanting to visit me regarding that matter then I can't see what excuse the Chief Constable can come up with to stop you visiting otherwise he's condoning the corruption, correct? He should be thanking you and helping you in your cause in every way." Well the fact is I still wait to get to see Paddy.

I have some personal experience of what the police can do and here is a short story to confirm that. In 1995 I set up CAPTIVE (Complaints Against Police The Independent Victims Enterprise.) What that was all about was, that a number of complaints made against the police, that were justified, by the victims of police wrongdoing had been dealt with by the police. My argument was how could the police investigate the police? Therefore it was my aim to challenge this type of procedure where someone would make a complaint to a police inspector and in the end the inspector would talk the complainant out of taking further action, thus the complaint went no further than this friendly chat. My intention was to become a voice for the weak, a voice for those that could not be heard.

I had some 10,000 leaflets printed and had them distributed around housing estates advising people of this new scheme where any complaint against the police could be submitted through CAPTIVE and they would take up the complaint on their behalf. Complaints of a hostile nature obviously would not be considered, as CAPTIVE was not intended as a tool for those that were out to seek their own revenge on the police. Credibility would have to be built up. The feedback was substantial enough to let me know that there was a need for this type of service, of course there were those that thought the scheme was loony and 'Why would people need such a service when the police never did any wrong.' I agreed with them, yes. 'Why' was the part I agreed with, that was all?

Anyway to cut a boring story short I just did not follow through and did not have the time to pursue the matter and it lay on file, nevertheless it is there as a landmark. So I thought anyway, until two researchers and I were arrested on deception charges, if you do not know what it was all about by now then you have not been reading any of the books relating to crime that I have written.

A big story was to have been covered on that side of things in a national Sunday Newspaper, a one with a big fancy name. The story had been done and the details submitted to the journalist who wanted proof of all he asked. The national newspaper contacted the police with regard to the nature of our arrest and so on, but you see somewhere along the lines the police slipped in that I had ran CAPTIVE and that put me down as some sort of activist. The story was dropped like a hot potato! Faster than shit off a stick on a summer's morning.

What CAPTIVE had to do with the story, about to be published, was as far away as possible, yet the police just dropped that one in there against me. SO you see I know how these things work. The reporter asked if I would be pursuing an action against the police over my arrest? My reply was that I was not above the law and the police were only doing their job, in that instance. Any actions would be against those who actioned the complaints against me. Those companies are to be pursued with regard to holding up the publishing of the last book, which has had a knock on effect of holding up this book, which is behind by the same amount of time the first book was. That is a direct result of the complaints made by national food companies to a central administrative body that check out fraudulent complaints made against the food and drinks industry in this country. Here are just a few of the names of the companies that I investigated with regard to their lack of quality control. Nescafe, McDonalds, Scottish Courage (Castaway), Asda food stores, Safeway, Hamlet cigars (Benson & Hedges Ltd), Carling Black Label, The Body Shop and many, many more. Some of them called in the police. Just imagine there you are sitting down to a meal and looking forward to a nice drink, something spoils it and the whole night's fucked up because of it. One of the items in the meal caused you to feel ill. Do you write and complain about the product or take it on the chin and avoid that product like the plague? Well considering some of the companies called the police in on me for doing exactly that, then you should be in your rights to call the police and make a complaint against, say, Castaway, because the bottle has rust around the neck, which you might have only noticed when taking a few guzzle straight from the bottle. The rest of the nigh is finished and you might feel ill, what would you do?

So you see for doing that I am assumed to be an activist. What of Amnesty International or Justice or Watchdog, are the people who work for them considered to be, whatever. Greenpeace has become a respectable household name; they were once classed as a load of cracker jacks up to no good. So be it then, let me stand accused of whatever, so long as it keeps them from talking about those who want to be left alone. From this I hope you can see that I have been working on other people's behalves for some while now and if I had just appeared out of the woodwork then I could accept that my role would be looked upon with suspicion.

Back to the Glover situation. There was a story going around that suggested that when Glover was on the run his wife had an argument with a neighbour, Glover was at home and on hearing the argument he went running out into the street, wearing only his boxer shorts, oh, and also brandishing a sawn off shotgun. The neighbour was threatened with the gun and the story goes that whilst this was happening a police officer drove past and saw what was happening. A few minutes later Glover's mobile telephone rang and someone told his wife to get him in the 'fucking house.' Of course this is only a story and therefore it has to be accepted as only that, a story. People will invent anything for sensationalism.

One thing is for certain though is that Glover became a transvestite, having to parade about in high heels and suspenders, so to speak so as he would not be recognised by those that knew him. Glover seems though, for a man who was most wanted, to have been able to move about with considerable ease. His garb of a long floral dress and a wig on his head did not protect him from being spotted by those that knew him. The word on the street was that he was out and about.

Eventually Glover, 25, was arrested in Middlesbrough, of all places! After six months on the run, Glover along with another Newcastle man were arrested when a routine enquiry was answered by police. A car was being broken into. What was Glover doing in Middlesbrough breaking into a car?

It does not seem logical that a most wanted man would put himself up for likely capture for such a stupid crime.

When Glover was found guilty of the kidnap and torture charges it was in a jury trial, the jury was not fooled into thinking that Glover had nothing to do with it.

When you consider that Glover turned up in his car and drove into a car park that Paddy had been sitting waiting in his own vehicle for some while it adds substance to what Paddy alleges about Glover having made the phone call to the police about Collier's tooth being snapped. How come Paddy had been sitting there, watched by PC Noble, yet Glover was nowhere in sight? What had Glover been up to? Paddy can account for his movements, Glover only had the word of a sighting by a police officer, how can this be proven that it was Glover that the policeman had seen driving about the West End? The jury certainly believed Glover had not been running around on errands for the police, yet the police testimony was all for Glover, but it fell on the deaf ears of the jury who were having none of it. The trial cost an estimated £1M and lasted seven weeks. Two other men were found not guilty. Nine witnesses had to be given police protection while five were re-housed and given new identities. Glover is now serving his time in a category 'B' prison while Paddy has to continue under the mentally arduous double Category 'A' tag, yet he only has three years of his sentence remaining. What stories he will be able to tell on his release, maybe that can be covered in another book, who knows?

This might all seem like a one sided story and that Glover is the victim here, I contacted a car sales pitch that Mr Glover, Snr was thought to have owned. I was just too late and the person there told me that Mr Glover was no longer there. I asked that my call be relayed to Mr Glover as I wished to speak to him about his son's incarceration. Affirmative, it would be passed on, Mr Glover did not get back to me. I also asked those close to Paddy to pass on my concerns to Mr Glover, Snr, obviously this has not been carried out obviously Mr Glover, Snr, wishes to have the privacy he is entitled to.

From all accounts David Glover, Snr, is a very likeable man and could be considered to one of the likeable rogues from the West End of Newcastle. A story that will have most prisoners grinning from ear to ear is when Davy managed to talk some prisoners officers into calling into one of his local pubs. 'Fine, have a beer old mate', except Davy was being escorted on an inter-prison visit from HM Prison Acklington in Northumberland to top security HM Prison Frankland in Durham to meet a co-accused inmate.

Davy was serving a prison sentence for his part in a £180,000 cannabis conspiracy. He received a seven-year prison sentence at Newcastle Crown Court in October 1991.

Two guards and a driver left Acklington prison escorting Davy to Frankland jail. The visit went OK and a likely future appeal was discussed, but on the way back, from what should have been only an hour's outing each way, Davy managed to get the party to stop off at the *Hydraulic Crane* public house on Scotswood Road, Newcastle. Maybe it was a visit of nostalgia as that was the last pub on Scotswood Road; they stopped off for beverages! Maybe now you can see the charm that such men possess.

Paddy made a bid for an appeal and he vowed he would be out on the streets within a year of September 1996. The prosecution said that the police gave all the tapes of the police radio transmissions to the Crown Prosecution Service. This may well be so, but that did not stop the trial judge pulling one of the tapes out of the game. It was suggested that the material was disclosed to the defence? Paddy would beg to differ on that account. His appeal was funded from the sale of his Happy House lodgings. The cost of his appeal was some £10,000, which he paid for himself.

In a bizarre incident Glover, from within jail, is supposed to have foiled a plot to have a Crown Court Judge 'done in. His Honour Judge Hoffman who sits on the North East circuit had an alleged £50,000 price tag on his head, the job was allegedly offered to a Sunderland based hitman. Glover foiled the plan when he learned of it in HM Prison Armley, Leeds while he was on remand in HM Prison Winston Green, Birmingham he tipped off police that he had been helping when he was free and a paid police informer.

The plot to kill the judge was said to have come from a Yorkshire based criminal whose wife was due to appear before Judge Hoffman. If the woman was jailed then in a letter that Glover had intercepted it was said that the criminal wanted Judge Hoffman done in and would pay £50,000 to have the judge 'done in' if the man's wife was imprisoned. Glover took the words 'done in' to mean the man wanted the judge killed.

Glover said he had acted on this information and told the police because he wanted to be located in a prison nearer home and he wanted to be given credit from his trial judge, hoping of course it would give him a lesser sentence. The judge was unharmed and it may have just been an elaborate hoax by Glover to win sympathy from his trial judge, however it was taken seriously enough to warrant a police investigation.

Paddy's appeal against his conviction went ahead and another twist came in to the story when Paddy refused to go into court because an excuse was offered up as to why PC Noble's radio transmission would not be allowed.

At the Court of Criminal Appeal there was to be presented an affidavit made by Mrs Janet Ann Anderson from West Denton, Newcastle. That affidavit explained in full detail certain goings on that took place at Newcastle Crown Court and in a later incident in which it was alleged that a party had taken place for the 'conviction of Paddy Conroy.' There was one problem, Paddy still had 2½ weeks of his trial to go! Mrs Anderson, of good character and a housewife, became involved in the appeal of a convicted torturer by accident rather than by choice. Mrs Anderson sparked a full red alert police inquiry ordered by a judge sitting at the Royal Courts of Criminal Appeal in London on 4th March 1997, following the dismissal of an appeal by Paddy against his prison sentence of 11½ years imposed by Newcastle Crown Court in December 1995 for the offences of: kidnap, false imprisonment and escape from lawful custody.

I have spoken with Mrs Anderson about this very important matter and with her permission the interview was taped. I also obtained a signed release from her allowing me to pursue certain inquiries I have made.

Taken from the recording of the interview Mrs Anderson has very graciously given me the following is her account of how she became involved in this case.

I ask about her first affidavit that she made to a firm of solicitors, in which she gave a full account of what she had been told by a work mate to a solicitor yet he only wrote the briefest of details on the first affidavit that she gave. Mrs Anderson: "That's true, yes." What was the name of that solicitor who took the affidavit? "Mr Bradley Stephens from Newcastle." Mr Conroy's defence team were not happy with the lack of detail in this first affidavit and wanted more comprehensive coverage. What was it you said in that second affidavit? "What I did say was exactly how things had been, I had been working and I had worked with this girl that had been on the jury of a different trial that was going on at the same time as Paddy Conroy's trial." What was the woman's name? "Julie Hislop." You were working with Miss Hislop and she had been on a jury, is that right? "Yes, she was on the jury, she was working with me all that week, it was Christmas time and we worked nights together." She had been on the jury? "She had been on the jury." How did it come about that she had mentioned it while you were working together at the Old Assembly Rooms in the bar? "She said that when the trial finished, 'they were taken by police car', this is what she told me. They had been taken by police car to Gateshead and that there was a buffet and drink on. It was supposed to have been for the finish of Paddy Conroy's trial, but it didn't finish, as planned. So all the jury or whoever now I know that there was only the two of them had went. The jury of this other trial were invited to this party." Also? "Hmm mh." Miss Hislop had obviously showed an interest in what she was telling you? "She was more complaining about having a hangover and being shattered, it was the next night." So her trial, when she was on the jury had finished? "Yes." She was in the Gateshead Police social club based in Gateshead police station, did she mix with any members of the Conroy jury? "I don't know. She was more telling me about having this night and all the drinks and everything. What I picked up on the most was that the party was supposed to have been for the finish of the Conroy trial. There had been a buffet and everything." Did Miss Hislop state whom the police officers were who invited her to the party? "No, they had gone to this party in the police station at Gateshead. I didn't even know there was a function room or whatever, it was on the top floor. But it hadn't finished so they still continued with this party." So she had not mixed with any jury members of the Conroy trial? "What she said to me was that the jury members were sick because they couldn't go to the party. That was said, but what I picked up on the most, because it made me sick to think that they had parties to celebrate the end of trials." Did Miss Hislop's jury mix with the jury of the Conroy trial, such as taking the same breaks and so on, did Miss Hislop suggest this? "No. I wasn't even thinking 'Paddy Conroy' I was thinking 'Eh, that's what they do, have parties.' That was the thing that really stumbled me."

This party was for the security on the Conroy trial and not for the murder trial that Miss Hislop was a juror. There was no security on that trial. The police and security staff were on the Conroy trial, therefore there was no need to invite a juror from a murder trial to a party for security staff on the Conroy trial. The security staff had built up a friendship and camaraderie whilst serving on the Conroy security side of things, that is accepted, but the need then to invite others who were not part of this security camaraderie shatters that explanation that is given in the ordered Police Report.

The special security police do not talk to any old Tom, Dick or Harry and if it were you or I there then they would not give us the time of day. I ask Mrs Anderson what age Miss Hislop was? "About 22 or 23 something like that." Was she what you would call a 'head turner'? "She was always bragging about 'When I was in Ibiza', she was that type of girl, nice girl mind, but we used to call her the gyrator." Obviously the invitation to Miss Hislop was given for obvious reasons, she was found to be attractive, would a 60 year old have been invited, doubtfully.

The mere fact that there was a party planned after such an important trial indicates certain improprieties. I ask if the whereabouts of Miss Hislop is known? "I only know she lived somewhere near Killingworth. In the report thing that afterwards That I had said it was near Cramlington, Killingworth all that area I don't know. It wasn't in Killingworth." Cramlington, Killingworth, even to me they are part and parcel of the same place, one is not much different to the other place, but the police report tries to show Mrs Anderson has made a mistake in her affidavit. What difference this made to what was told to Mrs Anderson said is hard to determine; yet the police latched on t this. Had it not been for Mrs Anderson's affidavit then the police report would not have been possible and this sort of thing would not have come to light. Yet Mrs Anderson has not even been approached by the police to include her statement in the report, this is found difficult to believe because without her actions in this matter the party would have largely went unnoticed and who is to say how it could have ended up at the end of trials.

When the trial at which Miss Hislop was one of the jurors ended on the afternoon of Friday 24th November 1995 eight of them went on to the *Baltic*

Tavern pub on the Quayside, opposite the court building. A near enough place to have a drink and say goodbye to each other. During that time a number of police officers had become part of the group socialising.

It became know to Miss Hislop, the report states, 'and Hislop accepts that she then requested of the two police officers whether herself and her colleagues could also attend the club and in consequence the four jurors travelled to the club in private vehicles.'

Miss Hislop invites herself to a party at Gateshead Police Social Club. A party intended for the security men of the Conroy trial. Big strong macho gun totting men splashing out money to caterers for a buffet spread? The foodstuff would have gone to waste if it was not used. The party was just a coincidence with the other trial finishing although it was accepted that the Conroy trial overshot by a couple of weeks.

The function was decided to go ahead regardless of the trial not coming to its planned end. Although the report says that private vehicles were used to transport Miss Hislop and three others to the party it does not state if the vehicles were actually vehicles owned by police officers! It would be a clever way of not actually saying the vehicles were not connected to the police when in fact they could have been, indirectly.

Mrs Janet Ann Anderson, the report clearly states, has no past convictions or cautions. Therefore what she says cannot be knocked because of past convictions. However in the report it states that she is the wife of Kenneth Anderson. Who has a prolific criminal record dating from 1957 for a wide range of offences including robbery, affray, grievous bodily harm and unlawful possession of a firearm with intent to endanger life. What the report is saying here is 'look we can't get anything on Mrs Anderson, but we have plenty of dirt on her husband, does that count in discrediting her testimony?'

There is also a mention of an association between Mrs Anderson, her husband and the Conroy family. From what I have found out this is a very loose association. If knowing someone generally is classed as an association then so be it. If not seeing someone for four years is classed as an association then so be it. If not even being able to recognise someone is classed as an association then so be it.

The Police Report goes on to say that this and that is incorrect about one of Mrs Anderson's affidavits, but it does not go on to qualify why parts of the affidavit are incorrect.

A slur against Mrs Anderson is without foundation when it is written in section 6.4 'It is an open speculation as to whether Anderson had a motive for deliberately 'massaging' her version of that conversation as per the content within her affidavit.' Mrs Anderson, from speaking with her, comes across as a woman that would not want to cause herself any needless aggravation at this stage in he life, after all why would she want to sully her good character for things she has manage to stay out of all her life?

Paddy Conroy – Trial or Fiction

Section 6.7 it is stated that 'Detective Chief Inspector Atkinson accepts that in hindsight his decision to allow the discharged jurors to congregate at the Police Social Club was perhaps unwise, albeit he was placed in such circumstances that to decline that visit may have caused embarrassment to the jurors.' The man who just could not say 'no'.

Certain things have happened that are too much of a coincidence to ignore in Paddy's case. When it came to Mrs Anderson making another affidavit because the first one she made was too basic Paddy's sister, Denise, took Mrs Anderson to another firm of solicitors who took instruction to prepare and affidavit for submission to Paddy's appeal.

Paddy takes up the story here, "I said take her to a solicitor that can't be nobbled. Mrs Anderson told them everything she knew and nothing was missing out of this statement, perfect. I got it sent straight to my solicitor in London. What had happened here was crucial to my appeal! Anyway three or four days before my appeal my solicitor told me the statement had went missing from his office and can I get another one. I phoned my sister up telling her to take Mrs Anderson back to the solicitor to make another one.

She went to the office and explained the problem and asked for another appointment to make a new one. The girl at the desk said that wouldn't be necessary as the most recent one was still on computer. Mrs Anderson would just have to go in to sign a copy that would be run off the computer. My sister said], 'great' and went back with Mrs Anderson, when they did though the floppy disc was missing! My sister then brought Mrs Anderson down tot he appeal court so she could explain directly to the judges about the party, but they wouldn't let her give evidence. My barrister took a statement from her, but it was another one missing all the details of what she had been told."

Here we have Mrs Anderson travelling to London from Newcastle having to probably appear in court as a witness. That must have been a daunting task to her especially since it took a lot of courage for her to meet me and talk about the case as she did. Suddenly she has to give the details all over again at the last minute to a barrister, he takes a quick statement and a lot of the translation is lost in the hurry to get it done.

The first affidavit taken from Mrs Anderson is pretty basic, less than one A4 page size in double space. The second affidavit was lost in London by Paddy's ex-solicitor three days before his appeal, and then it is claimed the computer disc went missing from Tait, Farrier, Graham Solicitors in Adelaide Terrace, Benwell, Newcastle. I wrote to them on two occasions before I elicited an answer. They cannot help in the matter and say that they have not got a computer disc with the affidavit on.

Paddy was told not to trust me, but he does not want to disclose who said it, this was in the beginning after he had been able to read the parts in the last book relating to him he changed his tune, but being in his position and having your mate betray your trust in such a way Glover did as well as how Glover

240

set him up it is understandable that he has so little trust left in anyone.

Paddy finishes off by saying, "I'm quite surprised how truthful the book is (last book) as I thought all along that no way is this man going to help me. One of the reasons I thought that was because everyone I spoke to told me not to trust you. A strange thing happened, about the same time you contacted me David Glover, Snr, was contacted and told to go and see his son's solicitor.

They arrived at his office, the solicitor was out, but the secretary told Mr Glover that they could not represent his son anymore and gave Mr Glover two large boxes containing all of Glover, Jnr's, case papers, he took them home and a couple of days later he phoned the solicitor to ask why he couldn't represent his son anymore? The solicitor replied that the secretary had made a mistake and asked him to fetch the boxes back in. I thought this was strange as a solicitor is not allowed to hand anybody's papers to a third party unless he has it in writing to do so, which he didn't have. About a month later my sister and friend contacted a new solicitor for me they then went to my previous solicitor to let him know this had been done and to tell him where to forward the papers on to. They waited at his office as he was out, they had not informed him or his secretary that they were calling. He arrived at his office about an hour later, he was told the new address of my solicitor taking over the case. They were not aware my solicitor could not give them my case papers, so asked for them. To cut a long story short he took them outside his office to his car, opened the boot and, hey presto, there's my case papers boxed up, which he gave them. What my sister found strange was he did not know why she wanted to see him and the fact he already had the papers in his car boot. Both mine and Glovers papers have gone out of legal hands without any permission, this was definitely no coincidence, Steve, and I have racked my brains to come up with an answer why this was done.

I've read what you have to say about Viv and you're correct when you say he was not involved in drugs. If he had of been I'm sure I would have known. It's also bollocks about the protection rackets the newspapers said he ran. The police don't like to be seen not to be able to do their job and that's exactly the case when the pubs and clubs are hiring others to look after their premises, it's the job of the police, ain't it? Having to hire a third party shows that the job of the police isn't getting done and the police always put this down to a protection racket in order to say this money is being demanded and it's not a case of them not being able to do their job."

Paddy told me he was withdrawing his offer of ever appearing in the Viv murder trial as he had stated he would so as to clear up some points. Paddy went through the typical 'I'm giving up routine' once during the months I have been in contact with him and his family, he seems to be over the worst hurdle now. He spoke of a man called Paul Ashton getting a raw deal with the courts and he is now doing 26 years (and expecting more porridge I understand) for trumped up charges that didn't deserve 10 years if he had of been guilty. The courts have went berserk, Paddy told me, these past four or five years and are dishing out jail like it is going out of fashion.

Paddy admits he gave Collier a beating in his car and that was it, he states as you are familiar with by now that he had caused damage to his father's gravestone. Here are a few examples to show that Paddy is not on his own when it comes to what he did. Tony Kidd, 42, of Scarborough caught a lout vandalising a gravestone and he ended up cuffing him. Tony was arrested for assaulting a boy of 15 who was in the graveyard with tow others. He saw one of the juvenile vandals takes a run up to a gravestone and he tried to kick it down he then took a kick at another. Tony clipped him on the head and ended up in court, the magistrates gave him an absolute discharge and the vandal was not charged as no damage had been done!

A baby's grave was robbed of beloved ornaments that were laid on the grave by mum Victoria Hudson, 21, of Washington said, "I don't know how anyone can do that, I felt horrible." The grave was in the baby section of the graveyard.

Widow, Margaret Reid, 69 was disgusted to find dog faeces on the grave of her late husband's grave. Thomas died seven years ago and she ad been tending the grave in all that time. She said, 'I was horrified when I saw it. It was clearly not a small dog.'

Newcastle's Old Eldon Square is experiencing difficulties because of drunks, skaters and the like who are desecrating a Tyneside War Memorial. Boozers just sit on the steps of the memorial and graffiti artists do not seem to know the meaning of the word respect when they daub slogans on it. The council plan to act over complaint received about this.

Florists have been charged with stealing graveside tributes at a Tyneside cemetery. Two former shopkeepers have elected for trial at Crown Court when they pleaded not guilty to stealing floral tributes from gravesides to re-sell in their former shop, Mary Scott Florists in North Shields. Bail conditions were imposed and the conditions were that the married couple stays away from cemeteries, their trial is still pending. Floral tributes left at the murder site where Viv was shot mysteriously disappeared during the night, days after he was gunned down. The council did not remove them, who did? Lee Paul Duffy's grave was vandalised in Middlesbrough in 1993.

Hopefully these examples will show what it is like to suffer such acts of vandalism and how incensed Paddy was so much so that he assaulted Collier, a convicted granny basher.

A teenager was trussed up like a chicken and tortured. 17-year-old, Darren Lynch of Burnopfield, had his private parts burned with a hot tin opener, and smeared with toothpaste and antiseptic. Darren had went to the flat of Stephen Neilson, 23, because he knew him. It was there that Darren was tied up so tightly that the rope cut into the sides of his mouth and caused it to bleed. Along with Neilson, Neil Spoor, 18 and Michael Young, 23 carried out a sadistic torture and at one point he was stripped so that some girls could look at him. The torture was attempted to be masked by the defence saying 'trails of strength and endurance' were regularly held at Neilson's home.

Darren had to be freed by burning the rope that bound him because it was so tight. A second torture session took place when 17 year old Leonard Giles was forced into Neilson's car and taken to his flat, they accused Leonard of stealing £2 in an earlier visit, Leonard denied this.

Leonard was then tied up and gagged while £1 coins were being heated up on the ring of an electric cooker. Spoor stood on the tips of Leonard's fingers and the use of pliers seems to have been the up and coming thing in 1988.

Neilson used the pliers to press the hot coins into his victim's hands, which burned the flesh until it sizzled like frying bacon. To top this salt and vinegar were poured onto the burns. Three men kidnap two young lads and decide to wantonly torture them, building up from horseplay to full scale torture tactics of actually going out and kidnapping one of their victims on the excuse that he had previously stolen money. Compare this to the punishment that Glover inflicted on Collier. Neilson received a ten-year prison sentence, Spoor was sent to detention centre for 3½ years. Michael Young who had assisted in the burning of Darren's private parts received a paltry two years imprisonment. Their trial lasted only six days and the jury was out for only a few hours. The three had been terrifying the village of Burnopfield for some time. Both Neilson and Spoor had previous convictions for violence.

Further use of pliers, and this time hot wax was also used in what was said to be invented torture. Spaceman, a nickname given to Geordie soldier John Reed, 19, was alleged to have invented stories of torture about himself. One particular story that he was accused of making up was that of having hot wax poured onto him. Corporal Mark Nesbit, 27 of the King's Regiment had denied ill treatment of John Reed with the candle wax, but he admitted using pliers on John's fingers. Reed left the army under premature voluntary release and he said he was called 'spacemen' because of the time it took him to understand orders. He was under pressure to join the army and keep his family tradition going. This sort of case shows how easy it is for people to become embroiled in acts of violence, Paddy says he did not authorise the use of pliers and other methods of torture on Collier. I believe that to be true, but only after seeing evidence myself and experiencing the authority's methods in frustrating my attempts to get to the bottom of everything.

John Sayers, 24, experienced the rough end of the law when he was facing trail charged with taking part in a £750,000 post office robbery in Sunderland. Sayers ran a fruit and veg shop way back then in 1988, he insisted on his innocence and when arrested from a house in Newcastle by early morning armed police he was not surprised. Police accused Sayers of being involved in the raid yet he gave an alibi that was difficult not to believe, he said the Regional Crime Squad were watching him and they could verify his story although he refused to give an account of his movements on the day in question when the West Sunniside Post Office was robbed in Sunderland, August 1997. It was only when was picked out of an ID parade that he gave an account of his movements on the day in question. His alibi was that he had visited his father and then later on he had met with a building society manager.

Sayers had a co-accused, Kenneth Sandvid, 33, who was also accused of robbing another post office in Washington, he was pleading 'not guilty' to both of the robberies. John Sloane, 19, was a witness in the trial and he said he had seen the driver sitting in a white van, with a mask pulled over his head and he had a shotgun. The only problem was that Sloane had problems of his own as he was serving a sentence in Low Newton Remand Centre. He said he saw the man again only minutes later, 'He came from across the road and was smoking a pipe outside the shop.' Sloane had been watching what was going on and he was certain it was the same man as he was dripping with sweat and he struck a match to light the pipe, but his hand was shaking so much the match went out. He had no doubt about whom the man was. Sloane helped piece an identikit together and it helped pick Sayers out of an ID parade. Sandvid was also picked out of an ID parade by sloane and he was identified as the man as the man standing guard while the raid took place.

Sandvid was also claimed to have been seen in town before the robbery took place by a 20year old woman who gave her name and address to court on a piece of paper. She later identified him in a police station.

Postal worker Frank Bell told how the cash bags from the West Sunnisde PO had just been unloaded from a van when the raid happened. A dark blue Range Rover burst through the gates, a man got out; he was wearing a mask. Three postal workers were taking the cash into the sorting office on a trolley. A man with a shotgun then appeared and he pointed it at them and without speaking he took control of the trolley moving it of.

During their trial it was said that a detective invented a confession from a man who was charged with taking part in the West Sunniside PO robbery. It was said to be a 'dishonest attempt to bolster a police case that did not exist', claimed Brian Higgs the defence for Sandvid. Constable William Watt vigorously denied this saying 'His record of interviews was correct.' Sandvid was arrested from Newcastle Airport about to board a plane bound for Majorca is alleged to have admitted his part in the robbery. Sandvid is alleged to have told police that he supplied the Range Rover that was used to batter the gates down, was this the first ever ram-raid? Sandvid was then said to have told DC Watt, 'You're getting no names off me I can't afford it.' He was also meant to have admitted being there when the robbery was talked of.

Unemployed Sandvid was found to have £2,000 in cash on him when he was arrested he explained it away allegedly by saying the Sunderland job had nothing to do with him, but it was for driving at the Washington job.

Sandvid was asked at what job it was he was driving and he is meant to have said, 'A post office, no names that's all I want to say. All I had to do with the Sunderland job was delivering the Rang Rover.' £76,000 was stolen from the Washington job, which he denied having anything to do with it.

The Regional Crime Squad was accused of falsifying logs to dispute the alibi given by John Sayers. David Robson, QC, alleged the falsifying had taken place. Crime Squad detectives had been keeping surveillance on a building society that Sayers said he had visited at the time of the robbery.

DC Leslie Hodginson said that Sayers had not entered or left the premises in the three hours of his watch, which took place at the time of the raid. David Robson cross-examined Hodginson and he denied suggestions that Sayers had arrived during the relevant times and not been recognised or the logs had been changed. Also DC Trevor Martin who had made the entries in the logs denied they had been deliberately changed at a later date to break Sayers' alibi.

Sandvid was shocked that he was said to have confessed to the raids, he told the court 'He couldn't believe it'. The first Sandvid had known of his miraculous confession was when he appeared at Sunderland Magistrates' Court and the prosecution outlined his confession. The admissions they say he made about taking part in the raids and supplying the Range Rover and taken part in the raids was news to him. He claimed police made up his confessions.

Sayers told the court that his younger brother was on the run from the police. He said that he and his younger brother, Stephen, 23, looked so much alike that their mother even had some difficulty telling them apart. He said that his brother had disappeared shortly after his arrest for the robbery and he had not seen him since. He denied he was shielding anybody, but he did say he would not have told the police who did the robbery anyway. Sayers was asked about the fact that he was picked out from the ID parade and he was seen smoking a pipe outside of a shop. He said he had never smoked in his life.

Both Sandvid and Sayers were found not guilty of robbery at Durham Crown Court. What was then classed as Britain's biggest post office robbery was cleared from their plates and they both smiled their way out of court when Sandviv was also cleared of the Washington raid. During the trial both men alleged that police fabricated evidence against them. The judge, Mr Justice Ognall directed both men should be discharged immediately. Both had been on remand for a year whilst waiting to be tried.

What happened to the police who were alleged to have falsified records of times and so on? As it happens Sayers was to receive more than his fair share of porridge in a later trial for which he is only just getting around to being free in about 15 months time. We have not got the space to cover it in here though. What can be said is that Sayers received a lengthy sentence, believed to be a one of fifteen years (a life sentence, just about). Not because of the offence he was charged with, but because he had escaped prison for this particular robbery. As has already been written, John Sayers is the North East's own John McVicar, in fact in the money stakes, if comparisons were made, John McVicar would have been behind on totals. It is claimed that Tony Leach, an associate of Sayers' had interests in a well known North East based footwear outlet, but because of some financial tangles he had to pull out and it is further claimed from an insider that John Sayers has become somewhat concerned as to this matter, obviously John takes a great interest in the welfare of his friends.

Right, here it is the bit that most of you have been waiting to read. My publisher has been asked many times about the incident I now write of. Sunderland's Ernie Bewick v Tyneside's Billy Robinson. That should please the Sunderland following that the previous book has had the support of. It was mentioned that Teesside had a piece of the action through the Lee Duffy chapter so it has been accepted that Sunderland should get a piece of the action although it was hoped to be able to give more comprehensive coverage of Ernie, but due to his awaited Crown Court trial it is not going to do anyone any favours by writing this and that about them, hopefully it can be covered in a future book in more detail.

The story that follows is only an alleged story and it was claimed to have happened by an insider. From now on what is mentioned has to accepted as a story, a novel, a piece of fiction. The reason for expressing this is that it would be wrong to say 100% that it happened especially with Ernie awaiting trial for a serious offence.

Gateshead's Billy Robinson is as hard as they come, ever walked into a lamppost, because that is what his punch was like. Billy has settled down over the years and for that reason he does not have to prove anything to anyone, he's been there, wore the T-shirt and now he's reading the book. Billy's durability is a typical Geordie in-breed thing, although he's older now he will remember his younger days when he and Paddy Leonard worked the doors together, Viv was only a young up and coming doorman and back then Billy had seen more action than Viv had hot dinners, Viv of course eventually caught up. As much as most local hard men have their following, so had Billy.

Ernie Bewick was a good amateur boxer, having fought in the ABA regional championship over two decades ago. At this point I have changed part of this article as Keith Bell contacted me via letter. Keith has changed his surname and it is not for me to question that or go into details of where he is, etc. Keith tells me that he was a close associate of Viv's and as far as he was concerned Viv was a gentleman. With regard to the alleged fight between Robinson and Bewick I have included some of the details Keith has provided, those details you will have to work out for yourself if they are true or not. Keith confirms what is already known about Ernie, that he did fight in an ABA championship bout, in fact Keith fought Ernie in the 1976 North East championships at middleweight, who won?

Ernie worked on the door at Sunderland's *Blue Monkey* club; it was predominantly a rave club then in 1992. Billy at times would go off on a drinking session and throw caution to the wind about the amount he would consume and in his jolly, but not drunken state he and some friends went to the *Blue Monkey* club. A confrontation took place between Billy and Ernie and it led to blows being exchanged, Billy come off second best and was sporting a black eye and other bruises as a result of this fight.

Some months had passed and it was now June of 1992 when Billy decided he wanted to have a 'straightener' (a fight to even it up) and he asked Viv if he could organise this and to get hold of Ernie. Viv contacted Keith Bell at South Shields asking if he could make Billy's wishes known to Ernie. Keith says, "Viv asked if I could get Ernie up to a gym in the Jesmond area of Newcastle. Ernie and I travelled up to Pandora's gym (name changed for legal reasons) in Jesmond for the bare knuckle fight." A W ran Pandora's gym a winner of a Mr Gt Britain body building title.

The fight was underway and the fitter of the two, Bewick, carried less body weight and he was getting the better of Billy, although Billy was no disgrace for a man of his age (in his 40s) up against a fitter, leaner man who had got through to the ABA finals. Viv intervened and knocked Ernie out with "a fats hard upper-cut, Ernie was out stone cold, hit from the side unawares, it was sad and unfair." 'Sad and unfair' seems to say it all, but Viv did not want to see his mentor get hurt, yes in his day Billy would have ate Ernie for breakfast and had him again for lunch, but Billy had become accustomed to the good life, who would not?

It was said by another insider that Ernie had a tooth knocked out by Viv and in compensation Viv threw him £200 and said, 'Get your tooth repaired', Ernie threw the money back saying he did not need his money. That part might be slightly untrue, but make of it what you will. The other side of the story goes that Ernie and Billy had the fight and were getting no where, when Viv intervened as Ernie left the Gym and gave him a blow to the head.

Ernie and Viv had made peace and each said their piece to each other some time after in a meeting in Keith Bell's home. Keith said, "To be fair, I know Ernie would not have lasted two minutes with Viv as Viv was some 17/18 stone while Ernie varied between 12½ to 14½ stone. Viv had it all: speed and super strength a natural fighter with a knock out punch in either hand."

Many thanks go to those of you who co-operated in helping me assemble this story and now we return to the land of fact.

We continue with a look at how things can be twisted from what they really are. You have read about how Paddy has not had a fair deal. This particular finding concerns a man that had a whiter than white past, until he decided to put right a wrong that he felt was too obvious to be left alone. Jim Richardson served with the RAF (Royal Air Force) in the Middle East from 1952 to 1955. He left the RAF and worked within the credit trade for some 25 years until he was tempted by a vacancy within Northumbria Police Force (NPF), he was successful in his application for the job and was now a civilian Warrants Officer (collecting/executing fine default warrants).

Superintendent Tom Nichol gave him the job in 1980, but the path of his job was paved with jealous people who did not believe that a civilian should be in the employ of Northumbria Police Force in such a position of power, nearly akin to theirs. He was sometimes referred to as a 'fucking civilian' and other crude names, Jim put up with this as after all he knew he had invaded their territory and it would take a little for him to be accepted by them. Female civilian employees were referred to as 'split-cunts' or 'slappers'.

Jim loved the job as it was mainly outside work so he did not really take it too seriously as he felt that here he was doing a worthwhile job, get on with it. His job took him to many parts of Newcastle and his visits to the homes of those on the top of the 'most wanted' list many a time. He was always civil with fine defaulters and in return he built up respect from those he pursued for unpaid fines, etc. He became good at his job and it became part of his life, it just did not seem fair then when it came to an end because of reorganisation within the NPF.

Jim was re-deployed to Gateshead police station as a counter clerk, OK it was not the same, but at least he had job security and was thinking of his retirement pension so he needed to get those years in to amass a decent sized pension; nothing was going to spoil it for him. He was in his fourteenth year of employment for NPF. When his position as Warrants Officer became obsolete it was done so suddenly, that was in December 1993. Jim told me, "In December the Newcastle Warrants Dept was suddenly closed down by Chief Superintendent Sweeney who wrote to Mr JS Young, Newcastle Justices' Clerk, by letter dated 18th November, 1993 'I regret short notice of our changes, but the process of restructuring has become so dynamic that it takes quantum leaps on an almost daily basis....In the short term it is hoped that there will little or no reduction in revenues collected from fine warrants. Indeed one unit commander is planning a warrant campaign in the run up to New Year, so income could possibly increase. The situation will be monitored closely but no guarantees can be given that revenues will not decrease.' Since December 1993 Fine Default Warrants are still being issued by our courts to the police, but the instructions (printed on the warrant) regards their execution are being totally ignored and consequently police moral is understandably low when the lawless are allowed to thumb their noses and show blatant contempt to our courts, police and all other forms of authority. The police may as well instruct their officers not to arrest anyone and close our courts down until a more positive attitude is taken to enforce the penalties imposed by the courts.

On many an occasion I have expressed my fear and concern to senior police officers that the non-collection of fines was having demoralising effects on officers and could lead to the breakdown of law and order, but I was told 'Don't' rock the boat, Mr Richardson.' I found this most offensive and difficult."

What Jim is really saying is that thousands of fine defaulters are getting off scott-free regardless of how much they owe in outstanding fines. Jim should know, as worked in what used to be one of the most feared places in Newcastle; the West End. He came up against some of the most feared crime families and names that used to turn people's stomachs just talking about them.

That though has changed along with the methods of collecting outstanding fines. The warrants officers could badger people into paying an could give them time to come up with the money, they could even put a warrant on hold for a few days grace until the money was scrapped together to pay it off. After all this was Newcastle, not Wimbledon. Credit cards were things that some people in the West End would use to go on a shopping spree with, so long as it was not their card! Money was tight Jim understood this. The courts were dishing out fines, but now that the warrant officers were no longer collecting the outstanding fines it was extra duties for the, already, over stretched police force.

The Lord Chancellors dept were going to review the procedures to find a more efficient way of collecting unpaid fines and compensation. Police officers told me that they have not got the time to run around after these fine defaulters as they are too busy trying to catch the criminals so as to put them into court where they get fined for basic criminal offences. Jim Richardson made it clear to his bosses that the situation was getting out of hand, even though he was no longer employed as a Warrant Officer. He was told to keep quiet and not to rock the boat. Jim had been involved in knocking on people's doors for some 39 years, it was not going to just dry up over night and no matter how he tried he could not let the situation go.

Jim says, "On 16th June I was called to NPF Headquarters to discuss the non-collection of fines with Assistant Chief Constable Alan Oliver and a summary of that meeting read: 'Mr Oliver then explained the sequence of events which had led to the changes in the method of fines collection and this was now definitely a Magistrates' Court's job.' At the same meeting with Mr Oliver he stated that if the courts refused to take warrants back NPF would adopt a non-collecting policy to force the courts to make an alternative collecting arrangement. More than 52 months have elapsed since he told me that and the changes he talked of have still not took place. This loss of revenue is costing taxpayers £Ms every year. Naturally I was most unhappy that Mr Oliver gave no assurances that fines would be collected – and that felons would pay the penalties of their crimes, so I immediately elected to take an official appeal to the Northumbria Police Authority (NPA). After lodging my appeal I was called to see Gateshead Superintendent David Warcup on 5th August 1994. He became most hostile when I expressed my fears regarding uncollected fines, uttering words to the effect that I was the only one showing concern on this matter.

Six days after seeing Supt Warcup I received a letter from Force Headquarters saying I had to take a medical, as a one had been arranged for me, this had been arranged without my knowledge or consent. I tried to find out who was responsible for organising it, but in vain. My appeal (against the non-collection of fines policy) was heard on the 30th November 1994 it was heard by the NPA at the Gateshead Civic Centre. A sitting magistrate, Mr Colin Dale, was a prominent panel member. In the two hours the appeal went on I voiced my concerns that fines being imposed by courts were not getting collected. The appeal was dismissed without a reason being given! I was promised minutes of that meeting, which were taken by the clerk Mr Gary Haynes, they have never been given to me as promised. I was barred from contacting Mr Haynes as I was writing letters constantly because I wanted the minutes as a record of my attempts to get the system changed."

Here we have a man who has 14 years experience out in the city of fines collections. He puts his point to the seemingly law unto themselves NPA appeal panel and is ignored as though he had the plague. Promises made by Mr Haynes of a transcript of the minutes did not materialise. Councillor George Gill the chairman of NPA has not offered up any defence after I forwarded Coun Gill a copy of the article I addressed to the NPA. I did, however, receive a letter from NPA's solicitor saying that they would not be happy at having Mr Richardson's article appear in this book and if it did then they would take the 'appropriate legal action.'

Well that is just hunky dory as the amount of people who have threatened legal action can form a queue around the Angel of the North to the Tyne Bridge, because there are so many of them now, get in line, buster.

On 3rd January 1995 Jim Richardson was called to see Supt Warcup at Gateshead to discuss the non-collection of fines and even though this was not a disciplinary matter meeting (Jim has this in writing) he was, however, warned/advised that this 'sensitive issue' should not be discussed with the press or his MP. No assurances from Jim were forthcoming.

On 10th May 1995 a final written warning was issued by Supt Warcup for what Jim describes as "…nothing more sinister than writing 12 letters to the NPA about various matters such as the promised minutes of my appeal and asking for their help in supporting me in the non-collection of unpaid fines. My response to this final written warning took the form of a letter dated 31st May 1995 it was not even acknowledged.

I had noticed an untaxed car in the area that I live in and I told the man who I thought was the owner, a local barman, to get it taxed. It bore a tax disc (Vehicle Excise Licence) dated 9/94, some seven months out of date. He made a complaint to the police by phone on 1st June 1995 saying that I had abused my authority. Some 28 days later I was suspended from duty, they were so unsure of what the grounds were for my suspension that the original report was dated 27th July 1995, some 57 days after the complaint.

The complainant refused to make a statement, but he did do a question and answer session. My disciplinary hearing took place on 4th August 1995 and the task of asking for my resignation was allocated to Chief Superintendent Davidson by his superior officer, Supt Warcup, but when I refused then the loss of pension rights was brought into play. He dismissed me on the strength of the final written warning."

It seems Jim was now considered a loose canon, he was asked to desist from his role as self-appointed taxpayers friend. What had actually happened was that Jim had done a vehicle check on an untaxed vehicle to see who the registered keeper was, because it was being used on a public highway without displaying an up to date vehicle excise disc.

Jim had been cleared by security many years previously to allow him to access details on the police computer. Even some senior police officers did not have the high level security clearance needed to check some details out so they would ask Jim, with his higher clearance, to check things out for them at times. So it was not a case of Jim abusing his power in relation to the Data Protection Act, an NPF letter told him that he had not breached the act. All what Jim had done was to act too keenly in the matter of having an untaxed vehicle off the streets. An untaxed vehicle means a number of things either the vehicle has no MOT or that it is not insured. If you have ever had a run in with a vehicle and the owner has no insurance cover you will know how difficult it is to recover your losses and if you have a personal injury claim! It could take years to get a payout from the Motor Insurers Bureau.

Jim fought his dismissal by appealing against unfair dismissal, but that was dismissed. He then went on to fight it at a tribunal, but again it was dismissed. He says a work record, which appraised his work (Staff Appraisal) was completed by Sgt McEnroe, but it went missing and was not seen by the tribunal. Jim says, "Would it have gone missing if it had been an unfavourable report?"

"Jim showed me evidence that fines collected by Warrant Officers collected in Newcastle had not been paid in until up to month later after the money had been collected by certain fines officers. That in effect meant that the defaulter was still at risk of being arrested if a warrant was still outstanding against them! I have seen the evidence with my own eyes and I have copies of the account forms that show how payments were not entered into the fines office for some considerable time after the officer had collected the money. On one occasion Jim had to go and see an off duty Warrant Officer at his home because he had been sent to get his record book because an audit was being conducted and the man was down by a few hundred pounds on his side of things, the man told Jim he needed time to get the money in, Jim wanted nothing to do with it, later that day the off duty officer came in and had paid the money in that was one month late, he had already been paid by a fine defaulter, pocketed the money and paid it back after a month.

Jim has shown this evidence to his MP, Joyce Quin, and other high-ranking figures, yet nothing has been acknowledged to him of the wrong doings and misappropriation of funds. This is so very important to expose because it meant that while some of you who owed fines money and may have paid it to a warrant officer pre-December 1993 you were still at risk of being locked up for non-payment of fines! Jim went onto tell me of how he was called in to certain meetings even though he was not medically fit to do so because of certain investigative tests that were carried out on him by his specialist at hospital, even though Jim gave warning that he was not fit enough it was said that certain meetings would still go ahead, even if he was not there! Jim had to be escorted back home by his solicitor from one meeting because of this lack of consideration shown to him by NPA.

Fair do's, Jim admits he was over zealous, but he did not use any of the information to his own advantage, unlike a female civilian working for North Yorkshire police who accessed personal details and passed them on to her boyfriend after he had given her lists of names his friends wanted to have checked out. That is a total breach of power and the Data Protection Act. Yet that woman is still as far as I am aware working for North Yorkshire police! I do not say that lightly and all of the above evidence from Jim's file as well as details of the female from North Yorkshire is stood by from me, even though others have not acted or given a toss, I have.

Just like people had underestimated Jim's resolve and inner strength they have also underestimated mine.

Just a quick mention here about North East drug dealer, Brian Charrington, he is currently facing extradition proceedings from Spain, he has been released on bail of £200,000 surety from Spain's National Court in Madrid. Middlesbrough born Charrington had been arrested from his Spanish villa and held for 16 months when charges relating to importing cannabis from Morocco into Britain, Spain, Italy and France.

You might recall that Charrington had a case fall apart against him when he was charged with smuggling cocaine worth £150M into Britain concealed in lead ingots back in 1992. It was discovered that he was a police informer and walked fee from court and moved to Spain. Barry Shaw the Cleveland Chief

Constable asked the Police Complaint Authority to carry out an inquiry into the background of the case. Thirty police from a southern force spewn two years sifting through paperwork in Operation Mantis. A number of police officers involved in Charrington's trial were investigated. The probe cost £1M with no results, of course that is the police investigating the police. A further investigation called Operation Teak was launched in 1996; as a result disciplinary notices have been served on a number of police officers.

Right, the final part of this chapter relates to the insurance policies of Viv. I obtained a signed release from Mr and Mrs Graham, Viv's parents, on that basis I wrote to their solicitor, Tim Gray, Sinton & Co, Jesmond, Newcastle.

Tim was kind enough to discuss certain aspects of the claim and I asked him what the objection was with regards the insurance company withholding one settlement? Tim: "Old Mutual state that there was a material non-disclosure also that Viv had failed to disclose a medical problem and that Viv did hazardous pursuits." What was it that Viv had failed to disclose about his medical history? "A boil he had on his buttock!" Tim went on to say that Old Mutual had tried to derail the claim by saying that the legal aid system was being abused with regard to the claim Mr and Mrs Graham are pursuing.

Tim covered some other points and one of those was the fact that Viv gave his occupation as a van driver and he says, "I am bound to say that there is a bona fide dispute here, which arises because of the fact that Viv gave his occupation to the insurers as 'van driver'. What they are saying in essence, is that there was a material non-disclosure based upon information that they have gleaned from two television programmes, from the police and from other sources as to Viv's alleged true activities.

I have my own views as to what has gone on here, but clearly I have to be fairly careful how far I go in propounding them, given that there is litigation, as I say, pending."

What I did find out was that the insurer's agents were also the agents for Viv's house purchase. That might not mean much here, but it does for the ordinary man/woman in the street because it is usual for agents in such transactions as house purchase to carry some associated product and it is, obviously, to their advantage to try and load you up with as much cover as possible. I am not saying that took place with Viv's insurance agent, but there were a number of people present when Viv signed his proposal form and because of that those agents have to bear some responsibility as to the contents of the proposal form. It could be argued that Viv was so well known in the North East that any agent signing him up would be aware of their position in this matter.

Moving on to what Tim Gray said about non-disclosure from Viv's medical background. Old Mutual is saying that because Viv did not disclose he had a boil on his buttock that they have good grounds for withholding payment. Oh, I see, so I should inform my insurers that I had an in grown toenail and I asked a chiropodist to trim it, oh, what about that filling in my tooth and the time I had the wax drained from my ears? Where does it end, because all of those things are medical procedures?

I wrote directly to Old Mutual International at Bartley Way, Hook in Hampshire. I asked a number of questions and enclosed a copy of the signed release I had obtained from Mrs and Mrs Graham, which allowed me to make this inquiry. I received a reply from Robin Aghovia – Legal Adviser. In that letter he says 'We would be grateful if you would set out in writing the specific information you seek and we may then consider your request.' I set out some 15 questions ranging from asking what were their guidelines about club doormen being covered by insurance to the fact that it was their own employees who signed Viv up, what had they to say about that?

I wrote to them asking all the questions under the sun some two months ago, still no reply! I can only take it that they have something to hide or are feared of what I might find out. I have found out enough to satisfy me that they are doing all in their power to withhold payment by hook or by crook, no wonder solicitors are fighting to get the money from them.

I would advise you the reader if you have an insurance policy stuck away in the bottom of your drawer, get it out and check it, because if you have failed to make a disclosure such as you helped your neighbour on Sunday afternoons to trim the hedge with a mains 240 volt revolving bladed hedge trimmer and you were to cut your finger off, you might find payment being withheld if you made a personal injury claim.

These insurance companies are too quick to take your money, but when it comes to waiting for a decision on the payout side of things it can rage on for years. Look at people like Rob Armstrong, he had his insurance cover withdrawn by his insurers because of what they gleaned from TV documentaries. Any insurance company covering him now will ask if he has ever been declined insurance cover, what is he going to tell them, that his friend was murdered and because of that... The whole insurance game stinks, it is all a flash front nice white smiling teeth, 'My roof blew off in a force ten gale and it was replaced the very next day', 'An elephant fell out of the sky and crushed my car, I was driving a new car the very next day' the sort of everyday occurrences that happen to everyone of us is used against us to make us spend even more money on something we might never need, well at least not for a long time.

The fact of it is that Viv signed to say he wanted £20,000 to go to his mam and dad and the other £40,000 to go to his two children. That was it, simple as that, he was murdered in cold blood, the way the insurance company are going on you would think that Viv died on purpose! Old Mutual Life Assurance Company are perpetuating the pain and suffering that Viv's family are going through right now by the fact that they are dragging this whole affair out to something that resembles a piece of elastic, how long can it go on for? I would ask any of the directors to come forward and talk to Mr and Mrs Graham and have this matter settled before it finally destroys these two wonderful people. J C R Collis and B A Marquard are the two British directors of Old Mutual International Ltd, would it hurt one of them to authorise an ex-gratia payment?

Insurance used to be a dirty word up to ten or so years ago, it had to buy respectability and win the public over by a different marketing strategy other than knocking on peoples doors asking them if they thought they needed insurance cover. There are a number of people who still go around businesses touting for new business. Avoid these like the plague because they are selling something that no reputable company would touch, read the teeny weenie small print, especially if it is a personal injury policy. '£50 per day if you spend more than two days in a hospital after an accident.' How many people do you know who have spent more than two days in hospital after an accident? '£50,000 lump sum payment if you lose an eye and a limb as a result of a car accident.' How many people do you know who have lost an eye and an arm as a result of a car accident?

I can make things sound just as good on paper:

'Buy: *Viv (Graham)* – *'Simply the Best'* and receive a free money off voucher for 12½% of the value of that book off: *Viv – and the Geordie Mafia (Vol 2)*

All what that means is: £1 voucher off the recommended retail price of Volume 2 enclosed in the first Viv book.

There are further insurance polices to settle and that is for those who are arguing over Viv's estate to contest.

15

Gary Ward – The Blackpool Beach Murder

Derek Bentley, 19, hanged for murder some 45 years ago has now had his conviction quashed by the Court of Appeal in July 1998. For those of you too detached from this case I give you a watered down version of what happened. A warehouse was broken into in Croydon, Bentley with an accomplice, Christopher Craig, 16, had a confrontation with police and gunfire was exchanged between police and Craig. Bentley was alleged to have said 'Let him have it'. A policeman was shot and died and it ended up with Bentley who had the mental age of an eleven year old being sentenced to death while Craig was too young to be sentenced to hang he served ten years in prison.

Bentley's sister, Iris, campaigned continuously over the years to secure a full pardon and in 1993 she had a partial victory when the Home Secretary granted a limited posthumous pardon. Sadly Iris died before the full pardon was granted, as the conviction was deemed unsafe after a three-day hearing. Bentley played no physical part in the murder of PC Sidney Mills a fellow officer, PC Robert Jaggs, received a commendation for bravery following the shootout.

What has been revealed now is that PC Jaggs took a secret to his alcoholic grave and he told a colleague that if they carried the secret he had for so long then they too would be an alcoholic. Robert Jagg believed that his colleague PC Mills was actually killed in crossfire by a police bullet and that Bentley was wrongly convicted!

Judge Barrington Black ordered a trial be halted when evidence that the prosecution had about the alleged victim of a drug fuelled rape failed to disclose to a man's defence that they had a doctor's letter warning them that the accuser had a drink and drugs problem. Judge Black sitting at the Old Bailey found out that the letter undermined the credibility of the alleged victim and the trial was abandoned in July of 1987.

These two examples are written here to draw the attention of those people that usually say that the law is all above board and no one who is convicted is innocent. These are two examples that attracted media attention and now I wish to draw to your attention to one case that is ongoing in the process of a man trying to prove his innocence. That is the case of Gary Ward, 23, who is alleged to have murdered newly employed Mark White working as a porter in Blackpool. Mark was walking back to his digs when it is alleged that Ward, a Blackpool club doorman, and his co-accused, James Docherty, also a fellow club doorman murdered White by beating him senseless and then drowning him in the sea.

How I came across this was due to the diligent eye of one of my three researchers working on the first book in this series. An article appeared in the Newcastle *Evening Chronicle* by Vince Gledhill a reporter at the Morpeth office. That article had the headline 'Help my son win freedom' and it was dated January 22nd, 1998. The article featured Viv Graham and because of that I got to work finding out what it was all about.

Gary Ward's mother, Sandy Ward, was making an appeal via the local newspaper to ask readers help locate possible witnesses that could help corroborate her son's story that he was actually fighting ¼ mile further up the beach with a man they knew to be called Viv Graham. Whilst this fight was allegedly going on between Ward and Viv Mark White was being murdered. Two other Geordie's were in attendance with Viv but they offered only token resistance.

'The family and friends of Gary Ward...' the article said, '...were fighting to clear his name by offering a reward for vital new evidence.' That is not what attracted me to this case as it turns out that Gary is penniless and his family are struggling to make ends meet. The then girlfriend of Gary, Nikki Scott, and her father put up the £10,000 reward. Since then the relationship with Gary and Nikki has come to an end. The article did not feature Viv's name in any of the titles and therefore it seemed a genuine article. The journalist was called and he was asked if he could contact Mrs Ward as I might have some information to help her son in his attempt to clear his name. Eventually after a further prompting to the journalist he did respond and pass on my interest to Mrs Ward. This was done before the Chronicle took to hating my guts because of what I had wrote about the reporting techniques in the previous book so it was easy to seek assistance from an unwary reporter then. It is a bit like being Roger Cook he cannot get away with much as he is known but before that the world was his oyster.

Sandy Ward said she was putting herself in danger by coming forward and bringing this out in the open. On face value it seemed a bit sensationalist and maybe it was all hype to attract attention to her son's plight but I thought it was worth going quite a way to see her to establish if it was worth pursuing as the interest was the connection Viv had to Blackpool. I made it my job to find out as much about Viv's activities as I could. The money has gone and I am still pursuing the matter so it has to show that my interest is not a one of personal gain although after the Viv fund put up £100,000 to secure the conviction of his killers and here I am again where money is mentioned it would, on the surface, give the impression I had an ulterior motive. Since both funds had been cancelled prior to my intervention I cannot now stand accused of seeking those sorts of riches and conjuring up evidence from out of the blue.

Sandy has written to the Prime Minister and local MPs, but up to now none of them has publicly lent their name or support to the free Gary Ward appeal. It is not for me to criticise his or her lack of support, but just to point it out in case anyone should jump on the bandwagon after I have set it in motion. That is just in case they should try to take all the credit for it if Gary is eventually proven innocent and released. They can fuck off, as it is I who will be seeking a knighthood or life peerage in the lords with a flat in Belgravia so that my better half can claim the secretarial allowance of so many grand a year for washing dishes. After all that is what most MPs do, they have their wife on the payroll as a researcher or secretary so they can claim those allowances, which are all above board of course?

After securing a signed form of release allowing me to work on Gary's behalf (dated 19/3/98) I could set about trying to secure the full story. A copy of the form was forwarded on to Gary's solicitor, Gabb & Co, in Powys to Glynn Maddocks who, I was informed by Gary, acted on his behalf. Since the Northumbria Police still have that letter on computer floppy disc amongst a lot of other Viv related items I am not able to quote directly from that and many other letters forwarded to Gabb & Co Solicitors. What was asked was if they could very kindly forward copies of all paperwork relating to Gary's case as a matter of urgency. One month passed by then two months passed by! I was a little pissed off to say the least. Gary had also written asking what the problem was. He was told the cost was prohibitive, I then wrote again asking what the hold up was and indicating my impatience to get started on the case I also asked if the solicitor had ever done any charity cases and if he did then to consider this to be one of those. Another month went by! By this time I had organised to go to Blackpool with all the required electrical gadgetry to try and get the required statement from the people who could help particularly about Sabre Security. A week was allowed in the planning to go and seek out witnesses as well as taking a minder to Blackpool that would have been a match for intimidation offered. A professional witness would be needed in case anyone at a later stage was frightened to go to court to give evidence against those we sought. Then the expenses of living there for a week so something in the region of £5,000 would just about take care of it. The money was agreed to be put up by my publisher, but then time passed without any news from Gary's solicitor so I had to ditch that and pursue other matters that were being neglected.

I informed Gary of the lack of regard his solicitor had shown this very important matter and to make matters worse Gary was going through an emotional time of it in HM Prison Wakefield due to his girlfriend indicating the relationship that was formed after Gary was sentenced would be coming to an end. The matter of pursuing evidence to obtain a renewed appeal was now in full swing and all of the tragedies of this case would be revealed to me in many different ways. I was now inside the jam jar looking out at myself looking in.

Viv was murdered on New Year's Eve, 1993 while the Gary Ward incident happened only months earlier on September 7th. The story in-depth is a lengthy one and it is covered in detail. Two club doormen stood in Preston Crown Court on 3rd May, 1994 and were facing a charge of murdering Mark White, 25. His naked and battered body was found on Blackpool beach near the Central Pier. The defendants, James Docherty of no fixed abode and Gary Stuart Ward of Lytham Road, South Shore were both only nineteen years old at the time of the incident, both worked as club doormen in Blackpool.

Docherty and his mother, Mrs Mary Docherty, also faced separate charges of acts intending to pervert the course of justice between September 7th and 11th. Mark White the victim in all of this had just started work as a kitchen porter at the Burroyd Hotel on Hornby Road but he stayed at his digs in South Shore the same area as Gary Ward had been staying. Mark had been drinking with friends at his workplace after he finished his duties and he left the premises at about 1.00 a.m. some three hours later at 4.15 a.m. his body was found opposite Barton Avenue, South Shore by a couple. He and Gary Ward both lived in the same area and Mark lived in the same area as he was murdered. The close proximity of all of these things shows that Mark was obviously near enough to home for it to be assumed that was where he was headed.

The post mortem revealed that Mark, the youngest of six brothers and one sister had sustained eight broken ribs and head injuries in the assault that had happened against him. There are further revelations about his injuries revealed later on in this chapter that are not for the soft natured. The parent's of Mark had to return from a holiday on the Canary Holiday Island of Tenerife when informed of his death.

A witness for the prosecution, Gail Lambert, appeared in court whilst pregnant, she was the girlfriend of Gary they had shared a flat together. Tear stricken Gail formerly Gary's bed partner was now standing giving evidence against him. Gail told the court how Gary had returned home on the morning of September 7th and his clothes were covered in sand and blood. She claimed that Gary had at first told her he had been fighting with three men. She then washed his jeans and T-shirt. Gail went on to explain to the court that the following day Gary had bought a local newspaper and said to her "Just read the paper?"

The front-page news that greeted Gail's eyes told a different story to what Gail alleges Gary had told her. The newspaper story went on to cover the details of Mark White's death. She said that Gary had told her that he held Mark White's head under the water while the lad was trying to say "Get off" but Gary had told her he could not stop himself – and then it was too late!

The prosecution looked to have an easy job here and told the court that both Ward and Docherty took it in turn to attack their victim and finally stripped him naked so as to make identification of his body more difficult. A further prosecution witness, Nigel Donsworth, seemed to put the final nail in Ward's coffin by standing in the dock. Donsworth owner of Sabre Securities swore on oath that Gary had confessed to killing Mark White. Gary had offered a plea of manslaughter at this stage, but the prosecution turned down this offer.

At this stage it would seem that with all of the evidence stacked up against Gary that this was the only option open to him. Armed with the advice that any defence barrister in the country would have given Gary at that time he offered this token plea to manslaughter that would have secured a less severe prison sentence than a conviction for murder. The motive for the murder was given that Gary Ward and James Docherty had been drinking all day and after a scuffle unconnected to Mark inside one of the clubs Gary had left seething with rage. It was alleged that Mark had bumped into Gary outside the nightspot in Blackpool. A fight ensued in which it is alleged that Gary had placed his foot on Mark's head to keep him under the water near to the Central Pier.

You have heard of the saying 'Throwing good money after bad'. Gary had previously offered a plea of manslaughter, which was turned down and now he was offering a 'guilty' plea. His hope was one of leniency in the sentence he awaited. Although a life sentence was unavoidable and the residing judge would apply a tariff to that sentence. Gary's hope was of a lenient tariff being applied to that life sentence expected. Maybe now you will understand how it seemed that Gary was chasing a falling domino circle. With each offer Gary made it only produced a counter productive effect of a small custodial sentence moving further away from him and he was vacuumed into having to make a guilty plea to the murder so as to lessen the severity of sentence.

Docherty his co-accused received a seven-year sentence of imprisonment after admitting manslaughter. This evoked anger from Mark's family when they slammed the lenient sentence given to Docherty. The presiding judge,

Mr Justice Gatehouse, was clearly shocked by the way the murder had been preceded by such brutality being inflicted on the victim and said "It's well nigh impossible to understand how one human being can so behave to another". Docherty was given a lesser sentence because it was accepted by the judge that he had played a considerably lesser part than Ward in the savage attack on Mark White and that he took no part in the drowning.

Docherty had passed all of the blame onto Gary within a police statement when he said that after Gary had told him he intended to 'whack' Mark after he had seen him on the promenade he had then said to Gary "I bet you don't". The prosecution case rested on what was said to be a motiveless attack in which detectives were sickened by the injuries Mark had suffered to every part of his body. It is alleged that the two men either dragged Mark to the sands or that he was already on the sands when they come across him and that the attack was not expected so he was caught unawares. His reason for being on the sands would be unclear if that was the scenario unless he was relieving his bladder. Police detectives believed that Docherty and Gary took it in turns to carry out a sustained attack on Mark using their feet, fists and knuckle-dusters while each of them went to the promenade stairs to keep a look out. Gary was alleged to have returned and stood on Mark's head until 'the bubbles stopped'.

The body was then stripped of clothes and they were thrown into the sea, so it was alleged. The tide washed the clothing back onto the beach near to where the body was found. (Author's note: how is it known that the clothes were washed out to sea? No one witnessed this!) It is then alleged that both men considered themselves 'hard men' because they were working as club doormen for a company called Sabre Security Services and that they had to live up to the macho image the job created. The reason for the attack on Mark, it was told to Preston Crown Court, was that Gary had singled him out, it is alleged, that he had threatened him a week earlier.

The police though had a different theory and that was that Docherty and Gary had called into the *Time Gap Club* a melee occurred with Gary and another club doorman, which resulted in Gary's coat being ripped. Detective Inspector Ian Kennedy said "That incident could have dented his hard man image and effected his ego and annoyed him. When they came out of the club they saw Mr White walking along the front and they decided he would do as a victim just because he was there."

The reason the duo had become suspects, it is alleged, is that they were bragging of their deed and this helped the fifty strong murder squad home in on them. Gary was arrested in Shrewsbury where it is alleged he 'fled to' and a day earlier Docherty was arrested from premises where he was working as a doorman. There was not a lot of detective work needed in this investigation and perhaps that was the problem.

What about the victim? It would be too easy to leave Mark White out of this and then you would not know what type of a person he was so as not to make you go all soft on the side of the Gary Ward who insists he did not have anything to do with killing him. Then I could be blamed of overlooking the victim so apologies are given to the victim's parents if they have this matter pointed out to them. It is stated in the Blackpool Evening Gazette that Mark a bachelor was an unassuming friendly type who had been working as a kitchen porter for a number of months. His family was from Radcliffe near Bury. Mark's death was shattering news to his family he was known as a quiet lad and had not been in any trouble, he got on with everyone and was not aggressive at all, he kept himself to himself.

Mark's father, Gordon, was, naturally, deeply shocked by the murder and he was appalled at the low sentence that Docherty received and he went on to say "Years ago murder would have been a hanging offence." I now ask you to recall what you first read at the beginning of this chapter about Derek Bentley? Mark's father has a right to say those things as his grief will never come to an end and therefore it is only understandable that he would want his son's killer/s to receive their just deserts and it is understandable that really nothing less would be wished on someone who committed such a violent vicious attack on a family member.

When someone suffers such loss and the alleged killer/s is/are apprehended and eventually receive punishment it could be said that justice has run its course. But what if the killer/s has/have not been apprehended for their crime? What if someone went missing without trace and you did not know if they were alive or dead? That uncertainty could keep a glimmer of hope alive that they were alive and well even if at the back of your mind you had a niggling doubt. That is what happened in the case of Carol Park's family when she went missing some 21 years ago.

Carol, 31, mother of three from Leece near Barrow-in-Furness had stayed in bed because it was alleged she felt too ill to join her husband and the children on a day trip to Blackpool. The hope of ever seeing Carol alive were dashed after her body was found at the bottom of the lakebed at Coniston Water in Cumbria by amateur divers putting an end to the mystery of her whereabouts. Her body was weighted down and wrapped in plastic sacking - this was now a murder inquiry.

The most obvious suspect was her husband, Gordon, now married for a third time. He was arrested and all looked cut and dried but there was insufficient evidence to bring about a prosecution. Carol's brother, Ivor Price, thought it was all over and the anguish he had suffered over the discovery that she was not ever going to come back was compounded by the fact that no one had been brought to justice over her murder. Ivor had tolerated 21 years of despair and hope of his sister's whereabouts and now what should have been the final torment of having her killer brought to justice was not to be.

Ivor a retired shipyard worker said 'You think it's all over, then suddenly the whole thing is dropped and you are in a crisis again and it keeps going around in your mind as to what happened.' His wife, Maureen, said 'You can't feel as though you've put somebody to rest until the person who killed them has been found – only then can they be put to rest.' The funeral service was arranged by Gordon Park's family and it was a daunting experience for Ivor and Maureen to attend he said 'The wife and I and the family will not come to terms with it until there is justice. Justice takes the aching away – somebody has paid the price and you know what happened. My faith keeps me going without it I'd have gone under totally.'

Ivor's belief in God gave him strength and that similiarity can be compared to some of those close to Viv. Their faith kept them going in similar moments to that what Ivor faced and still faces. The killer of a family member has brought suffering beyond what words can describe to those that are living; living victims. The similiarity between Ivor and Peter Connelly is uncanny and Ivor said 'I go on with it in the hope that in the end this will bring to justice the person who did it. I'll go to any lengths to do that, I've got to.' Peter is of the same mind and obviously the similarities will go on about a number of other things. Both men cannot rest and feel easy until the killer of their respective family member is brought to justice. Another similarity with Viv's family is that Ivor has suffered further tragedy in life with the loss of a sister, Christine, seven years before Carol disappeared! His brother died then he and Maureen lost their daughter, Debbie, 24, to leukaemia the toll was too much for Ivor's mother and she passed away soon after. To say Ivor has been to hell and back he says, 'I would like to think my family and I can rebuild our lives as best we can and that we will have greater peace of mind...it will be an end to this hell of hells.'

With new advancements in forensic science Ivor hopes that with the evidence the police have that it will bring the killer to justice and he finishes off by saying 'That person has seen me on TV and seen me suffering. Surely in their heart as a human being they must be feeling it now. If they had a heart, they'd feel some remorse for the family. Whoever committed the murder is not going to be safe. They have a life of hell ahead of them because that knock at the door can come at any time. The family of Carol still appeal for anyone around the Coniston Water area in the long hot summer of 1976 to come forward if they saw anything suspicious that could help lead to the conviction of her killer.

How does this tie in with the Gary Ward case? Should it turn out that Gary was not involved in the murder of Mark White then the anguish of Mark's father might only be increased. Justice is seen to be done when his son's killers are brought to, but what could be worse than that? The answer is an injustice! Knowing that your son's killers have been punished cannot lessen the loss but a sense of justice has prevailed and the pieces of everyone's lives can be threaded together even if only loosely. However if the conviction of one of the alleged perpetrator's of the crime seems unsafe then the sense of justice has been tarnished and if a wrong has been done then it must be remedied as fast as possible so that the pain that the victim's family is going through is not drawn out. The difficulty though is that British Justice, although the envy of the world is slow in re-examining possible miscarriages of justice.

Convicted child killer, Maxine Robinson, 30, imprisoned in the notorious 'She Wing' in HM Prison Durham at time of writing insists upon her innocence. Her crime it is alleged is that she murdered her two children as they slept five month old son Anthony and 19-month old daughter Christine were, the prosecution said, 'Suffocated by Maxine as they slept.' The family home was in Ouston just outside of Gateshead near Chester-le-Street and in June 1993, Maxine's husband, Peter, returned home to find his children dead. He was a key prosecution witness in the four week trial that led to his wife being convicted on very flimsy evidence if any at all. A top pathologist suggests that there is no evidence of suffocation. Campaigners suggest that the deaths were cot deaths. Maxine's first child, Victoria, was also the victim of a cot death.

Maxine has insisted from within her prison cell that she would rather die behind bars than admit to murdering her two babies who died mysteriously. She adorns her cell wall with photographs of her children and now waits for the Criminal Cases Review Commission to assess the merits of her case for a renewed appeal.

In the meantime she has the Justice group on her side and also the support of a convicted murderer's stepmother who successfully fought to have his conviction overturned. That case in itself created history when Phillip English was convicted of murder when he was held in custody by a police officer some ten yards away from PC Bill Forth when Mr English's associate, high on drugs, lashed out with a knife and stabbed PC Forth who died. This was very reminiscent of the Derek Bentley case that this chapter was opened with.

The ruling of joint enterprise caveat meant that Mr English was held also to be guilty of the murder of PC Forth at Sunniside just outside of Gateshead. Mandy English tirelessly campaigned for her step-sons conviction to be overturned and in her opinion, after having read some of the case papers she cannot see what evidence there is for a conviction. So there you have it a top pathologist, a leading body acting on behalf of unfair convictions-Justice and an experienced campaigner are all of the same mind which is that there is little if any evidence at all to support her conviction.

Continuing along the lines of convincing the doubting Thomas' out there here is a very celebrated case that took place in 1981 when it was alleged by the prosecution that top surgeon, Paul Vickers, now 63, murdered his sick wife, Margaret, 44, with an anti-cancer drug. The motive was that he was having an affair with a former beauty queen, Pamela Collison, a former political researcher for Michael Heseltine and his wife was in the way of his ambitions to become a Euro MP for Northumberland.

The claim made by Mr Vickers was that he was treating his wife with the drug because he thought she had a tumour in her brain. Ms Collison told police that she believed her lover killed his wife. Both she and Mr Vickers were arrested and charged with murder to cut a long story short she walked while Mr Vickers received a life sentence for murder after the 25-day trial at Teesside Crown Court.

Since Mr Vicvkers' incarceration he has appealed no less than four times: 1983 – turned down by a judge, 1988 – turned down by the Home Secretary, 1990 – turned down by the Home Secretary and 1994 when fresh medical evidence was produced by pathology expert Professor Laurence Henry the appeal failed despite this. Mr Vickers has maintained his innocence throughout his imprisonment although in his parole application he does admit a role in his wife's death he does not accept that it was murder. It is important to remember that in order to be eligible for parole consideration Mr Vickers and any other prisoner applying for parole must address their offending behaviour. In order to address their offending behaviour of course they have to start somewhere in terms of admitting their crime. A denial of the offence would naturally not go towards helping the parole board's decision hence Mr Vickers' stance in accepting that he accepts responsibility for the role he played in contributing towards his wife's death.

Jim Cousins, Newcastle Central MP, has spoken out about Mr Vickers sentence and has raised doubts about the conviction. He said that there was room for legitimate doubt and that he had doubt in his mind as to the safety of the conviction. Ms Collison does not wish to have any contact with the man that once wrote to her in a letter 'everything I can ask of a woman – love, lust and sex' was something she had combined within her. Parole looks a likelihood for the impressive surgeon who had it all he was dubbed Doctor Death. Mr Vickers a model prisoner has no intentions of returning to Newcastle when eventually released. Maybe in time forensic science will unveil the truth.

James Hanratty hanged for murder in 1962 for what became known as the A6 murder when it is alleged he murdered government scientist, Michael Gregston, 36, and then raped and shot Gregston's lover, Valerie Storie, 22. Hanratty's name has become the by-word for miscarriages of justice over the years. Only now has forensic science advanced enough to be able to carry out tests from semen stains taken from underwear that Miss Storie was wearing. Hanratty's mother, Mary, now suffering from senile dementia has had swabs of saliva taken from her so that cross matching the DNA can once and for all prove one way or the other if he did the crime. No news at time of writing on the results if any of that test.

These cases have been mentioned to show that miscarriages of justice do happen and that it can take years of campaigning to get the cases heard sometimes many years after the person's death. Maybe I could be accused of going overboard and giving my own opinions, this is not true, do not be fooled by what the press may report about this or the last book. I do not seek to curry the favour of arseholes and at the risk of having poor write ups if even any at all I continue with these important disclosures relevant to the Gary Ward case.

Stephen Craven convicted of the Penny Laing murder in trendy overcrowded Newcastle's *Studio* nightclub in which Miss Laing suffered at the hands of a sex pest maniac who slashed her across the neck severing her juggler vein. This was covered in detail in *Viv (Graham) – 'Simply the Best'* so I will only briefly cover it. Craven is currently appealing against the conviction and he is supported by his family as is expected but when it was discovered that Viv had felt it was a man from London allegedly connected with the Marines that had carried out the murder I was told by a senior police officer that Craven was the right man and they were not looking for anyone else. The officer went on to explain that Viv was advised by the police that they had the right man and that Viv was alleged to have left it at that and not pursued the matter any further. I was told that Viv had telephoned a man in London and asked him to come back and face the charge of murder but the two explanations clash and it has to be left at that since Viv is not here to prove what he did or did not do pertaining to finding out who Penny's killer really was.

Finally on the matter of Craven it can be revealed that it is public knowledge that blood on his shirt is the pivotal point that will be considered at his appeal and if it is concluded to be as I suspect then forensic science will have done its job.

Winding up the situation it is revealed that an ex-governor, Dr David Wilson, of Grendon Underwood jail in Buckinghamshire says that one in 50 (1,300) prisoners are innocent! This comes from a man that is a professional and on the other side of the law he has no axe to grind therefore what he says has to be listened to. What made Dr Wilson believe this? It was after Stefan Kiszko was freed in 1992 after serving some 16 years in prison because he was wrongly convicted of the murder of schoolgirl Lesley Molseed. Kiszko died one year after being released from the prison that Dr Wilson was a governor of.

Kiszko was one of many long term prisoners who refused to admit their guilt and in order for them to be considered for parole they would have to admit their guilt and address their offending behaviour which of course as previously pointed out is a prerequisite for being granted parole. It was revealed that Kiszko was advised by Dr Wilson to go on a sex offenders treatment programme and in the course of that he would have had to listen to other sex offenders going into detail about their crimes and had to have admitted his guilt about his offence and go into detail about murder of 11 year old Lesley. Dr Wilson said 'Of course he refused – it was absurd.'

Dr Wilson retired from his position and joined the Prison Reform Trust where he admits he was bombarded with pleas of innocence from convicted prisoners. The Criminal Cases Review Committee (CCRC) was formed and Dr Wilson saw an immediate 1,000 cases of alleged miscarriage of justice put to them. He is now a top academic at a university and his method of detecting that 2% of the 65,000 prison population is innocent has been worked out by a method known as triangulation. When CCRC was formed some two years ago it was an indictment against the British Justice system that it had failed and some prisoners were wrongly convicted.

It has been suggested that prisoners with cases pending at the CCRC should be treat like remand prisoners and presumed innocent which would give them better privileges such as more visits and not being forced to work for pittances of pay. The Government has no plans to change rules about prisoners awaiting appeal or for a hearing with the Commission, which can only add to the worsening plight of these appellants. It is not for me to judge the system or the Government, as it is the courts that administer justice yet there is no one to accept responsibility for the unprecedented delay in justice being seen to be done.

The Gary Ward case is no different to those mentioned. As long as he remains convicted and there is a doubt it will always be an unfair conviction. As usual you are shown the situation from as many angles as possible so that it does not become a biased view. The prosecution and Mark White's father were not pleased with the lenient sentence handed down to Docherty, Gary's co-accused. When you consider that Docherty also had further charges one was for kidnap and assault of businessman, Stephen Jeffrey, from Lytham.

In a later chapter Paddy Conroy has his case examined whereby he received a sentence of more than three times that of Docherty for alleged kidnap and torture of someone who desecrated his father's grave. Docherty received a three-year prison sentence to run concurrently alongside the seven years he received for the manslaughter of Mark. Should you not know the difference between a concurrent prison sentence and a consecutive prison sentence then I will explain: the sentence as it stands for Docherty was seven years for manslaughter and three years for kidnap & assault = ten years, but since it runs concurrently (at the same time) he only serves a seven year sentence. However should the judge have said, "The sentence is to be consecutive" I am sure you now know that it would truly be a ten-year sentence in total. It is not surprising then that the prosecution appealed against such a light sentence considering what was said in court about the way Mark White died.

Detective Superintendent Graham Gooch a serving police officer of some 23 years service said that Mark was murdered 'for an evil dare'. Comments made in court by Gary's barrister, Guy Whitburn, were refuted by Det Supt Gooch when he said 'Our evidence indicates Mr White didn't bump into Ward, we belive Docherty said to Ward "I bet you can't fill him with one punch" that's how it started.' Det Supt Gooch was not a man to be shocked easily and he went on to say, 'I'm hard to shock... but this was a horrible and motiveless attack. There was no reason or justification for it.' I'm sure we will get the entire piss head population of postgraduate criminal psychologists coming out of the woodwork now, well tough shit it has been done, too late!

The motive for the killing of Mark White has been attributed to the male macho characteristics of wanting to prove they are hard, as hard as nails some might say. Two young club doormen trying to outshine each other in a chain of events that led to a man losing his life. That is all newspaper hype so as to increase sales if such things really terrified people then no one would ever walk along a beach, particularly Blackpool beach, but that is not the case. People still do go out on to the beach without fear because it is known that not every testosterone kid out there is going to test his strength on your head with a knuckle-duster.

That is the reason though explained as to the motive for this attack, which I am sure you will now accept as being guesswork not that it is not possible though especially in the current climate of increased violent and sexual crimes. But all in all it has to be accepted that out of the millions of people who visit the Candy Rock Resort the chance of such a thing happening to them or the residents of Blackpool are pretty slim, when was the last Blackpool beach murder? So when it is alleged that Mark White was attacked for no other reason than for Gary and his co-accused to test their mettle that it would have to be deeply considered as to whether the two murderers should have been certified insane. Only a person who was insane would do such a thing to an innocent man walking back to his digs after a few drinks.

The proof of the pudding will be in X amount of years time if Gary has not been free by then due to his renewed appeal and he is still standing firm proclaiming his innocence because he would not be considered for parole at all until he addresses his offending behaviour. This must be a daunting prospect for those who are innocent. To know you will not be considered for release until you confess to having committed the crime in some way seems as barbaric as when an alleged witch was thrown into the river while their hands were tied. If they floated they were most definitely a witch and if they sunk and drowned they were innocent of the charge sounds a bit like 'heads I win, tails you lose'.

Action Against Injustice (AAI) was set up in 1996 on the tenth anniversary of Winston Silcott's unlawful imprisonment and a number of campaigns were launched to raise awareness of the plight of those who were wrongfully convicted. Protests were organised to put pressure on the Criminal Cases Review Commission and to expose police corruption. Nikki Scott took part in one of these campaigns outside of Winston Green prison her role then was as Gary Ward's Campaign. Alongside her were grim reminders of how the justice system had let down many and is still continuing to do so. Annie Whelan (Bridgewater Four), Valerie Davis (M25 case), Sue Caddick (Eddie Gilfoyle Campaign) and many more representatives of those who are undergoing injustice.

AAI had the support of many prisoners throughout Her Majesty's prisons they took part in a mass hunger strike amongst those was Gary Ward at HM Prison Wakefield along with Eddie Gilfoyle and prisoners from a further thirty two prisons took part to show their concern. This action was not against treatment whilst in prison but against the means to an end that got them there.

Gary's case, as he succinctly wrote it in his 33 page proof of evidence document, hinges on a number of issues. I have taken the liberty to edit that proof of evidence document and include some notes. Later on you will get to read of dodgy drug deals with counterfeit money and how some Geordies in a drug deal duped the Blackpool underworld.

Regina Vs Ward – Proof of Evidence

Early to mid August 1993 a deal had taken place at a businessman's address in Lytham, St Annes, Lancashire. The businessman whom is a one Mr XXXXXX XXXXXXXX (Author's note: name withheld for legal reasons.), was the mediator who brought John Barratt, Nigel Donsworth, John Herd and James Docherty (all 'Sabre Security' members/directors), to his business premises to take part in the following deal.

Two men, Stuart King and Hugh Christie, had brought some Geordies to town who wanted to buy £25,000 of amphetimines, cocaine and cannabis. Hugh Christie and Stuart King arranged for the Geordies to be present at the deal via XXXXXX XXXXXXXX bringing Barratt, Donsworth and Herd from Blackpool.

Docherty and myself were both doormen who worked for Barratt and Donsworth, all of us were present at the deal. I was armed with a Smith & Western 9mm authomatic handgun. Docherty had a Berretta handgun and Herd had a sawn-off shotgun (all concealed). The deal went good and peaceful. Barratt handed a parcel of drugs over after checking what appeared to be £25,000 in cash in a briefcase. The Geordies weighed the cannabis, tested the cocaine and the amphetimine powders. Barratt shock hands with the deal and we all left XXXXXXXX's premises.

I drove Barratt back to Blackpool in a green 'G' registration Ford Granada.

I dropped him off at 97 Ellesmere Road, Marton, Blackpool and drove to the Marlborough Hotel in Blackpool to collect Docherty, as he had travelled with Herd and Donsworth (in a white 2-door Toyota sports car) from XXXXXXXX's premises. The Geordies left Lytham in a blue Vauxhall Senator, Christie and King left Lytham in white Mercedes car.

After Docherty was dropped off in the town I rang Barratt on a mobile phone. He asked me to deliver the Granada to XXXXXXXX as a commission for his part in the deal, which I did. A few days later the police who found the Granada as a ringed car (stolen with its identity changed) pulled this businessman in a random stop/search. The man said that it had been bought in good faith from a man in a pub (authors note: not the 'man in a pub' story again!) and produced a bill of sale which got him off from being prosecuted for handling stolen goods. One day later this businessman was kidnapped by Docherty, Herd and Barratt. The reason was that the £25,000 that the Geordies had bought the drugs with had turned out to be counterfeit money! Barratt was none too pleased. I believe XXXXXXXX reported this to the Lancashire police and gave them a chilling account of what happened to him, as Barratt, Herd and Docherty wanted to know where Christie and King were. I assume this was so that they could trace the Geordies through them. XXXXXXXX was eventually taken into police protection and placed in a safe house with his wife XXXXXXX.

A day or so later Barratt was arrested from 97 Ellesmere Road. The police recovered handguns and forged documents. At the same time Donsworth's address, 8 Mayfield Drive, Rossall Beach, Cleavley's was raided by the police where they recovered a twelve bore double barrelled shotgun and from John Herd's address (a flat underneath the Marlborough Hotel, Central Promenade) a sawn-off shotgun and ammunition was recovered with various forged documents.

On the night of the kidnapping I was working as a security guard at Kirkham Grammar School. I finished at midnight and was home with Gayle Lambert by 12.30 a.m. I believe that the kidnapping took place between 2.30/3.00 a.m. that morning. Barratt, Herd and Docherty dumped XXXXXXXX in a village in the South Lakes. Whilst they did this Donsworth, with the help of some others, they had cleared this businessman's premises in Lytham of everything of value. He used a Ford Transit van borrowed from the *Jaggy Thistle* club in Blackpool.

Barratt and Herd were remanded in custody on several charges. Donsworth was released on 'Part 4' bail. Docherty had several warrants out for his arrest including the kidnapping and was not captured until the Saturday some days later on 11th September 1993. Even though Docherty was still on bail for an assault on a soldier, Nigel Penny, whom he also threatened with the IRA, it took some days to arrest him.

Saturday 4th September, 1993, I was working at the *Ardwick* pub on

Foxhall Road, Blackpool. I should have been on duty at 11.00 a.m. but I did not arrive until 12.30 p.m. I was late because I had been working at the *Palace* nightclub on Friday night. I had not finished until 4 a.m. on 4ᵗʰ September so it was understandable my being late luckily a fellow club doorman, David Maschitter, covered for me until I arrived.

David told me when I arrived that there was a group of Geordies at the top end of the pub that needed watching. I was annoyed at him for letting a gang of lads in, as the *Ardwick* was a family pub; normally I would ensure that gangs of lads were not admitted.

Starstruck Karaokes were on stage that afternoon run by Roger and Allan. In between 1.00 and 2.00 p.m. I had occasion to twice speak to the Geordies about their behaviour. At around this time, 2.00 p.m. David had went off duty for his hour-long break. Whilst at the front door of the pub the bell rang from the bar. It was a sign that trouble had started and I knew it had to be connected to the Geordies so I ran into the bar to the table where the five Geordie's were.

I disarmed one of them from a fire extinguisher because he was spraying it over other patrons, the club was packed at this point. I sent Antonia Watson for back up from the *Casablanca* club, *Uncle Peter Webster's* and the *Tavern*. Roger & Allan of Starstruck and Antonia witnessed me confront a man, six foot in height with black hair and wearing a navy/white rugby shirt, jeans and shoes. He weighed about 16-18 stone and was of heavy/stocky build. The man I took the extinguisher off was about 5'-6" tall he had short dark hair, wearing a shirt, jeans and trainers and he was of medium build. He punched me when my back was turned.

About eight doormen turned up acting, as my back up one of which was Docherty. Several of the doormen had Cromby coats on and the pub went quiet. The Cromby coats were opened on some of them revealing baseball bats. Four of the Geordies started humming and making silly apologies but the one whom I was locked in a confrontation with told me he'd be back to take me out, this I took to mean he would kill me. These sorts of threats are commonplace to any doorman. I cannot be absolutely sure about this but I believe that three out of the five Geordies were at the previously mentioned meeting in Lytham.

Two days later Docherty and I met up in town at about noon on Monday 6ᵗʰ September we went on a pub-crawl to many different pubs and clubs. The last pub we went into was the *Time Gap* on Central Promenade. An off duty doorman, John Radd, and I had an argument in there. He ripped my jacket to embarrass me and made it known that he thought I was too young to be working as a doorman. I invited Radd outside and Docherty told me that he would intervene and punch Radds associate, Malcolm Boyle, (another doorman on duty at that time) if he interfered. Docherty handed me a ringed knuckle-duster as we left the club assuming that Radd and Boyle were

271

following us out.

Immediately upon leaving the club I was confronted by a man with two others who had Geordie accents. Because of something said I recognised them as the men from the 'fire extinguisher' incident from the *Ardwick*. I threw the first punch wearing the knuckle-duster and Docherty dropped one of the other two men and chased after the third Geordie who ran off. The man I hit I will refer to as man 'A' the one Dochery hit as being man 'C' and the one he chased after as man 'B'. (See enclosed layout above heading *Gary Ward – The Blackpool Beach Murder.*)

I fought with man A at point 3. I was aware that Docherty might have been having difficulty with man C getting up and chasing him as Docherty was chasing man B. I ran to catch them up so as to even the odds. Man A was left semi-conscious at point 3.

I caught up with Docherty and witnessed him drowning a man. I assumed it to be one of the Geordies and upon my trying to stop Docherty he pulled a gun out on me. We had a scuffle after it was established that the man had died which resulted in me having a limp and a cut lip.

Docherty headed straight for an all-night café illustrated at point 5. As we walked along the promenade Docherty threatened to shoot my brother, Jason Cain, if I opened my mouth to anyone about the beach murder. I found it to be coincidental that our employer, Nigel Donsworth, was there who spoke with Docherty inside while I sat on a nearby wall. Donsworth came over to ask me if I was OK and he asked me for the knuckle-duster which I gave him. He gave me a £20 note and told me to get a taxi over to Gayle's flat. I was asked by Docherty to follow him around to a friend of his, Julie Bingham, so he could get cleaned up. We then walked around to Tyldsley Road at point 7. Julie would not let Docherty in when he shouted up so we went to my flat at 61 Lytham Road where I used a pillowcase to wipe what I can only assume was man A's blood off my ripped jacket. I think the police found the pillowcase when they raided my flat.

Docherty and I went up Lytham Road to the *Kettle of Fish* restaurant I went in while he waited outside. We parted company at Waterloo Road whereby Docherty had given me his knuckle-duster and told me he would pick it up the next day, as he did not want to get caught with it by the police. I was reminded yet again to keep my mouth shut. I immediately went to Gayle's flat leaving Docherty who, I had assumed would go on to his mother's at St Bedes Road.

When I arrived at Gayle's she was waiting up for me with my brother, Jason, as he was staying with us for a few days. I explained what had happened about the fight with the three Geordie's and I was fussed over by Gayle. I went to bed while Gayle waited up to see Jason off as he was leaving at 6.00 a.m. that Tuesday as he was catching the early morning train back to Scotland to see his girlfriend. Gayle washed my clothes in the sink by hand, so she says, and cleaned my boots which she told police were covered in sand.

Later that day Docherty called around for his knuckle-duster he told me that my boss wanted to see me. I refused to go. The following day, Wednesday 8th September the newspapers and the rest of the media were covering the beach murder and reporting that the deceased's penis had been bitten off and that the body had been identified as Mark Gregory White, 25, who was a hotel porter in Blackpool who had originated from Radcliffe in Manchster. After hearing this I was somewhat confused as I thought the man Docherty had drowned was in fact a Geordie. I then told Gayle everything that had happened including how I thought this was a follow on from the *Ardwick* 'fire extinguisher' incident with the group of Geordies. (Author's note: Peter Connelly told me how his potential brother-in-law Viv had liked to play about letting fire extinguishers off. Make of this what you will. Blackpool is only about 2 ½ hours away from Newcastle in a reasonably fast car. I did it in three hours taking my time.) I told Gayle how I had tried to stop Jim Docherty from doing what he did.

Nigel Donsworth (alias Max) came around the flat to see me at 5.00 p.m. He told me he was taking me to see a solicitor. I told him that I had told Gayle everything. I asked him about the knuckle-duster he said it had been destroyed. I was then taken to see Keith Cartmell of Cartmell Solicitors 201 Church Street, Blackpool. I believe that Donsworth and Barratt had used this firm of solicitors many times before given that Sabre Security were subject to lots of litigation matters I found out some two months before my trial. I told Cartmell all that had happened on the beach and during the night of the murder present were James Rawlinsoin, a partner in the company, and Donsworth. I was advised to go to the police by Cartmell and tell them what I had told him about Docherty.

Donsworth ran me back to Gayle's where I began packing because on the way back he said I should pack and leave town for a few days until the murder case had blown over. Docherty came over whilst I was packing and Gayle called him a "bastard", etc. for involving me in all of this. Docherty asked to speak with me outside and warned me to tell Gayle to keep her mouth shut otherwise he would arrange a nasty "accident" for her. I asked Gayle to stay quiet and that I would ring her to let her know where I was so she could come and join me. Docherty took me into town.

I phoned Helen Louise Kamadu in Shrewwsbury from the *Ardwick* pub I asked her to come and pick me up, although she was not a girlfriend she was a close friend. She set off almost immediately to pick me up. I told her that there was some gang rivalry taking place and that I would be doing myself a favour by keeping well out of the way. When I arrived in Shrewsbury I stayed with Helen, her brother and mother, Brenda. They were aware that there was a good reason for me staying with them. I had decided to go back to Blackpool and hand myself in and as we were pulling out of the drive the police pounced and I was arrested by armed police in unmarked cars whilst marked cars blocked off the road ends.

I was cuffed and frisked and then asked if Docherty was in the premises that we had just left. By this time the cuffs were digging into my wrists and two plain clothed officers tried to get me into a Montego. I would not because the cuffs were too tight. I asked that they be loosened and refused to get into the car until they were. In an effort to get me into the car I was kneed in the stomach so that I would bend forward but that did not work and I remained upright. A senior officer came over and I explained what the problem was at which point he ordered that the cuffs be released a bit and once this was done I co-operated.

At 1.30 p.m. I was in custody inside Shrewsbury police station. I refused to sign any forms, which included the custody record, my property sheet or the fact that I was informed of my rights. By 2.30 p.m. I was being driven at high speed under armed escort up the M6 back to Blackpool. Detective Inspector Turnbull asked me where Docherty was. I asked why and was told, "I want him off the streets before anyone else gets hurt or killed."

Upon my arrival in Blackpool's custody/charge room Keith Cartmell was waiting for me. We had a chat in the interview room. He asked me why the West Lancashire Drugs Squad was waiting to interview Nigel Donsworth, as he was acting on Donsworth's behalf. I assumed given that he voluntarily went into the police station on the morning of Saturday 11th September and told the police a bullshit story that I had confessed the murder to him. His knowledge of the facts would have come from the pre-arrest meeting I had with Keith Cartmell on the previous Wednesday in his office on the 8th September. His story as I will explain later hides his involvement/conspiracy to the murder by the way he assisted James Docherty.

Keith Cartmell had told me that he had spoken at length with Donsworth. He also said that he had been told to remind me of the word "Ricki"! 'Ricki Laine' is my brother's (Jason Cain) stage name for showbiz work he does. Cartmell asked me what it meant? I did not answer him although I did know exactly what he meant – it was a reminder to Docherty's threat on Jason's safety being good on the night of the murder. The inference to me was "keep quiet about the murder"

Saturday 11th September 7.50 p.m. Det Insp Turner, Det Sgt Gill, Keith Cartmell and I are present but I refuse to answer any questions about the murder as I am still in shock from being arrested six hours earlier. I learn that the police know about the incident in the *Ardwick* on Saturday 4th September 1993. They ask me questions about John Barratt being in prison. Thus, the inference is they are aware of the connection in the drug deal, the kidnapping and the Geordies. I also learn that Gayle had been brought in for questioning earlier in the day. Her flat and mine had been raided simultaneously.

Gayle has supposedly made a statement twelve pages long. I am suspicious of this statement given that I knew she was supposed to be in Bolton at her mother's on Friday 10th September. She says I came home resembling something out of a horror show! The police are aware of a fight with three lads. (Men A, B & C.) I feel intimidated by the police's oppressive questioning. Under duress I refuse to answer any questions. Bite marks are discussed and the police went on to say that this attack had all the hallmarks of a "gay attack" and they go on to accuse me of being gay. (Author's note: this does not tie in with what was said later on by Det Sup Graham Gooch when he said this was a 'motiveless attack'. If it was thought to have been a gay bashing attack or a gay lover's tiff at this stage of questioning how did it suddenly become a motiveless attack?) I also learn that Max (AKA Nigel Donsworth) had also been into the station voluntarily, whereas Gayle had been cautioned.

My solicitor, Cartmell, tells me in the break that Docherty is in custody and that he has got a message via Docherty's solicitor, Michael Ball, that I am to admit to fighting with one of the three men. Cartmell asks me if I want to tell the police what I told him. I then briefed Cartmell about the drug deal mentioned earlier on. He told me it would be OK to admit to fighting with one of the men, obviously to extract information from the police to see how much they did know.

My second interview was at 9.00 p.m. and it soon becomes clear that the police are talking about someone very different to any Geordies! I am trying to establish my side of what happened. I am persistent and insist that the man I fought was one out a group of Geordies. I am trying to establish my side of what had happened. I am persistent and insist that the man I fought was one out of a group who was at the Ardwick on Saturday 4th September 1993. I point out that I assumed the man out of the three came back looking for me in relation to the events of Saturday 4th. I deny any involvement in killing someone. I also make every effort to keep Docherty's name out of my interviews given that I feared for my brother's safety. I learn how the police are more informed than I am. Helen Kamudu told them specifically what I had said about the gang rivalry.

The third police interview took place on Sunday 12th September at 12.30 p.m. I am still insisting that I did not drown man **A** whom I say I was fighting with opposite the *Time Gap*. The police mention two other names of suspects they have in mind and I still do not spill the beans on Docherty. My story does not add up to the police as it is obvious we are talking at cross purposes, I am talking about man **A** and the police talking about the deceased.

I learn that Mark White died around 3.00 a.m. because that was when the tide was in. The couple who found his body said they called the police at

4.40 a.m. It has been verified by the police that at that time (4.40 a.m.) I was at Gayle Lambert's flat so I could not have witnessed the couple's discovery of Mark's body. That was even though I had said that I saw them find the body that was in fact information I had extracted from newspapers before I left Blackpool.

I was rather weary from all the interviewing and constant pressure so at the end of statement number 3 I admitted killing the man on the beach just out of stress and frustration so as to get the interview over with. I did the same in interview number 4.

Whilst on remand in a hospital unit awaiting location I wrote to my mother and in that letter I made an admission of the murder in that what was said to the police. Prison officials intercepted the letter and later used/unused or it could have been additional evidence in the case papers. Only four pages were used and the other four pages 5, 6, 7, & 8 are not there therefore the letter had only part of it used out of context but was meant to do damage and help the prosecution.

Whilst awaiting trial I made application to have better conditions and each time I did this I was put in solitary confinement. It took a letter of complaint to Dame Ellaine Kellet Bowman, MP for Lancaster, to have these abuses of remand rights stopped.

Gayle Lambert regularly visited me in prison from September to late November 1993. In early October she told me that she thought she was pregnant and if she was then I was definitely the father. She told me that Donsworth had been to see her quite a few times telling her that she was not to go anywhere near the forthcoming trial. Gayle had no intentions of going to court anyway. Visiting arrangements were that whenever Gayle visited me he (Docherty) also received a visit at the same time from his sister Kirsteen. It became apparent to me that Kirsteen was actually watching Gayle for Docherty. It seemed more than just a coincidence that Docherty received a visit every time I did.

Keith Cartmell gave me a copy of the depositions (legal paperwork and witness statements). This happened when we were in Blackpool magistrates' court. I went to the toilet leaving the paperwork in the cell that Docherty and I shared. When I got back to prison I looked through the paperwork and realised that there was some documents missing. I telephoned my solicitor and asked how many statements Docherty had made to the police he said, "Four", I knew then that Docherty had stolen parts three and four out of my paperwork whilst I had visited the toilet when we shared a cell together at magistrates' court. Docherty obviously had an ulterior motive for doing this?

Returning to my wing I had all of my case papers removed from my personal possession and they were placed in the wing safe by the governor Mr Parfitt. I challenged this decision and because of that I was placed once more in solitary confinement. (Author's note: this is left in for you to read and for possible future litigation against the authorities for breaching many of the rights that Gary was allowed under Home Office rules and the European Convention for Human Rights.)

On October 20th 1993 a parcel arrived for me from Cartmell I believe it clearly stated 'Rule 37A – Legal Correspondence' on the package. (Author's note: this means that it is sent directly from a legal representative and contains paperwork directly connected to the case of the person it is addressed to. Prison officials can look through it to ensure there is no contraband within the pages and then it has to be handed over to the prisoner.) I was asked to sign for this, but could not have it. (Author's note: this sounds quite feasible since mail I personally forwarded to Patrick Conroy was interfered with by prison officials and Patrick was asked to sign for mail before he had even seen it and then it was not given to him which of course would give anyone the impression he had in fact received the mail!) Then the solitary officer Mr James Anthony Lively claimed that he had placed it into my property. The next thing I am aware of is an additional bundle (pile of legal papers) being served on Cartmell. Officer Lively apparently wrote a security report saying that I had confessed the murder to him in a one-to-one counselling session. I believe Officer Lively had without any authorisation censored the bundle that was sent to me which contained parts 3 & 4 of Docherty's statements that were previously missing.

Late November 1993 I stopped Gayle Lambert from visiting me, the reason for this was that Docherty had told me whilst we were both in the exercise yard that she had grassed him up to the police in her statement for the murder. I would not have known what she said as I had not read her statement due to Governor Parfitt relieving me of my paperwork and having it put into the wing safe.

On visits Gayle would tell me how she wanted me to come home to her if I was released and that she loved me. She said she was not going to go to court and that the police later threatened her by saying if she did not go to court they would charge her with perverting the course of justice just like they did with Docherty's mother. She had refused to make any incriminating statement against her son. I was concerned that Docherty had said he was going to punch Gayle on a visit for grassing him up. That is the reason I stopped her from visiting me. In late November/early December Barratt and Herd were released on court bail.

The first day of the trial saw John Barratt, John Herd, Mary Docherty, James Docherty and myself in the dock. Barratt, Herd & Docherty pleaded not guilty to their charges. Mary Docherty pleaded not guilty to perverting the course of justice and I pleaded guilty to involuntary manslaughter. My plea was rejected in an improper speech to the jury whereby the prosecution

In an improper speech to the jury said, "This plea is not acceptable to the Crown." I gave Cartmell an instruction to retract all of my statements at the committal hearing for trial on February 4th 1994. I gave him a list of witnesses to trace, which he failed to do so. One month before the trial I wrote to Preston Crown Court requesting a transfer of legal aid to a new solicitor in an addition to this an adjournment was requested so as to brief new counsel. His Honour Justice Lockett refused this application. (Gary gives reference to: Regina v Harris, Crim LR 244 C.A. (page 874 – Ss 7 – 86), Archibold Case Law – Criminal Pleading March 1997 Edition – wrongful denial of legal representation.) I actually sacked all of my defence team because I discovered my barrister, Timothy White, was representing Barratt and Herd in relation to Docherty's other charges. This was one of my reasons I gave to the Crown Court in my request to seek fresh representation. I also offered up for the consideration the fact that it was Donsworth that had secured the services of Cartmell and not myself.

Donsworth was heard by my father, George Ward, asking Cartmell for advice as to whether he should say he had amnesia or not. When I confronted Cartmell about this he confirmed Donsworth had in fact said that. Donswortth took the stand and gave evidence against myself only he mentioned nothing about Docherty.

Barratt and Donsworth actually went to the cells in Preston Crown Court to speak with Docherty after the trial. This is when my first real suspicion was proved that they had all colluded against me and set me up for a 'life' sentence for murder. The court cells visitors register will confirm this visit took place. Gayle Lambert appeared for the prosecution heavily pregnant and my defence, Guy Whitburn (QC) said that if he cross-examined her it would lead to the jury taking an extreme disliking to me. Therefore Gayle's evidence went unchallenged for that reason alone. Guy Whitburn knew that Gayle was a hostile witness due to her having visited me but this was left as it was.

(Author's note: what Gary writes immediately after this should be considered in his favour as it pertains to club doorman registration scheme where potential club security staff are vetted and have to attend a course to prove their reliability and temperament as potential door staff.) My father also spoke to Det Insp Turner and he was asked if the policemen were generally getting on with the doormen in Blackpool. Turner replied: "Very well. Relations have improved since we introduced the licensing/registration scheme for doormen." My father then enquired if I was registered. Turner said that I was not. However the fact is, I *was* a registered doorman with Blackpool Town Hall. Licenising Sergeant Paul Degnan at Blackpool police granted me my licence to work on the doors. Paul Degnan actually ran a course at the *Savoy* hotel in Blackpool. I attended that course in March/April 1993. My licence was given to me in August 1993, after I had been vetted by Blackpool police. Had I a criminal record with offences of violence or drugs I would not have received my licence. The fact I had neither on my record (apart from petty/minor motoring offences) meant that I was eligible for a licence.

Upon pleading guilty to murder on the second day of the trial the jury returned a verdict of guilty. Docherty pleaded guilty to manslaughter and a series of other charges. Barratt and Herd were bailed to appear in court at a later date. Mary Docherty was dismissed from the dock after the Crown Prosecution Service said it was willing to allow her charge to lie on file! The pleas were accepted by the CPS rather than independent verdicts from the jury. I understand that the following case law applies:

The Proviso – Conviction Unsafe (page 857 – Ss 7 – 45) Archibold Case Law Book:
>Regina V Manners – Astley 52, Cr App R, 5 (Non-direction)
>Regina v Ashley 52, Cr App R, 42
>Regina v Gambling (1975) Q.B. 207, Q.B. 207, 60, Cr App R25
>Regina v McVey (1988) Crim L.R. 127 C.A.
>Regina v Gibson 77, Cr App R, 151

Conduct of Trial Judge
Page 872 (7 – 81) See Regina v Matthews & Matthews 78 Cr App R, 23

Venire de Novo
(Page 879 7 – 103) Regina v Baker 7 Cr App R 217, CCA

Practical Application
Regina v Ditch 53, Cr App R, 627
Regina v Kemble, 91 Cr App R, 178 at 7 – 215 (Page 926)

Docherty received a total of ten years (seven years for manslaughter) and three yesars to run concurrently for other offences he pleaded guilty to. On 5th May, 1994, I heard on the radio that Det Supt Graham Gooch from Blackpool says that the courts should never have allowed Docherty out on bail to kill Mark White. (Author's note: there is currently a case where a man from Gateshead is pursuing a complaint against the police authority because his son was knifed to death by a lunatic who had been given two police bails for offences of violence. This man's son was murdered over his coat and had the perpetrator of the crime not been given bail then he would not have been out on the streets to kill this defenceless sixteen year old boy. Two police officers have already been reprimanded for this. Understandably the boy's father is still not happy at this and is pursuing the matter further. This could leave the door open for Mark White's father to pursue a line of action against Lancashire Police Force. It is a considered fact that those who have been bailed for acts of violence are likely to commit further acts of violence whilst on bail.)

Docherty and myself were moved to HMYOI at Castington, Morpeth next door to Acklington Prison. (Author's note: Castington is considered to be the most secure type of prison for long term sentenced young offenders as both were under the age of 21.) I was involved in a fight with another inmate called 'Kennedy'. This resulted in me being taken to the block (segregation block) where I accidentally lashed out when I was pinned to the floor by the block screws. My elbow caught one of them and for this I paid a dear price it ended up that I had to be taken to Ashington hospital the following day for treatment and a head X-ray. I wrote to a local solicitor in Ashington at Albion Way but the next day I was shipped out (ghosted) to HM Prison Moorland. I had passed on plans of the prison to another inmate at Castington who wanted to escape, as I knew the area pretty well since I had family living in the area so the prison regime wanted rid of me ASAP.

On arriving at Moorlands I was given what was left of my depositions and on close scrutiny it was obvious to see that I was not guilty of all the police made me out to be. I then contacted Max Gold & Co in Hull. They went about arranging for me to have a full set of case papers. Cartmell advised me that I had no grounds for an appeal. It was in November of 1994 when I started making enquiries of whom it was I was actually fighting with on the night of the murder. I would like to point out that there are no eyewitnesses or forensic evidence linking myself to the murder. However there is forensic evidence linking Docherty to the murder.

Nigel Donsworth's Statement/Testimony CPS Hearsay witness

Nigel Howard Donsworth was a director/business partner with John Barratt at Sabre Security Services, 20 Queen Street, North Shore, Blackpool. He stated that I appeared outside the cafeteria window on the night of the murder, looking agitated and upset and I was limping. He alleges I rang him on his mobile phone and he called around to Gayle's flat where he heard my confession that I had done it. This of course is a lie and I in fact told him what I have always said happened. Donsworth then goes on to say things about Docherty, asking me if Docherty had bitten Mark White's penis, etc. I told him I did not see Docherty biting or fighting with the lad on the beach, whom I assumed, was a Geordie. I told him I had only saw Docherty drowning the lad I told Cartmell the same story when Docherty was present.

Donsworth visited Docherty while he was on remand at a place called Lancaster Farms and he was also visiting Barratt and Herd at Preston whilst they were on remand. Donsworth was the only person not charged with any offence connected to drugs especially since West Lancashire Drugs Squad had been keen to speak with him. Apparently he had done a deal with the police and later on his connection with the police was confirmed by an investigator. (Author's note: this sounds a similar equation to the David

Glover, Jnr, situation whereby it is alleged he had done a deal to get off with certain charges he faced because of his involvement with the Geordie Mafia. More of this later though.)

A brass knuckle-duster was shown to Gayle Lambert in the course of the trial. It had been cut in half but Gayle had still identified it as being the one that I had come home with on the night of the murder. My defence, Guy Whitburn; QC, was instructed to ascertain how Donsworth had handed over the knuckle-duster in the condition that it was in to Docherty's solicitor, Michael Ball. I later learned from my case papers at Moorlands that this knuckle-duster was consistent in its symmetries to various head injuries the deceased received. Docherty had let it slip that Nigel had bleached the knuckle-duster and had also cut it in half to dispose of any blood or DNA that might link the deceased. The last time I had seen the knuckle-duster was on September 7th, 1993, when Docherty collected it from Gayle's flat.

April 1996 Mick Atken of Direct Investigations in Hull acting on the instructions of Max Gold & Co Solicitors went to Blackpool and confirmed the following:

    1 <u>Yes</u> – Donsworth was the subject of an investigation by the West Lancashire Drugs Squad

    2 <u>Yes</u> – He was bailed on Part 4 for the kidnapping of Steven Jeffries

    3 <u>Yes</u> – He had been a paid police informer since the trial in May 1994

    4 <u>Yes</u> – Sabre Security had disbanded

Mr Aitkin actually called at Donsworth's home and interviewed him. Donsworth stated to my private investigator that if I called him to my appeal he would tell the court that he actually witnessed me killing the deceased. I would dearly love to take Donsworth's challenge up in order to call his bluff and to theoretically prove he lied in his statements & testimony.

Gayle Lambert CPS Hearsay witness

The excuse for not having Gayle cross-examined at trial was because of her pregnant state. Gayle, just like Donsworth was inconsistent in her statements and testimony. The QCs failure to cross-examine her now prevents me from calling Gayle back to give evidence. Thus I am questioning the material irregularities at the trial in the sense that cross-examining Gayle in her pregnant state would have prejudiced the jury in deliberation. Clearly the issue in question is to discover the truth and not be sympathetic to an acclaimed (convenient) pregnancy, which actually prejudiced my case. As my QC stated that he could foresee problems arising of that nature had he cross-examined Gayle at the trial.

(Author's note: Gary is actually right because the minute his defence had started to pursue the witness in the dock then the jury would have taken a dim view of Gary. The problem is that the jury had eyes and would see Gayle Lambert's state of pregnancy and Gary's case would have been prejudiced even more. Looking at this he did not really stand a cat in hell's chance of winning his case. A QC too frightened to pursue a pregnant woman that held the key to be able to turn the trial in Gary's favour was let off lightly considering she had changed her tune and was now a hostile witness. In instances like this were it is blatantly obvious that the jury would be sympathetic towards someone just because of their state it should be pointed out to them by the judge that the defence has just as equal a right to pursue the line of innocence for the accused as the prosecution has used that witness to their advantage to help them prove guilt regardless of their state. After all it was the prosecution that called a heavily pregnant Gayle Lambert and no reflection on their case was prejudiced by Gayle's state so why should Gary's QC, Guy Whitburn, have acted in such a way?)

I stopped Gayle from visiting me for her own safety and she insisted she would not be going to court to give evidence against me just as much as Docherty's mother had promised him faithfully. Gayle broke her promise out of spite because I had stopped her visiting me. Gayle holds some of the answers to this and she may yet come forward of her own accord.

Whilst on remand Gayle sent me lots of love letters. Around November 1993 she started work at the Jester chip shop on Lytham Road. Anne Stanley owned the chippy and she let me phone Gayle there. Anne did not believe I was guilty and for this reason I believe that Gayle may have confided in her about what I really told her. (Author's note: Hell hath no furry like a woman scorned. What made Gayle change her allegiance of loyalty from being the faithful girlfriend of a man awaiting trial for murder to becoming one of the star prosecution witnesses? Maybe Gary has the answer.)

I remember Gayle saying to me that the police had harassed her after my arrest. She was apparently told that if she did not help the police they would charge her with perverting the course of justice for washing my clothes and assisting an offender. (Author's note: this is on par with what Mary Docherty was charged with as she did not take sides against her son and she paid the price of being charged with a serious offence. No such charges were brought against Gayle and for this reason it seems likely she took the soft option of becoming a prosecution witness.) I wonder if the police threatened Gayle with giving birth in prison if she did not testify against Docherty and I. (Author's note: this is a favourite ploy of the police and I have a researcher that was told she had her children to think of when the police were pursuing a line of inquiry against myself with reference to another book I was and still am working on. Children are mothers' Achilles heal and a way of getting them to co-operate. Mary Docherty was charged with perverting the course of justice because she laundered Docherty's clothes and she refused point blank to help the prosecution incriminate her son in any way. Surely the prosecution did not think that Mary Docherty was so stupid as to think that she could wash her son's guilt away when really if she thought about it she could have just dumped her son's clothes. Most sons would not want their mother to think the worst of them that they had in fact carried out a murder and therefore they would not say, "Oh! By the way, mam, I've just murdered someone by standing on their head until they drowned do me a favour, wash my clothes so as to remove any DNA." What the prosecution believed was that Mrs Docherty was told about the murder and tried to cover her son's guilt by washing away any evidence. Mothers are very clever creatures and would not for one-minute go against their sons when a bond was formed so why should the prosecution pursue a mother's love? A mother's pain for what her son has done cannot be washed away in a court of law.)

It is worth mentioning that Gayle Lambert's statement appears in case papers against Barratt, Docherty and Herd for the kidnapping of Steven Jeffries. Additionally she once worked as a chambermaid in a hotel on St Chads Road where she stole a Lloyd's credit card in August 1993. I took £240 out of the card's account in Lloyd's Bank on Waterloo Road. Gayle told the police she had never stolen anything!

Jason Richard Cain – Alias Rikki Laine

In his statement Jason said he had only met me two years before I moved to Blackpool in 1993. I can call several witnesses who can confirm we first met in 1982 in Canvey Island, Essex. Jason was then estranged from his natural mother, who is also my mother, Mrs Sandra Neil, although we do have different fathers. Jason's father, Bobby Caine, died in 1980. As a result of this he was reunited with his natural mother via the efforts of a Mr Paul Hedges, Jason's legal guardian.

In November 1992 I worked as a security officer/dog handler for Guarda Security Services in Osborne Road, Newcastle upon Tyne. I left the same year and went to Blackpool and had a night out with Jason. I returned to Blackpool in February 1993 where I began working for Hill's Northwest Security Services in Church Street, Blackpool. They enlisted me on a doorman's registration scheme run by Blackpool police. Jason set me up with accommodation at the Gainsborough Hotel on St Chads Road; the proprietors Ray and Bonnie Lee were Jason's agents for his entertainment profession. I shortly after moved out to another accommodation and by this time Jason was at the *Jaggy Thistle* club on York Street.

I eventually left Hill's security over a pay dispute and it was around April/May 1993 that I arranged a meeting with Sabre Security via the phone. I met Nigel Donsworth and John Barratt at a cafeteria and Donsworth agreed to my employment on a self-employed basis. He gave me the *Ardwick* pub to work on Foxhall Road, the *Palace* nightclub on Central Promenade and *Annie's Bar* at the Winter Gardens.

Jason told me that he thought I was making a big mistake by working for Sabre Security as they had a reputation in Blackpool for being extreme and dishonest. I met Docherty through this job. I was given a job by Barratt to protect a girl called Antonia Watson. I had to keep an eye on her twenty-four hours a day as she had witnessed a murder outside of *Mr B's* arcade and she was to give evidence against Michael McDonnagh, 19. McDonnagh's friends had threatened her so my job was to protect her if they ever approached her. Jason expressed his dismay over this. The nephew of the owners of the *Jaggy Thistle* nightclub (Michael Campbell) was also a witness to the murder outside Mr B's arcade except he was a friend of Micky McDonnagh.

Jason had to stay with Gayle and I because he was evicted from his abode. He stayed with us for a few weeks and after my arrest he moved into an empty flat above Gayle's. He did not stay long and left owing a few weeks rent. Jason visited me on remand. He told me that the police statement was not his own words but the words of the police. He said he had been held in custody for some nine hours and had refused him a phone call and would not let him go until he signed a statement. It appeared at later inspection to be 100% collaboration with Gayle Lambert's statement. I repeatedly told Jason to leave Blackpool after John Herd was released on bail. Jason insisted that John also known, as the 'Midget' was his friend. I disagreed with this as I believed that John Herd was actually watching Jason for Docherty. I later received proof of this in letters where Docherty makes several admissions in 1995 and 1997. I tried all ways to get Jason to leave Blackpool and I wrote to him saying I would 'kick his fat arse when I got my hands on him.' My direct concern was for his immediate safety.

Early in 1997 my new girlfriend, Nicola Scott, contacted Jason after tracing him to Didsbury, Manchester. He told her that I had phoned him in the presence of Docherty on the same phone call while we were on remand in Lancaster. He alleged we had both verbally threatened him not to go to court. My defence of this is that Docherty and I were never kept on the same wing at Lancaster farms. Jason also told Paul Hedges, George Ward, Sandra Neil and Trevor Neil that he had made his statement to the police under duress and it was not his own version of what happened on the night of the murder.

Marie Cummings – Alias Maxine (Stripper)

She worked as a stripper at the *Casablanca Club* in York Street, Blackpool and was friends with Antonia Watson and Clare Curry, Docherty's girlfriend. On the night of the murder (Monday 6th Septmenber/7th September 1993) Docherty said in his statements that he was under the impression we were supposed to have met Maxine and Claire at the flats of 61 Lytham Road. This is the first I had ever learned of this supposed meeting. My defence of this is that I stated that I called at my flat to wipe the blood from my jacket, which I had assumed, and still do, that it was man **A**'s blood.

According to Maxine, Docherty had confessed the murder to her on the dance floor in the *Casablanca Club* on Friday 10th September 1993. In 1996 I briefed the Private Investigator, Mr Atiken, about the stripper named Fiona whom I asked that she be traced as she was working at the *Time Gap* on the night of the murder. Mr Aitken told me he had traced Marie Cummings to a club in Soho, London I thought he had traced the wrong stripper. I wrote to Mr Aitken to say that Marie Cummings was not the stripper working at the Time Gap. Thus he had found the wrong person and I instructed him to abort his inquiry into Miss Cummings.

However it was only until my meeting with Elizabeth McCusker (from Max Gold & Co) and barrister Rodney Fern that I understood my indiscretion concerning Marie Cummings! As Marie has made a statement saying that Docherty confessed the murder to her before his arrest. So it is now vital that she is found in order that her fresh evidence can be introduced for my appeal. The same applies to Docherty's girlfriend that her testimony could be classed as new evidence although she was traced she was never spoken to by my PI.

Barrister Rodney Fern clearly stated in his 'Advice to Appeal Grounds' that original solicitors had acted and served me very badly indeed. (Author's note: this in itself is not the grounds for a renewed appeal but contributes.)

W J Copley – Forensic Odentologist

The police released a statement to the Watson Press Agency, the Evening Gazette (Blackpool and Granada television saying that the deceased penis had been bitten off.) Upon my arrest the police asked me in interviews if I had bitten the deceased and if I was homosexual. I had no inclination of anyone being bitten. When I caught up with Docherty I did not strip the deceased although Docherty did and I certainly did not bite the deceased. I gave an impression of my teeth to the police appointed odentologist. I was unaware that the odentologist had made a report that eliminated me from having bitten Mark White. Even though I do not agree with homosexuality this does not mean I had a motive to kill someone because of sexual preferences. Besides, I had no prior knowledge as to who or what Mark White was before my arrest.

I never actually knew of the report until October 1994, which was when I received my case papers back in Moorland prison. However pre-trial I did voice my concerns about the press alleging that the deceased penis had been bitten off. In fact I told my barrister at the trial to argue that I did not bite anyone. Had I of known about the odentologist's report then I would have pursued that matter more vigorously? The odentologist also named two other suspects. The police also mentioned one of them to me in interviews. I would like to know exactly what part, if any, these two played. Elizabeth McCusker (Max Gold & Co) seemed to think that they could have interfered with the body after Docherty had drowned and stripped Mark White. When the couple had found him the police thought he had been dragged around the beach. Only speculation could explain that line of thought. I do not know if this odentologist's evidence was available at my trial or knowledge to my barrister. If it was then why was it not used in my defence?

Forensics

There was no forensics on my clothes linking myself to the deceased. This is because I swear on oath that I never touched the body. However blood was found on Docherty's clothes which correspond with the deceased's. Docherty was found to be of the same blood group as Mark White although it was not precise as to who's blood it was on his clothes they did say it was very clear that Docherty had come into contact with the deceased whilst he was bleeding.

DNA testing was suggested by Elzibeth McCusker, which would mean having the body of Mark White officially, exhumed. I agree with this being done and instruct legal representatives to seek permission to carry out such action. However I would first want to be sure the deceased's family understand the nature of the inquiry to my defence, as I would clearly not want to upset the family any further. I do feel a great deal of pity for them, but I cannot allow deep feelings to deny myself justice. If it is proved that Docherty's clothes do have the deceased DNA on them then new evidence like that would determine Docherty's true guilt and my innocence. I am sure the deceased's family would want justice to be done to Docherty and have myself vindicated if I can prove my account.

Mary Docherty laundered her son's clothes at a local launderette. The clothes were machine washed yet failed to remove all the evidence of blood stains on her son's clothing. One week later the clothes were examined and discoveries were made by forensics. My clothes had been washed by hand and if Gayle Lambert's accounts of the state of me are to be believed that I was covered in blood it is hard to believe that her hand washing could remove all stains leaving none for the forensics to find! Hand washing v machine washing? It either means that Gayle Lambert can wash cloths by hand far better than machine washing or that her statement is of a false or pressurised nature made under fear!

There is further evidence to suggest that Mark White was hit a number of times (85 times). Forensic findings are inconsistent from my point of view. It is hard to believe that Docherty caused some 85+ head injuries and 14 broken ribs to Mark's body on his own in just ten minutes. This would give rise that others as well as Docherty had caused injuries to Mark's body.

There was a crowbar that was eliminated from the murder yet a one-foot line mark was found on the deceased back surely the crowbar had been used to administer the mark?

The prosecution alleges my shoeprint to be on the deceased back. In the photographic evidence there was no sign of this? There was however a photograph of a print in the sand of what I believe is a left shoe print; forensics said this matched my footwear. In response to this I offer the following theory to disperse the argument.

A boot print made in the sand before the tide would bare the chevron designs and details of the boot. Now if the tide came in covering that print, would it not remove most if not all of these same designs and details? I do not profess to be an expert in such matters science or scientific theory but the example just given is plain common sense. The fact that the print size is a size 11 (my own UK shoe size) does not determine that I was the person who made this impression on the sand. The crucial point that everyone has forgotten is that thousands of people pass through Blackpool every day. Anyone of them could have made the print. A tide comes in once every twelve hours thus cutting the thousands down to a few hundred, maybe, therefore that print could have been made by one of hundreds of people whilst the tide was out in those twelve hours. It therefore might have nothing at all to do with the murder scene. If there is only one footprint in the photograph (circled) then where is the other footprint? The scientist was not 100% that the print was mine. He said in his statement that he would have to reinvestigate his findings if new evidence came to his attention requiring him to do so. I ask now that he put my theory to the test and look at the points I have just raised.

Finally, Prison Life

Docherty arrived at Moorland prison in November 1994. Docherty was placed in solitary confinement for making knives in a workshop. It is not known whom the knives were intended for, but as a result Docherty was 'starred up' and moved to HM Prison Garth, Preston in February 1995 when he was still only twenty years old. 'Starred up' is prison slang for a dangerous young offender being re-classified to adult status.

While I was at Moorland the name Viv Graham was mentioned to me by a prison officer called Rick Midgely. I started asking Geordies on my wing questions about who Viv Graham was. I was told he was gunned down on New Year's Eve 1993 in Newcastle-upon-Tyne and it was something to do with bouncers! I also asked friends at HM YOI Castington about this man. Indeed a girl named Terri Cooper began visiting me in strange circumstances. I discovered she was a friend of Alan Tams (a North East gangster) she asked me many questions. I actually asked her to bring Alan Tams on a visit because I wanted to talk to him about a Geordie I thought he might know of.

(As he was an alleged friend of Viv Graham.) Unfortunately this did not happen and Terri disappeared from my life for over a year. However I did hear that she had showed up in Edinburgh and later moved to Jasper Walk, Moss Side, Manchester. My suspicions were raised about Terri as I was not sure if she had anything to do with Docherty, the police or Tams?

She did express great interest in helping me find the answers to my case. In 1996 she made several enquiries in Blackpool. She told me almost every doorman she spoke to could not understand how Docherty was only found guilty of manslaughter and me of murder. The last I heard from her was January 1997.

After February 1995 I received many letters from Docherty. One in particular dated April 1995 warned me to stop my appeal from proceeding any further. In July 1995 I went to Garth prison for accumulated visits where I survived an attempt on my life at the hands of Docherty, Bernard Travasari, Lee Hughs and Johnny Turner. All of them were obsessed with Docherty's reputation. Travasari was released in November 1993 from Lancaster Farms. He came back in early January 1994 for resisting arrest and pointing a firearm at a police officer in Blackpool. Travasari was free while Viv Graham was murdered as was a man called John Herd. (Author's note: neither of these men had any connections with the murder of Viv.)

The specific letter I received from Docherty pre-July 1995 stated that John Herd was very anxious to keep me silent. I certainly think that Docherty knew I was on the right road to making the connection to the beach murder at the time he wrote the letter to me. It has taken me a long time to make the connection.

In December 1996 I went to HMP Strangways for accumulated visits. By chance I found out more information about my case. I had to share a cell with an inmate called Wayne Henry (Cell A1-20, 'A' Wing). By coincidence Wayne was on the same wing as Docherty in Garth Prison during 1996. He told me that Docherty was forever bragging that he had got away with murder and that he had set me up for it. He was even displaying photographic exhibits of the deceased on his wall!

My girlfriend, Nicola (Nikki) Scott, appeared in the Blackpool Evening Gazette on Friday 13th December 1996. The article explained how she was fighting to help me obtain a re-trial. On January 21st 1997 I received another letter from Docherty. He told me he was aware that of Nicola being in the Gazette and warned me to stop my appeal otherwise he would send someone to the university he named that she was at to hurt her. The Gazette had printed her personal details including the university she attended and the particular course she was on. Docherty also threatened my brother's life once more. Two weeks after I received that letter Jason rang my new solicitor in Liverpool saying he would not be going to my appeal. I certainly think that Jason was approached by one of Docherty's associates or is this just another coincidence to finalise a large number of coincidences over the last four years which I am very aware of!

On February 3rd 1997 I had a police visit from Det Supt Holt of Northumbria police I gave him a recorded interview and passed on information about the unsolved murder of Viv Graham which he said he would pass on to the regional inquiry unit at Newcastle. I did not pass Docherty's letters on to that police officer though for my own reasons. Det Chief Insp Felton (Author's note: now promoted to Superintendent Felton.) wrote to the appeal court saying he would not be acting on my information. Thus Viv Graham's murder will remain unsolved if my claims are not looked into. I was hoping that Northumbria police would force Blackpool police to re-open the case that I am involved in given that they never did dig deep enough to start with; or am I being naïve to think that one police force will investigate another.

My brother, Jason, has since stated that he will attend my appeal to give evidence and to say that his statement was not his own as he signed it under pressure from the police, he is also willing to say that he has received phone calls of a threatening nature from Docherty.

I can wait 18 years just as the 'Bridgewater Three' did and I will never give in to the system. I will not even accept parole until I am given a fair re-trial. If my health continues to suffer as it has then I want the authorities to know that the reason for it is because they are denying me justice. A life sentence can mean as long as 99 years what I do know is that if I do not address my offending behaviour the state has the right to keep me locked up until I do. (Author's note: what Gary writes here is correct and that applies to every single life sentence prisoner regardless if they are still insisting they are innocent even after thirty years of being banged up. The state wants them to address their offending behaviour even if they have not committed the crime they have been sentenced for. Rather like the old witch-hunt. Tie the witch up, throw them in the river and if they drown they were innocent! The analogy is that if you are innocent in prison and insist on that then you will remain there! Admit you did the crime and go through the motions of crocodile tears and you will go free.)

Gary continues. However, there is NO CHANCE WHATSOEVER, THAT I WILL BOW DOWN TO THE SYSTEM'S DEMANDS! Because until I am fairly re-tried and vindicated, the system is just a corrupt figure to me. I am no longer a doorman and I doubt I will ever return to that trade. I never denied I was a carefree 'fuck with me and you'll get hurt' type of individual. I do not have that type of attitude anymore because I know exactly what it is I have lost, including my liberty. I took things like that for granted! I would have eventually ended up in prison from working the doors at some stage in my career and YES had I been guilty of an offence I would not be complaining. The police did not realise that I could have been a star witness who could have helped them smash an organised crime syndicate in their jurisdiction, to the letter of the law.

My co-accused had over 40 serious charges recorded against him including the manslaughter of Mark White. So how is it that he is in category 'C' prison (open prison) when he has not even reached the half way stage in his ten-year sentence? (Author's note: looking at the light sentence Docherty received and the easy prison conditions he was in it does seem that Docherty had done something to earn this light handed treatment. When you consider that Paddy Conroy from Newcastle is serving 11 ½ years for a kidnap and torture charge it makes Docherty's sentence look so light I could win the slimmer of the year award. Paddy Conroy is still a double category 'A' prisoner even though he only has a few years left to serve yet Docherty with his past antecedents (record) is having a comparatively easy time? Work it out for yourselves.)

This proof of evidence was dated 27th April 1997 and signed by Gary Stuart Ward. We now recommence and I take over the pen, so to speak.

Stephen Jeffrey (Gary calls him Steven Jeffries) was described as a Lytham businessman when he was kidnapped by Docherty and Co. Jeffrey was not as clean cut as that label indicated. He was in fact a porn shop owner with porn in the wall facilities for people who hired sleazy videos showing perverted sex acts in pornographic blue movies.

Gary has alleged that Jeffrey was kidnapped for a totally different reason than was suggested in the defence of his kidnappers when they appeared in court charged with kidnap and assault. Docherty, John Heard and John Barratt gave an account that differed to what Gary suggests was the reason for the kidnap. Who can blame the accused for changing the story somewhat because if it was found out that the kidnap was connected to something more sinister and connected with organised crime then the case would have been looked at more seriously than it was.

It was alleged by Barrat and Herd that Jeffrey had shown two sample videos to them so that they could judge the quality for themselves before becoming distributors. One video was a 'snuff movie' showing a real murder and the other was child porn! You have to consider here that both Barratt and Heard knew Jeffrey's background and obviously had to know they were not going to see Walt Disney type films coming from this guy. Anyway to continue their allegation…they were so incensed by this that they decided to teach Jeffrey a lesson.

That lesson actually happened and although it was put across as a terrifying assault Jeffrey did not have a mark on him after it took place! His premises had been burgled prior to the kidnap and in a pretext to get Jeffrey to go with the two kidnappers they told him they could get his stock of dildos and other marital aids along with sexy lingerie, cosmetics and cheap jewellery back for him if he went with them. He fell for it and they travelled in his car to this non-existent fence (handler of stolen goods). Docherty was picked up along the way and when he got in the car things became a little more nasty for Jeffrey when he was prodded by a machete that Docherty produced and then threats of violence from all three were directed at their prey.

Jeffrey had been what is commonly called amongst criminals, 'taxed'. He was forced to sign a receipt handing over his car and to sign a letter of complaint that Barratt had intended to use against the police. Jeffrey was dumped and the three drove off thinking they had covered all the angles. It was not a classic style of taxing similar to the NorthEast's Geordie Mafia Bud Armstrong who used to tax other criminals of their goods. He had a good run of it until he taxed a businessman and it all came on top for him and everyone came out of the woodwork with complaints that got him locked up for a long time.

All the kidnappers knew that Jeffrey was going to start up a brothel and distribute child porn & snuff videos in Lytham, that is what was alleged in court by their defence. Maybe that was true but the real reason for the kidnap is hidden in Gary's 'Proof of Evidence'. All three pleaded guilty to the charge of assault and falsely imprisoning Jeffrey. Docherty received his three year sentence and also admitted having a machete and other offences of forgery, deception, handling stolen property and robbery and he only received a total prison sentence of ten years which would mean serving just over 4 ½ years imprisonment whilst Barratt and Herd were released on bail? That prison sentence is just so unbelievably lenient that when you look at it in context it meant he had a licence to commit crime and continually received bail and ends up with a seven and a three = 7 years concurrent?

That is not the end of it yet! Docherty also faced a charge of Robbery with violence! What prison sentence do you think he got for this one? Wait and see. Nigel Penney was a serving soldier with the British Army in Germany and whilst on leave he decides to spend a bit of time in Blackpool. He goes out for the night and in a short time picks up what he thinks is his date for the night. He gets to her home and after a short while she suggests sex! Penney is all set for a night to tell the lads back at camp when suddenly in stepped Docherty with another man. The classic set up was achieved. Boy meets readily available girl who takes him home. Girl's angry boyfriend catches them at it just before the vital moment and feigns anger whilst robbing the victim. Docherty seemed to have his finger in every little scam going, so there was no reason to think this was not another one of his scams. Penney had taken the bait and was set up good style by the look of this scenario.

Docherty, along with an unidentified man, set about Mr Penney. The knuckle-duster allegedly used later in the Mark White murder was used by Docherty to beat Mr Penney about the body and legs. Hot liquid was thrown in his face and lighter aerosol fumes were sprayed in his eyes. Docherty then threatened Mr Penney with an IRA hitman from London saying he would find him and kill him if he told the police what had happened. Later Docherty's flat was searched by the police looking into a matter of deception and personal items belonging to Mr Penney were discovered.

So there you have it, Mr Penney has hot liquid thrown in his face after being beaten with a knuckle-duster and for good measure he has liquid gas squirted into his eyes and is robbed of personal possessions and to top it all he, a serving soldier, is threatened by the IRA from the unknown accomplice. What would you expect the prison sentence to be for this sort of violent offence against one of Her Majesty's soldiers? 10 years imprisonment? 12 years imprisonment? Maybe 15 years imprisonment? No! None of those, Docherty got off Scott free because the three year prison sentence dished out was to run concurrently (alongside) with his two other prison sentences; seven years for manslaughter and three years for kidnap & assault.

Docherty's defending barrister, Richard Henriques, told the court that the violence was in temper and that the injuries received by Mr Penney were comparatively modest! Oh, well…that is all good and well then? I would have put it to the jury that this in fact was dummy run for Docherty to test out the damaging power of his knuckle-duster. He hit Mr Penney about the body the same way that he hit Mark White about the body while breaking nine of his ribs on Blackpool beach. Docherty lashed out in temper when he attacked Mr Penney just as he did against Mark. He had an accomplice with him because he needed the support just like he needed the support of a number of others when he assaulted Gary Ward in prison. He cannot work alone yet when faced with someone who would stand up to him like Gary did on the night he stood on White's head he pulled a weapon on Gary because that is all he knew. Suddenly the unidentified accomplice of Docherty gets the blame for the IRA threats and the aerosol attack just like he threw it all at Gary when it came on top for him. He could not get his own way so he threatened those close to Gary, his girlfriend and brother, with violence so that Gary had to go along with what Docherty wanted.

Gary was in a vulnerable position in life, alone and in prison - facing a murder wrap. So why the fuck would he piss his pregnant girlfriend off from continuing to visit him? You may have read earlier about Viv threatening to smash HM Prison Durham up because Anna Connelly walked out on him whilst on a visit. Gary's latest girlfriend, Nikki Scott, has walked out on him and I can tell you that I had to telephone the wing officer at his holding prison (Wakefield) to advise that Gary would need watched because he was feeling low in himself because of the situation. No man in his right mind is going to stop his girlfriend who is carrying his baby from visiting him! Not unless he feared for her safety from another inmate who had threatened to plant her one as soon as he seen her on a visit. Gary acted accordingly and advised her to stop visiting and because of this Gail Lambert (Gary calls her 'Gayle') became vexed at Gary and went against him in the court case.

Gary told of how he was involved as hired muscle in a drug deal between Blackpool underworld members and Geordie Mafia. He told of how counterfeit money was used by the Geordies to buy the £25,000 value of mixed drugs from the Candy Rock boys. In May of 1994 a drug swoop by armed police on premises in Thornton Cleveleys uncovered a stash of drugs, a handgun and counterfeit money! Three homes were raided in this protracted investigation by the Fleetwood police drugs team. The interesting thing about this raid is that it happened not long after Docherty was imprisoned for such a short stay for such heinous crimes. The fact that counterfeit money was found in some way confirms what Gary has wrote earlier on in his proof of evidence.

The testimony of Nigel Donsworth is called into question in a leaflet distributed by Nikki Scott. She alleges that he became a paid police informer after agreeing to be a prosecution witness.

Gary told me how he came about the fact that he knew it was Viv he had the fight with in Blackpool. "In April 1995 I received a letter from Docherty, which named Viv Graham! Prior to that letter I didn't even know who man A was. I only knew what he looked like. I was actually asking other inmates from the Newcastle region, who were in Moorland, if they knew who the person was that I was drawing and could they put a name to it. I had actually drawn a picture of man A whilst I was on remand awaiting trial, that is now in the possession of my solicitor.

The next thing I knew I received the letter from Docherty. (Mentioning Viv.) I started asking then, 'Who was Viv Graham?' It was in April/May of 1996 that I picked up a book relating to gangsters and in that book I discovered that Viv had been shot and murdered three months after Docherty and I were arrested. The in July I went to Garth prison for accumulated visits, whilst there I had a deep conversation with Docherty, after receiving his letter I asked him who Viv Graham was. He gave me every indication that he was a rival of John Barratt in Blackpool and was trying hard to put him out of business. Docherty didn't say Viv was dead at that time. I turned around to Docherty and said, 'Look if you don't go down to the appeal court in my defence and tell them I wasn't fighting with Mark White, I'm going to find Viv Graham and the two guys who were with him and I'm then going to go down to the appeal court and explain story and I'll tell them you killed Mark White!' I then went for a piss in the toilets on the field in Garth and all of his mates run in and kicked me unconscious, not that I felt very much. One dirty bastard hit me on the back of the head with either a stick or a piece of wood and that rendered me unconscious. When I came a round I staggered outside onto the field, blood pissing out of my head, and I was sore, my ribs felt as if they were broken and I was having problems breathing. Prison officers escorted me off the field to the prison hospital where I lost consciousness for two days. I woke up eventually back at Moorland prison in a hospital bed. I remained on the hospital wing for three weeks.

So I think it's safe to assume that I touched a raw nerve with Docherty. I started to build up my own theory as to why Docheryty and John Herd (AKA 'Midget') and John Barratt (AKA 'Slim') were so desperate to keep me from obtaining a trial. Blackpool's nightlife is a multi £m industry, that nightlife has its own guardians; just like Viv was a Guardian of his own interests in Newcastle. I think if he had of stayed on his own turf instead of trying to muscle in on Leeds, Manchester, Liverpool, etc and of course Blackpool. Now in Blackpool, you have three main players. One of them does business legitimately, the other is quite small whilst the other controls all the drugs and the supply to the town dealers. One clue I can give you also who is shipping handguns and drugs safely into the town is the IRA! A lot of money is changing hands in that town. Do you think someone like Sabre Security was going to let Viv Graham walk in on something like, I don't think so, because there is a saying in that kind of industry, 'there is enough to go around'. People like Viv were greedy, and I am certain that one of the Sabre crew in Blackpool went over there, to Newcastle, not only to put Viv in his place, but to also establish one clear message. 'You don't rip off people with £25 grand worth of drugs!' If it was Viv who was involved in the Lytham drug deal in August '93 then they had every reason to want to take Viv out! Docherty's letters to me indicate two people know a lot more about Viv's murder than I do. The power of the pen will get me out of prison, Violence wont. Viv Graham could stop a riot, I can't.

In 1988 I was trained to box by ex-Irish International Patrick Long. My father built a gym, a boxing ring and a weights room for me and another boxer called Adrian Bush. I never stuck at being a good boxer. It didn't interest me; my dad wanted me to be something I wasn't.

Nicola's dad offered a ten grand reward for information leading to my being granted bail and finding the two men who were with Viv when the fight took place. Man **B** and man **C** should come forward if they have anything about them. If they are the type of men I think they are, they wouldn't let a man do a life sentence especially if my account manages to secure a conviction on who shot Viv! Right or wrong Viv was a bastard from what I've read and heard about him. I don't think he deserved to die in the same way. I don't believe Mark White deserved to die either. I don't disrespect Viv, in fact I admire the guy. Had I known anything about Viv Graham at the time he fronted me I would've backed down, but you can ask any doorman what the ethics of not giving a fuck is about? Being a doorman is about being fluent in two languages – diplomacy or violence! If a guy says to me, 'Hey, do you know who I am?' I'll say, 'I couldn't give a fuck who you are, you're on my doorstep, I'm the boss in here nobody else!' It's much the same everywhere else in the world. Some people will say I wasn't capable in my profession as a bouncer, everyone is entitled to their opinion. But not being capable and not wanting to reveal your capabilities is two different things. I threw my life away to protect others close to me, that's the difference between me and a lot of so called gangsters. I actually care about innocent people where a lot of them don't.

My last appeal failed because I wasn't represented at the hearing in November 1997 and I wasn't present either. My last solicitor in Liverpool claimed over £3,000 in legal aid and it ended up where I had to prepare my own grounds for appeal in handwriting. One of the three Courts of Criminal Appeal judges criticised the fact that the grounds were submitted in my own handwriting. No wonder everything went wrong.

On June 28th 1998 I had a visit from Superintendent Keith Felton of North Shields police and his colleague, John Comber, who both had in depth knowledge of Viv's case as both were involved in the murder inquiry. Comber came across as arrogant whilst Keith Felton came across as very likeable and easy going. It was Comber who allegedly interviewed Viv's last fiancée, Anna Connelly, about Viv's movements in September 1993. Apparently she was quite specific about his movements between 1st September and 8th September 1993. Comber looked down his nose at me when he said, 'We know Viv was in Newcastle on the dates you say he was in Blackpool, Gary, and the reason why we know that is a close friend of Viv's was quite specific about his movements.'

Here's where I shut him up and shocked him by telling him straight away, that someone in Wallsend wasn't telling him the truth and here's how I interrupted him from his little ' I know better speech'. 'Well, first of all, I'll tell you that 'Anna Connelly' accounted for Viv up until the night of 1st September, and to be more specific, it was in fact someone's birthday who was close to Viv wasn't it? Later that evening Viv and Anna had a lover's tiff, and Viv was not seen again in Newcastle/Wallsend until Wednesday 8th September '93 which was another person's birthday and Viv showed up for it! Mr Comber, bear it in mind my intelligence is on par with yours, and don't think because I'm locked up in high security that I can't gather intelligence! Because I'm telling you that I'll prove Viv was in Blackpool and once I do that... you're obviously not as informed as I am 'cos your close friend/reliable sources aren't being straight with you are they?'

I also gave Keith Felton copies of Docherty's letters naming Viv Graham to me. I also indicated that Blackpool CID have had in their possession a CCTV video tape of me and Viv exchanging blows outside of the *Time Gap* club because the *Foxall* pub cameras caught it all. Further to that I received a letter in March 1998 from Wakefield Police Force Intelligence Officer DCI Colin Sutton he was writing that Detective Chief Inspector Turner of Blackpool CID was aware of the tape's existence and Information I had passed on to Blackpool via Wakefield liaison, Turner knows of many other matters in existence as well including Docherty's connection to the IRA!

That letter from Wakefield CID suggests Blackpool CID are harbouring a great deal of information and evidence which tells the truth about my case. It may very well help you and Keith Felton solve Viv's murder! That letter is however in my solicitor's hands, not mine! I was unable to show it to Keith Felton at the time of the visit. I also handed other documents to him to take away and study. The one very significant document he did find intriguing was the private eye's report, which has Det Chief Inspector Michael Turner's comments in it relating to what he had thought all along. You'll find his comments in that report hold the key solving the mystery and the link between my case and Viv's murder.

My old man's philosophy on respect, he was saying to me, 'Son, there are two ways you can gain respect, buy it or fight for it. I can't exactly buy it if I've got nothing to buy it with, can I?" I tell Gary that there is a third way to gain respect and that is by earning it. Gary: "I'm going to forget being polite and diplomatic about it and resort to fighting my way out of with my nut, elbows, feet and fists because in a nutshell, Steve, that's all I've got left.

Once I utilise those last defences people will get hurt and I'll end up in the block somewhere with mechanical restraints on and nothing left whatsoever then. Because, the state will own me lock, stock and fucking barrel, and the only thing I have left then is my mind. Once that's gone, my friend, because of one liquid cosh too many, that's it, the game is all over I am then a forgotten number in a file with a photo in it, sat in a dusty fucking shelf for another decade or two.

The girl 'Terri' I know where she is, how long she has been there and what for. My certain friend helped me out on that one, and the bottom line is this, she was there in Blackpool on the night of the beach murder, she saw me fighting with Viv, and she knows who the two men are from Wallsend who were with Viv on the night! She also mentioned she was told to latch on to me to find out what I knew about Viv's murder. Interesting as fuck that isn't it? This Terri looks like the same bird as the one in the poster with Viv, I've got photo's of her, how do you think my mate found her and correctly identified her before coming back to me and asking me, 'What needs to be done next?' To which I replied, 'Nothing needs to be done next.' That's where I'm leaving it for now, at least until I financially recover, my health gets better and until the CCRC grant my brief legal aid to follow all this shit up. As I say, that will be at least two years, not even my MP, Gordon Marsden, can speed that decision up, although he said he'll try.

James John Docherty of no fixed abode, so he told Blackpool police when interviewed over the murder of Mark White, had been in Blackpool since November 1992. His mother, stepfather and sister had previously moved from Port Glasgow in Scotland and Docherty had followed them. He started work as a kitchen porter in the Ulvescroft Hotel, then moved on to Sabre Security as a doorman. He had only been working a couple of months for

Sabre yet here he was well in with all the right connections, a fast worker. He considered Gary to be a friend, but not a close friend who he could really confide in and that was through his own admission to police. Docherty's territory covered *Webster's* on Foxall Road, *Annie's Bar* at the Winter Gardens, the *Palace* and *Cross Foxes* in Prestatin, Wales. He had not worked with Gary on the doors, although he had worked for the same company.

Docherty had been back to Scotland the week before Mark was murdered, returned to his mother's in Blackpool and went on to stay at the Richmond House Hotel. The following Monday he went out drinking with Gary and he states '…it was early evening…' They ended up at the *Time Gap* after calling at a number of pubs, particularly a one where Gary's brother, Jason, was a comedian; the *Jaggy Thistle*. Docherty recalls leaving at between one and two o'clock in the morning (Tuesday). Docherty then tells the police he and Gary left the club and went straight to a 'girl doorman that stays up'. She was later to describe Docherty as being in a state and covered in sand. He tells the police that he went up the beach later on by himself.

What follows now is very crucial and is taken directly from what Docherty told the police in a statement. Detective Sergeant (DS) Wright asks Docherty if he can remember going up the beach?

Docherty: I did myself, later on.

DS Wright: Yeah. How have you come to go on the beach, Jim?

Docherty: I was down at the, er, I was going to go to my mother's and I walked in, er, Waterloo Road crossed over to go to the toilet and er, I thought they were closed, but I can't remember and I do know I was sick on the beach and I fell asleep now.

DS Wright: Was Gary with you then?

Docherty: No, he went home.

DS Wright: Gary tells us a different story than that.

Later on the interview continues and we reach the part in which Gary is said by DS Wright to have told him that he had trouble with four men and one said he would batter Gary. This fits in with what Gary has said all along. Docherty's shoes were recovered from his mother's house; they had blood on them. Docherty had no explanation as to how blood got on to his shoes! Docherty mentions a stripper in the *Time Gap* who used a cigar in her act!

Here Docherty is in the middle of a murder interview relating about a stripper who used a cigar in her act! He was asked if he picked something up from Gary on the Tuesday morning? His reply was: 'Pick something up off him? No!' Gary and his girlfriend, Gail Lambert, had actually told the police that he had called to pick the knuckle-duster up. Docherty denies all knowledge about ever owning a knuckle-duster even disputing his girlfriend's statement saying he had a one. Three people have made statements saying Docherty had a knuckle-duster, yet here he is still denying the ownership of it.

Docherty related to the police how he fell asleep on the beach as the tide was coming in, yet the tide at that place comes all the way up to the slipway, which meant Docherty would had to be like Jesus and walk on the water to stay dry! Docherty carried a machete around with him, although initially he denied this, but later on admitted to the police he did.

Julie Bingham was the club doorlady where Docherty had called to looking for the stripper, Maxine, and his girlfriend, Claire. Julie shouted down to both Gary and Docherty that they could not come up. Although Julie noticed that Gary was dirty it was not discernible from her point of view if it was sand on Gary. It was noticed that Gary was limping and this fits in with what he said about the fight with Docherty that caused him to limp after he tried to stop the murder of Mark.

Docherty's suede shoes were soaking wet and this can only mean he had been in water with them. Mark White had his head kept under the water by Docherty's foot, Gary alleges. To top it all Docherty confesses to Maxine, the cigar fondling stripper and his girlfriend, Claire, that he did kill the man on the beach. He particularly told Maxine the part about him holding Mark under the water. His exact words were, 'Guess what? I did murder that guy on the beach by drowning, I held him under the water!' At this point when Maxine gave her statement she did not know the victim had been drowned! Therefore what Docherty confessed to her was first hand knowledge that only the killer could have known.

Eventually on the third interview Docherty confessed to the killing and tied Gary in with it. Gary was blamed as the instigator, while Docherty played down his role to that of simply throwing a few punches and a few kicks. Mark was then stripped of his clothing and neither Docherty or Mark admitted to biting Mark's body. There is a possible explanation that the area may have been a one used by homosexuals. Just say someone stumbled across Mark's body or that Mark was still alive after the assault. A crowbar was found nearby and there is some allegation that two other men had some involvement in the dragging of Mark's body around the beach? Whose was the T-shirt that lay nearby next to the crowbar? Has this been examined for blood spillage? What if it belonged to a third party that did bite Mark?

There was blood on the sea wall yet Docherty says that he cannot recall Mark being hit off the wall although he was near it. This might support the conjecture that others were involved after Mark was originally assaulted.

Docherty had arrived in the West Coast of England's holiday resort. Shaved his head and started acting like a prodigy of Jimmy Boyle's. He was trying to impress upon the locals that he was of a higher echelon within the criminal world than he really was. A softhearted lad turned nasty by the expectations of others, this sounds like how Viv started out in life. Docherty might change because of this, but if he does not then the likelihood is he will become just another statistic. Hopefully his mother can talk some sense into him as she sounds a sensible enough lady in some of the things she says. Nigel Howard Donsworth (Max) gave a statement to the police, in which he says that Gary confessed to the murder. Of course Gary confessed to the murder, as he believed he had actually killed the man **A** who he was fighting with on the beach. Man **A** is alleged to have been Viv. Keith Cartmel from Rawlinson Cartmel, a firm of solicitors, was brought into play. Donsworth thought that he would be doing all a favour at this stage. Gary told Donsworth about the previous Saturday afternoon when 4/5 men had caused trouble and one of them threatened to come back and cause him trouble. The very story that Gary has consistently stuck to all along, right up to this day. Here though it seems that Donsworth embroiders somewhat on what Gary told him? Donsworth had heard Gary give an account of the incident to Cartmel and because of this he was privy to things that even the police would not be allowed access to, yet here Donsworth was listening just as intently as Mr Cartmel. Therefore when it came to him making a statement he was relating and repeating some of the things said in confidence by Gary to Cartmell.

Donsworth said, Gary had told him he concocted a story about fighting with two or three men and battering one of them. Gail accused Gary of having an affair; it was then that he spilled the beans about the fight. Spilling the beans on which fight, the three men incident or the murder of Mark White? Looking at this it seems that Gary was prepared to say anything to keep his girlfriend; all the more convincing that Docherty had threatened to hurt her. That is why Gary stopped her from visiting him whilst he was on remand.

Consistently through their statements both Gary and Docherty deny having bitten Mark White. Docherty was a weapons man and Gary had his macho image to think of at that time although it does seem to slip into a Freudian type theory. All of the barrack room psychologists can fuck off back into their tiny little holes as we had enough with the two cheese eaters from Sunderland University letting us down because the last book (*Viv (Graham) – 'Simply the Best'*) was not thought to be academic enough for them to waste their breath on. Does the Oedipus complex raise its head here, to pardon a pun? Was Mark used as a type of proxy to complete this inner desire from one of the killers? Does Munchausen by proxy come into it? Causing someone else to suffer something chilling to him or her and thereby attract the public interest so as to feel good within oneself.

Robert Eric Brodie has known Docherty since secondary school and he went

299

out with his sister, Kirstine for a couple of years. Bridge of Weir in Scotland was a place they both frequented, Docherty had tempted Robert to Blackpool, he ended up staying there for three months; February to June 1993. Even though Robert had received a few beatings at the hands of Docherty over the years they still seemed to maintain a connection. Docherty's pal, 'Kit-Kat' was introduced to Robert at Blackpool.

Robert said of Docherty that he was, 'very violent when drunk. I would describe Jim Docherty as mentally unstable.' Docherty used to stay in Kilmacolm when in Scotland. Robert returned to Scotland because of a Scottish warrant being issued for him otherwise he might also have ended up within this situation somehow.

Robert saw kit-Kat in Quarriers Village when he was sent by Docherty to knock on Robert's door. Robert's parents did not allow Docherty near their son because he was a bad influence on Robert. Kit-Kat gave the message that both, he and Docherty, were picking up mores stuff for Docherty's mother who was moving to Blackpool. Robert and his girlfriend, Karen Tenant, from Renfrewshire drove to meet Docherty where he was waiting in a large whit hire van. Another man was there; he introduced himself as Gary.

Docherty gave a greeting to Robert saying that he should step out of the car and give his big mate a 'cuddle'. Obviously Robert was suspicious of this greeting and stayed in the safety of his car. A friend of Robert's was there, Tony Morgan, who was sitting on the bonnet of his own car. Docherty suddenly, for no reason, pulled a gun out of the back of his jeans and pointed it at Robert's penis! (Author's note: does this indicate that Docherty had a thing about male sexuality? Was he confronting his own fears?) Docherty said nothing during this action; he just laughed and then pulled the gun back out of the car and held it in his left hand. He then proceeded to, pull out a cartridge containing eight brass bullets. The cartridge was slammed into the handle of the gun - later identified from pictures as being a 9mm automatic self-loading pistol. Robert drove off immediately when Docherty had finished this procedure.

The man called Gary was spotted with a large machete; over one-foot in length, he was just idly hitting trees with it. Karen was crying when they drove off, as she was really upset. Kit-Kat was described as 5'-11" tall, heavy/fat build, dark blond short hair, balding at the front, he was wearing glasses with square type lenses, clean shaven and he spoke with a Manchester/Blackpool dialect. About two weeks after this Docherty was spotted in the *Milwheel* pub in the Bridge of Weir when he met a friend of Robert's, Brian McGreash, he was asked to phone Robert so as to arrange a meeting, but Brian did not co-operate. Docherty phoned the number himself and on hearing Docherty's voice Robert's mother put the phone down, Robert was going to be invited for a drink. Robert said that he would be unable to identify the person called Gary if required to.

Brian James Kerr McGrish knew Docherty, but was not as close to him as Robert Brodie was. His story confirms the phone call from the *Milwheel* pub. Maybe Docherty wanted to make amends for the gun incident a few weeks prior to this.

Anthony Morgan another acquaintance of Docherty's from Quarriers Village said that he bumped into Docherty when he had the same two in his company as Robert Brodie mentioned. This time Docherty told him he was working in Blackpool as a bouncer. Obviously this was a big feather in Docherty's hat and in a way he was doing his best to show them he had made it to where he wanted to be in life. He bragged that he had been involved in some robberies down in Blackpool and to reinforce this he pulled the handgun from his jeans once more to show Anthony. The gun was thought to be a fake until Anthony handled it and Docherty pulled the magazine out of his pocket to prove it was capable of working. That was when Robert Brodie pulled up in his car and Docherty re-acted the event just described.

Docherty told the slim English guy, he had in tow, to show them his 'toy'. Gary (Described as being 5'-7" tall by Robert Brodie, makes it unlikely to be Gary Ward.) obliged by pulling out a machete over one foot in length. Anthony says that he thinks Bobby (Robert Brodie) said 'What the fuck are you going to do with that?' The fat guy (Kit-Kat) showed Anthony a knuckle-duster that he was wearing it was brassy with rings that your fingers went through. No one said anything about him wearing it.

Docherty was visiting his old stable and showing off with his new down to the knuckle hairstyle while he was carrying the main weapon and his two henchmen were carrying weapons of a lesser type. What was Docherty's motives for showing off to those in such a small village? It seemed he needed this type of acclaim he sought from those he left behind in such a sedentary place as Quarriers Village.

In sharp contrast to this Gary had a slight run in with club doorman, John Rad, in the *Time Gap* club. Gary had no qualms or fears about saying that Rad had tore his leather jacket in a disagreement about how Rad looked upon Gary as a weak type of doorman. Gary did not feel uncomfortable with the fact that he was able to say what had happened in the *Time Gap* club between him and Rad. Rad says he was not drunk yet he cannot remember ripping Gary's leather jacket! Leather is leather and it has to be pulled quite hard to tear it or even break the seam. Rad would have to have been as drunk as Gary suggests he was for him not to have noticed he tore Gary's jacket.

Rad and Gary became acquainted when Gary joined Hill's Security, whom Rad still worked for after Gary had left to work for an opposing security company in Blackpool, Sabre Security, and at the time this confrontation took place. Gary started working at *O'Malley's*, which is the Irish bar underneath the *Clifton Hotel* . Rad explained that he believed the reason Gary went to work for Sabre was that nobody at Hill's would work with him. His reason was that other club doorman felt that if there was trouble then Gary would not be able to back it up. 'He was more likely to run the other way', said Rad and he went on to say, 'You only had to shout at him and he would back down.' Rad had noticed Gary on the door of the *Ardwick* though for about four or five weeks. For a man so disinterested in Gary he seems to have taken a direct interest in Gary. On that night in the *Time Gap* he took pleasure in asserting himself on Gary he humiliated him by tearing his jacket in typical club doorman fashion. Even though he was off duty enjoying a drink.

Rad had been drinking at the bar with another off duty club doorman, Malcolm Boyle, who worked the door of the *Lifeboat* pub on Foxhall Road. Rad suggest that Gary approached him in a drunken manner and he told Gary to go away and pushed him and in doing, so he says, he might have caught Gary's jacket with his hand, but he cannot remember if he did. Pull the other one!

POST MORTEM

Dr Edmund Tapp Home Office Pathologist carried out the post mortem examination on Mark White. Adult male 5'-10 ½" in height and of average build, light brown hair and blue eyes.

Irregular scars on the deceased's knees and shins noted past injuries. Recent injuries were present. The face had a split in the middle of the forehead, a laceration ¾" in length on the right side of the forehand, a scratch of some ½" in length on the right side of the forehead and a line abrasion above the eyebrow. This sort of injury was found at some 24 four areas on the face.

The head had 12 injuries while Marks upper body limbs had twenty injuries one particularly was described as an irregular abrasion, which could be a bite mark on the front of the upper arm just below the shoulder. A group of irregular abrasion's which could be a bite mark on the front of the right upper arm close to the anterior axillary fold. Also three rather distinct areas of bruising in the back of the right upper arm could be bite marks.

With regard to the penis of the deceased being bitten off here is the official report. The external genitalia: a bruise 3/8" across on the foreskin anteriorly at a point ½" from the tip with several irregular bruises, the largest ¼" across on the shaft of the penis posteriorly. The testes were found to be normal. The cause of death was found to be Drowning and Multiple injuries. Frothy fluid in the airways concludes that the immediate cause of death was from drowning. The physical injuries are suggested to have disabled the deceased enough to cause partial or full loss of consciousness. That is only conjecture and what is said by Dr Tapp after that is more a layman's guess than anything when he says, 'This would enable an assailant to hold him under the water more easily and hence to drown him.' What a clever man! That sort of report should be scrapped and put in as hostile, because he suggests by guesswork that Mark White had his head held under the water, surely it also suggests that because he could have been unconscious then his head would naturally, without control fallen under any water flowing above it. That suggestion could be just as equal to what Dr Tapp suggests.

Bite marks are thought to have been responsible for some of the lesions on the deceased's body. There is no conclusive proof of this and it may have been given over to the media as publicity to make the murder seem more repulsive than normal.

Gary's footwear was examined by a forensic scientist, Mark Daly, from the Forensic Science Service at Chorley. Three pairs of Gary's footwear were examined, those that he had been wearing on the night in question and others that were taken from Docherty. The conclusion was that Docherty's footwear was not found to be a match to footwear marks taken from the deceased's back and from photographs taken of the beach. Gary's footwear though offered this finding: 'In my opinion the findings in relation to a mark on the back of the deceased and the left boot taken from Gary Ward would support that this mark was made by this shoe.' Looking at this information it would seem that Gary's goose was cooked, so to speak. But when you hear the conclusion you will know that the forensic evidence is not worth the paper it is written on and therefore should not have been submitted until conclusive proof one way or the other was found such as in Docherty's case.

The report ended, 'There is no conclusive association between the footwear taken from Ward and any of the marks and as such I cannot totally rule out the possibility that these marks have been made by another pair of boots or shoes of the same pattern, size and general wear as the boots taken from Ward.' There you have it, no forensic evidence here to support the prosecution. Further evidence in Gary's favour is forthcoming from this scientist when he states, 'There are footwear marks from the beach, which could not have been made by any of the footwear submitted for examination.' What does he mean by that? Your guess is as good as mine is, here.

Docherty's clothes were posted to Glasgow and recovered from the sorting office by police who searched the place high and low for them during the night when it was closed. These well travelled clothes that had been washed, in a laundry, by Docherty's mother prior to posting were now on their way back to the forensic laboratory for their findings to be disclosed. Also the knuckle-duster was being scientifically examined.

Mouth and anal swabs were taken from the deceased's body to look for traces of semen – none was found. Head hairs from the deceased did not conclusively match hairs taken from the sea wall where it was alleged he had been battered against. Blood groupings from the scene failed to provide results.

Items relating to Docherty and particularly his leather jacket had blood on the outside of the right cuff. This blood did not originate from the deceased. But, results of grouping tests carried out on hair roots taken from Docherty show that his blood could have originated from him. However Mark White could be the source of the blood on Docherty's cuff, but Docherty is unable to be eliminated as a possible source. This stands in Docherty's favour just as much as the shoe test stands in Gary's favour. Docherty's clothes passed the test and turned out to be clean although there were signs of a probable presence of blood, but that was all. Docherty was clean in all respects of the forensic side of things, up to now.

Gary's turn to go under the microscope and he came out as clean as his co-accused and likewise had a probable presence of blood on the left knee of his jeans, his boots passed the test with flying colours as did his T-shirt. When you consider, if someone had kicked a window in there would be a strong likelihood that particles of glass could be found on that footwear by forensic experts to tie them in with the damage it is difficult to see how something as adhesive as blood could escape the scientist! The knuckle-duster passed the test and came out clean! The pillow that Gary wiped himself down with at his flat also passed the test and came out clean! But, something in Gary's favour has come out of all of this and that is, the blood on the pillow that was found by forensic scientists has been discovered not to originate from the deceased, could it be Viv's blood as Gary suggested to me? DNA testing can prove this one way or the other if Viv's DNA is compared it might match up.

Back to Docherty's leather jacket, DNA profiling was inconclusive, but there was support for the proposition that the leather jacket has come into contact with Mark White whilst he was bleeding. However, the possibility that some of the blood on his jacket could have originated from Docherty himself. What does this mean? In real terms it really means nothing other than there is a strong likelihood that Docherty's jacket, which he was wearing came into contact with Mark White while he was bleeding. That I cannot fully understand because, just assuming that Docherty had slept rough on the beach and lay innocently in blood that was not of his making then how could he be blamed for the murder just because his jacket had come into contact with the deceased's blood. There was nothing conclusive, though.

Traces of blood were found on clothing belonging to Gary and Docherty but no conclusive proof of whom the spillage came from! After looking at the blood grouping results there seems to be no proof against either men on the forensic front.

Detective Inspector Turner suggested to Gary that the attack on Mark had all the hallmarks of a gay attack especially with the biting on the penis. It has been suggested that a woman asked Gary immediately after he left the *Time Gap* club that Mark be attacked because he had some involvement in a sexual nature against her daughter. Gary had allegedly said he would sort it out for nothing, this seems highly unlikely. Gary in his statement to the police said he remembers whacking a man and then jumping up and bringing his foot down on his back. In the forensic side of things there was a foot print on Mark's back although it was inconclusive as to whether it was Gary's you, the reader, have to make your own mind up about this.

During Gary's interview he was asked if he held Mark down by standing on his head, so as to drown him. Gary replied: 'I'm telling you straight now, the guy was left in the sand, he was not dragged into the water. You see there is something else an all, before I carry on me and Jim, oops fuck it.' Gary at that point had dropped his co-accused in it albeit his co-accused was already in custody and spilling the beans in his final interview, but Gary was not to know that. His slip up in some way indicates his concern at keeping Docherty out of it, but everyone has something inside of them that makes them spill the beans in some way or another. In a book entitled *The Compulsion to Confess* it is said that everyone has the need to confess and therefore, when a crime has been committed, there are tell tale clues that the perpetrator usually leave behind so as to be caught. Det Insp Turner put it to Gary that he knew what Docherty was like, but since Gary had just named him on tape it was a bit of a farce not naming Docherty. The point here is that Det Insp Turner is admitting what Docherty is like and that there could be reprisals because of what is said.

A man called 'Fawcett' is brought into the equation in Gary's interview, the reason being that he came on the scene after the young courting couple had found Mark's body. Gary says: One guy was with me, said to me that he saw this guy who was on the beach, with the body undressing himself to an extent, trousers around his ankles.' Det Insp Turner says, 'Well alright, but er we're talking about how the body got faced down in the water, because the man you're talking about who we think is a man called Fawcett, come on the scene after the couple, didn't he? They gestured him down.' Gary's reply was: 'I, I, I'm only telling you what the guy I was with told me.'

Steve Hill who ran Hill Security is mentioned because John Rad is brought up in the interview. Gary is telling Det Insp Turner about the incident in the *Time Gap* when his leather jacket was slashed. Det Insp Turner: 'Who was that?' Gary: 'He was called John, he's from *Gaeity's* bar. He works on.' Turner: 'Who does he work for?' Gary: 'Steve Hill.' Turner: 'Do you know his second name?' Gary: 'No. Got a brumy accent.' Turner: 'What was that over?' Gary: 'He's one of the piss takers, one who'd walk all over me he had been fucking punching me in the bollocks every time he sees me and stuff like that.' Turner: 'And he's another doorman?' Gary: 'Yeah. An older doorman.'

The interview goes on about how Gary has had to put up with two years of being walked over and now he doe not want the piss ripped out of him. He confesses to the murder, but insists he did not stand on the man's head to drown him. Gary is saying he did not realise who Viv Graham was and that he believes it was him who he attacked. That leaves a question mark about who attacked Mark? Since Gary says he was fighting ¼ of a mile away from that incident and only came across Docherty committing the murder when he chased after him to check he was not out numbered by Viv's two associates.

When people go to Blackpool they get off the coach and head for a bar, they are expecting a good night out and that could be at the cost of anything. They are in a group and the drinking goes on and on until they are ready to get back on that coach. Trouble could flare at any time and the size of the group varies so club doormen face a difficult job, particularly stressful. But when club doormen give each other a hard time it makes you wonder if they are really cut out to be in the job. Gary was just doing a mundane job that looks glamorised because of the status it brings, girls, girls and more girls. But that is it and at what price?

The final police interview with Gary was the one in which he admitted, after a final consultation with his solicitor, Mr Cartmel, that he murdered Mark by holding his head in the sea water on Blackpool beach. Gary said he held Mark's head down while holding his arm and putting his knee behind his neck. Two bubbles came out of the water and that was it, less than two minutes and he was dead. Hearing that you will now think it is the final nail in Gary's coffin, not so. The meeting that Gary had, in private with his solicitor, was the one in which Gary alleges that Cartmel said to him that Docherty had told him to recall his brother's name. This is alleged by Gary to have been a veiled threat against the safety of his brother.

Violet Walker Wolsey ran the *Burroyd* Hotel in Blackpool for some six years. Mark White had taken up employment as a kitchen porter from 2nd July 1993. During his time working there Violet noticed he was a good worker who was quiet natured, he did not discuss his private life in any detail. It was however noticed by Violet that Mark sometimes spoke about a person called Paul, who he always referred to as his friend. He said Paul was a fat scouser who worked at the *Bond* Hotel in Blackpool, she thought as a kitchen porter. Violet says, 'Mark's referring to Paul as a friend and occasionally the way he spoke or acted led me to think he may have been a homosexual, although he never told me this or did anything I could positively say confirmed my suspicions.'

Violet continues, 'Approximately 1.00 a.m. on Tuesday 7th September, 1993 I called last orders in the bar, left in the bar at this time was myself, Ian Bootham (karaoke machine operator), Janet Barclay (barmaid), Mark and approximately four middle aged couples who were resident guests at the hotel. I noticed Mark was leaving and I asked him if he wanted a taxi, but he declined…I did not consider him to be drunk, he was steady on his feet and only what I would describe as merry.' Had Mark accepted the offer of a taxi home…well, it would have been a different story.

Nicholas Bollington a carpet fitter from Derby was holidaying in Blackpool, maybe looking for a holiday fling, which he soon acquired. He and his newly found partner went for a walk along the beach when they came across what was thought to have been a large doll. 'As we walked along the beach I suddenly saw a body lying face down in the sand. On first seeing this I thought it was a doll as it was naked. I didn't want to touch it at all, but I could see it had bite marks all over the back of this body. I then just nudged the left shoulder with my foot right foot…I then really knew it was a body and not a doll.'

What could the naked body of a young man be doing on the beach at this early hour of the morning? Certain areas of Blackpool are the cruising grounds of the gay community. The alleged bite marks on the body and particularly the penis suggests a gay motivated attack. Mark was thought to be gay by his employer, although this is only conjecture and is not with any foundation. Although that is what the forensic side of this case is all about, suggestion without foundation, yet that is accepted as evidence and probability plays a big part in all of this. Had Docherty and Gary Ward not said anything then, I believe the prosecution would not have had a case against either of them, but each being played off against the other won the day for the prosecution side of things.

Gary accepted he had taken some part in an attack on a man and he had threats of violence hanging over his girlfriend and brother, the only two people in his life in Blackpool. Gary assumes it was man **A** that the police say he attacked so he went along with it, so he says, and has continually said from day one, throughout all of this. His witness could have been Gail Lambert, but because he did not call her or have her cross-examined it negates her from being called in an appeal. New evidence though would allow her to be called, in the right circumstances.

Gail Lambert was a hostile witness, Gary says, she had been visiting him whilst he was on remand, but she had given a statement to the police before Gary was charged and that gave her the status of being a prosecution witness. It was unfair of Gary's counsel not to cross-examine her just because she was heavily pregnant as if she had been asked certain questions it may have altered the course of events. She said in her statement that she felt Gary was very much influenced by Docherty and his personality made Gail very wary of him. She says, 'His personality used to change noticeably from being sober to when he had been drinking. When he had a drink he was frightening. Gary used to jump when Docherty told him to. Docherty used to visit Gary at my flat, I didn't like him and I was frightened of him. Docherty came around with a small handgun. It was silver in colour and had a revolving chamber. I don't know anything about guns, but I remember that. He also brought a big knife, a machete. He wanted Gary to keep it in the flat for him. Gary obliged and put them under the wardrobe in the bedroom. I was frightened, the gun and the machete were in my flat for two or three days before Docherty collected them.'

The contrast between Docherty and Gary is plain to see by what Gail said about Gary, 'I would describe Gary as a kind person. He was funny and made me laugh when I was sad about something. He was generous when he had money and would try to help anyone who needed it. Having said that when Docherty was around he tried to be something he wasn't. I saw him try to act like the hard man and not be frightened of anyone. Gary was happy to stay in and watch TV with me, but Docherty would be constantly coming around and badgering him to go drinking with him all night. If he didn't go along with something Docherty wanted him to do Docherty would turn violent; Docherty would change his voice and swear at Gary. Gary used to tell me he was frightened of Docherty and thought that if he didn't go along with something, Docherty was capable of harming him.'

Here we have proof that Gary was genuinely concerned at Docherty's threats of violence against Gail when both were on remand and just after the beach murder. Why else would Gary stop Gail visiting him? Docherty had Gary so frightened that he just had to go along with it. There was no return and Gary was riding the tiger's back like there was no tomorrow. It is easy to say that Gary should just have told Docherty to 'Fuck off and sling your hook', but these sort of situations cannot be handled like that. It was not a dispute with a noisy neighbour or someone parking in his space, this thing went deeper than that. Rather like the Hindley/Brady scenario, both on a helter-skelter like the followers of Charles Manson. One was the ringleader giving the instructions to the other one and even though the things asked to be done were, maybe, not liked they had to be done because that was the way it was and if the pack leader had of demanded that the trainee should jump off a cliff for them then it would be carried out to the letter without question. You just do not get out of it by turning your back on the situation because wherever you turn the situation is there. As someone, once famous, in political circles said just before his Government lost the General election 'When your back's against the wall and the going gets tough you turn around and fight.' That is what it was like, wanting to fight, but being all muddled up against the brain washing that had taken place. (Just because Myra Hindley has been mentioned it is no good jumping on my wagon using this as your own stage, so fuck off. She and her situation were only used as an example.)

When Gary returned home in the early hours of the morning, when Mark lay dead on the beach, Gail noticed he was caked in blood. The T-shirt he was wearing was splattered in blood, which had run. Remember that Gary had also gone into a café for a kebab in that state. However he got in that state it was as if he had tribal markings on him and he had come of age and this blood was rather like a display to tell all and sundry that he had made the grade. That applies to most people out there, how many drunks have you seen that have cuts and bruises? They just go about things as if it were normal to bear these injuries; a primeval instinct takes over.

Docherty asked for the knuckle-duster that was allegedly used in the attack on Mark. Gary handed it over in Gail's flat from the drawer where Gail had put it a few hours before. Gail could not stand to look at it, it really made her sick and that was before she knew of the alleged injuries it had inflicted on Mark only a few hours earlier! Gail had washed Gary's clothes and cleaned his boots. She says, 'Had I known that he was responsible in any way for something like that I would never have washed them.' Gail gave this statement before Gary was found guilty in a court of law based on the evidence available at that time, but Gail had only known Gary for a few months and had wanted a full commitment by the sounds of things. This was going pear shaped for her so she could only feel one thing and that was, let down. She did not face charges like Mary Docherty did due to her statement.

Nigel Donsworth received a telephone call from Gary and he went and met Gary in Gail's presence, Gail says, 'I did hear Gary say that he put the lad's head underneath the water and held it. Max (Donswortth) said "C'mon, Gary, you know Jim (Docherty) is well known for biting, did he bite him?" Donsworth took Gary to a solicitor and they both returned about an hour later and Gary was told to hand himself in within 48 hours or Donsworth was finished with him. Docherty turned up later that night and met with Gary outside of Gail's flat. When Gary came back in he said to Gail, 'Don't say anything please Gail or you will get hurt, I love you and I'll be in touch.' Docherty had again threatened those close to Gary with violence in the conversation they had just had. Gary was caught between the devil and the deep blue sea. He had to leave so as to ensure those close to him were not hurt in any way by Docherty.

Claire Louise Curry was the girlfriend of Docherty and on Friday 10th September 1993 she was in the *Casablanca* celebrating her birthday with a friend, Maxine, when Docherty came in on his own. Claire had mentioned in conversation about the body found on the beach and asked Docherty if he had heard about it? He said he had. Maxine jokingly said to Docherty, he might have done it. Docherty looked at Claire and asked her if she thought something like that? Claire replied she 'did not' and then Docherty said he had done it. They stayed at the *Casablanca* and had a late drink, after that Docherty walked Claire home, they kissed goodnight. During the evening Docherty told Claire that he had battered Gary 'for opening his big mouth.'

Jason Richard Rain, Gary's half brouiei, made a statement to the police, but it is believed by family members that he had been got at. Make of this what you will. Gary disputes some of what was said in the statement. Apparently Gary had bragged to Jason that he had dropped a Pakistan lad in a £100 bet with Docherty. Docherty had bet Gary he would not be able to drop the lad with one blow. Jason says, 'Gary had said he had done the job and he had hit the Pakistani and put him down with one blow while wearing the knuckle-duster. Jason Rain had identified the knuckle-duster shown to him by police as being a one that Gary had a few weeks earlier. The difficulty here is that the knuckle-duster was handed to police by a solicitor and the exact source it came from is not fully established and should have been looked into a lot more than it was. Gary alleges that it was Donsworth who handed it in to a solicitor. Who then cut it and put it in a pan of bleach as it has been alleged? Whoever did this obviously perverted the course of justice and should have been charged accordingly. How many knuckle-dusters of this type must there have been in Blackpool, floating about in the circles of club doormen? How can anyone be sure it was the exact knuckle-duster that Gary and Docherty were seen with? Anyway, most knuckle-dusters are brass/gold coloured with rings to put your fingers in and graduating from large to small with a flat edge.

Marie Cummings was employed as a dancer at the *Casablanca* club in Blackpool. She and Gary had dated for a week in July, 1993 she was also a friend of Docherty's because she was friendly with his girlfriend. She says, 'We thought that because Jimmy has been a violent person in the past and because we both (Claire, Docherty's girlfriend at that time) know him well. What I mean by that is that if, for instance, he was to see a lad eyeing me up, he would want to beat them up and talk about waiting for them outside the club. I next saw Jimmy (Docherty) on the Thursday evening when he said that he was going to drink all weekend until Monday when he was going to hand himself in to the police. He has been sought by the police previously.'

The night passed by and eventually Claire went away to play pool and the subject of murder was broached again as it had been talked about previously with all of the publicity. Marie takes it up again, 'Jimmy brought the subject of murder up again, just out of the blue saying, "Do you think I did the murder?" I said that I didn't and I was only messing about (what I had said previously that he had done the murder) and Jimmy then went all serious and took my hand in his and said quietly to me that he was responsible. He said, "Guess what? I did murder that guy on the beach, I drowned him, held him under the water!" This was said whilst he and I were alone sitting at a table.'

Remember the compulsion to confess that was mentioned earlier? Here we have Docherty admitting to the murder and confessing to someone he looks up to in some way and he can reinforce his masculinity by telling of his dastardly deed to someone he sees as ultra feminine.'

There is a clash of statements between Claire Curry and Marie Cumnings. One indicates it was a different date that they were in the Casablanca. Claire gave the date as Monday 8th September and Marie said the date was Monday 6th September. Since it was Claire's birthday on Friday 10th September, it seems her mistake in identifying the correct date is a little unusual. (Check out what Hitman based in Manchester said about not doing a hit on specific dates, such as people's birthdays and so on in *Viv (Graham) – 'Simply the Best'.)*

Julie Bingham, doorwoman employed at the Foxhall pub, was from Kilbarchan in Glasgow, Scotland. Julie recognised Docherty's face when she started work in Blackpool. Although she did not know his name she had recalled seeing him in Kilbrachan. Easter Bank Holiday, 1993 Julie worked the door at the *Beer Keller* with a man called Ricky who was the head doorman at the *Castle* pub on Central Drive. After work she went on to a nightclub with Ricky and his friend Gary Ward. (This defeats what John Rad said about Gary having no friends within the doormen of Blackpool.) W Mandy Simpson was with them, Gary went out with her after that night until July of 1993.

Sunday 5th September 1993 Julie worked the door at the *Raikes Hall* pub from that afternoon. When she finished she, Docherty, Gary and a number of others went to the *Casablanca*. After about 11.00 p.m. Julie left with Darren the doorman from the *Casablanca* at this time Docherty and Gary were still there. The next thing she can recall is, being woken up in the early hours of the morning by Gary shouting up at the window. She looked out and saw that Gary was very dirty, as he was illuminated from a nearby street lamp, although she could not see if it was sand. 'I noticed that Gary had a very bad limp.' She told them she was not letting them in and that the two girls they sought were not there, Claire Curry and Maxine. Gary said they had been fighting and needed to get cleaned up.

Julie met Gary, Wednesday afternoon, at the *Casablanca* and she had a go at him about waking her up, he said he was sorry. Julie says, ' At the time of talking to Gary I was with Paul Kirby who's a friend and is a doorman at *Gaeitys*. From what I know of Gary he is usually noisy and likes to be the centre of attention, but on this occasion he was very quiet, he only stayed for a quick drink of orange before leaving. He had a video with him in a bag that he was trying to sell for £20. Since I have known Gary I have seen on several occasions a piece of wood that he keeps in his coat. I would describe it as about 14" long and the thickness of a chair leg. He has got it out on several occasions bragging about it and showing it about to everyone.'

Both Docherty and Gary came from broken homes. Docherty adopted the surname he now uses, which formally was Lepick. His mother although never re-marrying started a relationship with Charles Docherty in 1980 that is where Docherty adopted his surname. Docherty was living with his girlfriend, Lesley Muirhead in Inverlocky when his mother decided to move to Blackpool in July 1992. Docherty soon followed, but he did not get on with Charles Docherty, his mother's common-law-husband. So he soon found his own place.

Docherty's mother, Mary said of her son, 'James got a job working for Sabre Security as a doorman in different pubs in Blackpool. I did not like him working for them his nature changed and he wasn't the same, he became cheeky, he became very hard to talk to and I asked him to leave Sabre. Monday, 6th September 1993 I recall the doorbell awoke me. It was dark and I did not know what time it was. It was James and I noticed he was dirty, I got the impression he had been fighting.' Later that morning her husband, Charles got up to go to work and Mary checked on her son and spoke of him going to Scotland to visit his pregnant girlfriend, she would find out the bus times. She noticed his clothes were filthy and there was no time to have them washed for him leaving to go to Scotland so she laundered them and posted them to his aunt's home where he had left for. Nothing wrong in that as she was being a good mother or was she? For this she was arrested and charged. Wednesday evening Docherty had returned to his mother's telling her his aunt did not want him in the house. Not surprisingly Mrs Docherty was not amused and when he was asked about the clothes Docherty said, 'They did not arrive.' He told his mother to throw the split shoes away that she had tried to dry. They were put in the kitchen bin liner by Docherty's mother.

Mary Docherty sent the clothes parcel to an address that she knew would not be suspected of anything being sent to. In fact it was the first time ever it was known for her to send a parcel to any address in Scotland. Mary had told an old work mate, June Mary Cattermole, of her concerns. They used to work together at the *Rewa* Hotel in Blackpool. Mary broke down on seeing her former work mate return to the hotel to pick some damaged linen up that she was going to sew. On seeing Mary Cattermole Mary Docherty broke down and told her of the concerns she had over the Blackpool Beach Murder and that she believed her son had been involved in it. That was the basis for charging Mrs Docherty with attempting to pervert the course of justice and how she ended up in the dock. She panicked just like any protective mother would, but in doing so revealed a darker side of her son that not many people knew of. The following Saturday Mrs Dochery was arrested, when she appeared in court her charges were allowed to lie on file.

The urine sample put in to the science laboratory was messed up because not enough preservative was put in with it therefore it was not possible for the lab to determine alcohol levels. It seems all the tests on every aspect proved inconclusive.

All of those who are close to Viv denied that he was in Blackpool at the time Gary states he was. Understandably there is a concern to protect Viv from any further controversy by his family. It would have been easy to leave it at that and pursue other matters, but I did not. From a source of the highest nature I have been informed that Viv was indeed in Blackpool and came off second best in a fight. I now await the details that will confirm the dates and who went there with him from Newcastle. I have written to Crispian Strachin, the Chief Constable of Northumbria Police Force, seeking permission to visit a double category 'A' prisoner. His junior replied in a letter advising me to contact the prison governor concerned. I have done so over two weeks ago and I still await a decision as to whether I am allowed a visitor's pass. I fear it may be too late in this matter, as this book is so far behind its publication date that I am now being pressurised to move on with things. I wrote to Docherty at his prison some months ago asking for him to contact me in relation to Gary's situation, naturally he did not reply. I also wrote to Miss Teresa Cooper (Couper), she is currently serving a prison sentence, again, as in the case of Docherty, I did not expect nor receive a reply. Anyone with any evidence to shed further light on the matter is advised to contact Gary's current solicitor: Susannah Arthur of Gabb & Co Solicitors, Old Bank House, Beaufort Street, Crickhowell, Powys, NP8 1AD.

I can advise that I have acted within the Criminal Cases Review Commission's guidelines by not pressurising anyone to change any statement at any time or to retract any statement made. I have presented the facts of the case, that is all. Any further evidence that comes to light will help Gary and if I have been a catalyst in this then I will have served my purpose to secure justice, if it needs securing. I am not the judge and jury, you can decide for yourselves if this case is an unsafe conviction by the elements I have raised.

I have left this matter until now as if I had started with it you would have thought a sympathy vote was asked of you. Gary's mother, Sandy, is suffering from a number of illnesses and this situation has only caused extra stress. She has not managed to visit Gary in a long time because he is a considerable distance away from her home. Gary has only had the support of his ex-girlfriend when she was visiting him, but now that has stopped he is all alone. His mother believes he is innocent, but that would be the case I can hear your minds thinking, especially since Docherty's mother tried to cover for him. I cannot change your natural assumption, but assumptions are dangerous and since some of you might have or could be sitting on a jury in the future it would be dangerous for you to think that all mother's cover for their sons. Mrs Ward is an honourable woman and in her state of health has no need to write letters to the Prime Minister and other personages of similarly high positions. What about the mothers that shop their sons to the police if they have done wrong, are they to be dis-believed?

What about the Michael Stone appeal? 'What about it', I hear you ask. Lifed up for nothing more than testimony from his fellow inmates in prison whilst he was on remand awaiting trial. One of them now retracts what he has said; saying, 'It was all lies!'

Staying in Blackpool for a while, I raise the case of Stephen Akinmurele, 20, charged with murdering Eric and Joan Boardman. He was also, later on, charged with the murder of his former landlady Jamimah Cargil, she died in a house fire in Blackpool in October this year. A further charge of arson to endanger life was added to his list of charges. Since the case is sub judice it cannot be written about therefore I can only say that he is being investigated for four more possible murders over the last two years. Detectives are examining fires started over the last two years in the Lancashire Force area as well as on the Isle of Man. It would be dangerous to comment on such a case without first examining the full details. What have you, the reader, decided from reading this? Does it seem that Akinmurele is guilty just by this small piece? The majority of you would have assumed him to be guilty just because it is in print. I would ask that you consider the Blackpool Beach Murder case tried at Preston Crown Court? Most jurors would have been aware of this high profile emotional case; therefore I cannot see how Gary received a fair trial just by virtue of that alone. Usually high profile trials are shifted out of the area so that the defendant can have a fair crack of the whip.

Finally the Michael Stone case has seen some twists and turns that only a down hill skier on the Piste would be capable of navigating. The latest is that detectives are investigating the possibility that two prosecution witnesses in the murder trial had been threatened and warned off from giving evidence at the trial. Police were treating the matter with great concern. What then when defence witnesses are warned off, as in Gary's case? Docherty has not been pursued over this allegation by Gary, is it to be accepted that when a case is wound up that these allegations are overlooked simply because a man received a life prison sentence?

Gary has told a lifer Panel Board on 24th March 1998 that he would not be addressing his offending behaviour or attending any programmes and that he did not want re-categorisation or parole. They say pride comes before a fall. Gary is likely to serve twelve years plus if he addresses his alleged offending behaviour. The proof of the pudding would come if Gary pursued his line of innocence throughout his imprisonment, like many others in the system who are still refusing to address their offending behaviour, therefore they are not considered worthy enough for parole. Strange sort of custom! Just like the past monarchs of this country who would keep prisoners locked up in the Tower of London until they signed a confession, even if they prisoner had not done the crime. That still goes on today in the modern British penal system, "Henry the V111; eat your heart out."

We finish off the chapter with an extract from a letter that was sent to Gary allegedly by Docherty although hand writing analysis has to confirm this. 'Midget is also getting pissed of about those questions you've been asking about that cunt Viv Graham, look Gary that's none of your business do you understand me!

You're a good lad, Gary, and I'm sorry I had to put you under the pressure I did, but you know this thing is much deeper than Mark White and it's only you who's thinking of fucking everything up in Blackpool! You know what happens to grasses do you? Now when the police fuck off and stop showing an interest in the Pool I'll send someone down to see you.

You took the wrap and saved a few of us…'

The letter is only alleged to be from Docherty and until proven that it is it can only be suggested that it might be. Make of it what you will. Is it a letter that has had its structure planned or is it genuine. Docherty is to go free soon, having completed his sentence what has he to lose. What do you think?

16

Kenneth 'Panda' Anderson – *The Original Geordie Mafia*

The best chapter has been kept back until last because I believe it is the best one in terms of putting across how Viv was not as bad as he was made out to be. When you meet someone for the first time it is usual for that memory to be embedded in your subconscious. Equally as much as that so are the goodbyes in life remembered just as well. This chapter is the goodbye bit, where we hug each other while looking sheepish and trying not to betray our feelings of mutual loss. I discovered Panda through interviewing his wife, Janet, with regard to her affidavit submitted to the Paddy Conroy legal team. After talking to Mrs Anderson I was stunned to learn from her that her husband was THE Kenneth Panda Anderson that I had heard so much about.

For those of you who do not know who Panda is and what he stands for it would take much more than a small chapter to reveal his connections with the criminal underworld. The North East has had to be content with throwing around the names of Sibbet, Luvaglio, Stafford, Landa and Co for the last 30 years or so just like every time the football World Cup comes around we have to re-live the English success of 1966 all over again, it wears a bit thin playing the same old record. Then all of a sudden along comes success when England nearly won the European Championships, all of a sudden 1966 was kicked into touch and the ghosts of the past had been laid to rest. The same is said of Panda, except if he were the England football team he would have won the World Cup a number of times over, laying to rest the continuous use of past gangster's names. Kenneth 'Panda' Anderson will become just as well known as those from the past, now it is his turn to be written about.

Kenneth has a criminal record stretching back to 1957 and there is no one in

Big time British crime that he does not know or know of. Anyone who is anyone in British crime will know of Panda Anderson, the man has connections and is the connection of others in the criminal underworld. Panda was asked if he would like to give some comment for the Viv book. His first reaction was abhorrence that he would be in the same book as Viv. I thought at first that it was because Panda had a disliking for Viv, but Panda made it perfectly clear that Viv was not a leading criminal figure and that he did not want to be in a book that elevated Viv up to Panda's own level of criminal activity, that he had worked so hard at to get where he is now. Of course when I explained that Viv was not going to be portrayed as a leading crime figure from Tyneside Panda relented and was more than happy to offer his support to this book by way of granting an interview.

For all that Panda has the same status as his colleagues from London he has kept a low profile, until now that is. His friends list like a British Who's Who of Crime, Freddie Foreman (The Managing Director of British Crime co-author of *Respect*), the late Mr Lenny McLean (co-author of *The Guv'nor*), Frankie Fraser (socialite, actor and retired criminal underworld figure), and many more names that roll off the tongue so fast you would need an A-Z book to keep track of all their names.

To start the chapter off I relate a story that an alleged insider told me in which he claims that Panda was in a pub on Newcastle's Quayside when a man walked in who owed Panda a few grand. The *Redhouse* pub was a haunt of known criminals on Tyneside, so when in walks this man, Panda spotted him almost immediately with his razor sharp instincts. It just so happened that Viv was in the pub at the same time and Panda goes up to him, it is claimed, and says 'Viv, get a hold of that man over there and bring him upstairs as I need to have a word with him, there's a monkey in it for you.'

Viv acted without hesitation and within minutes the man was being held in Viv's vice like grip and he was sat in a chair while Viv held him there. Unbeknown to Viv or the man being held Panda pulled a serious looking knife out from behind his back that he was seen to keep in trousers. The blade was heavy and sharp and without anyone having time to react the knife came down so fast that not even Viv's reactions could have pulled the man he was holding away from the harm it was about to do to the man's finger end. Swishhh! Viv let go of the man so fast and scampered off down the stairs leaving the scene faster than a bishop out of a brothel's window during a police raid. The man's finger end lay there, a lonely looking thing!

This shows how Panda was set apart from people like Viv and the following day it is alleged that Viv met up with Panda and said to him, 'Hey, I couldn't go through that again it turned my stomach all last night just thinking about what happened, never again.'

We talk a bit about characters that Panda has met through his chequered past and Charles Bronson is mentioned whereby Panda says of him, "I hate to say this, but he was potty, poor Charlie he just used to fight screws that's what made him barmy, he's alright though, a canny lad. He got stabbed by some London fellahs you know, what a shame. He struggled really, you know, but it was just that he was bad inside (prison), nobody worries about inside now, it's outside."

Panda tells me he knows a little bit about law (what he does not know about criminal law could be written on the back of a stamp) when I mention the Paddy Conroy situation to him and it leads to him talking about Juries that serve in criminal trials. "One thing that I've learned is that you cannot touch a jury, I used to watch for any move or anything that they could overhear. I got the first trial stopped by getting my co-accused off in front of Judge Marella Cohen, she stopped the trial because of a policeman's notebook I had managed to get hold of. One thing about a jury is that they are sacro sanct, you cannot touch a jury, nobody can touch a jury, nobody." Panda talks like he is a seasoned professional, all that is missing is the barrister's gown and wig and it would transform what he says into something as acceptable as any top barrister would say. Panda says that he realised the significance of his wife, Janet, making an affidavit in the Conroy appeal he says, "I knew they would have a pop at me because of who I am."

We watch a recent video recording of a wedding that Panda and Janet were invited to in London. Panda gives a commentary, "I'm looking for another great fellah, Micky, they used to call them 'murder incorporated' and they **were** murder incorporated, but only bad people they'd never hurt anybody decent. Everybody was frightened to go near the mad axeman, Frank Mitchell (murdered in London on 24th December 1966). They took him outside and murdered him." Tony Lambrianou and Charlie Kray appear on the same wedding video that Panda attended and as Panda says, "You'll see them all. With these people you couldn't have a row to save your life, if you were drunk and worked it they would say, 'Come on!' Nobody would fall out."

Panda, though, says about proper fallout's, "It's serious because the other people are serious, but otherwise if they can talk they'll talk at first." Panda is distracted by another name on the video, "Dave Courtney, he's so quiet he was on *Vanessa* (morning talk show – UK TV, now discontinued.) a few weeks ago. He put the security on for the wedding, the place is in Foxhill, Surrey, 32 acres worth £2½M."

Panda was around when Reggie Kray visited Newcastle in the 60s and there is so much talk about why he came to the North East and that he had his arse kicked out of Newcastle's Central Station. It would be easy to let that rest but some people are just so full of shit that the story had to be looked into and although Panda was around at that time he put me on to a rival source who gave me the following account of Reggie's visit to Tyneside. Should anyone want to disprove what is written her then I will gladly consider what they have to say and include it in the next 'gangster' book. They came up and it was Vince Landa who brought them up. The key to Vince Landa's fortune was fruit machines. I was told that Reggie visited Whitley Bay, first the club *Go-Go* and then went to the *69 Club*, which had not been open very long it was owned by Joe Lyle. ('Lucky' Joe Lyle) He had just come back from the Isle of Man and he used to own racehorses and was never a crook, but he made money from fruit machines. There was John Heanan (Heannan?) who used to play for Newcastle United years ago, he works in the Gosforth Park Hotel. Eddie Campbell, Tommy Whitehead and Eddie Lenny, who is an uncle of the West End Sayers family, were also there. Vince Landa come in with a few others and Reg. Vince was in front paving the way for Reg he said, 'Alright, Joe, I've got Reg here.' That was their style, having doors opened for them. They had just wanted a night out whilst visiting the area, they were not as famous in the North East as they were down South. Joe said, 'You cannot come in here.' Joe was in a state of panic, 'You cannot come in here, you're not welcome here, the police station (West End police station) is just ten yards down the road.' Vince said, 'What's wrong, Joe?' Joe made out that he had an alarm in the club that went direct to the police station. Reg was still standing in the door looking at Joe with his ice cold eyes and he said, 'I won't forget you Mr Lyle!'

Joe asked Panda Anderson what he thought about it all? Panda is alleged to have told him, 'I think you're in trouble!' Joe then said, 'What have I done, what have I done, there's a grand go and give them a grand.' What Joe had said about the alarm being connected to the police station had been believed, but that was not the way to treat someone like Reggie Kray as they were used to being treat in a slightly different way back home. The only intention of the visit was to call in for a drink. Vince Landa (Formerly known as Vincente Luvaglio lived in Sunderland and he had a big manor and was boss of Social Club Services Ltd – fruit machines.) It was Landa's gig and he had to go somewhere and he was talking to Reg and rabbiting on and Reg said, 'Son, stop the car, stop the car.' He then went on to say, 'You're doing me nut in', Vince pulled up and Reg is said to have dragged Landa out of his car and drove off leaving him standing at the roadside. He gave him his car back eventually, but Reg could not be bothered with having his ear filled with the noise of Landa's mouth.

Panda, for a man of sixty, still has in his system what a man of 25 would have, he has lost none of his sharpness, and he has added an array of new modern weaponry to his already fine honed arsenal. That weaponry is the ability to read people's body language with a startling accuracy that would have psychologists looking on with admiration. Panda has the ability to read people's eyes with his direct eye contact that would scare off most Rottweilers. But that is not what makes Panda different to the common crook, what does make him different is his quick thinking and being able to turn any situation around to his advantage, I have only ever seen this in two other people in my whole life. One was an SAS soldier of the highest calibre and the other person cannot be named because of a promise I made him, that man had allegedly murdered five people and kneecapped at least a dozen or so others, he had never been charged or convicted of any offence whatsoever in his life, not even being booked for speeding!

Panda has been pulled in by the law on numerous occasions whenever there was a shooting incident or a tie up then he would be pulled in. Most recently, three years ago a man was shot in the head whilst he was running around looking for Panda. My source tells me that the man had not cared a less who Panda was although Panda, it is claimed, was at a loss to understand what the man's argument was with him. The man was driving in the vicinity of Panda's home when someone ran out into the road stopping the van. The window was opened and words exchanged then a bullet entered the man's head, the bullet was thought to be a .22 calibre. The van stuttered forward coming to a halt, the passenger in the vehicle was too scared to say anything to the police. The police pulled Panda in over this shooting which resulted in the man being left in a permanent state of vegetation and no charges were ever brought against Panda and a number of other's arrested. It was suggested that the man that pulled the trigger was an 18-year-old as he was dressed in designer sportswear and a fashion hat.

I am told a story by an alleged associate of Panda's, he says "The way people go on, 'I'll shoot him' and 'I'll do this' people just talk, Panda had some hassle and these people went to a buy a gun they were asked if they needed any bullets, this man knew Panda by the way, they said it was for Panda to see what he would say. This man frightened them when he said, 'Have you ever used a shotgun? Well, I'm going to tell you something, don't miss.' They asked 'what for?' The reply was, 'He never does.' So they left, they didn't want the bullets and then, the gun, it is claimed, ended up with Frankie Donnelly and he fired it into the air and got five years in an incident.

The video is still running and Panda points out Joey Pyle who faced a murder charge some years ago in 1960 when Selwyn Cooney, manager of a London club had a run in with Vicky James ('Blonde Vicky') and it resulted in their cars colliding, causing 54/9d worth of damage, in old money, to Cooney's car. He sent the bill to Blonde Vicky and because of this a number of ensuing incidents turned into something more severe when Cooney ended up being shot in the head, at point blank range. The jury sitting at the trial of Pyle and three others had been changed by the judge due to a number of incidents and the public gallery was full of 'faces' to help deter the jury by virtue of the faces just being there, the Kray twins, the Nash family and more. Pyle was acquitted of murder, but he received an 18-month prison sentence, the last large sentence he had received until thirty years later. In the meantime he was alleged to have been involved in all sorts of activities, but he was coated in teflon. He had run-ins continuously with the law and was cleared of connections with a murder in which he was charged with perverting the course of justice, nothing stuck. Pyle is thought to have connections with the right people and had an interest in running unlicensed boxing bouts. Just from this you will be able to determine that Panda is set apart from Viv and should anyone wish to still hang the 'gangster' tag on to Viv then you have not been reading this book. Pyle, just out of interest. said he was not a gangster!

Freddie Foreman is in the Video, in fact the video looks to be a collection of gangsti (my own word for a collection of gangsters.) and Panda says of Foreman, "He wouldn't be there by being a bluffer, if he was a bluffer he wouldn't be there." Roy Shaw is pointed out. "He broke Millsies (Freddy Mills) jaw in Rampton, Lenny (Lenney McLean) mentions him and he beat Lenny in a fight. There's Chris Quinton, who used to be in Coronation Street, Mad Frankie and Charlie Richardson are going into the main wedding reception tent." This would make an interesting social studies video; I point that out in jest to Panda, but seriously it might work.

From looking at this video I can see that it portrays affluence and the luxuries of life beyond what average people will ever amass in their lives. If this is what being a gangster is all about then it seems to be the life worth living, if you could avoid the prison terms on offer. These people do not rob grannies or burgle houses, yet they are feared people, you would be in very safe company with these people compared to a room full of louts convicted of boring crimes that the police have to pick people up for every minute of the day. How often is a big case in court with a big name? Not very often compared to your burglar. Panda is in constant touch with all of the characters mentioned and he regularly travels to visit his southern friends.

Panda points out certain body language of a particular guest he says, "Look, he cuddles him, but he doesn't cuddle him back." I point out that he must do a lot with body language and Panda says something that shows what it is that sets him apart from ordinary mortals, "You've got to, it keeps you alive." Bill Murray out of *The Bill* (UK TV Series) amongst other TV celebrities could be seen mixing with the guests. From this commentary you will see that Panda is one of the faces with the connections that others can only pretend of having.

From this video I can see that the only romantic notion ever attached to the North East about crime was Vince Landa, no one can be in the same league as those in the video, except for Panda who sees Vince from time to time. Apologies given for the Vince Landa/Reggie Kray allegation as Panda did not know I had discovered these details from someone he had put me on to.

John Cook is mentioned and Panda says of him, "Cookie, Cookie, don't mention him, I used to throw things at the telly whenever I saw him. He didn't even do a proper murder. He informed on his co-accused. When I was in Hull prison we had a five day riot and Cookie went through to get somebody out he said, 'Leave it to me lads, leave it to me', one was supposed to go off out of the riot because he had a bad heart, an Irishman; heavy IRA. Cookie said, 'Do you mind moving a bit more', because the screws were on the other side with riot gear on, 'He can't bend with his bad chest.' Cookie pushed the geezer back and went whoosh straight through the gap, he was off."

The IRA is mentioned, Panda says of one man, "He's innocent of bombing, I'll tell you why, go through all your IRA men not one of them pleaded 'not guilty' except the ones who were innocent. They refuse to recognise the court. I was with the Birmingham Six (wrongfully convicted) and I knew they were not guilty, they didn't accept it, but they took it well."

The Harry Perry (Tyneside face from the 70s & 80s) era is touched on and Panda enlightens me with his knowledge of the case. "Jacky (Jacky Patterson) shot Harry because he was terrified of him, but Jacky had a bit of a bad name and he was a loner as such. Harry was like the governor then, was the governor then. I had shot Snowdon so it looked like Jacky had followed suit with Harry. It was 25 years since I shot Snowdon."

The Snowdon shooting is related to me by Panda, "Snowdon was a hero to a lot of people because they thought he was unbeatable, he was violent, he used to break people's legs. People were terrified of Bobby Snowdon, he got five years for running a geezer over, Snowdon could fight for fun, when you went down he broke your legs, he could beat anybody. He would have beat Viv; nobody ever beat him in a fight. I was told once that I had put a gun through his letterbox, cobblers.

Everybody knows what happened really. There was a fall out at a bookmaker. So I go up to the bookmaker and say, 'Leave him alone', I was referring to a man who had some trouble with him, he said 'Well I've told Snowdon now'. I said 'Never mind Snowdon', but I was going off Snowdon a little bit, we used to be pals Snowdon and me. He wasn't a villain, he was something like Viv, but he was nastier than Viv hew would do things for fivers, break peoples legs and that and interfering in domestics and things. If his pals fancied somebody he would go and chin the woman's boyfriend, he did some terrible things. I was just starting to drift away from him, right, and I went into this bar and the little mob set about me with everything, Snowdon wasn't there but all his crew were, nine or ten of them. The police came and broke it up.

The next thing I know Snowdon's knocking at the door about ten handed, I opened the door and said who is this, Snowdon said 'You want a fight with me', there were about nine or ten at the door, I just couldn't believe it. I said 'Give me a week or so to heal up', and that was it. A week later the same crew were back with iron bars, crowbars, they were hiding around corners. When the police interviewed him they said why hadn't he had a fight with me on the moor (boxing booth that used to be run by Ron Clark on Newcastle's once a year Town Moor show.), he said that he wasn't sure, I was sure. And then that night come and I had got a gun, I had a one shell and a six shell. He had been to the house the week before and gave Janet a shock and when she went to shut the door they were hiding behind the wall. I thought I'm going to kill this geezer, nobody comes to my door like he did.

It was big then and it's big now to serious people, believe me. They went to John Hindmarsh, five of them, one of them, Algar, had two fights with Viv, they went in the five of them, with masks, on knocked on his door where his little bairn was and John was sitting with a pump action shotgun, wallop he killed one stone dead two got it in the chest and Algar got it in the neck. It was only four years ago; he got off with it. People who come to the door just go and that's the way it should be.

I looked at the size one and size six shells. Janet said to me, 'You're dead calm.' He never lost a fight, but when he came to the door the week before with a team then I knew he wasn't sure, mind. I was at home on my own as I didn't want to be looking out for others that way I knew everybody out there was my enemy. Snowdon phoned me from the bar and said, 'A straight fight one to one', but he was four handed up to then, tooled up. They were supposed to turn up at 12.00 o'clock, but it was quarter to one. (In the morning.) I was making plenty of money then, but he was still breaking people's legs for a fiver, a gangster's not a thug, you don't break people's legs for nowt, you don't do that, you cannot.

One of then come to the door and there's a shed at the back, they tried to entice me out and they had their bars hidden. I was going to put my bali (baliclava) on, but I thought 'He's not a grass', imagine that, he's not a man at all, he did tell the busies. I wished I'd put it on. The smallest one, Burns is knocking on the door, it shows you his mentally sending the smallest one to the door when he's just phoned up to say he's coming around. That must be the end of the story as far as Snowdon's concerned, he thinks I'm that silly I know he's coming up and he sends the little one, I open the door, what does he think? That made me angry. So I got the gun and went after him, he put his hands up and I put the gun in his mouth, he was saying, 'Don't kill me', I thought he's not even tough, that's why I didn't kill him. If he had of went 'Go on then!' I would have shot him there and then have no doubt about it. He couldn't match me in any way, one of his crew was standing there frozen with something in his hands, I said 'What's that in your hand', and he threw a bar away. I said to Snowdon 'Right I'll let you off,' he went 'Oh, thanks', I was never going to let him off, I let him off with his life, I put the gun to his leg and shot him. His pals picked him up and took him to the RVI, nobody come out, none of the neighbours. He was in bad way in intensive care, but he was strong and overcome the shock.

I've been shot at twice, I thought it was good, it didn't catch me it missed, it was a buzz, but if it hits you it would be a shock, I was shot at with a shotgun and a gun. There was a little write up in the papers about a well-known gangster being shot at. And then I get eight years, three months later the police come with guns and nicked me there was no evidence or nothing. They asked him why he came with a gang and he said it was in case I had a gang of them. There was no forensics or nothing.

They brought a judge up, a London High Court Judge to have me over. So when I went into Hull prison for it and we had the riots so we got the documents out of the office. I thought I was going to get parole first time, you get a write up from the police to submit with your parole application. I had a look at mine and it said: Responsible for major crimes in the area, a violent man, wouldn't hesitate to shot the police. I always remember the bottom line it said: A multitude of friends in the London underworld. That's the way they talk, you know; jargon. So this judge that was brought up slaughtered me. When I went for the committals I still didn't think, they wouldn't give me bail or nothing. The busies said to Snowdon, 'He'll get fifteen years, you'll get fifteen grand'. I didn't get fifteen years and his money was stopped because they said he was violent. (Criminal Injuries Compensation.) All of his assaults were against police, evil.

When the police came and I was told that Snowdon had grassed me, the bars they all brought with them to do me in was said to be debris after they were found lying about. I was naïve in court then and should have done it a different way. Snowdon had to give evidence against me as he was told otherwise he was going into the ground because he wanted me out of the road.

The comparisons here between this and the Viv murder charges that were not brought is that the police say that some of the witnesses in the Viv murder case would be unreliable as some of them have criminal records, yet here Snowdon was used as a direct witness against Panda regardless of his record. There was absolutely no evidence at all against Panda other than the word of Snowdon who had went team handed intent on smashing Panda's bones and body up as much as they could with the iron bars that they had dumped. They would have used them against Panda there is no doubt about that, you don't back the likes of Panda into a corner, so they learned. Panda was the first one to use a gun in such a way in the North East as such a thing was not heard of before. Now though this is a common event.

We talk of the hit on Viv and how the professional hitman I had interviewed told me that it was common to put one in the head and one in the heart Panda says, "Two in the chest and one in the canister." The conversation covers a whole range of shootings there was the tragic loss of a young man who was accidentally shot in the head by his best friend who was so well liked that he was classed as a brother of the victim. Davy Glover's father-in-law had been shot and the man got twelve years for that.

The riot of Blackett Street 1963 is something that should be mentioned here it is a piece of criminal history from Tyneside. Davy Finlay is fighting with John Sayer's dad. All of a sudden I'm walking down the street, this is a terrible thing it's worse than any shooting, one of the witnesses the Taxi driver said 'I was in Dunkirk and there wasn't that amount of blood there.' You should get the write ups, how he lived I don't know. Frankie was my pal; he was the boxer a little tough fellow. I said 'They've got hammers' to one of the parties. They were training, but there was no steroids back then.

Frank Sayers was going to fight Davy Finlay. The town was full of all these lights, big yellow buses and one way traffic, big old buses and the Haymarket was packed on a Saturday night. And up they come, we had an alibi for the Dolce Vita, we went there and come back to do the business.

Finlay had a big Alsation dog, it's true this mind, he went 'one on to one' and he just released it. Frank whacked it straight away, there's a geezer standing next to me he said, 'Go on Dave'. He got hit in the head with an axe, whack it was as quick as that. One of the men with them was Keith, who owns *Julie's* and all that. He was the doorman on the *Go-Go Club*, he just got inside, and he shut the door and left his pals on the path outside the club. Cars were stopped the axe had actually stuck in the door. There was a little scuffle and this Billy Finlay went, 'Come on', he put his hand in his pocket, I thought he had a gun, so he lifted it out, but it was a sword from the war caught on his pocket. He was hit on the head with an axe, quite hard and it stuck in his nut, he shock his head and it fell out. When it was up in court they said it wasn't possible, but they said because he had an extra thick skull it saved him. Anyway Davy Finlay is trapped and NODA (Newcastle Owner Drivers Association) taxis had just started then it was just a little pre-fabricated thing. In he goes he runs in the corner Frank Sayers, John Sayers, Snr and George Shotton move in on him. Davy is stuck in the corner and he says he has had enough. Davy had his hands on his head and seen an axe being swung towards him when he tuck them off his head and the axe sounded like it was hitting hollow rock, he was hit about fifteen times and he was sinking lower and lower as the axe was swinging hitting him more and more. Finlay was given the last rites as he was in a bad way and there was blood everywhere.

The defence was an ordinary barrister, Peter Taylor; he eventually became Lord Chief Justice Taylor. There were charges of affray and wounding, the judge was a High Court judge, Frank got six months for wounding, the judge said 'If it was anyone else but the people involved they would have got years.' What he meant was that the people involved were all criminals or people connected to such things and therefore it was an in-house thing.

The case of Nigel Abadom using the fact of Viv's murder against a man he and his associates Michael and Stephen Sayers were blackmailing was raised as Abadom had told the man that they were the ones responsible for killing

Viv and that the man had better pay up. This fact was later used in the prosecution's case against the three of them. Panda tells me, "I know who didn't kill Viv, but I don't know who did, I know it wasn't Michael Sayers, Stephen Sayers or Abadom. It wasn't me, I was away."

The propaganda machine of the Sayers seems to have accepted that they were responsible for every crime in the North East so as to give the impression that they were the ones in power.

Panda says, "Viv was starting to get a bit like Snowdon and that's when you get shot. I asked Viv if he ever carried a gun, he said 'The only weapons I need are these', he stuck his fists out." If the world was so perfect.

The comparison here between Viv an Snowdon shows that Viv could had headed in that direction as people said he was just starting to throw his weight about. There is an incident in which Viv is said to have given a substantial loan to a man to buy some ice cream vans. The money was to be paid back with interest over an agreed period. The man failed to keep his word and it resulted in Viv taking all but one of the ice cream vans off the man to settle the debt.

The other claim is that a Newcastle based Rolls Royce dealer was having difficulty in being paid from a hardman for a roller he supplied. So in order to speed the payment up and get some money from the man he ignorantly used Viv's name saying that 'Viv had been told about the debt and if the man did not get it paid then Viv would be making a visit to collect the money.' Viv found out that his name was used therefore he requested a commission on the amount that his name had successfully help recover. The car dealer paid up. But when Viv was murdered a nearby printer to the car dealer printed some T-shirts with the motif on the front saying 'THREE SHOTS FOR THE PRICE OF TWO'.

As much as Viv was said to be a gentleman, Panda is as gentlemanly as they come and all reports of him being mad are a bit exaggerated, Although it was claimed that Panda went looking for a man called Paul Ashton (now serving 26 years for violence). Panda is alleged to have said to Ashton who was looking out of the window to see who it was knocking on the door so early in the morning, 'Come down here, mug.' Ashton came down barley dressed and when he saw Panda pull a gun out he turned and ran away shouting 'You're a psycho, you're mad.' Indeed, Panda is the Original Geordie Mafia.

Authors Note

Look out for a future title that I might be working on called
Goosey Goosey Gander (possibly) or 'Goose' or 'Panda'
Relating to Kenneth Panda Anderson

Viv (Graham) 'Simply the Best'
ISBN No: 1-902578-00-7
The above title is the book that precedes this volume 2
Should you have difficulty in purchasing the above title then
please forward a cheque to the publishers for £8.99 includes P+P
Offer applies to UK only if in Europe then send
Int Money Order for £11.99 Stirling

A3 Full colour poster featuring Viv is available
For £2.99 includes P+P UK only

Future titles proposed from Mirage Publishing

RAMRAIDERS NORTH EAST Ltd
Ramrading spectacular

STAMPS
Blows the lid off the proposed sell off of the Post Office by the Government
Stamp Fraud is costing the post office £Ms in lost revenue and the post office
are powerless to stop the loss! Sex, violence and scandal

PUBLIC *consumer* ENEMY
The author and two researchers were arrested by police after exposing
how you the consumer of everything from fags to booze get ripped off
by the big name companies.

MURDERERS SQUARE MILE
A square mile full of murders, what has been the cause of this change in
such a tranquil area? What evil lurks behind this violence?

A chapter has been withheld from this book because there was insufficient
room for it to be enclosed in the binding, should you wish to purchase it as a
loose leaf addition then please send payment of £2.99 includes P+P to the
publisher. Offer applies to the UK only.